Great Crossings

Great Crossings

Indians, Settlers, and Slaves in the Age of Jackson

CHRISTINA SNYDER

OXFORD

UNIVERSITY PRESS

OXFORD
UNIVERSITY PRESS

Oxford University Press is a department of the University of Oxford. It furthers the University's objective of excellence in research, scholarship, and education by publishing worldwide. Oxford is a registered trade mark of Oxford University Press in the UK and certain other countries.

Published in the United States of America by Oxford University Press
198 Madison Avenue, New York, NY 10016, United States of America.

Library of Congress Cataloging-in-Publication Data
Names: Snyder, Christina, author.
Title: Great Crossings : Indians, Settlers, and Slaves in the Age of Jackson / Christina Snyder.
Description: New York, NY : Oxford University Press, [2017] | Includes bibliographical references and index.
Identifiers: LCCN 2016024418 (print) | LCCN 2016029255 (ebook) | ISBN 9780199399062 (hardcover : alk. paper) | ISBN 9780199399079 (Updf) | ISBN 9780199399086 (Epub)
Subjects: LCSH: Great Crossing (Ky.)—History—19th century. | Great Crossing (Ky.)—Race relations—History—19th century. | Johnson, Richard M. (Richard Mentor), 1780-1850—Homes and haunts—Kentucky—Great Crossing. | Choctaw Indian Academy—History. | Choctaw Indians—Kentucky—Great Crossing—History—19th century. | African Americans—Kentucky—Great Crossing—History—19th century. | Slaves—Kentucky—Great Crossing—History—19th century. | Community life—Kentucky—Great Crossing—History—19th century. | Imperialism—Social aspects—United States—History—19th century. | United States—Territorial expansion—History—19th century.
Classification: LCC F459.G73 S68 2017 (print) | LCC F459.G73 (ebook) | DDC 976.9/425—dc23
LC record available at https://lccn.loc.gov/2016024418

1 3 5 7 9 8 6 4 2

Printed by Sheridan Books, Inc., United States of America

In memory of Michael D. Green and Charles M. Hudson

CONTENTS

ACKNOWLEDGMENTS

This project began many years ago with a conversation in a sunny Chapel Hill courtyard. It has since taken me on a long and sometimes dark path, guided by an incredible wealth of archival sources that tell stories of hope, joy, and humor but also violence, dispossession, and suffering beyond comprehension. I hope that this book, in some small way, captures the rich, complicated lives of those who made Great Crossings, especially those whose voices are typically silenced. Any shortcomings are my own, of course, but I'm extremely grateful to the many people who have helped me along the way.

I write this book in memory of Michael D. Green and Charles M. Hudson. Mike, along with Theda Perdue, served as my advisor in graduate school. I appreciated Mike and Theda's key, early feedback. My trips to Kentucky helped me reconnect with my undergraduate mentor Charlie Hudson, who had retired to Frankfort. It was wonderful to catch up with Charlie at the Coffeetree Café and other Bluegrass spots over the next few years. He and his wife, Joyce Rockwood Hudson, generously shared their time and local knowledge with me. I have tremendous love and respect for Mike and Charlie, and I am grateful for their mentorship over the past two decades. Their contribution to the ethnohistory of the Native South is incalculable.

Among the greatest pleasures during the course of this project has been connecting with Brenda Brent Wilfert. Ms. Wilfert is a direct descendant of Julia Chinn and Richard Mentor Johnson and an accomplished historian who has done a tremendous amount of genealogical research on her family. After corresponding for several years, I finally met Brenda and her husband, Tom. They welcomed me into their home, and Brenda most graciously allowed me to conduct research in her family collection. Because much of the documentation on the Chinn-Pence family has been destroyed, Brenda's collections were crucial in helping me to learn more about the lives of Julia, Adaline, Imogene, and their descendants. She also offered valuable research tips on enslaved people at Great Crossings and freedpeople who later settled in Kansas. Thanks, too, to Bill Jackson, another Pence descendant, who generously shared his knowledge of material culture relating to Choctaw Academy.

I'm deeply grateful to the many archivists, librarians, and curators who shared their time and expertise over the years: at the Filson Historical Society—Jennie Cole, Heather Fox, James Holmberg, Judy Miller, Sarah-Jane Poindexter, Heather Potter, Michael Veach, and Mark Wetherington; at the Kentucky Historical Society—Tony Curtis and R. Darrell Meadows; at Transylvania University Special Collections—B. J. Gooch; at the Georgetown and Scott County Museum—Ruthie Stevens; at the American Antiquarian Society—Ashley Cataldo, Paul Erickson, Vince Golden, Lauren Hewes, Jackie Penny, Kimberly Toney, and Laura Wasowicz; at the Tippecanoe Historical Society—Kelly Lippie; at the Speed Art Museum—Lisa Parrott Rolfe; at Indiana University's Lily Library—Erika Dowell and Cherry Williams; at the University of Kentucky Special Collections Library—Jason Flahardy; at the Mississippi Department of Archives and History—Ann Weber; at the Oklahoma Historical Society—Jessica Lundsford-Nguyen and Rachel Mosman; at the Gilcrease Museum Archives—Renee Harvey; at the Spencer Research Library at the University of Kansas—Deborah Dandridge, Caitlin Donnelly, and Kathy Lafferty; at the Smithsonian Museum of American Art—Richard Sorenson; at the Museum of Fine Arts, Boston—Marta Fodor. Thanks, too, to Chris Clements, for your brilliant work as a research assistant at Indiana University. I am also grateful to Ian Byers-Gamber for his outstanding work on the maps.

Many source materials for this project required translation or linguistic analysis. I am grateful to those who shared their expertise with me, especially Daryl Baldwin, David Costa, Sean Gantt, Ben Frey, and Tim Williams. Thanks also to George Ironstrack and John Bickers, who corresponded with me about Myaamia culture and history, provided documents and references relating to Choctaw Academy students, and corrected misspelled names.

Visits to historic sites enhanced my understanding of Great Crossings and the people who once lived there. I am especially grateful to Ann Bevins for sharing her deep knowledge of Scott County, and to William "Chip" Richardson for his efforts to preserve the original Choctaw Academy site. Timothy Baumann also located and shared archaeological information. At Wheelock Academy, I learned a great deal about Choctaw educational history and current preservation efforts from Wanda Howard, Stoney Trusty, and Thomas Williston.

Many colleagues and institutions have provided essential support throughout this project. I am grateful for the generous support of the American Council of Learned Societies; the University of California at Davis Humanities Institute; the American Antiquarian Society; and several granting institutions at Indiana University, including the New Frontiers Program, the College Arts and Humanities Institute, and the Office of the Vice Provost for Research. I received invaluable feedback from colleagues over the years, particularly at workshops, including the Columbia University Early American History Seminar, the Kentucky Early American Seminar, and the Creative Intelligence Lecture Series at Transylvania University. For their insights, feedback, and encouragement, I especially thank Zara Anishanslin, John Bowes, Colin Calloway, Frances Clarke, Glenn Crothers, Christian Ayne Crouch, John Demos, R. David Edmunds, Matthew Guterl, Katie Johnston, Clara Sue Kidwell, Karen Kupperman, Michael LaCombe, Malinda Maynor Lowery, Edward McInnis, Mary Mendoza, Brian Murphy, Michele Currie Navakas, Jessie Morgan Owens, Theda Perdue, Dan Richter, Kelly Ryan, Honor Sachs, Rachel St. John, Gabriela Serrano, Jenny Shaw, and Timothy J. Williams. Indiana University has been a supportive institutional home and vibrant intellectual community throughout this process. Thanks, in particular, to Cara Caddoo, Brian Gilley, Peter Guardino, Allison Madar, Jason McGraw, Michelle Moyd, Amrita Chakrabarti Myers, John Nieto-Phillips, Dina Okamoto, Ougie Pak, Chris Pelton, Eric Sandweiss, Scot Wright, and Ellen Wu. It was a delight to share ideas with two colleagues working on similar topics: Nicholas Guyatt, congratulations on your amazing book *Bind Us Apart* (Basic, 2016); Amrita Myers's work-in-progress on the Chinn-Johnson family promises to enhance our knowledge of kinship and race in antebellum America.

Sometimes inspiration came from unexpected places. Thank you, Boston Fluevogologists and especially Rachel Jayson, for sharing your creative energy with me: your title ideas were awesome.

Many thanks to the readers and editors who challenged and inspired me. My agent, Jill Kneerim, was an early champion of this project, and her advice about prose and audience were invaluable. Thanks, too, to Lucy Cleland of the Kneerim & Williams Agency for her ongoing assistance. I am very grateful to the anonymous reviewers who offered helpful feedback at a critical stage. One of the highlights of this project has been working with my brilliant editor, Susan Ferber, who offered incisive comments and unfailing support. This manuscript also benefited tremendously from the suggestions of Kathleen DuVal, Theda Perdue, and Josh Piker, who read it in its entirety. Theda, thanks for correcting my mistakes and pointing me toward additional useful sources—I promise to locate and use that anecdote one day. Kathleen and Josh, I couldn't have asked for a smarter or more thoughtful set of reports: thank you for sharing so generously of your time and expertise.

I could not have completed this project without the love and support of my family. Much love to my parents, Dan and Janice Snyder, and my brothers, Danny and Matt, for your encouragement and for accompanying me on much-needed getaways. Dan and Linda Lee, thanks for your enthusiasm and insights about Kentucky history over the years. My husband, Jacob Lee, helped every step of the way, offering research tips, brilliant editorial suggestions, and the best company. I knew it was love when, as an archivist at the Filson, you searched uncataloged manuscripts for me.

Great Crossings

Introduction

The Great Path?

On July 19, 1827, more than seven hundred visitors gathered at Choctaw Academy, the first national Indian boarding school in the United States. From across the state and beyond, they had traveled to a village called Great Crossings in Scott County, part of the rolling bluegrass country of central Kentucky. They crowded beneath the arbors of sugar maples, looking at the stage that had been erected at the front of the grove. The audience was diverse, though mostly white: twenty local boys, classmates of the Indians; trustees who had overseen the students' final examinations the previous day; clergy who preached to some of the boys in church on Sundays; and Lexington intellectuals interested in the cause of Indian reform. Indian visitors included newly elected Choctaw chief Greenwood Leflore and James McDonald, the first accredited Native American lawyer. In addition to these invited guests, the exhibition was open to the public. Some visitors were interested primarily in the free picnic dinner that slaves would serve at midday. But most came for "no other purpose . . . than to see Indians," said the school's superintendent.[1]

A generation earlier, a gathering of dozens of male Indians would have been cause for alarm. Old-timers needed little provocation to tell "stories without end" about violent clashes between pioneers and Indians that began when the Cherokee warrior Dragging Canoe famously promised land speculator Richard Henderson and his guide Daniel Boone that Kentucky "was the bloody ground, and would be dark, and difficult to settle." The orchestrator of the event was one of America's most famous Indian-fighters, Richard Mentor Johnson, whose family leveraged its wealth and influence to claim vast estates in the Bluegrass while the region was still a contested borderland. In Kentucky's early days, they

1

Figure I.1 Great Crossings, with a view of the former Johnson plantation, as seen later in the nineteenth century. Courtesy of Brenda Brent Wilfert.

defended their claims with blood and fire; even the Johnson women were legendary Indian-fighters. Richard Mentor Johnson was only an infant when his parents and older siblings built their first stockade, but he, too, would grow up to battle the region's Indigenous people, reportedly killing the Shawnee warrior Tecumseh during the War of 1812. Richard Johnson capitalized on his fame, becoming a career politician as well as master of Great Crossings.[2]

At 11 A.M., Johnson appeared, leading a group of students who seemed a sharp contrast to war stories Kentuckians had heard at the knees of their elders. Under the American flag, one hundred students marched in neat formation to the sound of drum and fife. Their dress, too, was military, fashioned in Washington by the same tailors who made uniforms for the army: dark gray woolen pantaloons with matching jackets, white shirts, shiny black boots. This group looked like underage officers, young gentlemen who might have fought against rather than alongside Tecumseh. Earlier reports should have prepared visiting whites for the spectacle. After all, part of what drew them to Great Crossings that day was the seeming paradox of "children of the forest" who could recite Cicero.[3]

Some of the older students, distinguished by large silver medals that hung around their necks, briefly addressed their schoolmates in languages that most of the crowd did not understand—Choctaw, Creek, and Potawatomi. The leading Choctaw that day was likely Peter Pitchlynn or Hatchoctucknee. His sharp, handsome features and self-confidence were apparent, though only the Choctaws knew that his authority came from family ties back home, not from school. The crowd was also limited in its ability to understand the short speeches by the student leaders. Only the Indian visitors were aware that these "were exhortations to good order and decorum, and to a proper self-confidence to all such as intended to address the audience."[4]

Next came the main event, a series of oral performances designed to show the audience some of the skills the students had mastered during the academic year. Mostly, the scholars displayed their progress in English, delivering speeches they had memorized as well as those they had composed. One spectator said that "several of the addresses were not the less interesting that they were delivered in imperfect or broken English." Grammatical mishaps, he thought, merely added a "zest" to exercises that otherwise might have bored the audience. Not surprisingly, the most advanced scholars gave the most impressive speeches. Displaying skills in elocution and knowledge of classical history, they lectured on morality, temperance, and other serious subjects.[5]

The audience responded most enthusiastically to the last exercise of the day. Choctaws and Creeks, who spoke related but distinct languages, took turns reciting identical bits of dialogue in their native tongues "with the view of giving the audience an idea of the difference between the two languages." The audience, ideally, would come away impressed with the students' advancement as scholars, but they might also learn something about Native cultures. School administrators hoped that such exercises eroded the "prejudices of our population."[6]

Meanwhile, several slaves trekked from the kitchen to the exhibition area, bearing trays laden with barbecue and fixings. They worked under the supervision of Julia Chinn, an African American woman in her thirties. Chinn was the concubine—some said "wife"—of Richard Mentor

Johnson, the mother of his children, and the manager of his plantation. Used to hosting balls and Fourth of July parties, Chinn was well prepared to feed a crowd of seven hundred. She might have seen this exhibition as particularly worthwhile, for Choctaw Academy enabled Johnson and Chinn to covertly educate their young daughters, Imogene and Adaline.[7]

While the status and aspirations of Julia Chinn, her daughters, and other enslaved people at Great Crossings remained secret—or, at least, half-hidden—those of the Indian students were the dominant topic of conversation that day. Such exhibitions, popular at all American academies, were public rituals that allowed students to demonstrate the skills and virtues they would need to exercise rights in a republican society. During dinner, members of the audience approached the students to ask questions or offer them "advice and encouragement." Others talked among themselves, evaluating the students' performances. Many whites expressed "utter astonishment at the performance of the Indian youths." One young military officer wagered that if his fellow Americans could have seen the exhibition, many more would support Indian education. The board of trustees were mightily pleased with the examinations and exhibition that year, predicting that graduates of Choctaw Academy "will at no distant day be an ornament to this Republic." Doubtless, others in attendance disagreed, though they may have concealed their views from the school trustees and Indian visitors who recorded what happened that day. Perhaps some agreed with a critic who, after attending the previous year's exhibition, asked, "What is the use of thus educating their children, if the Choctaws are doomed to meet the common fate of their red brethren. . . . Is it not inhumane to educate them, and then plunge them into the wilderness . . . ? Better it is that they should remain as they are, than, by education, become unfit for savage life."[8]

Famous in its day, Great Crossings was an experimental community in which America's diverse peoples lived together and articulated new visions of the continent's future. Great Crossings got its name the previous century, when bison habitually crossed Elkhorn Creek at that shallow spot. By the nineteenth century, the bison had disappeared, but Great Crossings became a different kind of meeting ground, a small place that embodied monumental changes then sweeping North America. The United States was quickly transforming from an East Coast nation into a sprawling empire. The consequences of this shift extended across the continent, prompting Americans of all backgrounds to consider their future in a rapidly changing world.[9]

Great Crossings embodied three sorts of convergence: the crossing of geographic space, the meeting of cultures, and the traverse of time during a pivotal period. The village had an apt name, for Americans often used travel metaphors to discuss their relationships during that dynamic era. Common in treaty negotiations, many of these terms derived from Indigenous diplomacy. "Great paths" were shared by different groups of people, who strove to make them "white" or "clean" by maintaining peace. "Dividing paths," sometimes made "red" through violence, indicated a parting of ways. People of varying cultural and geographic origins came together at Great Crossings. Some were there by choice, others by circumstance or force, but they all looked for ways forward during a time of rapid change. Many hoped to forge a clean path, maybe even a great path, to the future.[10]

The plantation and the school at its core belonged to Richard Mentor Johnson, who was one of the architects of his nation's transformation. When Johnson joined Congress in 1807, Kentucky and its neighbor Tennessee were the westernmost US states. But Johnson, like his constituents, sought to enhance his nation's territory by defeating imperial rivals as well as Indian nations. A hawk who pushed for the War of 1812, Johnson was catapulted to national celebrity after he reportedly killed Tecumseh during the Battle of the Thames; to many Americans, that act symbolized the destruction of Indian resistance to US settlement of the West. After the war, the United States imposed punishing treaties that forced Indian nations to cede hundreds of millions of acres. By 1823, the United States announced the Monroe Doctrine, warning European powers against interference in the Americas. Increasingly confident, the young nation sought to embark on an imperial project of its own.[11]

Since their victory in the Revolution, many citizens had dreamed of conquering the continent, and they were less reticent than modern-day

Americans to call their country an "empire." As early as 1776, John Adams wrote a treatise that positioned the United States as Britain's imperial successor, claiming dominion over its former colonies in eastern North America and even the Caribbean. In 1789, geographer Jedidiah Morse argued that "the God of nature" intended the United States to stretch far into the West, much farther than the bounds dictated in the Treaty of Paris that concluded the Revolution. Soon, Morse predicted, the United States would build "the largest empire that ever existed." Some were less enthusiastic. Federalists, in particular, worried that expansion would destabilize their nation, triggering an eastern exodus that would populate the West with headstrong, uncivilized frontiersmen who might foment costly wars, form a breakaway nation, or join a rival empire. Still, federalists were interested in controlled growth and sought to craft policies that would build a "respectable empire." Though they debated the details, the many founders who favored imperialism imagined incorporating new territories into a realm of divided sovereignty, where power would be shared by the federal government and an ever-growing number of states.[12]

These aims remained aspirational until after the War of 1812 but were realized with startling speed thereafter. By the time Choctaw Academy closed in 1848, the United States stretched all the way to the Pacific coast, encompassing the formerly Mexican possession of Alta California and the once-British Oregon Territory. In explaining their rapid growth, Americans adopted a phrase coined by journalist John O'Sullivan, ascribing it to their "manifest destiny to overspread the continent allotted by Providence." Contrary to the doctrine of manifest destiny, however, there was nothing foreordained or natural about US expansion: the new American empire was forged through the conquest of other nations and colonies. In addition to the War of 1812, other wars of expansion included the Seminole Wars, which brought Florida under US control; the Blackhawk War, crushing Indian resistance to the settlement of the Midwest; and the Mexican War, which transferred more than half of Mexico's territory—over 500,000 square miles—to the United States. This territorial expansion corresponded to a surge in the US population, which leaped from 9.6 million in 1820 to more than 23 million by 1850.[13]

As it grew in territory and population, the United States confronted people from diverse cultures, ranging from Irish and Haitian refugees in port cities to Métis fur traders of the Great Lakes to plantation-owning Cherokees. Emerging from a collection of disparate colonies, the United States was young, still crafting and debating its identity. The chartering document of American identity, the Declaration of Independence, declared that "all men are created equal," a notion that encouraged Americans to think expansively about citizenship. For all their soaring rhetoric, however, those in power were often unable to imagine how to build a great path that might bring culturally diverse people together. Some were skeptical that certain whites—especially immigrants, Catholics, and the working class—could be trusted with rights of citizenship. The place of people of color also provoked heated debate. Might they be incorporated as citizens? Should they be treated as inferior subjects or even commodities? Or excluded from the nation altogether and deported to distant places?

Richard Mentor Johnson believed that the "empire of liberty" would extend freedom in its march across the continent. In 1820, during the debates leading to the Missouri Compromise, Johnson argued that emancipation and westward expansion went hand in hand. He imagined that freed slaves could resettle in the West, where they would build farms, schools, and churches, becoming assimilated into US society as full citizens. Johnson acknowledged that white racism was an obstacle, but he embraced a progressive view of history, arguing that his fellow citizens would overcome prejudice in time. Many other influential leaders agreed that slavery was on the decline and that gradual emancipation was inevitable. Thomas Jefferson argued that territorial growth would weaken slavery by creating a nation of yeoman farmers, while devotees of Adam Smith reasoned that the institution would die out in the face of an increasingly modernized economy.[14]

Julia Chinn, though legally enslaved, was one of many African Americans who sought a greater measure of liberty—if not for herself, then at least for her children and future generations. African Americans expected an expansion of their citizenship rights in the aftermath of the War of 1812, since so many had served bravely in the US army and navy. Julia's brother Daniel may have been the slave, unnamed in the original accounts, who accompanied Richard Johnson to the Battle of the Thames. Meanwhile, Julia Chinn and many other Americans took part in the Second Great Awakening, a series of diverse religious revivals that supported the notion of an inclusive and progressive republic. Stressing equality in the eyes of God, the revivals inspired women and people of color seeking a share of liberty. The Second Great Awakening also popularized postmillennialism, the notion that Americans, having severed Old World chains, could build the most progressive nation on Earth, so perfect that it might, quite literally, bring on the Second Coming.[15]

Many Americans worked to turn these lofty ideals into reality. The federal government restricted slavery, banning it in the Northwest Territory and prohibiting the importation of new slaves by abolishing the Atlantic slave trade. Manumissions accelerated throughout the nation, even in the South, and many northern states outlawed slavery altogether. For a time, free men of color could vote in many northern states as well as Kentucky and North Carolina; even women, provided they held property, could vote in New Jersey. Cities like Philadelphia included prosperous black communities, which included a professional class—doctors, ministers, teachers—and also skilled craftspeople who owned small businesses.[16]

At Great Crossings, Richard Mentor Johnson and Julia Chinn championed the notion of a diverse society. Their logic fell in line with the thinking of most early US intellectuals, who believed that, above all else, humans were shaped by their environment, meaning their climate, diet, and lifestyle. This so-called environmental theory of race suggested that by changing the circumstances in which immigrants and people of color lived and learned, they could acquire republican values. Johnson and Chinn knew from their own experience that different races could co-exist and mingle. In a speech before the Senate, Johnson upheld a unified vision of humanity, claiming that only social inventions—namely, slavery and prejudice—divided people. Meanwhile, Chinn embraced American middle-class values as a path to inclusion. She attended a local Baptist church, educated her children, and developed a local reputation as an "exemplary and pious" woman.[17]

In forging an interracial family, Chinn and Johnson opted for what was then considered the most radical means to integrate American society. Some US leaders supported the practice, which was then called "amalgamation." Drawing on their knowledge of European imperial history—the Spanish in Mexico, the Portuguese in West Africa, even John Rolfe and Pocahontas in early Virginia—they suggested that whites might pacify and "civilize" people of color through interracial marriage. President Thomas Jefferson encouraged frontier whites to marry Indians: "Let our settlements and theirs meet and blend together, to intermix, and become one people." Jefferson and other leaders believed that intermarriage with Indians would enable the United States to peacefully acquire title to Native land. The benefits of intermarriage with African Americans, who lacked sovereign territories in North America, were less obvious to white policymakers. In the wake of the Haitian Revolution, many whites feared that emancipated slaves might stage a similar uprising against their former oppressors in the United States. Among this group was Thomas Jefferson, who claimed that white-black amalgamation "produces a degradation to which no lover of his country . . . can innocently consent." Sex between whites and blacks was common in antebellum America—Jefferson himself fathered six children with his slave Sally Hemings—but many powerful whites demonized the practice, citing it as a major concern in debates over abolition. Still, some intellectuals, like Kentuckian Gilbert Imlay, argued that white-black unions were inevitable and, indeed, beneficial, for they would erode slavery and prejudice, helping Americans from diverse backgrounds create a more cohesive empire. Due to Richard Mentor Johnson's political prominence, he and Julia Chinn would emerge as the most visible symbol of amalgamation, their family a topic of debate throughout the United States.[18]

A fitting home for the Chinn-Johnson family, Kentucky was then the West, and it occupied a special place in the American imagination as "the land of promise." Because Anglo-Americans did not come to Kentucky until the Revolutionary era, they associated it with the spread of freedom and democracy. Kentucky became a laboratory for the American dream, an augur for the nation's future. Settled more quickly than other frontier regions, Kentucky reflected Americans' firm commitment to western growth, but it also provoked critical thinking about citizenship and race as the empire expanded into new territories. In 1792, at Kentucky's first constitutional convention, the commonwealth considered a proposal by Presbyterian minister David Rice to abolish slavery. Although the measure was defeated by a vote of 16 to 26, Kentucky's constitution became famous for its democratic principles, granting all free men, regardless of their property, the rights of citizenship. Visitors believed that Kentucky's social relations, like its politics, were more democratic—people of different classes socialized, Catholics lived alongside Protestants, whites and blacks shared stagecoaches. Kentucky never outlawed black education, and many of its white citizens actively supported emancipation. Thomas Henderson, later superintendent of Choctaw Academy, first came to Kentucky to found a community for freed slaves, one of many utopian projects in the commonwealth's early days.[19]

Kentuckians embraced the sense of opportunity and reinvention associated with the West, but they were eager to overturn other aspects of frontier identity. Seeking to dispel the stereotype of the Kentuckian as a rough redneck—"half horse, half alligator," according to a popular song—many sought to bring "civilization" to the frontier. The Bluegrass, fashioning itself as the "Athens of the West," was the epicenter of this movement, home of the first college west of the Allegany Mountains, a symphony orchestra, public libraries, and a wide range of private academies, including some for free African Americans.[20]

Like many Americans, Kentucky reformers were eager to extend "civilization" not just to white and black Americans, but also to Indians. This represented a change from post-Revolutionary policy, when the US army and state militias waged a series of border wars with neighboring Indian nations in an effort to gain land that Britain had supposedly ceded in the Treaty of Paris. As Indian armies scored key victories in the West while American casualties and costs mounted, policymakers considered ways to turn bloody paths into peaceful ones. In 1795, Secretary of War Henry Knox implemented the Civilization Policy, which sought to remake Indians, changing their cultures, languages, religions, family structures, and gender roles to conform to those of Anglo-Americans so that they might become US citizens. In a report commissioned by the federal government, scholar Jedidiah Morse concluded, "Indians are of the same nature and origi[n] . . . with ourselves; of intellectual powers as strong, and capable of cultivation, as ours."[21]

While the War of 1812 demonstrated that the United States remained willing to use violence to gain Indian land, the work of "civilization" resumed after the war. Drawing on a circular printed by a Kentucky missionary society, a federal employee named Thomas L. McKenney outlined a plan for schools in Indian country. Backed enthusiastically by progressive evangelicals, the Civilization Fund Bill passed by Congress in 1819 provided $10,000 annually for Indian schools. This funding was part of a broader expansion of education in the wake of the war, for policymakers believed that schools might transform a heterogeneous group of Americans "into republican machines." Yet schooling for Indians served a special purpose. One general declared, "Educating the children . . . will go further to keep peace on our frontiers than all the armies that has been or may be sent there." Policymakers imagined the policy as an alternative to warfare, but they disagreed about the ultimate goal: Would "civilization" make Indians eligible for citizenship in the "respectable empire"? Or would civilized Indians remain outside the United States, acting as "good neighbors and faithful allies" who would pave the way for America's imperial march? Whatever the next step, policymakers believed that educated Indians would be more pliable "in yielding to the policy of the government, and co-operating with it."[22]

The debate over the place of "civilized" Indians demonstrates that many whites disagreed with inclusive ideals, doubting that Indians and African Americans, in particular, could ever overcome their "heathen" backgrounds or the stain of slavery to become citizens in a free republic. Like many states, Kentucky retreated from some of its Revolutionary principles to restrict rights for people of color. In the late 1790s, Kentuckians revised their constitution to bar "Indians, negroes and mulattoes" from voting and enacted an expansive slave code, for the economy was increasingly wedded to slavery. The rich Bluegrass country, home to the commonwealth's largest free black community, was also the site of its biggest plantations. Maintaining close economic ties to their southern neighbors, Kentuckians used slave labor to produce staple crops, tobacco, pork, bourbon, and hemp. They shipped all of these products and more down the Mississippi River to New Orleans, then the capital of the growing cotton kingdom.[23]

Even if they supported emancipation, many whites could not envision a multiracial citizenry. Many joined the American Colonization Society, founded in 1816, which offered a solution to those who favored gradual emancipation but feared race war and amalgamation by promoting the emigration of former slaves to Liberia. Led by famous statesmen, including President James Madison and Congressman Henry Clay, the colonization movement was particularly strong in Clay's home state of Kentucky, where a diverse coalition of whites supported the cause. But the Kentucky Colonization Society, established in 1829, sent only 658 African Americans to Liberia in its thirty-year history. Few were interested in "returning" to a continent they had never seen. Philadelphia pastor Richard Allen explained that the vast majority of African Americans were determined to remain in "this land which we have watered with our *tears* and our *blood*, [which] is now our *mother country*." To govern the vast majority of free African Americans who refused to leave the United States, most states imposed extra taxes and heightened property requirements for black voters.[24]

For Indians, the Civilization Policy seemed to offer the possibility of US citizenship, but was, in fact, Janus-faced. Thomas Jefferson explained that he hoped for assimilation as the "most happy" arrangement but threatened that those who could not or would not change would be forced to "remove beyond the Mississippi." Parallel to African colonization, the threat of removal was another sign of the possible limits of citizenship. The United States provided pathways to inclusion but also created obstacles, demanding that people of color meet heightened standards to qualify for citizenship.[25]

Indians, however, occupied a different legal and political position from that of African Americans, for they were citizens of their own sovereign nations and were not necessarily interested in US citizenship. Indians and Europeans had lived together in North America for nearly three hundred years, and Natives were used to European schemes to change their cultures and lifestyles. Civilization Policy echoed aspects of earlier attempts by the Spanish, English, and French empires to remake Indians in the image of Europeans. Although Native Americans adapted aspects of European culture, they were selective, attempting to choose elements that enhanced their own power.[26]

Schools, in particular, emerged as a battleground. Indians and Europeans alike used education to transmit the culture of their ancestors and prepare their children for the future, and thus both groups connected education to the survival of their nations. Treaties, as nation-to-nation agreements, confirmed the sovereignty of Indian nations, but the United States still tried to pressure Native people to adopt Anglo-American culture. When the federal government asked Seminoles to send their students to American schools, leaders responded, "It is better for us to remain as we are, red men, and live in our own way." The Ho-Chunk agreed, saying, "If the Great Spirit had made us like white men, he would have given us a way to be educated like them." Dakotas told their agent that teaching their children English and other white ways would offend their relatives and ancestors and might even invite the spirit world to "destroy them." These nations agreed with many white Americans that separate paths were the best course.[27]

By the 1820s, however, a growing chorus of Native leaders argued that radical education reform was necessary for Indian survival. Many believed that they were living in an era of accelerated history and unprecedented change. "America is the country of the Future," declared the popular writer Ralph Waldo Emerson. "It is a country of beginnings, of projects, of vast designs and expectations." Indians agreed that the United States had ruptured the course of history, but they did not share Emerson's celebratory tone, for the explosive growth of the United States had inaugurated an era of crisis in Indian country. As a Choctaw named David Folsom observed, "The circumstance of my nation is changed, the game is gone, our former wilderness is now settled by thousands of white people, and our settlements are circumscribed and surrounded." Yet Folsom believed that Indians, too, were a people of change, a people fit for the future. To endure, Folsom believed that it was "necessary that my nation should change the custom, and leave our forefathers' ways."[28]

Choctaws were at the vanguard of the education movement. In that nation, leaders like David Folsom linked schooling to coexistence with whites. The United States actually conquered few Indian nations on the battlefield; as Native leaders knew, most of their land had been usurped in treaties demanded by ever-growing numbers of invading white settlers. These treaties were written in a foreign language through imperfect and usually corrupt translators. As the United States had become increasingly aggressive in its territorial ambitions, Indians desperately wanted new solutions for peaceful cohabitation, including more effective mediators. By becoming "learned people," as one Choctaw put it, his nation believed that they could remain in their eastern homelands and train the rising generation to better defend Indian rights.[29]

Though Choctaw Academy began as a collaboration between the federal government and the Choctaw Nation, the school appealed to Indian leaders from across the continent. By the time Choctaw Academy opened in 1825, there were thirty-eight other Indian schools, but this academy was different from the rest in its mission, scope, and scale. While the others were run by missionaries, Choctaw Academy was the first controlled by the US federal government. Specifically, Choctaw Academy fell under the purview of the War Department, the branch that oversaw Indian Affairs. The only other school directed by the War Department was West Point, a telling link, for both were conceived of as elite institutions that offered secular education to aspiring leaders. Over the course of twenty-three years, Choctaw Academy educated more than six hundred Indian students representing seventeen different nations, making it by far the largest and most diverse antebellum Indian school. Potawatomi chief Noonday explained the appeal: "I wish our children to be instructed like the whites; then these educated children will become capable of assisting us in the transaction of business with white people." Indians wanted more than the proselytizing, vocational education that the few mission schools in their own nations offered. Native leaders demanded a school advanced enough to prepare their children to compete with whites in the realms of law, politics, and the sciences.[30]

At Great Crossings, Americans' diverse dreams and competing goals converged. Then at the crossroads of North America, Kentucky was a gateway to the West and a borderland between North and South. Kentucky embraced America's imperialist spirit as well as its contradictions, for it was home to gentlemen and half alligators, slaveholders and abolitionists, and at least one Indian-fighter who became schoolmaster to the children of his former foes. It became a meeting ground of Native cultures as well. Choctaw Academy's students included plantation grandees from the Deep South, bison hunters of the Great Plains, and fur traders hailing from the Great Lakes. Collectively, the residents of Great Crossings spoke more than a dozen languages and counted ancestors on three continents. They included settlers looking to extend the dominion of the United States to incorporate distant lands and foreign people, Indians from across the continent seeking new ways to assert anciently

Figure I.2 Native Nations and Choctaw Academy. Shows the tribal homelands of nations that sent students to Great Crossings. Map by Ian Byers-Gamber.

held rights, and people of African descent hoping to cross the threshold from slavery to freedom.

⚬⟡⚬

Great Crossings embodied the meeting of space, cultures, and time that distinguished the period between the War of 1812 and the coming of the

Civil War. Usually, the history of this era focuses on whites who turned west to conquer a continent, extending liberty as they went. This story, instead, begins in the interior of the continent and looks outward to reorient our perspective and broaden our gaze. It includes Indians who faced east and met Americans in the middle and African Americans who challenged the empire of liberty to live up to its rhetoric. "We hope for better things," explained one resident of Great Crossings.[31]

The American Revolution plays a leading role in the origin story of the United States, but the Jacksonian era gave birth to the empire that would eventually transform global history. But before it looked overseas, the US empire first grappled with North America, which was not an empty wilderness but rather a complex continent shaped by competing sovereignties and diverse populations. The Jacksonian era marked the first time that the continental balance of power shifted away from Indian nations in favor of the United States. US dominance, however, was not a foregone conclusion but rather a contingent process born of battles waged in blood and ink. The Jacksonian era was both much more and much less than an expansion of democracy born of the Revolution: it was a time of profound social, economic, and political change that brought the diverse peoples of North America closer together than ever before. Intimacy forged common ground but also conflict.

Americans hoped that time would bring progress. In justifying its expansion, the United States claimed to spread democracy, economic opportunity, and peace. "The theory of your government is justice and good faith to all men," Choctaw leaders reminded Congress. "Impressed with that persuasion, we are confident that our rights will be respected." But the empire of liberty was also driven by darker impulses: tyranny, exclusion, and war. The story of Great Crossings reflects, in microcosm, the large-scale forces then shaping North America, but the place itself animated some of those changes, profoundly impacting those involved and influencing national policies in the United States and in Indian country.[32]

Great Crossings provides an intimate view of the ambitions and struggles of Indians, settlers, and slaves who came together at a crossroads and tried to forge paths ahead. Dividing paths, often red with violence, are perhaps more familiar to us. Studies of the era typically focus on one of three journeys: the expansion of US territory and democracy, the spread of slavery, or the expulsion of Native Americans during Indian removal. Though often treated separately, these issues were deeply entwined, as the story of Great Crossings demonstrates. Great Crossings also offers less familiar stories of once "great" paths shared among many that were later abandoned and forgotten. Incomplete crossings might be lesser known, but they are still significant, for they help us recover past mindsets as well as alternate paths to the future.

Anticipating "a perfect system of roads" that would bind North America, Congressman John C. Calhoun declared, "Let us conquer space." Soon, the United States would complete the westward expansion that Calhoun envisioned, and the empire's formative era would profoundly shape subsequent ideology, both at home and abroad. But Indian-derived metaphors remind us that roads are never "perfect," in the sense of completely formed or finished. Rather, roads are dynamic because they are shaped by ever-changing human relationships. Paths that connected the US empire were forged and maintained by an uneasy federation of the enthusiastic, ambivalent, and unwilling. The story of Great Crossings suggests that US history is not progressive but rather cyclical, a recurring debate over competing visions of America. The territorial growth of the United States forged a multicultural society, but that diversity also gave birth to a thousand anxieties over race, citizenship, and America's destiny—anxieties that remain with us still.[33]

Warriors

A long time ago, in the Choctaw town of Yazoo, a handsome son was born to a war chief. The boy was strong and courageous. All the elders said that he would be a great warrior one day. But he was unlucky in battle. Other young men who had slain enemies and taken captives earned new names—war names—to commemorate their feats. As he grew into adulthood, he followed the custom of shedding his childhood name. Still, as the years went by, he failed to earn a war title to replace it. His relatives called him the Nameless Choctaw.

The Nameless Choctaw loved a young woman from his village, and she returned his love, but she could not become his wife until he had won a name. One summer, the Choctaws were at war with a nation to the west, the Osages, and the Nameless Choctaw got another chance to prove himself. His countrymen gave him the honor of leading four hundred warriors in the dances before the expedition. A few nights later, as the war party neared Osage country, they slept in a cave. A stealthy Osage hunter discovered them and soon returned with other warriors, who made a fire and sealed off the cave, smothering the Choctaws to death. From afar, a Choctaw scout witnessed this and ran back to his own country to reveal the sad fate of his brother-warriors. The lover of the Nameless Choctaw heard his story and she fell into a deep sorrow. Before the new moon came, she passed away.

But she did not meet the Nameless Choctaw on the path of souls, for he was not dead. The war chief had asked him to spy on the enemy, and he was away at the time of the massacre. Osage warriors tracked him down, chasing him over their vast prairies, all the way to an unfamiliar land of forest and mountains. The Nameless Choctaw managed to evade his pursuers, but he was lost and asked the Great Spirit to guide him home. A giant white wolf appeared and led him back. The Nameless Choctaw, transformed through great suffering, was unrecognizable to his people, who were still mourning the loss of his betrothed. This seeming stranger asked the people to repeat the story of her death, and he wailed a mourning song. On a cloudless night, the Nameless Choctaw visited the grave of his lover. Overwhelmed with grief, he collapsed and died. The white wolf howled, again and again, and the sound remained—it remains still—in the pine forest where the lovers lie.[1]

Peter Pitchlynn heard the story of the Nameless Choctaw in his youth, and he repeated it as an elder. It stuck with him because it was, in many ways, a cautionary tale for his own generation. He and his peers were the first to come of age in a new era of Choctaw history. For the first time in hundreds of years, there were no wars to fight. And yet, in many Native cultures, warfare was an essential part of masculinity. Boys could grow tall and strong, and begin to wish for wives and respect and other privileges of adulthood, but without proving themselves in war, could they ever become true men? To avoid the sad fate of the Nameless Choctaw, Pitchlynn and his generation, with the help of their elders, had to imagine a different future, another path to manhood, a new way to to earn their names.

Peter Pitchlynn, or Hatchoctucknee ("Snapping Turtle"), was born on January 30, 1806, into a prominent Choctaw family of Indian and European ancestry. Peter's grandfather, Isaac Pitchlynn, was in the British navy, and his grandmother, Jemima, gave birth to Peter's father, John, at sea, on board a ship in the Caribbean. Years later, after Jemima's death, Isaac and John were traveling across the South, when Isaac fell ill and died, leaving a teenaged John orphaned among the Choctaws. John remained in the Choctaw Nation, where he learned the language. Although he had no formal education, John could read and write passably well, and these skills, combined with his linguistic talents, helped him become a translator, a job he would hold for the rest of his life. After John married a Choctaw woman and fathered several children, he became more integrated into the nation. John initially brokered knowledge, but he added trade goods to his repertoire, becoming a cultural and economic liaison between whites and Indians.[2]

But the real power came from Peter's mother, Sophia, who married John after his first wife died in 1805. Because the Choctaws were matrilineal, resources and power followed through the maternal line. Political offices, too, were influenced by heredity, usually passing from an uncle to his sister's son. Sophia was related to Puskush and Mushulatubbee, two of her nation's most powerful mikos, as Choctaws call their chiefs. John and Sophia's marriage was seemingly affectionate, but it was also strategic. John benefited from Sophia's connections, which allied him with some of the most powerful leaders in the Choctaw Nation, while Sophia and her family, with John as a go-between and skilled translator, were able to communicate more effectively with US officials and gain privileged access to trade goods. John and Sophia's marriage epitomized the hopes of those who imagined a future of peaceful coexistence for whites and Indians. The two were by no means exceptional. For centuries, Native people used the bonds of kinship to build bridges with other nations, a practice they extended to colonial newcomers. Many elite Native women, with the encouragement of their families, married white traders or colonial officials. Such ties conferred power, for they eased trade and diplomacy among nations.[3]

Although he had three half-brothers from his father's first marriage, Peter was the first child born to John and Sophia, making him a favored son from the start. The Pitchlynns lived in the Northeastern District, which was ruled by a succession of chiefs related to Sophia. John built a trading post at Plymouth Bluff on the Gaines Trace near the junction of Oktibbeha Creek and the Tombigbee River. Over time, the Pitchlynns expanded their wealth, becoming cattle ranchers, cotton planters, and investors in a stagecoach line that connected the Choctaw Nation to Mississippi Territory. Peter grew up in what he called a "cedar log mansion," a two-story house distinguished not only by its large size and comparative grandeur but also by the impression of a wayward cannonball, launched in celebration of the conclusion of the War of 1812 by a careless neighbor.[4]

Enslaved African Americans did much of the work around the Pitchlynns' estate, planting corn and cotton; tending to herds of cattle,

Figure 1.1 Há-tchoo-túc-knee, Snapping Turtle (alias Peter Perkins Pitchlynn),
George Catlin, 1834. Courtesy of the Smithsonian American Art Museum.
Gift of Mrs. Joseph Harrison Jr.

horses, and hogs; carrying letters; clearing land; and digging wells. A personal servant whom the Pitchlynns called "Black Peter" usually accompanied Indian Peter on hunting expeditions and other trips. Slavery was
legal in the Choctaw Nation, though not exactly commonplace. In 1831,
the first comprehensive Choctaw census counted 521 slaves among
nearly 20,000 Indians. The Pitchlynn family, with sixty slaves, were the
largest slaveholders in the Choctaw Nation.[5]

Because Peter's father John was of English descent and influenced by European notions of patriarchy, he acted as a co-parent to his children, something that seemed strange to the matrilineal Choctaws. Even so, young Pitchlynn still experienced many elements of traditional Choctaw education. Peter's maternal uncle Mushulatubbee fulfilled his traditional obligations, educating the boy in Choctaw ways, teaching him the stories and songs and prayers that Peter's biological father could not. What young Peter thought of as play was also a kind of education. With his brothers and other Choctaw boys, Peter camped in the woods, rode horses, and hunted deer, bears, and the occasional alligator. Although Peter would never get a chance to prove himself in battle, he could still hunt, just as his kin had done for hundreds of generations.[6]

Before he learned to draw a bow or fire a rifle, however, Pitchlynn learned the work of a cowboy, tending cattle alongside his male relatives as well as enslaved men. Although Indians acting as cowboys might seem incongruous, it was, in fact, fairly typical among southern Indians. As far back as the 1600s, Native boys and men had herded cattle belonging to the Spanish in Florida. By the late 1700s, many southern Indians had become serious ranchers in their own right, owning herds that compared with those of their white neighbors and exporting beef to emerging markets in Pensacola, St. Augustine, Mobile, and New Orleans. By the time Peter was born, Choctaws who could afford it gave each of their children "a mare and a colt, cow and calf, and a sow and pigs." An educational tool as well as an investment, these livestock were supposed to be raised by the child and then given to him or her at adulthood. By the early nineteenth century, animal husbandry had become "traditional" for Choctaws, who proved more than capable of incorporating aspects of European culture into their own society, on their own terms.[7]

Just as Choctaws adjusted their economy, they also adapted their political organization to meet changing demands. The Choctaws' ancestors lived in several independent chiefdoms, and while their dialects differed, they spoke a common language. With European contact came disease, warfare, and slave raiding that decimated the populations of these chiefdoms. Seeking protection, the survivors came together in what is now Mississippi and, several decades before their American neighbors to the east, forged a new nation. Ruled by three chiefs—one for each district—the Choctaws adopted a government that preserved some of the autonomy of their ancestors' chiefdoms. Each district retained its own council and laws, but the Choctaws' unified government could project power in foreign affairs. Because the Choctaws were one of the largest and most powerful nations in colonial North America, they were a valued partner in trade and warfare. For much of the eighteenth century, the Choctaw Nation allied with the French empire, though they also forged relationships with the British, Spanish, and other Indian nations.[8]

Continuing a practice developed with other imperial powers, the Choctaw Nation signed their first peace treaty with the United States in 1786. Thereafter, the Choctaw Nation acted as a strong military ally. In 1814, during the Red Stick War, as the United States sought to defeat an anti-colonial faction of the Creek Nation, seven hundred Choctaw warriors helped them win two key victories on the Black Warrior River, a feat that earned Chief Pushmataha the rank of brigadier general in the US Army. Later that year, fellow general Andrew Jackson again called on Pushmataha and the Choctaws to serve in the War of 1812 at the Battle of New Orleans. Commanding more than one thousand warriors, Pushmataha led a flank attack against seasoned British regulars, earning high praise from grateful Americans. In the eyes of Choctaws, such experiences—"your blood having mingled with our blood in wars"—bound the two nations as allies. Through a blend of cultural persistence and innovation, Choctaws endured the tumult of early colonialism to emerge as a formidable nation.[9]

As a child, Peter learned about politics and the history of his people. He shadowed his father as John went about his work, visiting the homes of prominent Choctaw leaders, translating letters for them, and discussing trade prices and foreign news. Uncle Mushulatubbee also took Peter under his wing. Because Peter was Sophia's oldest child and, as was increasingly obvious, the most politically inclined of all her sons, Miko Mushulatubbee began to see Peter as his heir. After promising to sit quietly at a distance, Peter was even allowed to watch meetings of the Choctaw General Council. Young Peter was captivated by what he observed: the eloquent power of those elders, resplendent in brightly colored hunting shirts and sashes, as they debated the issues of the

Figure 1.2 Mushulatubbee, by George Catlin, 1834. Courtesy of the Smithsonian American Art Museum. Gift of Mrs. Joseph Harrison Jr.

day in an ancient dialect of Choctaw using literary turns of phrase and vivid historical allusions. Inspired, Pitchlynn decided that he wanted to cultivate the life of the mind in the hopes he could emulate these poet-kings.[10]

Pitchlynn was more ambivalent about his first exposure to Western schooling. The first date he ever recorded in his journal was in 1815, when, at the age of nine, he copied out guidelines for surveying property. Rote copying and memorization was hardly inspirational, but surveying was an increasingly useful skill for a people determined to hold on to every acre of their ancestral land. Peter's first teacher was probably not his father, who was determined to give his children the education he never had, but rather a distant cousin of John's, Gideon Lincecum. Lincecum, who was a surveyor and naturalist of some note as well as a correspondent of Charles Darwin, took a great interest in Peter. But Lincecum had little time to devote to Peter's education—he later said he sent Pitchlynn off "half fixed to school"—so John and Sophia decided to send their boy to an academy in Tennessee. As the only Indian at school, Peter recalled that he was "talked about and laughed at, and within the first week of his admission he found it necessary to give the 'bully' of the school a severe thrashing." After only one term, Peter returned home.[11]

Pitchlynn became more serious about school a few years later, at the age of thirteen, when word got around that another teenager, Peter's cousin Israel Folsom, had written a letter to the president of the United States, James Monroe, expressing his desires for the Choctaw people. Folsom, then attending school in New England, told the president of his plans after graduation.

> It is my chief object, when I finish my education, to return to my dear Nation, and endeavor to persuade them to forsake their ancient customs, habits, and manners, and lay hold on the culture of the land, after the example of their white brethren; to lay their guns and tomahawks down, for the plough, hoe, and the axe; to cultivate their lands, and exchange their whiskey, that detestable liquor, to which they are perpetually devoted, for the coffee, and the tea; and the war whoop for the praises of GOD.

In short, Folsom hoped that the federal government's Civilization Policy would help his people prosper. Israel's brother, David, had actually visited the president at his "palace," as the Folsoms thought of it, and he, too, endorsed radical culture change. David had less Western education than his brother—only six months at a white school in Tennessee. He lamented, "I labour so much difficulty for not having a good learning." Still, he wrote to US congressmen and officials in the War Department, campaigning for greater Choctaw access to schooling. "I . . . wish young rising generation may be educated" so that they might "transact business for the Nation." The Choctaw Nation, that is.[12]

Peter Pitchlynn may never have read his cousin's letter to the president, though he certainly had a general sense of its message. In any case, what Pitchlynn found most arresting was that someone as young as Israel, only five years older than he was, could speak to a foreign leader on matters of Choctaw national policy. As Israel demonstrated, Western schooling offered new sources of power and influence, seemingly a solution to the predicament of his generation. Peter vowed to become a scholar, though he would never lose sight of the Choctaw intellectual traditions that first inspired him.[13]

The desire for schooling was not limited to wealthy and powerful families like the Pitchlynns. One observer noted that "the poorer class" were especially "anxious to have their children educated." It might offer their children a better future. Most Choctaw families, however, lacked the connections and resources to send their children to faraway private schools. Driven by their people's demand, the Choctaw chiefs looked for ways to expand access to Western education.[14]

Missionaries provided one solution. Back in 1810, Presbyterians and Congregationalists in New England had founded the American Board of Commissioners for Foreign Missions (ABCFM). Born of the religious fervor and postmillennial ideology of the Second Great Awakening, the ABCFM was at the vanguard of a group of voluntary societies collectively known as the "benevolent empire." The ABCFM sought to convert and educate "heathens," and it focused especially on the foreigners closest to them—Native Americans. The ABCFM's mission to spread Anglo-American, Protestant culture fit squarely within the Civilization Policy of the federal government, which provided some financial support for missionaries venturing into Indian country.

In 1817, the ABCFM sent a representative to the Choctaw Nation, where he found "not only a readiness but an ardent desire" to receive missionaries. The following year, Chief Levi Perry donated land in the Western District for the first mission. Called Elliot, it was named after John Eliot, an early missionary among New England Natives. One missionary at Elliot related how Choctaws from across the nation had such great "anxiety to have their children educated" that they sent them hundreds of miles away to Elliot, where the ABCFM had to turn away dozens of potential pupils. To accommodate Choctaw demand, the mission system expanded dramatically over the next several years, so that there were multiple branches in every district. Each of these missions had two schools, one for boys, another for girls. The missionaries hosted after-school education programs for adults and, a few times a week, they traveled to more distant villages to teach and preach the gospel.[15]

The Choctaw Nation paid the lion's share of the cost. Within the first two years of the missionaries' arrival, the Choctaw Nation appropriated about $70,000 (the equivalent of $1,500,000 today), about three times more than either the US government or the ABCFM contributed. Most of this sum came from treaty annuities—money that the federal government paid annually to Indian nations for ceded land—but many wealthy families also donated cash, livestock, or the labor of their slaves. The Pitchlynns, for example, helped found Mayhew, the first mission school in their district, by giving $1,000. Families of more modest means cleared land, constructed buildings, cooked, and nursed the sick. Families, rich and poor, from across the Choctaw Nation, bound together to invest in their children's future.[16]

According to the terms of the contract between the ABCFM and the Choctaw Nation, the Choctaws, if displeased, could discontinue the missions, at which time "the privileges granted . . . shall cease, & the use as well as the right of said shall revert to the nation." To maintain the agreement, the missionaries found that they had to adjust to Choctaw expectations. Initially, they tried to teach and preach in English, sometimes employing bilingual Choctaws as translators, but they quickly discovered that, to be effective, they would need to learn Choctaw. Cyrus Kingsbury, the ABCFM's head of missions in Choctaw country, directed a few of the missionaries to gain proficiency in the language. The most able of these linguists proved to be another Cyrus, Cyrus Byington. Hailing from Stockbridge, Massachusetts, Byington was inspired by the Indian mission set up by John Eliot in his hometown, though, growing up, Byington thought he would pursue a career in law. A few years after his admission to the Massachusetts bar, however, Byington went to a revival and had a profound conversion experience. A few years later, he was in the Choctaw Nation, working as an ABCFM missionary. To learn Choctaw, Byington moved in with David Folsom and his family. His previous linguistic training, in Greek, Latin, Hebrew, and French, helped him think about the mechanics of foreign tongues, and soon Byington was working on a dictionary and translating Christian hymns. In 1825, Byington, in collaboration with fellow missionary Alfred Wright and Choctaw friends, including David Folsom, wrote the first book printed in the Choctaw language, *Chahta Holisso*, or "Choctaw Book," which taught beginning students how to spell in their own language.[17]

All the missionaries in the Choctaw Nation attempted to emulate Byington's success, though few gained his proficiency. A fellow missionary, in his early attempts to preach in Choctaw, "by a slight mistake once asked God to eat up all the children." The incredulous Choctaw audience may have gasped, or exchanged worried looks, or even laughed knowingly, but, in general, they appreciated missionaries' attempts to learn their language. It was a sign that the foreigners were willing to bend their expectations to accommodate Choctaws' demands.[18]

Despite these early signs of promise, problems quickly emerged. Although the missionaries proved accommodating in some ways, they remained, first and foremost, evangelicals who believed that they had a divine mandate to convert heathens. Leaving their New England towns to live and, in many instances, die in a foreign land, they expected to spend most of their time saving souls. Choctaws, however, had other plans. As one missionary complained, Choctaws manifested "great indifference" toward Christianity: "The expectation of this people has been that all our efforts would be directed toward the commencement of a school." As missionaries moved into new areas of the Choctaw Nation to preach the gospel, Indians reminded them of why they had been invited in the first place: "some have even gone so far as to say that if we do not get a school in to operation by such a time, we must quit the country."[19]

Choctaws wanted education, not conversion, but they found that the missionaries refused to separate the two. Once schools were in operation, parents and tribal leaders expected their children to learn useful skills—literacy, arithmetic, surveying. But they were sorely disappointed to hear very dissonant daily accounts from their sons and daughters. Missionaries regarded the schools themselves as "usefully principally as a means of communicating religious truth to the surrounding population." The Bible was the focal point of the curriculum. Students spent much of each school day hearing about it, reading it, and reciting it.

Missionaries bragged that one scholar at Elliot memorized 476 verses, a feat that many Choctaws likely regarded as remarkable, though a waste of time. Some even made it plain to missionaries that they "despise[d] the religion of Jesus."[20]

When the students were not bending over the Bible, they seemed to be doing chores for white people. Religious and cultural conversion, missionaries thought, went hand in hand. Believing that Indians were lazy and backward, missionaries made manual labor part of the curriculum, emphasizing "proper" gender roles. The girls made clothing, soap, and candles, and did other domestic work, while the boys cleared fields, planted crops, milked cows, and chopped wood. Joel Wood, a schoolmaster at the Elliot mission, admitted that students sometimes spent up to half of their workweek engaged in chores and that he found it very hard to teach grammar to students who spoke little to no English. Believing that some of their students were suited *only* for manual labor, the missionaries called one boy "stupid," noting he "will make a better farmer than a scholar."[21]

In the early nineteenth century, Indians debated what role, if any, manual labor should play in education. A federal official among the Ojiwbe asserted, "Indians are averse to any kind of manual labour & despise to see their children thus engaged." But many saw the value in teaching children "the mechanical arts." Blacksmiths were in particularly high demand in Indian country. In 1828, for example, one district of the Choctaw Nation set aside $1,500 to pay and supply an American blacksmith, for whom they also built a house and shop. They were delighted when mission graduates began to fill such positions. Native nations, though, protested when their children were put to servile work, such as cleaning for or waiting on whites.[22]

Boys' engagement in agriculture also caused an uproar. In many eastern Indian societies, including the Choctaw Nation, farming was considered women's work; although men might help women clear fields, women traditionally did all planting, cultivation, and harvesting. Although Indians welcomed some cultural innovation, they saw male engagement in agriculture as emasculating, a dangerous inversion of their own gender norms. When elite Mohawk Molly Brant learned that her brother Joseph, then enrolled in an Indian preparatory school affiliated with

Dartmouth, had to work on the farm, she wrote to him in Mohawk, telling him to withdraw immediately. In the Cherokee Nation, a chief who was considering sending his son to a mission school "offered to find a slave who should work all day, if the missionaries would excuse his son from agricultural labour between school-hours."[23]

In the Choctaw Nation, Robert Cole, heir to Chief Apuckshanubbee in the Western District, led the protest against manual labor in schools. Initially, Cole supported the introduction of mission schools, sending five nieces and nephews to Elliot. When the children's father, Daniel McCurtain, asked to place another child at Elliot, the missionaries refused, saying the school was full. Angry, McCurtain withdrew all of his children. Cole, assuming the traditional authority of a maternal uncle, interceded on the children's behalf, asking the missionaries at Elliot to take them back. Still, they refused. Cole, too, turned against the school. His dismay mounted when his daughter told him of all the work she did at Elliot and of how the missionaries whipped her when she misbehaved. Although white men considered corporal punishment normal for wives, children, and other social subordinates, Choctaws stigmatized whipping, reserving it for criminals and slaves.[24]

When tribal leaders looked to the grounds of the mission schools, they saw new buildings, large herds of stock, cultivated fields, and, most galling, stores selling food and clothing produced by the children. Such riches represented a huge outlay of Choctaw capital, and many felt that they had not made a wise investment. Kingsbury himself admitted, "There is hardly a council but that some of the Choctaws talk about the cattle they have given the missionaries, and say they ought to take them back; that their children in the mission schools do not learn anything, etc." What, exactly, had the Choctaws gotten out of their $70,000 investment? Some began to suspect that the missionaries had come to swindle them, a theory bolstered when several applied for licenses to trade in the Choctaw Nation.[25]

Miko Mushulatubbee's grievances went deeper, beyond questions of money and curriculum. Several years earlier, Mushulatubbee, like the other two chiefs, was eager to found a school in his district. On April 30, 1822, Mushulatubbee got his wish with the creation of Mayhew. Mushulatubbee sent his four sons and several nieces and nephews, including Peter Pitchlynn, to Mayhew. After only three months, however,

Pitchlynn was expelled for some unnamed offense, recorded only as "disobedience." The next closest mission school—closer than Elliot—was Charity Hall, located in the Chickasaw Nation. Mushulatubbee and the Pitchlynns were pleased when Charity Hall and the Chickasaws made a place for Peter, but harbored a grudge against the overly strict missionaries at Mayhew. Shortly thereafter, Mushulatubbee helped establish a school at his house. Naturally, Mushulatubbee planned to have a stronger hand in shaping "Miko Mushulatubbee's School." Save for $100 from the federal government, Mushulatubbee paid for everything, and the teacher and all the students boarded in his home. Soon, though, Mushulatubbee clashed with schoolmaster Adin Gibbs, a Delaware Indian educated in New England who reprimanded Mushulatubbee for hosting drunken gatherings at his house.[26]

Peter's expulsion and Gibbs's admonishment were part of the ABCFM's broader aim to reshape Indian cultures in the mold of middle-class, respectable whites. This meant that, in addition to proselytizing, the missionaries sought to suppress a broad range of "heathenish" behaviors, including ball playing and dancing—social activities that also held religious meaning for Indians—and sexual practices, especially polygamy, a marriage pattern common among elite Choctaws. Missionaries also complained that "Indian parents are generally indulgent to their children, and seldom control them." In school, missionaries compensated with corporal punishment or verbal lashings, or by isolating unruly children or denying them meals. At the time, white Americans deemed such treatment "normal" for disobedient children, but Indians thought it abusive. Seeing the ways in which missionaries disregarded their tribal culture, Choctaws called them "intolerant," "bigoted," and "overzealous." Choctaws who fed and housed the missionaries resented the overbearing foreigners whose instruction extended far beyond the schoolhouses. Annoyed, Mushulatubbee once told Cyrus Kingsbury, "I never can talk with you good missionaries without hearing something about the drunkenness and laziness of the Choctaws. I wish I had traveled over the white man's country; then I would know whether my people are worse than every other people."[27]

After Gibbs repeatedly nagged him, Mushulatubbee lashed out, reportedly "abusing" Gibbs in some unnamed way. In response, Cyrus

Kingsbury removed Gibbs and closed Miko Mushulatubbee's School. Desperate to educate his four sons, Mushulatubbee apologized, and Kingsbury reopened the school. Thereafter, however, Mushulatubbee cast a more critical eye upon the missionaries, resenting the ways in which they meddled in familial and tribal affairs.[28]

Critics like Mushulatubbee began to consider other ways to educate their children. A few Choctaws, including Peter Pitchlynn and David Folsom, had left the nation to attend private academies. Though unusual, this was not unprecedented; since colonial times, Indians—especially elite Indians—had attended school alongside white children. Pitchlynn's experiences, however, reveal how racism and bullying dissuaded many Indians from leaving home. David Folsom's brothers, Israel and McKee, attended a different kind of institution, the Foreign Mission School in Cornwall, Connecticut. Established in 1817 by the ABCFM, this school enrolled "heathens" from around the world—including American Indians, Native Hawaiians, Chinese, Maoris from New Zealand—as well as some whites with a goal of training them to become missionaries, interpreters, and cultural liaisons. Israel Folsom, in particular, fulfilled the expectations of his teachers at the Cornwall School by becoming a zealous Presbyterian minister, but most Choctaws remained uninterested in Christian conversion and showed "no disposition . . . to send their young men to Cornwall."[29]

The most accomplished Choctaw educated abroad was James L. McDonald. James's white father gave him his Scottish name but little else; the boy was reared by his Choctaw mother, Molly, who managed her family's farm. Molly decided early on that James would have a Western education. By then, she may have been a widow, but even if her husband was still alive she would have been the one to make this decision. As one shocked white observer noted, matrilineality gave women "much more influence in educating children than men, particularly amongst the Choctaws." When James was about nine years old, Molly sent him one hundred miles from home to attend a white school in Washington, Mississippi. There, McDonald learned the basics—reading, writing, cyphering—enough to give the young boy, in his own words, "a great relish for learning." Molly then sought out higher education for James, working with the Choctaws' federal agent to place him in a succession of private academies in Baltimore, Maryland: first, a Quaker school, and, after he graduated, a mathematics institute, where McDonald learned algebra, mechanics, astronomy, and natural and experimental philosophy.[30]

By 1818, when McDonald was sixteen, his academic accomplishments came to the attention of high-ranking US officials. Secretary of War John C. Calhoun pulled McDonald from school and took the Choctaw to Georgetown, placing him in the home of an official in Indian Affairs, Thomas L. McKenney. McDonald's good manners and handsome grace made him, in the words of McKenney, "the idol of my servants, and the beloved of his school-fellows, and of all who knew him." McKenney adopted McDonald, then about the same age as his biological son William, and the young Choctaw accompanied the family everywhere. "His book was his constant companion," observed McKenney, "whether on the road, going to or returning from school, or in the garden, or the fields, or in alcove, or grove, it was in his hand, or about his person." McDonald was so far ahead of his white classmates in Latin, Greek, and math that the headmaster told McKenney that he had to privately tutor the Choctaw in those subjects. If ever there was a poster boy for the government's Civilization Policy, he was McDonald. As a delighted McKenney told his colleagues in the federal government, "The acquirements of this young Indian afford a gratifying evidence of Indian capacity. . . . To such as question the capacity of Indians for civilization and improvements in science, no better argument need be offered."[31]

The United States would act "the part of a kind parent for him," and, in turn, McDonald would be expected to take a job in the federal government's Indian Office. Initially, McDonald trained as McKenney's clerk, writing letters for him, filing, keeping track of accounts. But the work bored McDonald. McKenney observed, "he loves to keep his intelligence in operation but dislikes drudgery, and forms." McKenney was genuinely fond of McDonald and did not want to force him into an unfulfilling career. Noting that "No young man in the District [DC] writes more, or with apparently more pleasure," McKenney urged McDonald to compose a letter about his future plans. McDonald, "much surprised" by McKenney's suggestion, worried about displeasing federal officials who had financially supported him. His first instinct was to ask to return home and help his mother manage the farm. But that was not why she had sent him away for ten years of schooling. Ultimately, McDonald decided, "I have an ambition to distinguish myself, some disposition to be useful." McDonald thought about the condition of his countrymen—the treaties that continually pushed US boundaries west-ward, greedy whites who sought to hoodwink Indians out of their prop-erty, Choctaws' desire to protect themselves and their homeland. What they needed was a lawyer.[32]

In the early nineteenth century, there were few professional schools in the United States; most aspiring barristers simply interned with practicing lawyers. McDonald, too, followed this path, benefiting from mentors who were among the brightest intellectuals in the country. First, the young Choctaw improved his Latin and Greek by attending a nearby seminary run by James Carnahan, a classically trained scholar who would soon become president of Princeton. McDonald then moved to Lebanon, Ohio, where he studied law under another Princeton man, John McLean, a progressive thinker and anti-slavery jurist who would later serve on the US Supreme Court. In 1824, James McDonald, ready to pursue a career in law, returned to his people.[33]

Shortly after James McDonald came home, Choctaw leaders were pre-paring to depart for Washington, DC. Back in 1820, during the Treaty of Doak's Stand, Choctaw leaders had agreed to part with several million acres of their homeland in exchange for 13 million acres in the West. But, once surveyed, it became clear that this new acquisition included some 5 million acres promised to white settlers in Arkansas Territory. The United States, seeking a quick-and-dirty resale, dispatched two commissioners to try to pressure the Choctaws to cede even more land. But Choctaw lead-ers refused, demanding that a formal negotiation with the "President and heads of Departments" take place in Washington. Because this was an important matter of state, the treaty delegation included all three district chiefs, Apuckshanubbee, Pushmataha, and Mushulatubbee, plus other key leaders, including David Folsom, Robert Cole, Daniel McCurtain, Talking Warrior, Red Fort, and Chilahihumma. The delegation asked James L. McDonald to join them, and the newly minted lawyer accepted.[34]

The journey, in those days, was a month-long, thousand-mile trek across the heart of the South, northward on the Natchez Trace, then up to the Ohio River, and, finally, east to Washington. At Georgetown, Kentucky, where the delegation relaxed before catching a stagecoach, they met with Senator Richard Mentor Johnson, who sought to curry favor with friendly words and Kentucky barbecue. While resting, Mushulatubbee asked someone—probably James McDonald—to write a letter on his behalf to his nephew Peter Pitchlynn. Mushulatubbee reminded Peter that as his heir and captain of the Lighthorse police force, he must "use all your exertions to maintain order and sobriety in my district." Mushulatubbee himself was decidedly rowdier. He and other delegation members overindulged in Kentucky's storied whiskey, and Apuckshanubbee, chief of the Western District, fell off a cliff at Maysville, Kentucky, high above the Ohio River. Incredibly, the elderly chief survived the fall, but died two days later.[35]

Another battle-hardened chief, Pushmataha, completed the journey but developed pneumonia and died a few weeks after the delegation arrived in Washington, on Christmas Eve of 1824. The most revered chief in Choctaw history, Pushmataha was born into a non-elite family in 1764. His parents died when he was still a child, and Pushmataha made his way in the world as a warrior, gaining respect for his courage, eloquence, and sound judgment. In 1811, when Tecumseh visited the Choctaws and urged them to join his multinational Indian alliance against the United States, Pushmataha denounced him as an outside agitator who sought to compromise Choctaw sovereignty and his nation's alliance with the United States. Alongside Americans, Pushmataha led Choctaw troops during the War of 1812 and the Red Stick War, during which time he befriended Andrew Jackson. When the chief died, Jackson paid homage to Pushmataha as he lay in state. More than two thousand whites attended Pushmataha's funeral at the Congressional Cemetery, where the miko was laid to rest with full military honors at the rank of Major General. The mourners, white and Indian alike, agreed that Pushmataha had been a hero.[36]

During treaty negotiations, however, relations between the former allies turned adversarial. Popular American culture often depicts treaty payments as trifling tokens paid to uncomprehending, naïve Indians, but Choctaws and other Native leaders considered treaty annuities investment capital and attempted to secure the best deal possible. Up to that point, however, no Indian negotiator had proved as able as James McDonald. Taking a leading role, the twenty-three-year-old lawyer squared off against his adoptive father, Commissioner of Indian Affairs Thomas McKenney. McKenney was shocked at the young lawyer's abilities and audacity: "I found him so skilled in the business of his mission, so prompt, and so competent, both in verbal discussions, and with the pen, as to make it more of an up-hill business than I had ever before experienced in negotiating with Indians."[37]

The Choctaw delegation stated at the outset that they would cede no more of their homeland, but, for a worthy price, they would consider selling their Arkansas land. Secretary of War John C. Calhoun started off with $65,000, a sum they considered insultingly low, and the Choctaws scoffed, presenting a laundry list of counter-demands. The United States, accustomed to using strong-arm diplomacy and the language of legal-ese to gain maximal land for a minimal price, was forced to give up much more than usual. Ultimately, the Choctaw Nation received a package worth $216,000, more than three times Calhoun's opening offer, plus $6,000 a year *forever* for education. This sum included payment for 843 Choctaw veterans of the War of 1812, who had never been properly compensated for their service, plus additional money for individual Choctaws whose property had been stolen by American citizens. For the Arkansas land, McDonald and the delegation secured $96,000 cash over the course of the next sixteen years.[38]

Perhaps not surprisingly, the treaty's largest expenditure—the education annuity—would prove most consequential. In a letter to Congress, McDonald explained the delegation's rationale: "We have become sensible that one great reason of the power and prosperity with which our white brothers are so eminently favored, has been the general diffusion of literature and the arts of civilized life among them." Citing his people's peaceful alliance with the United States and their desire for education, McDonald asked, "Should not inducements be held forth to our young men to qualify themselves to become useful citizens of your republic?" Certainly, McDonald was not blind to racial prejudice against Indians. Like Peter Pitchlynn, he had probably experienced racial discrimination at school or heard slurs as he stepped out of the McKenneys' carriage and into the streets of Washington. McDonald's brother Thomas, one of a growing number of Indians who served in the US Army, wrote him letters about the discrimination he had faced from fellow soldiers. But, as McDonald addressed Congress, he called upon America's better angels. Education, McDonald hoped, would afford future Choctaws the opportunities he had enjoyed, an ability to move between Indian country and the United States, a kind of dual citizenship in the new American empire.[39]

After the Treaty of 1825, as it came to be called, was signed, surviving delegation members made their way back to the Choctaw Nation. Choctaws were generally satisfied with the treaty—a rare occurrence and a testament to the skill of its negotiators. James McDonald reported, "All the intelligent men of the nation are gratified that the *money* is to be applied for the purpose of education." But one important question remained: What kind of education?[40]

When fervent Christian David Folsom signed the Treaty of 1825, he assumed that they would add these new funds to those they already gave to mission schools within the Choctaw Nation. Fellow delegation members had other plans, but Folsom did not know this because he had stopped speaking to them. Disgusted with his fellow negotiators' enormous Washington bar tabs, which included champagne, oysters, brandy, and gallons of whiskey, Folsom blamed the deaths of Apuckshanubbee and Pushmataha on drink, saying, "God is just and right in taking those chiefs from among the people, so that there may be better men raised up in their places." Departing in a huff, Folsom left Washington before the others. Back home, Folsom talked to missionaries and fellow Choctaws, trying to gather support to use the school funds to build a new school near his house at Pigeon Roost in the Northeast District.[41]

While David Folsom had been fuming in his Washington hotel room, other members of the treaty delegation, possibly over drinks at the bar, discussed how they wanted "to try some other plan" with the education funds. The two most powerful members of the delegation were Mushulatubbee and Robert Cole, who had succeeded his uncle Apuckshanubbee as miko of the Western District, and both had serious grievances with missionaries. Once Mushulatubbee returned home, he vowed to reassert authority over his namesake school and its overbearing teacher, Adin Gibbs. He hosted many visitors at his plantation home, discussing the treaty, opening kegs of rum, and trying to counter David Folsom's growing influence. On July 1, 1825, Cyrus Kingsbury once again closed Miko Mushulatubbee's School—this time for good—citing the chief's "intemperance, and the concourse of drunken Indians at the place, and his overbearing disposition." Furious that these new-comers would attempt to usurp his authority, handed down from gener-ations of mikos, Mushulatubbee threatened "to break up all the schools in the nation."[42]

After Mushulatubbee's school closed, he and Robert Cole accelerated their public relations campaign against the missionaries. Mushulatubbee charged, "We have never received a scholar out of their schools that was able to keep a grog shop book." This turned out not to be true; several mission school graduates became accomplished bootleggers. As a rhe-torical flourish, however, it captured many Choctaws' dissatisfaction with the schools' high costs and seemingly low yields. Cole, meanwhile, reminded Choctaws of how the missionaries worked their children in the fields and whipped them for trivial infractions. Conjuring a terri-fying metaphor, Cole told people in his district "that the children were allowed only two hours in a day for study, and that the balance of the day they were driven in the field in the same manner that negroes were on the plantations in the Southern states." Calling the missionaries "cheats and liars," Cole concluded by accusing them of "encroaching upon the rights of the nation." In the view of Mushulatubbee and Cole, these high-handed missionaries threatened Choctaw sovereignty.[43]

Mushulatubbee told the Choctaws' federal agent, William Ward, that he wanted to create an academy outside of the nation, possibly in a nearby southern state like Tennessee or Kentucky. Ward wrote to his brother-in-law, Senator Richard Mentor Johnson, who was interested in over-seeing an Indian school, especially one as well endowed as that of the Choctaws. Partnering with Johnson, in particular, had its appeal. Ward likely revealed to Mushulatubbee that the congressman strongly sup-ported the separation of church and state and that he rarely attended Sunday services. Johnson also told Choctaw leaders in no uncertain terms that "if you have any business in Congress, I will be yours," a position he may have articulated as early as fall of 1824, when the treaty delegation visited Great Crossings en route to Washington. As a powerful member of the Senate's Committee on Military Affairs, Johnson could prove an invaluable ally in this politically tumultuous era. By late August of 1825, when the General Council met to discuss how to spend the new school funds, Mushulatubbee and Johnson had a gentleman's agreement that the whole amount would be spent on their proposed Choctaw Academy on the senator's property at Great Crossings.[44]

Luckily for Mushulatubbee and due, in no small part, to his influence as the most senior chief, the General Council reached the same conclusion. Some in the nation, including David Folsom and the missionaries, knew about Mushulatubbee's backdoor deal and expected others to be as outraged as they were. It is difficult to gauge the reactions of ordinary Choctaws. Some opposed the schools and refused to send their children. An even greater number complained about Folsom's beloved missionaries. But did they agree, along with David Folsom, that the proposed Choctaw Academy was too expensive? As James McDonald observed, those selected for a pricey boarding school education would need "friends and influence." Commissioner of Indian Affairs Thomas McKenney had similar critiques, pointing out that a local school could educate more students and have a greater economic and social impact by keeping money and Choctaws within the Choctaw Nation. He urged Choctaw leaders to endorse David Folsom's proposed mission school at Pigeon Roost. General Council member Greenwood Leflore acknowledged the War Department's position: "It has been intimated to me that some persons and perhaps members of Congress were dissatisfied with the location of the Choctaw academy." But the Council was firm in its decision. As Leflore told the secretary of war, "as the school is established at our request and upon our money we hope that the experiment [we are] now making will not be interfered with." The commissioner of Indian affairs noted that he could not, with propriety, dissuade the General Council.[45]

Choctaw Academy was indeed an "experiment," one that held great appeal for Choctaws looking for a new kind of education. An alternative to the mission schools, it would be less religious and provide a more advanced education for the most promising youths. Moreover, because the school would be located outside of the nation, its teachers and administrators would be less able to change the culture of the nation itself. Instead, the new academy would be a kind of study-abroad experience. By "being placed in a white community," one Choctaw explained, the children would learn the "customs and manners" of the Americans "and at the same time receive a liberal education." Useful foreign customs or knowledge could later be filtered into the Choctaw Nation, by way of educated Choctaws rather than meddling missionaries.[46]

When sending boys to Choctaw Academy, one tribal official told them to "make every effort to obtain a knowledge of the English language so that you can speak it and write it perfectly." In this era when conflict moved from the battlefield to the treaty table, Choctaw leaders were most anxious that their sons and nephews learn English. Many Choctaw men knew enough English to trade deerskins or exchange a few words at a tavern, but only a handful were fluent. During negotiations for the Treaty of 1825, James McDonald had proven how valuable such knowledge could be, how a fluid speaker, reader, and writer of English could beat whites at their own game. Because mission school students studied English only for an hour or two each day and then returned to a Choctaw social world, they rarely achieved advanced proficiency. In another contrast to mission schools, Richard Johnson promised to enroll white students to help expose Indians to American language and culture, though the contract he created with the Choctaws ensured that whites would always be in the minority, presumably to avoid the sort of bullying that Indian students experienced at white-majority schools.[47]

Because Choctaw Academy was five hundred miles from the Choctaw Nation, students could not easily go home, nor seek the protection of their parents. Predictably, this fact dissuaded many families from enrolling their children, but others believed that such a journey paved the way to manhood. As elders gathered Choctaw Academy's first students, they told the boys: "Do something that is noble—great things are expected of you." Like the Nameless Choctaw, the rising generation could not fight to earn their names, but they could follow the Natchez Trace to a distant land and train to become a different kind of warrior, armed with the weapons their people would need to survive in a changed America.[48]

2

A Family at the Crossing

Men, women, and children, white and black, lined the road for fifteen miles, from Lexington all the way to Georgetown. They had abandoned farms, shops, and schoolrooms on this joyous day, May 18, 1825, to welcome a great Revolutionary War hero, the General Marquis de Lafayette. Muskets fired and cannons boomed as the crowd cheered on the parade, led by prominent citizens of Lexington, several generals, Governor Joseph Desha, and finally, Lafayette himself. Commissioned a major general in 1777, Lafayette earned his red badge of courage at the Battle of Brandywine and, after the war, championed liberty in France, enduring a five-year prison sentence for his convictions. A close confidant of George Washington, the Marquis was the closest living embodiment of Americans' beloved founding father.

The citizens of Georgetown expressed their enthusiasm by presenting the Marquis with a cheese weighing five hundred pounds, an impressive if eccentric gift that would prove useful at the evening's main event, the ball hosted by Richard Mentor Johnson. Local papermaker Ebenezer Stedman described it as the grandest party he had ever attended: "All the young girls in town were dressed on this occasion, the poor as well as rich . . . the excitement was so great that all forgot that they were poor or rich." Stedman could not help but notice that two of the most striking women were Johnson's teenage daughters. "They were dressed as fine as money could dress them," Stedman observed as Imogene and Adaline played the piano for the Marquis. The music and dancing went on well into the night, fueled by punch, barbecue, and that famous Georgetown cheese, as locals from every walk of life celebrated the spirit of 1776.[1]

Lafayette's visit coincided with the fiftieth anniversary of the Revolution, giving Americans an opportunity to reflect on the past and consider the future. During the celebration, the congressman's twelve-year-old nephew and ward, Richard M. Johnson Jr., recited a speech in honor of the Marquis. Dressed in a white uniform with a red sash, a scabbard holding a sword at his side, Richard commanded a veritable children's army of two hundred similarly dressed boys. Addressing Lafayette as "Father," the boy promised, "we will endeavor to imitate your exalted virtues . . . by shedding our blood in the field of the valiant . . . by devoting our lives and our fortunes in the defense of the liberties of our country." These boys enacted a spectacle orchestrated by their elder kinsmen, but, in time, they would take up this charge to extend the "empire of liberty" into Mexico and the far west. But who would benefit from their service? Not surprisingly, the diverse crowd that gathered at Great Crossings—girls rich and poor, old veterans, a young papermaker, two Richard Mentor Johnsons, and the Marquis himself—harbored different visions of America's future.[2]

～ও ৯ৎ～

The Johnson family hailed from Virginia, part of the great westward exodus from that colony that began during the Revolution. Richard's father, Robert, had served in the House of Burgesses as a representative of Fayette County, and his mother, Jemima Suggett, came from a wealthy and politically connected family. Alongside Daniel Boone, Robert Johnson had surveyed Kentucky before it was open to white settlement, and he took that opportunity to secure some of the best land for his own family. In 1779, Robert bought several thousand acres on Elkhorn Creek from Patrick Henry, who, like several other founding fathers, had a side career in land speculation.[3]

The fortunes of the Johnson family were intimately bound up with those of Native Americans. Though Robert Johnson held the title to Great Crossings and much of the surrounding region, Indian resistance prevented the family from moving there for several years. After leaving Virginia in 1779, the Johnsons first relocated to a fort called Bryan's Station six miles east of Lexington. Richard, their fifth child, was born shortly thereafter, on October 17, 1780. Away fighting Indians in the western theater of the American Revolution, Robert missed the birth and much of his son's infancy, leaving Jemima and the older children to defend the family. In 1782, when a multi-tribal Indian army from the Ohio country laid siege to Bryan's Station, the fort ran low on supplies, and legend has it that Jemima saved the day by leading a group of women to a nearby spring. As intended, Jemima's actions both supplied the fort with water and drew the enemy's attention, providing an opportune moment for the settlers to attack.[4]

After the war, Britain conceded vast swaths of eastern North America, including Kentucky, to the United States, and the Johnsons, having more secure title, left the fort at Bryan's Station to claim their Bluegrass estate. But Indians had not been invited to the Treaty of Paris, and a multi-tribal coalition contested US claims to the region. The Johnsons built a stockade around their house, while Richard's father and older brothers fought Indians in a lingering guerilla war. An early Kentucky poet claimed that the Johnsons and other pioneers' blood "washed from thy soil their murderers' guilt."[5]

After the border war concluded in 1794, thousands of settlers joined the Johnsons in Kentucky, lured by stories of the "best poor man's country," "flowing with milk and honey." The Bluegrass state derived its nickname from its most famous region, where underlying calcium-laden limestone enriched a bluish grass that nourished America's finest horses. In Kentucky, one promoter promised, it was "impossible that we can experience anything like poverty." Kentucky's white population skyrocketed, from less than 200 in 1776 to more than 324,000 by 1800. Contrary to popular myth, however, Kentucky was far from the best poor man's country; only one-quarter of white men owned any land at all. Meanwhile, the wealthiest 1 percent, which included Richard's father Robert, owned one-third of Kentucky. The Johnson family's fiefdom grew to exceed 65,000 acres by the early 1800s, including some of the region's the best farmland and pasture.[6]

A member of one of the wealthiest and most powerful families in the state, Richard Johnson was expected to extend his family's influence. As a teenager, Richard Mentor Johnson studied law at Lexington's Transylvania University, where his father was a trustee. Admitted to the bar in 1802, Richard briefly practiced law, but like his father before him, he was drawn to politics. The young Jeffersonian Democrat championed the "will of the people" as "the supreme law," and in his first public speech, he celebrated the Louisiana Purchase as a measure that "enlarged" the "boundary of freedom." In violation of the Kentucky Constitution, Richard Mentor Johnson was elected to represent Scott County in the state legislature when he was twenty-three years old, one year shy of the age minimum. Two years later, in 1806, he became the first native-born Kentuckian elected to Congress, taking over his father's seat in the House of Representatives.[7]

As relations with Britain strained, Richard Mentor Johnson urged Congress to declare war. In speeches before the House of Representatives, Johnson claimed that the British provoked "the savages against our infant and innocent settlements upon the frontiers." As long as the British retained a foothold in Canada, Johnson argued, they would continue to ally with Indians to threaten US national security. Johnson pushed for the conquest of Canada: "I shall never die contented until I see her [Britain's] explusion from North America, and her territories incorporated with the United States." Johnson and his fellow Kentuckian Henry Clay emerged as leading War Hawks, their fervor an accurate reflection of that of their constituents. Kentuckians, largely poor and landless, were desperate to forge a red path of war to British-allied Indians in the Old Northwest and Upper Canada so they could seize those territories. Fellow citizens in the Northeast and Chesapeake, worried about further interruption of trans-atlantic trade, had a more tepid response, but the War Hawks and their constituents prevailed, and Congress declared war in 1812. Richard, who said that he cherished tales of his family's "gallant deeds" against Indian foes, welcomed the chance to distinguish himself as a warrior.[8]

The defining moment of Richard Mentor Johnson's life came on October 5, 1813, when he was thirty-three years old. Having raised a mounted regiment of Kentucky volunteers, Johnson commanded his battalion against combined Indian and British forces at the Battle of the Thames, just east of Detroit in what is now southern Ontario. General William Henry Harrison gave Colonel Johnson permission to charge the enemy. Richard told his brother James, a fellow officer, to attack the British regulars while he engaged Tecumseh's Indian forces who were concealed in a wooded swamp. Asking for twenty volunteers to lead the first charge, Richard led them into the swamp. Meanwhile, Tecumseh told his men to be patient, to wait until the enemy drew close. When

Tecumseh gave the order to fire, most of the first twenty volunteers fell from their horses, dead. Indian soldiers rushed to engage the survivors in hand-to-hand combat.

What happened next lives in the shadowlands between history and myth. We know for sure that Richard Mentor Johnson, wounded and senseless, emerged from the woods on a staggering mare, once white but now mottled with pink and red, and that the body of Tecumseh lay lifeless in the swamp. At first, confusion reigned, for the battle was still hot. Johnson's second and then third wave of troops rushed the swamp before Indian forces had time to regroup. Tecumseh's troops held out longer than their British counterparts, but they, too, retreated, leaving Americans to claim one of their greatest victories of the war. The next morning, American troops scoured the woods for Tecumseh, and finding a man with an engraved British medal around his neck, skinned his thighs, intending to make war trophies out of the fallen warrior's body.[9]

Over the months and years that followed, American accounts of the death of Tecumseh solidified into two distinct categories. Johnson's political opponents felt sure that this soft-handed plantation grandee could not have killed America's greatest Indian warrior in single combat. He was merely a "great *wind mill*," full of hot air, claiming the glory to endear himself to the common folk he pretended to champion. It must have been one of the young privates, David King or David Gooding, or perhaps the old Indian-fighter Colonel William Whitley: anyone but Richard Johnson. This, however, was the minority view. Aided by books, pamphlets, and popular broadsides, most Americans came to identify Richard Mentor Johnson as Tecumseh's killer. Johnson himself was largely silent on the matter, allowing friends and political allies to spread the story for him. Forever after, Johnson was intimately linked with the Shawnee general in the American mind, so much so that "Old Tecumsey" became his nickname.[10]

Johnson's cronies were not the only ones who gave him credit. Many Indians also believed that Richard Mentor Johnson had killed Tecumseh. Those who fought alongside the great Shawnee at the Battle of the Thames told of how Tecumseh, sword in hand, advanced on the man who rode the white horse, and how the wounded officer managed to draw his pistol and fire a deadly shot. Joseph Bourassa, a Potawatomi who attended

Choctaw Academy, had heard such a story from his uncle Shabbona, one of Tecumseh's lieutenants. Shabbona pointed out that Kentucky troops were mistaken in thinking that they had skinned Tecumseh; that poor vessel belonged to Tecumseh's nephew, whose uncle had given him a British medal. However, Americans were right in identifying Richard Mentor Johnson as Tecumseh's killer, according to Shabbona.[11]

Despite the US triumph at the Battle of the Thames, American victory in the War of 1812 was far from assured. In the spring of 1814, the United States needed to call on Cherokee and Choctaw allies to help them defeat the Red Stick faction of the Creek Nation, and, a few months later, British troops sacked and burned the capital city of Washington. The United States also failed in one of its basic objectives—the conquest of Canada. In December of 1814, the war ground to a stalemate, and both sides agreed to resume peaceable trade and return all territories taken during the war. Those most hurt by the war were Native Americans. The United States failed to comply with Article IX of the Treaty of Ghent that promised to restore Native lands. Instead, the United States imposed punishing treaties, seeking to extort the maximum amount of

Figure 2.1 Battle of the Thames, John Dorival, c. 1833. Dorival rendered this fanciful image in the run-up to Johnson's vice presidential campaign. Courtesy of the Library of Congress.

land from nations still reeling from the population loss and political divisions engendered by the war. In the war's aftermath, most eastern Indian nations felt that they could no longer challenge the United States militarily and so looked for other strategies to retain power.[12]

Americans, casting about for a redeeming story to tell about a gloryless war, fixated on Richard Mentor Johnson. One Kentucky resident recalled, "That was all the talk, that Johnson killed Tecumseh." Recovering initially at home, Johnson soon returned to Washington, where he received a hero's welcome. "After vanquishing the enemy," one socialite wrote, Johnson, "covered with glory and wounds, and more than ever beloved by his countrymen . . . is now without comparison the most popular and respected member from Kentucky." Contemporaries, who estimated that Johnson had received anywhere between five and twenty-five bullet wounds, observed his mangled left arm and crippled gait. Christ-like in his suffering, Richard Mentor Johnson, in the words of one colleague, "has served the republic faithfully, in both the Congress and the field, pouring his blood out like water, in defense of his country's rights." In killing Tecumseh, called by white contemporaries "the greatest Indian warrior ever known, the most formidable enemy that the white man ever encountered in the savage wilds of America," Johnson had symbolically destroyed Indian resistance, thereby unlocking the gateway to the American West. In retrospect, as one popular history recalled of the Battle of the Thames, "Never was victory so complete or its achievement so glorious."[13]

Lafayette visited Great Crossings during what one local described as the "noon tide" of Richard Johnson's prosperity. In the decade since the Battle of the Thames, Johnson rose from the House of Representatives to the Senate. To mark the occasion, President Monroe gave the warrior a ceremonial sword. As a senator, Johnson sought to empower common whites: middling craftsmen now poor, victims of the first wave of American industrialization; European immigrants who poured into eastern ports by the million; whites seeking a better life on the western frontier. As chair of the Committee on Military Affairs, Johnson pushed for higher pensions for veterans. He also supported a more liberal land policy to make it easier and more affordable for average Americans to buy land newly wrested from Indians. By upholding the right of preemption, whereby squatters had the right to purchase land at the minimum price once it entered the public domain, Johnson encouraged whites to seize Indian land before treaties were even negotiated. Johnson allied with one of the most rabid US imperialists, fellow Democrat Andrew Jackson. During the First Seminole War, Jackson illegally seized Spanish territory in Florida and executed several Indian and British military officers following a sham trial, which earned him censure from Congress. In the Senate, Johnson became Jackson's leading defender. Congressional observers counted Richard Johnson's speeches on Jackson's behalf some of the best of his career, the presentation enhanced "from beholding those honored scars . . . which had so essentially contributed to prostrate our combined enemy."[14]

Johnson's most famous political issue was his quest to end imprisonment for debt. His home state outlawed the practice in 1821, and Johnson, believing that the federal government should follow suit, brought the issue to the Senate floor every year. Imprisonment for debt, Johnson argued, was simply un-American. "The debtor becomes the slave of the creditor," affording "the creditor this sovereign power over his person." The freedom of white men was "too sacred to be annihilated," especially for something so trivial as money. Embracing the millennial rhetoric popular in the young empire, Johnson argued that this measure was necessary to preserve the moral power of the United States: "We should give an example of the world worthy of our character, that may profit foreign states and distant ages." As the industrial revolution widened the gap between rich and poor, northeastern city dwellers, in particular, cheered Johnson. Reprinting Johnson's speeches with detailed addenda, the Boston Society for the Relief of the Distressed cataloged 1,442 cases of imprisonment for debt in 1820, most of them for less than $20.[15]

Richard Johnson knew a thing or two about debt, his arrears being far in excess of $20. Though he came from a wealthy family, Richard was one of eleven children, and he could not count on a substantial inheritance. Moreover, senators, in those days, were paid a per diem of only $8 each day that Congress was in session; the rest of the year they earned nothing. Johnson, however, could leverage his political appointment to supplement his income. A political enemy of the Johnson family over-stated his case but captured a kernel of truth when he wrote, "Scarce a federal dollar has passed through Kentucky, that has not first been their property." The management of Indian affairs, in particular, offered for-tunes in money and land. In 1818, following in the wake of Lewis and Clark's expedition, the United States sought to extend its influence by developing trading and military posts among the Indian nations of the northern Plains. Richard and his brother James won a federal contract to outfit four steamboats to transport and provision troops during what was dubbed the "Yellowstone Expedition." In exchange for the $267,000 required to finance the expedition, the Johnson brothers expected to secure a lucrative federal contract to continue supplying the forts. The expedition, however, proved disastrous. The Missouri River ran low that summer, stranding the steamboats at Council Bluffs, and the sup-plies proved too paltry, resulting in a rash of scurvy and fever among the soldiers. The Johnson brothers managed to recover much of their initial investment from the federal government, but never all of it.[16]

By 1821, Johnson and his business partners owed the Bank of the United States over half a million dollars, the equivalent of $12 mil-lion today. Johnson's congressional colleague and fellow Kentuckian Henry Clay, acting as a representative of the Bank of the United States, described Johnson as an overly credulous dreamer, explaining, "Acting under the illusions of his strong imagination he believed that he could command, among his friends and connections, property to almost any amount." Johnson and his partners managed to sell or mortgage enough buildings and acreage to satisfy much of their debt, though Clay admit-ted that he was overly generous in evaluating those properties. Still, Johnson owed an additional $100,000 to the Baltimore branch of the Bank of the United States, plus tens of thousands of dollars to various Kentucky banks and creditors.[17]

Johnson's astonishing debt came in part from the Yellowstone Expedition, but he dug the hole deeper in another venture with his brother James. During the War of 1812, the brothers had scouted the Fever River, on Mesquakie and Sauk land near modern Galena, Illinois, learning about the region's rich lead mines. Bringing twenty laborers, including free and enslaved African Americans, James and Richard began to work a mine. Although the brothers had negotiated a contract with a local chief, most Mesquakies regarded the Johnsons and the thousands of other whites who poured into their country as intruders. Conflicts that would eventually lead to war disrupted and then destroyed the Johnsons' mining operation. Once again, Johnsons' creditors came calling, exerting additional pressure by detailing his debts in a Kentucky newspaper as Johnson fought to retain his seat in the Senate. Johnson's political fortunes held strong, but his finances plummeted. By 1824, Johnson had mortgaged his plantation, big house, adjoining property, tavern, mills, livestock, and most of his slaves.[18]

The following year, when brother-in-law William Ward told him of the Choctaws' desire to found a school, Richard Johnson seized upon it: "Fortune for the first time, in my life, seems to open some advantages to me, by the providential friendship and confidence of the Indians." Publicly, Johnson cast this as a philanthropic venture, in line with his "duty to do all I can for others consistent with principle and my power and influence." At the same time, Johnson believed that he could take advantage of this "legitimate" opportunity to "disenthrall" himself from debt. Yet again, Richard Johnson looked to Indians to make his fortune, thinking that this, perhaps, was the most golden of all his opportunities.[19]

Johnson's interest in education did not begin with Choctaw Academy, however. Beginning in 1815, Johnson, as chairman of the Military Affairs Committee in the House of Representatives, sought to establish three national military academies across the country. One of these, he hoped, would be in Kentucky. By bringing institutions of higher learning to Kentucky, Johnson sought to combat stereotypes that depicted Kentuckians as rustic and primitive. The Kentucky of Johnson's imagination was genteel, aristocratic, and progressive. Much to his disappointment, Columbia College in Washington, DC, which later became George Washington University, was the only one of his proposed academies actually built. Still, Johnson maintained that establishing prestigious schools would enhance Kentucky's reputation and, by extension, his own political capital.[20]

In 1818, Johnson partnered with the Kentucky Baptist Society to establish an Indian school on his property at Great Crossings and circulated a letter, via federal agents, throughout Indian country, offering to educate Native children at no cost to their families or tribes. By

Christmas of 1818, school was in session, though it enrolled only eight students, mostly young adult Shawnees from nearby Missouri who were, perhaps, enthusiastic about returning to their Kentucky homeland. Johnson failed to secure additional support from private donors or the federal government, and the school folded in 1821. Moving forward, Johnson realized that he would need the support of tribal governments to create a successful school.[21]

⁓ℰ⚬⧕⁓

Never was Great Crossings busier than in the months between Lafayette's visit and the opening of Choctaw Academy, and Julia Chinn lived in the eye of the storm. She had hosted visiting dignitaries before—President James Monroe and Major General Andrew Jackson had visited several years earlier—but the Lafayette gala was far larger and grander. The first of August brought another kind of celebration, then called the "Colored People's Fair." Enslaved people from Great Crossings and nearby settlements held this annual event. They told white people that they were celebrating the harvest, but Chinn knew that they also used the holiday to commemorate the abolition of the Atlantic slave trade. Even if Chinn wanted to join her relatives and neighbors at the fair, she was probably too busy. Chinn was then hosting Richard's sister Sally and Sally's husband William Ward, who had traveled north from the Choctaw Nation for a long visit. Ward, the Choctaws' Indian agent, brought news that sent Great Crossings into a flurry of activity: Miko Mushulatubbee had authorized the creation of Choctaw Academy. Richard, then home for the congressional recess, had ordered his slaves to construct new buildings and to make dozens of pieces of furniture. Julia checked their progress and then gave orders of her own. She managed a group of women, including her daughters, sisters, and nieces, who sewed bedding and tablecloths. What they could not make Julia purchased at a nearby dry goods store, drawing on Richard's line of credit. In November 1825, when the first Choctaw students arrived, Richard Johnson had already left for his Senate chamber in Washington. Julia Chinn and the new headmaster welcomed the inaugural class at Choctaw Academy to Great Crossings.[22]

Julia Chinn was born into slavery around 1790. Contemporaries called her a "mulatto," meaning that she had both African and European

Figure 2.2   Colonel Richard M. Johnson, 1818, by Anna Claypoole Peale (American artist, 1791–1878), 6.98 by 5.46 cm, watercolor on ivory. This pendant may have once belonged to Julia Chinn, for it was later owned by Imogene Johnson Pence, Chinn's daughter with Richard Johnson. It was passed down to Imogene's descendants for generations. Photograph © 2017, Museum of Fine Arts, Boston. Courtesy of the Museum of Fine Arts, Boston, Emma F. Munroe Fund.

ancestry. She and her siblings took the surname "Chinn," likely in acknowledgment of their white father. Sources do not speak to the identity of this man. "Chinn" comes from an old English geographic term meaning chasm, and it became a British surname, though not a common one in the United States. However, there were a few Chinn families in the Bluegrass, including that of Richard H. Chinn, a prominent white resident of Lexington and law partner to Henry Clay. Whoever he was, this man must have had some significance to Julia and her siblings, for many enslaved people chose not to acknowledge their white fathers, who were not legally bound to provide for their enslaved partners or children. Julia's mother was owned by Richard Johnson's parents Robert and Jemima, and oral tradition holds that she was named Henrietta. Following the condition of her mother, Julia became a house servant and was favored by Jemima, who taught Chinn to read and write. Julia grew up in the same home as Richard, and the two doubtless knew one another well. When Richard moved out of his parents' house, his mother suggested that Julia act as his housekeeper until he married.[23]

By 1811, when Julia was about twenty-one and Richard was thirty-one, the two had become lovers. Oral tradition, from both the Johnsons and the slaves who served in their household, suggests that Richard's mother Jemima tried to pressure Richard to marry an upper-class white woman. This strategy, as Jemima probably explained, would uphold the family's station while also alleviating Richard's debt. Some society women in Kentucky and the District of Columbia expressed interest in Johnson, then "a fine handsome fellow that rode horseback gracefully, danced well and was popular among the young set." But Richard rejected them, becoming even more devoted to Julia after the birth of their first child, Imogene. According to Johnson family slaves, Jemima told Richard to send Julia back to the slave quarters or sell her, "because no one wants a maid dragging a young one with her." Richard refused, supposedly responding, "I don't want my child raised in the quarters among the slaves." It is difficult to gauge the accuracy of these conversations, which were passed down and recorded much later. Even if exaggerated, they likely record elements of truth, for Richard, as the scion of one of Kentucky's wealthiest families, made a bold choice, not in having sex with an enslaved woman, but in acknowledging Julia and the children as his family. "I think every normal man is proud to know that he is a father," Richard supposedly told his mother. Richard's father Robert passed away a few years after the birth of Adaline, Julia and Richard's second child. By that time, Robert had perhaps accepted Richard's decision—at the least, he passed on the opportunity to sell Julia and the children—because he left Julia to Richard in his will.[24]

Interracial sex was very common in antebellum America. Perhaps the most famous interracial couple was Thomas Jefferson and Sally Hemings.

Several years after the death of his wife, Thomas Jefferson began a sexual relationship with the black teenager, who served as a maid in his household. Describing the terms of their long relationship, one of their six children, Madison, claimed that the couple had arranged a "treaty." Presumably, Hemings agreed to a relationship in exchange for Jefferson's promise to provide for their children. Although Virginia law would never recognize their union, Sally Hemings acted as a substitute wife, or concubine. In Hancock County, Georgia, a wealthy planter named David Dickson forced one of his young slaves, Julia Frances Lewis, into a sexual relationship and, in time, she became his concubine. In 1849, the two had a child, Amanda America Dickson, whom David openly acknowledged as his daughter. When David died, he left the bulk of his estate to Amanda, making her one of the wealthiest women, white or black, in Georgia. Elites are more visible in the historical record—they were more often literate, held greater property, and were the objects of gossip. But court records, census data, and other documents indicate that interracial relationships were also common among middling and poor people: in North Carolina, some white women of ordinary means married free black men; in Tennessee, some Cherokee women married white men; interracial sex was ubiquitous in American cities, ranging from rape to paid sex work to long-term unions.[25]

Hysteria over interracial sex is actually the product of a later historical period, the Jim Crow era. After the collapse of slavery, those in power had to come up with new means of maintaining a racial hierarchy, and they did so with elaborate segregation laws undergirded by the threat of vigilante violence. The one-drop rule (meaning that someone with any amount of African ancestry was considered black) was not developed until 1910, when Tennessee incorporated it into state law; many southern and western states followed suit. In the antebellum era, whites did have some anxiety about interracial relationships, especially regarding the place of mixed-race children born of those unions. But slavery was so widespread and those who benefited were so powerful that they did not need to create elaborate racial codes to maintain white supremacy.[26]

The Johnson family brings out some of the most profound contradictions in slavery, namely that kin could also be property. Such relationships should not be romanticized because, given the grossly unequal power dynamics inherent in slavery, it would have been extraordinarily difficult, if not impossible, for a slave to resist her master's sexual advances. Many masters forced their slaves into sex, but others coaxed, claiming that "he will always consider her to be his wife, and will treat her as such; and she, on the other hand, may regard him as her lawful husband; and if they have any children, they will be free and well educated." Former slaves William and Ellen Craft, who paraphrased this speech, noted that most masters "care nothing for the happiness of the women with whom they live." Harriet Jacobs, another enslaved woman, added, "the offspring are unblushingly reared for the market." The Crafts, however, felt compelled to include a caveat: "there are those to be found, even in that heterogenous mass of licentious monsters, who are true to their pledges."[27]

Slavery fostered intimacy, paving the way for a range of familial and quasi-familial relationships. In the French Caribbean, many planters employed a free black woman as a *ménagére*, meaning the manager of a household. White masters often engaged in sexual relations with these women, who also served as go-betweens, directing the labor of enslaved people. In Louisiana and Florida, white men and their black or Native American lovers negotiated contracts that entitled the women to property and, in some cases, freedom. Americans tend to imagine that such practices flourished only in places like New Orleans, where exotic French and Spanish colonial customs persisted, but Anglo-American bachelors and widowers had similar relationships with their "housekeepers." In the United States, receptions of such unions varied from one community to the next, but neighbors and even census-takers sometimes regarded them as common-law marriages.[28]

Richard Johnson was exceptionally open about his relationship with Julia Chinn. In contrast to Thomas Jefferson, who was extremely guarded, Johnson often mentioned Julia Chinn in letters to close friends and at least once called her "my bride." Indeed, some locals claimed that the two were "secretly married" by the Reverend Thomas Henderson, later superintendent of Choctaw Academy. In an oral tradition passed down through the generations, other slaves at Great Crossings remembered the work they had put into the wedding: making a silk dress for Julia, baking a cake with cream custard, playing the violin and singing as a small group of guests enjoyed the reception. Kentucky law did not recognize interracial marriages or marriages of any kind by or between enslaved people, but Johnson and Chinn certainly acted like a married couple. As one contemporary noted, "he lived in the same house with her, and had children by her, whom he [treated] in every particular as his legitimate children." Not only was Chinn his "plantation wife," she was, on occasion, Johnson's "parlor and dining-room wife." When the Marquis de Lafayette visited, Johnson made no attempt to hide his family. Knowing that Lafayette was an abolitionist and international advocate for black education, Johnson may have been more open and more comfortable buying his daughters ostentatious dresses for the occasion. Neighbors, hostile and friendly, called Julia Chinn the "wife" of Richard Mentor Johnson. Although Richard took other lovers after Julia's death, he never married a white woman.[29]

Fewer sources speak to Julia Chinn's side of the story. Julia was literate and often wrote letters to Richard when he was away in Washington, but those letters do not survive. They were likely destroyed by a member of the Johnson family after Richard's death. Yet Richard's surviving documents sometimes quote Julia's letters and these combined with other sources reveal aspects of her life.[30]

Chinn spent much of her time in and around the plantation's big house, a well-appointed two-story brick home. As a helpmate and mother, Julia cared for Richard and their children Imogene and Adaline. She also directed the labor of the household staff, a position that allowed her to socialize with some of her relatives, including her brother Daniel and his wife Patience. When visitors came calling, the big house was even fuller. In addition to Richard's colleagues, Julia often hosted members of the Johnson family. Before Richard's sister Sally and her husband William Ward moved to the Choctaw Nation, they lived with Richard and Julia for several years. For honored guests and for other special occasions, Chinn organized lavish meals featuring goose or roast lamb and threw parties with music, dancing, and, occasionally, shooting contests. Chinn also acted as the plantation's doctor and later ran the medical ward at Choctaw Academy. According to Richard, "Julia is as good as one half the Physicians where the complaint is not dangerous." They called in outside doctors only on rare occasions.[31]

For at least six months of every year, while Richard was away in Washington, Julia Chinn managed the estate. Then, her purview expanded dramatically into many households and businesses, including at least 2,000 acres of farmland and pasture; a tavern; grist, saw, and hemp mills; dozens of cabins that housed enslaved field hands and mill workers; and, starting in 1825, the campus of Choctaw Academy. Certainly, Chinn consulted Richard on important decisions via her regular letters, but some matters simply could not wait the month it took postal carriers to get to Washington and back. And since meetings and social events left Richard only late-night hours for responding to mail from home, Julia managed mundane matters on her own.[32]

To accomplish this herculean feat, Julia acted as Richard's representative, temporarily crossing lines of gender and race. The work outside of the big house was so varied and extensive that Chinn could not take a hands-on approach but instead acted as an estate manager, directing the labor of several white employees and up to seventy-three slaves. Richard, confident in her fidelity and abilities, fully endorsed this behavior, making it clear to everyone at Great Crossings that when Julia was in charge they should "act with the same propriety as if I were at home."[33]

In addition to managing people, Chinn handled money. At that time, economic transactions were largely credit-based. Typically, a patriarch established lines of credit with local merchants and authorized family members and sometimes slaves to make purchases. Merchants in and around Great Crossings recognized Julia as an authorized user on Richard's accounts. They likely welcomed the business, for Chinn bought lots of supplies—furniture, bedding, tools, and more—for the plantation, school, and mills. Chinn's use of Johnson's credit indicates that he placed a high level of trust in her, for Richard was ultimately financially responsible, and he could scarcely afford additional debt. Before leaving for Washington each year, Johnson also entrusted Chinn with large amounts of cash that she used to pay white employees at the school and tavern as well as the occasional contracted laborer. Even if the money was not technically hers, Chinn's access to hard currency was impressive in a cash-poor economy. More broadly, shopping was empowering because it connected her to an increasingly important world of commerce. Improvements in transportation and the rise of industrial manufacturing meant that goods flowed more readily and were more affordable than ever before. Women of Chinn's era valued "mastery of money," priding themselves on financial savvy, thrift, and bargaining.[34]

The work of managing a large estate was complex and ceaseless, yet it afforded Chinn some independence. Even though she shared a house and—at least at some point—a bed with Richard Johnson, she also had her own "stone house" on the plantation. This stone house fits the description of a building still standing in Great Crossings, yet its original purpose remains mysterious. Was the house Chinn's refuge when disapproving guests came to visit? This is possible, but there are many written accounts from visitors—disapproving and otherwise—who identified Chinn as the mistress of the big house. If Chinn's relationship with Johnson was a secret, it was a poorly kept one. It seems just as likely that Chinn wanted the stone house as a retreat, a place of her own. We do not know how her relationship with Richard Mentor Johnson began, but perhaps Julia Chinn, like Sally Hemings before her, negotiated a kind of treaty. Chinn provided Johnson with sex, children, and labor, and in return Johnson offered her a measure of autonomy and empowerment. Regarding Julia Chinn, Richard Johnson explained to a white employee at Great Crossings, "you must support her authority."[35]

Chinn used this authority to shape the lives of others at Great Crossings. As plantation manager, she assigned her family members favorable work roles that allowed them to live close together. Chinn's sisters and nieces worked indoors at domestic tasks like housekeeping, sewing, and serving meals. Such labor preserved their femininity while clearly separating them from other enslaved women who toiled in the fields and at the mills. Julia also had at least a few male relatives at Great Crossings, including her brother Daniel and her nephews Marcellus and Romulus. They, too, worked inside the big house for much of the year, acting as valets for Richard Johnson.[36]

Because of Julia's role as manager, the Chinns' lives were markedly different from others of African descent at Great Crossings. With privileged access to the kitchen, pantry, and smokehouse, the Chinns almost certainly had a better diet than those who worked in the fields. While other female slaves wore what amounted to a uniform—dresses made of cheap cotton or, occasionally, linsey (a coarse linen-wool blend)— the Chinns' wardrobe included fancy dresses that turned heads when Richard hosted parties. As a shopper who also commanded a team of seamstresses, Julia Chinn bought and modified clothing that allowed her daughters to dine, dance, and mingle in polite society. The Chinns enjoyed other material delights. Addie Murphy, a slave who worked in the Johnsons' big house, was incredulous at the bounty she observed at Christmas: "they had pretty stockings with all kinds of strips, blue, red and all colors. They had oranges, candy, hoar hound and stick candy . . . kisses wrapped up in pretty papers . . . holiday packages and pies." Murphy may have secretly enjoyed something here or there, but these gifts were not for her. When Murphy wanted a treat, she resorted to eating boot blacking, for, as she recalled, "it was kinda sweet."[37]

Julia's role required her to supervise the work of other slaves. Richard did not hire an overseer until a few years before Julia's death, meaning that she managed the plantation for most of her adult life. We do not know how she felt about this, but surviving documents record some of the perspectives of other slaves. In general, Addie Murphy remembered "Col. Dick" as a kind master who refused to separate families and took care of slaves too elderly to work, building them cabins at the back of his property. Some white neighbors agreed that slaves at the Johnson plantation received "kind and easy treatment." One white employee of Johnson's even said that "they were an expense," suggesting that Johnson did not work them hard enough. In reality, it was Julia, not "Col. Dick," who ran the plantation and mills for half or more of each year. Perhaps she tried to manage as humanely as possible by taking care of the elderly, assigning reasonable workloads, and shielding others from the horrors of the auction block. Recollections from slaves and white employees alike must be taken with a grain of salt, because both received some pressure to emphasize the benevolence of their master and overseer, yet they still offer rare insights into a private world that is otherwise difficult to access.[38]

Some sources yield more critical insights. House servant Addie Murphy labeled Julia and her daughters "negro wom[e]n" and her Christmas memories suggest that she resented the way they were elevated above her. Never was the line between "family" and "property" clearer than in times of acute economic stress. Contradicting her earlier statement that Johnson never sold slaves, Addie Murphy also remembered seeing "slaves sold, hand-cuffed in twos." To satisfy his creditors, Richard Johnson repeatedly mortgaged and sometimes sold his slaves. Never did Julia, Imogene, or Adaline appear on those lists.[39]

One segment of the Great Crossings population that continually resisted Julia's authority were the enslaved men who worked in the fields. When Richard was away, the male field hands skipped workdays, left the plantation without permission, and refused to help Julia treat the sick. Julia told Richard that she asked "friends"—probably white male neighbors from nearby plantations or Richard's relatives—to punish these slaves with the "hickory or cowhide," but no one would agree. Julia reported these problems to Richard, but she was unwilling or unable to physically punish these enslaved men.[40]

These issues illuminate the limits of Julia Chinn's power at Great Crossings and in antebellum America more generally. She was an enslaved black woman in a nation that prized freedom, whiteness, and patriarchy. White neighbors who were called upon to apply the lash may have declined because they did not want to uphold Chinn's authority. Perhaps they disapproved of the power that she already wielded and did not want to enhance it. Knowing this, male field hands took the opportunity to enjoy a little autonomy for themselves, at least while Johnson was away. Even when Julia managed Richard's estate, she did so as a representative who supported, rather than challenged, his authority. Moreover, whatever power Chinn held was dependent on the will and whims of a white man who legally owned her. She was perhaps reminded of this reality in October of 1821, when Richard Johnson mortgaged Julia's brother Daniel Chinn and Daniel's wife Patience to pay off some of his debt. Richard probably told Julia that he would not actually sell the couple, and he did not. Still, Julia likely knew that a master's debts put enslaved people in constant jeopardy because they, like other property, could be seized by the courts. Whatever power Chinn held at Great Crossings, she alone could not challenge the institution of slavery or overturn the government that supported it. Instead, like many people of color in antebellum America, Julia Chinn focused on what she could control: Chinn sought out autonomy where she could find it and worked for a better future for her family, especially her children.[41]

~≈ ⁂ ≈~

A career democrat, Richard Mentor Johnson was a champion of frontier populism who would eventually become part of a pro-labor camp called the Locofocos. Known as "a friend of tolerant and liberal principles," Johnson cultivated Kentucky's open spirit. According to a family friend, "One thing I have often remarked, that when his house has been crowded with gentlemen and ladies, of the highest rank, who had visited for the sake of visiting, and the poorer classes, together with the suffering old soldier, widow and orphan, on business, they all received the same courteous and friendly attention." The visit of the Marquis de Lafayette was such an occasion when social hierarchies were blurred. Richard Johnson's political career was built largely on extending liberty to whites, but he held out the possibility of inclusion for people of color.[42]

Johnson believed that gradual emancipation was the will of Providence. In 1820, when discussing the Missouri Compromise, Johnson addressed his fellow senators: "No person in existence more detests this abominable traffic in human beings than myself." Yet Johnson argued in favor of the Missouri Compromise, claiming that expanding the American empire would create a western land of opportunity where emancipated slaves could "enjoy the rights of man, without convulsing the empire or endangering society." Here, Johnson departed from his friend Lafayette, who believed that emancipated slaves should form their own colonies overseas; remaining close to their former masters would expose blacks to unceasing prejudice and might foment war. Lafayette's stance was popular among those who joined local chapters of the American Colonization Society. Although Richard Johnson approved of the Colonization Society's efforts toward gradual emancipation and acknowledged their concerns by conceding that former slaves might need distance from their former masters, he did not think that resettlement in Liberia was necessary. Instead, Johnson believed that emancipated slaves could remain within the United States and, like Indians, walk the great path of "civilization" that would lead to citizenship.[43]

Unlike many of his white contemporaries who saw the United States as a purely white republic, Johnson argued in favor of meaningfully incorporating people of color into a multiracial empire. Surely Julia Chinn influenced Johnson's thinking about race. Chinn, Johnson asserted, was the equal of her white contemporaries, capable of "everything . . . which human nature can do." Rejecting the theory that blacks and Indians were inherently different from whites, Johnson saw emancipation and education as steps toward a shared future.[44]

Johnson's Senate floor speechifying cannot be taken at face value, but his personal life demonstrates that Johnson sometimes turned rhetoric into reality. In May of 1828, Johnson sold his slave Patsy and her daughter Frances Anne to Patsy's husband, Thomas Miller, so that the family could live together as free people. Moreover, Johnson facilitated this by asking for a very low sale price, $150, when the average cost of the two on the open market would have been more than $500. Over the next few years, Johnson freed another adult woman named Phebe and a thirty-year-old woman called Milly. Julia almost certainly worked behind the scenes, for Milly was one of her relatives. For both Milly and Phebe, there is no indication that Johnson received payment from either the women or their loved ones. He simply asked the court to grant them freedom certificates.[45]

Despite Johnson's efforts to liberate other enslaved African Americans, it does not seem that he ever legally emancipated Julia Chinn. In Johnson's private correspondence, he referred to "my bride" and "our family," suggesting that conjugal ties transformed Chinn's status, at least in his eyes. Still, Julia's name does not appear in the Scott County court records that documented the emancipation of other Chinns, and a document written a few years before Julia Chinn's death describes her as "belonging to Col. Johnson."[46]

Johnson could have had a number of motives for keeping Chinn as his legal property. Perhaps most obviously, he might have feared that liberty could erode the ties that bound her to him. Given the chance, Julia Chinn might have sought a new life somewhere else. If she had stayed in Kentucky, Chinn would have had to carry her freedom papers at all times; otherwise she would risk being arrested and even possibly re-enslaved. For free black women, decent jobs were extremely difficult to find but more readily available in cities, where they might become teachers, seamstresses, laundresses, domestics, or cooks. The closest urban areas were Lexington and Louisville, but Chinn might have also chosen a city outside of her home state, one with a higher free black population, like Charleston, New Orleans, or Philadelphia. But it was not merely the bonds of slavery that kept Chinn in Great Crossings. She was also fiercely loyal to her children and to her many family members, and she used her position to make their lives better.[47]

Richard Johnson saw himself as a benevolent patriarch. He may have reasoned that since he and Chinn could not legally marry, enslavement was the best way to keep her close, under his protection. Now, it seems absurd to credit Johnson for caring for his partner and children, but at the time, such behavior distinguished him from most masters who fathered children with slaves. Indeed, Richard may not have seen his role as father and master as conflicting, for families, like plantations, had ingrained inequality. In Richard's words, he sought to enforce "order and decorum of black and white and red upon the premises." Johnson felt that he was "kind . . . to a fault," but in return he demanded that all of his subordinates, including his family, "act in their proper place." He expected Julia, Imogene, and Adaline to be "mild," "faithful," "obedient," a source of "happiness and comfort to me."[48]

Whatever passed between Julia Chinn and Richard Johnson, Johnson would remain forever devoted to their daughters, whom he called "my dear children." When Julia Chinn became Richard Johnson's lover, her status changed, and yet, even if she had wanted to, she could never legally take his name. However, Richard insisted that his daughters be called "Imogene Johnson" and "Adaline Johnson." Even after they married and took on their husbands' names, both women retained "Johnson" as a middle name. Richard claimed his daughters, along with their white cousin Richard Mentor Johnson Jr., as his heirs.[49]

As children, Imogene and Adaline were legally slaves, but their parents started to prepare them for a future as free women. Richard taught them at home, focusing on basic literacy and morality. Also literate, Julia must have aided in this process. Someone also taught the girls to sing and play piano. As they became adolescents, however, Richard and Julia wanted their daughters to receive regular academic lessons. When Johnson began to interview candidates to take charge of his Indian school, he asked them whether they believed that African Americans should have "sufficient learning . . . to enable them to read the Bible."[50]

Although many masters fathered children with enslaved women, few sought to improve their lives. In providing education, Richard Johnson went beyond Thomas Jefferson's provisions for the children he fathered with Sally Hemings. Considering that Jefferson believed education to be essential for republican citizens, this omission is all the more shocking because it demonstrates that he saw African Americans, even free people like his own children, as living outside the bounds of meaningful citizenship. Intellectually, Richard Johnson paled in comparison to Jefferson—political opponents mocked the westerner as folksy and "slightly educated"—but he esteemed education as a means of social improvement for Americans of all races.[51]

African Americans themselves overwhelmingly viewed education as a vehicle for liberation. Education opened economic doors, including new jobs for free blacks and increased opportunities, including clandestine tutoring, for enslaved people. Slaves also associated education with freedom of movement, since it allowed them to forge traveling papers and enhanced their ability to pose as free people in order to liberate themselves. Even for those forced to spend a lifetime in servitude, literacy facilitated intellectual freedom, the ability to consume and exchange ideas.[52]

In the early nineteenth century, an increasing number of schools catered to African American demands for education. Some cities with large African American populations, like Philadelphia, had black public schools. Miami High School urged a wide range of parents, including masters, to send "colored youth" to school in the border state of Ohio. "The fact is undeniable, that many masters of slaves . . . are also their fathers. They are fully able to educate their offspring, and we doubt not, are in many instances, desirous of doing so." Even in the slave state of Kentucky, black schooling expanded in the 1820s and 1830s, especially in the Bluegrass and Louisville. Catering to free children of color, most were private grammar schools or church schools, though some Sunday schools or underground schools offered instruction for slaves.[53]

Along with black demand for education came heightened white anxiety. South Carolina passed the first American anti-literacy law in 1740 in the wake of a major slave uprising, the Stono Rebellion, because many white residents believed that slaves had used writing to conspire against them. In the nineteenth century, especially following David Walker's 1829 call for black liberation, *Appeal to the Coloured Citizens of the World*,

many other southern states outlawed a wide range of "mental instruction" for African Americans. Enforcement varied from place to place; a
free black teacher named Julian Troutmontaine held classes for fifteen
years after Georgia's ban, and the Louisiana state assembly supported an
orphanage that included black children. Kentucky never banned black
education, though most masters deemed intellectual learning dangerous and instead stressed manual labor and, sometimes, apprenticeship
in skilled trades.[54]

Stories from Great Crossings reveal that, in defiance of masters' bans,
many slaves actively pursued education. Scott County masters commonly leased the labor of enslaved men to nearby hemp factories. At one
such factory, the overseer used a chalkboard to tally how much rope each
slave produced each day. If a slave failed to achieve his quota, the overseer beat him before locking up the factory, leaving the enslaved men to
sleep on the floor. To avoid the lash, the enslaved men carefully observed
the way that the overseer figured sums, then used their nightly break to
teach themselves arithmetic. One night, their lessons were interrupted
when an unknown black man broke into the factory. Introducing himself, Tenn said that he was a runaway who needed a place to sleep: in
exchange for allowing him shelter during the nights, he offered to teach
the men to read and write. Tenn stayed long enough to teach the basics,
and thereafter the enslaved workers sneaked in newspapers, books, paper
scraps, whatever they could get, and read far into the night.[55]

John Samuels was one of the men who worked at that hemp factory,
though he was forced to return to the fields before he became a proficient
reader. One day, an enslaved boy belonging to a neighboring planter was
down by Elkhorn Creek when he spotted a book—it was thick, with
a dark blue jacket and gold lettering on the front. He picked it up and
brought it back to his mother. Knowing how deeply her master disapproved of slave literacy, his mother asked John Samuels to get rid of the
book. Samuels took the book, but dared not destroy it, for he knew it
was a Bible. Samuels's master must also have been disapproving, for he
hid the book in an old sugar-making cabin in the woods. Samuels and
another local slave, named Hense, turned the old cabin into a secret
library, nailing clapboards to the windows, so that they could return,
night after night, to read by the firelight. Building on the skills he had

learned from Tenn at the factory, John Samuels became an avid reader and, after emancipation, helped organize black schools. Stories like that of Samuels suggest that some of the field hands who "dodged" work under Chinn's authority may have been sneaking away to seek out education.[56]

Over the course of several years, John Samuels found ways to educate himself, but most African Americans of his day were not so lucky. Kentucky masters often punished slaves who smuggled writing slates into their cabins or met secretly in the woods to learn. During the antebellum era, an estimated 5 to 10 percent of enslaved people learned to read. Free blacks were not immune to this discrimination; throughout the South and, indeed, much of the North, law, custom, and discrimination combined to block most African Americans' access to education.[57]

Fearing that his neighbors and constituents might disapprove, Richard Johnson decided to educate his daughters at home, a move that Julia Chinn, mindful of her children's safety, probably endorsed. After Johnson discovered that a local schoolteacher, Thomas Henderson, was "much in favor" of black literacy, he hired Henderson as superintendent of Choctaw Academy. Little is known about Henderson's youth, but he hailed from Albemarle County, Virginia, where he received a liberal education and was ordained as a Baptist minister. Henderson, like many Virginians of his day, favored gradual emancipation. A fellow Albemarle County resident, John White, named Henderson a trustee in his will and authorized the young man to purchase 200 acres along the Green River in Kentucky, escort his emancipated slaves there, and then deed them the land. Henderson followed through and then decided that he, too, would remain in Kentucky. In 1812, he moved to the Bluegrass region, where he taught school in Great Crossings and nearby Stamping Ground, worked as a storekeeper, and sometimes preached at the Baptist church. Henderson was curious about the world and concerned about the welfare of "heathen" people. Although he believed that Africans, in particular, lived "in the lowest state of barbarism," he stressed that this condition was "greatly aggravated, if not solely occasioned, by those Europeans who frequent the coasts, and encourage the nations to kidnap and sell each other." Henderson believed colonialism, not some innate inferiority, was responsible for African—and presumably Indian—misery. But

Henderson reasoned that a different sort of colonialism, namely Western education, might also provide a cure.[58]

Richard Johnson paid Thomas Henderson an additional, under-the-table portion of the Choctaws' funds—$330 per year, to be exact—to educate Adaline, Imogene, and some of Julia's nieces. Johnson wanted the group "instructed at least sufficiently to read the scriptures." Henderson made it clear that Imogene and Adaline both received more advanced instruction than the other African American students: "I soon discovered such uncommon aptness in those two girls to take learning, and so much decent, modest and unassuming conduct on their part, that my mind became much enlisted in their favor. . . . I continued to give them lessons until their education was equal, or superior, to most of the females in the country."[59]

A "superior" education would prove valuable for Imogene and Adaline because, in the antebellum era, free blacks faced extra economic hardships, including head taxes and scarce job opportunities. Those who failed to support themselves could be arrested and, in some states, enslaved under vagrancy laws. Education would help Adaline and Imogene avoid such fates. Johnson also told Henderson that his older daughter Imogene's "principal study" should be "grammar including punctuation." At Choctaw Academy, this was an intermediate subject for those who had already mastered the basics of English literacy. This course would make Imogene a more refined writer and speaker and thus more socially respectable, while Henderson's instruction in bookkeeping would help both girls manage the property they would soon inherit. From his Senate chamber in Washington, Johnson wrote frequently to Henderson, reminding him to prioritize his daughters' education.[60]

Outsiders held wildly divergent opinions about the family at Great Crossings. Some applauded Johnson for doing "his duty as a father and as a Christian," but others wondered how anyone could respect a man "who has reared up a family of mulatto children under his roof." A pastor at the local church called Julia Chinn "one of the most exemplary and pious women," while others castigated her as a "negro wench"—a sexual object, perhaps, but not a suitable wife. Whites who wanted a clearly defined racial hierarchy found Imogene and Adaline most problematic, for they blurred the lines between black and white, free and

Figure 2.3 Reverend Thomas Henderson, by John James Audubon.
Courtesy of the Filson Historical Society, Louisville, Kentucky.

slave. According to one local, "no stranger would have suspected them
to be what they really were, the children of a colored woman." They also
"really were" the daughters of a white man who called them "my dear
children."[61]

⁂

Much like Mushulatubbee, the Choctaw leader with whom he collaborated, Richard Johnson transitioned from warrior to politician. It might

seem strange that Johnson, the famed Indian killer, later collaborated with Native nations, but Johnson was always intimately tied to Indian affairs, whatever the affairs of the day might be. Johnson's friend William Emmons, who wrote an early biography of him, claimed, "Col. Johnson, having been engaged in the war against the Indians, was led to a deep consideration of their character and condition. . . . As soon as the war had ended, his mind was employed in devising the most effectual method of civilizing and reforming them." Unlike warfare, which Johnson characterized as "a system of annihilation," education offered an "amelioration of their condition." Choctaw Academy appealed to Johnson's colleagues as a peaceful conquest, part of what former Secretary of War Henry Knox, the architect of Civilization Policy, called "expansion with honor."[62]

Johnson hoped that Choctaw Academy would aid his political career but also improve his personal life. As Johnson knew from his own family's experience, there were fortunes to be made in Indian land and resources. The senator also linked Choctaw Academy with his family life by imagining himself as a benevolent patriarch who ruled over Great Crossings. Johnson claimed Imogene and Adaline as his actual kin, but he also claimed a fictive kinship to all of his slaves and to all the students at Choctaw Academy, acting as father to a diverse brood of metaphorical children. Indeed, Richard Mentor Johnson may have believed it beneficial to his "bride" and daughters to further heighten the racial complexity at Great Crossings by locating Choctaw Academy there. But Johnson was not the sole architect of social relations at Great Crossings. From the big house, Julia Chinn managed dozens of workers, several mills, a school, and a plantation. In the privacy of her stone house, Chinn likely strategized her family's future, considering routes to education, financial security, and a fuller freedom. Great Crossings was an environment that frustrated those who thought that each race should walk a separate path, but it intrigued others, like the Marquis de Lafayette, who wondered if Americans might live up to the democratizing rhetoric born of their Revolution.[63]

3

Scholars

In early fall of 1826, the students sat together on long picnic tables under the cover of a shady grove, looking forward to a meal free of the rigid discipline of the dining hall. They had joined to welcome twenty-six new students to Choctaw Academy. Before they dug in, however, the boys turned their attention to an elevated stage and prepared to listen to invocation speeches from two advanced students, George Harkins and Pierre Juzan. These names were already familiar to the Choctaw students: Harkins came from a prominent family of traders in the Western District, while Juzan was even more famous, having descended from a line of Southern District chiefs that included Pushmataha. Johnson had chosen them not for their lineage, however, but because they were the "best speakers," fluent, even graceful, in English. Juzan was particularly poetic that day: "With great anxiety and solicitude, we have expected your arrival at this place, the location of the Choctaw Academy. Although we have been separated from you a long time, by space and time, we have been united in our friendship and affection and our prayers have been constant that the Good Spirit might protect and smile upon you in your journey through a land of strangers." Harkins spoke of the honor that they, as students, brought on themselves and upon their nation, and looked forward to the day when brother Indians from across the continent would converge at Great Crossings "to partake of the blessings we enjoy."[1]

During its first decade, Choctaw Academy increased tenfold, from twenty-one students to nearly two hundred. The academy's earliest students were Choctaws, who, along with some of their southern neighbors, acquired a reputation in the United States as "Civilized Tribes" because they adapted some elements of Anglo-American culture into their own societies. But interest in schooling was not limited to the South's "civilized" nations. Enthusiasm for schooling was widespread, even among western Indian nations who had little experience with it. This demand produced an incredibly diverse student drawn from across the continent. All told, they represented seventeen different nations, some of which were further subdivided into smaller tribes or bands. Having no common tongue, the students could not initially speak to one another. Even at the greatest of treaty councils, it was rare to have so many tribes represented. Pierre Juzan exhorted his Choctaw peers to welcome newcomers from other nations, "to live together as a band of brothers." Even if the new students could not understand this greeting, they understood it as a friendly gesture, meant to bless their shared mission: the empowerment of Indian America through a new kind of education.[2]

Pierre Juzan concluded his invocation address with an optimistic forecast for the future. His experiences with local whites—classmates, teachers, and neighbors—offered "conclusive evidence" that "our white brethren . . . are the friends of the Choctaws" and that education would result in "profit and prosperity to our nation." Great Crossings, Juzan reasoned, might presage a bright American future, where the gulf that divided its diverse peoples might be bridged by education. "Nothing, my friends, is wanting, on our part, but industry and correct conduct."[3]

From the outset, Choctaw Academy was an ambitious experiment in education, but initially its small student body represented only a tiny sliver of one Native nation. Miko Mushulatubbee handpicked the first twenty-one students. The majority were from his district, and most were related to him through blood or marriage. Mushulatubbee had usurped his authority, provoking an outcry in the other two districts. Thereafter, the three chiefs agreed to send an equal (or nearly equal) number of students from each district, so that by the fall of 1826 there were sixty-two Choctaws at the Academy. According to their contract with the War Department, Choctaws were supposed to select the most promising

graduates of mission schools to send to Choctaw Academy, where each
would have to present his certificate and a letter of recommendation in
order to be admitted. This clause, inserted by the commissioner of Indian
affairs at the last minute, was designed to decrease competition between
the mission schools and Choctaw Academy. In practice, however, the
chiefs chose from among their kin or other elite families. Because heredity played a strong role in Choctaw politics, the chiefs figured that elite
boys would lead the next generation and therefore deserved privileged
access to education. Some of these students were indeed "among the best
scholars." Others were spoiled troublemakers whom missionaries were
happy to have out of their classrooms. Class, more than ability, determined admission to Choctaw Academy.[4]

The reputation of the mission schools further declined, while
Choctaw Academy, as missionary leader Cyrus Kingsbury admitted,
was "in high repute." Choctaws continued to critique the quality of the
curriculum as well as the intolerance and duplicity of the missionaries
themselves. This criticism reached a fever pitch during the summer of
1828, when Choctaws discovered that missionary Stephen Macomber
had repeatedly raped one of his pupils, teenager Susannah Lyles, who
became pregnant. When questioned by missionaries and tribal leaders,
Lyles reported that Macomber "said he wanted I should forgive him, he
said it distressed him a great deal, and he prayed God to forgive him, he
hoped God would forgive him." Lyles also revealed that this was not an
isolated incident; teacher Adin Gibbs, with whom Mushulatubbee had
quarreled, had also sexually assaulted her. Presumably, Lyles was not the
only victim. Chief Greenwood Leflore railed against the missionaries,
"I will publish the case to the U.S. so they may see what you do here
in civilizing the Chahtas Indians." This revelation of sexual abuse only
deepened Choctaws' distrust of missionaries. Even students enrolled
at prestigious institutions like the Foreign Mission School at Cornwall
wanted to transfer to Choctaw Academy, and some parents who had initially opposed the Academy sought admission for their children.[5]

Such dissatisfaction with missionaries and mission schools was widespread in Indian country. Missionaries tried to cover up cases of sexual
abuse, but other grievances were well documented. Chief Togwane, who
led the Senecas of the Sandusky Valley, told their agent "that they had a
religion of their own handed down to their forefathers by the great spirit,

that with this they were contented and wished for no other, that they had already been visited by our preachers and wanted me to stop their coming in future." The Creek Nation invited missionaries to open schools, but stipulated that they could not preach. When the missionaries violated the agreement, a group of Creek men reacted violently, storming the mission and whipping the small crowd of slaves who had gathered to hear the sermon. Of their mission schools, Chickasaw chiefs complained, "There is not one of our children that is half a scholar." Several ambitious Chickasaw scholars, seeking to perfect their English, were "anxious to live a year or more, among the white people and go to school."[6]

Seeking higher enrollments, Richard Mentor Johnson told his colleagues that "wild" tribes might become civilized, not only through exposure to white society, but also by learning from "civilized" nations like the Choctaws. Through his connections in the War Department, Richard Johnson knew of other nations' complaints about the mission schools, and he sought to capitalize on them. He wrote to the president, secretary of war, commissioner of Indian affairs, and individual Indian agents, recommending that they "use every reasonable exertion" to induce tribes with education funds to send their children to the Academy. Johnson and Superintendent Thomas Henderson argued that a multi-tribal school would "cultivate union and friendship among those who were once hostile to each other." Moreover, Johnson argued that without any shared Indian language, the students would be forced to speak to one another in English. Federal officials were persuaded that such a school would support Civilization Policy by pacifying "warlike" nations.[7]

Though they did not share the War Department's rationale, many Indian leaders hoped that schooling would help their nations retain land and fight corruption. The Creeks, a fellow southern nation, were the first to seek a contract with Choctaw Academy. They were still reeling from the 1813–1814 Red Stick War, which forced the Creek Nation to cede 23 million acres of the South's richest land to the United States. More recently, in 1825, a duplicitous leader named William McIntosh (or Tustunnuggee Hutkee) secretly sold the Creeks' remaining Georgia lands. McIntosh's education played a role in the debates that followed: some Creeks wanted to avoid schooling altogether, though others argued that a more literate populace would be able to check corruption, vis-á-vis both the United States and fellow Creeks. The following year, Creek chiefs seeking to overturn McIntosh's fraudulent treaty went to Washington and endorsed the latter position, telling the secretary of war, "Our Lands are circumscribed and we must now seek resources from science to combat successfully, as the Cherokees have done, the intrigues of our white neighbors." The chiefs appropriated $24,000 to send their youth to Choctaw Academy and asked two educated Cherokees, John Ridge and David Vann, to help them negotiate a contract.[8]

Around the same time, the Potawatomis also sought to make a deal. Hailing from the Great Lakes, these "Keepers of the Fire" maintained the intertribal council fire that linked them to their Anishinaabeg neighbors, the Ottawas and Ojibwes. Beginning in the seventeenth century, the Potawatomis also allied with the French, incorporating traders into their families, Catholicism into their religious traditions, and French into their linguistic repertoire. By the eighteenth century, the Potawatomis controlled important international trade routes, and several families became wealthy entrepreneurs in their own right. After the War of 1812, however, Potawatomi power declined as the United States demanded massive land cessions from those who had been allied with the British. Over the next twenty-five years, various Potawatomi bands signed twenty-eight treaties, more than any other Native nation in American history, ceding valuable land that included the city of Chicago. Potawatomis used part of the treaty annuities to fund Western schools, a move that fit into their long history of global engagement. By the mid-1820s, they had a mission school system of such high quality that some graduates went on to medical school in the United States. In the Treaty of 1826, tribal leaders set aside $2,000 per year so that the promising mission students could continue their education at Choctaw Academy.[9]

After being approached by Richard Johnson and Native leaders from other nations, Choctaw leaders agreed to expand their academy, welcoming the enrollment of "students from any other Indian tribe." Tribal identity was paramount for Native Americans, but over the past century, as whites increasingly invaded their lands, these disparate groups had also come to embrace a shared Indian identity as well. For the Choctaws, this was an opportunity to lead the way in Indian education. Choctaw teenager George Harkins rejoiced, "This reflects great honor upon our Nation, and when we have left this residence, we shall leave behind us the children of other tribes who will sing the song of praise to our Nation." The Creeks, Potawatomis, and many other nations signed contracts with the War Department, agreeing to pay an average of $225 annually for each student's tuition, room, and board. Soon, the student body of Choctaw Academy would include Indian boys and young men from throughout the East and Midwest, including Cherokees, Chickasaws, Ojibwes, Creeks, Dakotas, Iowas, Menominees, Miamis, Omahas, Osages, Ottawas, Potawatomis, Quapaws, Sauk and Mesquakies, Seminoles, and Shawnees.[10]

In the school's early days, selection of students fell to each nation's governing body. Although political structure varied from one tribe to the next, most vested executive authority in one or more chiefs, who usually picked students. The situation was slightly different among the Cherokees, whose legislative body—the National Council—controlled admissions, and among the Chickasaws, whose chiefs consulted with an education committee consisting of seven high-ranking men. These Indian leaders, just like the Choctaws, generally chose from among their own families or other elite families. As one father, a well-to-do trader, explained, Indian leaders chose students who they believed "will soon be influential among their people." Though chiefs controlled the selection process, they consulted the parents and families of potential students. Consent from Indian mothers, who, in most nations, exercised much greater authority over their families than contemporary white women, was especially important. Although leaders of the Kansas Indians were initially enthusiastic about Choctaw Academy, they could not find any mothers willing to send their children so far away, and so they abandoned the idea. Of course, plenty of others chose to do so, and a few families whose children were not supported by their tribal leaders even paid tuition and fees out of their own pockets. Although they would be the most directly affected by such decisions, the students themselves had less power than their elders. Nonetheless, some tried to determine their own future: a Creek boy named Ned Crowell begged his parents to allow him to go away to school, while, on the other side of the spectrum, many boys hid or ran away before they were set to depart for Kentucky.[11]

Richard Johnson, ever eager to increase enrollments, asked Indian leaders to consider sending girls and young women, but the answer, invariably, was no. Most Indian nations maintained co-educational mission school systems at home, and many of them had nearly equal numbers of male and female students. Except for manual labor, which was strictly divided along gender lines, the schools' curricula featured similar academic work for boys and girls. In fact, seeking to spur competition, the Choctaws' Indian agent once sent a packet of girls' examinations from the Mayhew Mission School to Choctaw Academy, instructing the superintendent to "show them to the boys." Indian girls needed education because they were reared to take on leadership roles in their households and communities. Especially among matrilineal people like the Choctaws, well-respected women advised male politicians, particularly when it came to land, which belonged to female-headed clans. The source of women's power came from domestic ties—orderly households, productive fields, and sacred bonds to the homeland. Although Choctaw families often approved of schooling for girls, they believed that such education could be acquired closer to home. Men, as society's warriors, traders, and diplomats, traditionally went abroad more often. Sending boys to Great Crossings also made sense because Choctaw Academy offered specialized training for businessmen, lawyers, and politicians— roles that tribal leaders believed men would play. Perhaps, too, Indians thought of the abuse of Susannah Lyles. Distance held power as well as danger, and hundreds of miles would multiply the risk of exposing young women to male strangers who were not bound to respect them.[12]

Boys, however, came from across the continent. Dakotas hailing from the far north waited for the frozen Great Lakes to thaw before lashing canoes together and paddling the first leg of their 1,200 mile journey to Great Crossings. Four Quapaws, whose nation controlled the Arkansas River Valley where the South met the Plains, arrived at the gates of Richard Johnson's plantation with a trunk and four blankets. A group of slaves saw their strange wagon pass by and let them in. Only one of the Quapaw boys could speak a little English, though he could not explain how they had gotten there "except that they came in a steamboat." A group of Choctaw teenagers who spoke no English managed to complete their month-long journey, aided by their wits and a note written by some of their literate countrymen "to the public": "As they have no supervisor, and understand very little of the English language, and have a very imperfect and limited knowledge of the world, it is hoped that the good people on the road will aid in furthering them on, and not see them imposed upon, nor allow them to drink any spirits." Eight Seminole boys, who had grown up in the warm embrace of Florida's panhandle, benefited from the help of a bilingual escort. Chief Vacca Pechassie had ordered one of his slaves, probably his translator Jim Walker, to take his sons Jack Vacca and Orsler, as well as several other local boys, to school and help get them settled. Before leaving, Walker bribed the head cook Jerry to give his young masters extra-generous portions. William Lewis, a young Osage originally from the Missouri Valley, probably spoke better French than English when he arrived at Choctaw Academy. The most well traveled member of the student body, Lewis was part of an Osage delegation that had just spent three years in France, where they met King Charles X, attended the theater, and rode in a hot-air balloon.[13]

When new students arrived at school, school administrators rarely recorded their names. One agent who dropped off eight Potawatomi boys explained that he did not think "Indian names" were "worth noting down." Names were the first thing to change at Choctaw Academy, the earliest sign of cultural transformation from savagery to civilization, at least according to the federal government. All students at the Academy were required to go by a two- or three-word Anglicized name, which, in theory, had a doubly "civilizing" effect: first names were often Christian, and last names, meant to be passed to future generations, disregarded many Natives' emphasis on matrilineality in favor of patriarchy. School administrators usually renamed these Indian youths after American politicians, military heroes, or trustees or teachers connected to the school. Thus did Chickasaw Hotantubbee become Zachary Taylor, while Potawatomi Shahwnuk transformed into James K. Polk, and the son of Creek chief Opothle Yahola was thereafter known as Richard M. Johnson. Sometimes, even those who already had Anglicized names were forced to change them. A Chickasaw whose recorded "Indian name" was John Brown was redubbed David Porter, a naval hero during the War of 1812 who later became US ambassador to the Ottoman

Empire. The white Richard M. Johnson used the names to flatter his Washington colleagues, and some of them began to take a more active interest in the school. Senator Thomas Hart Benton, for example, asked his Creek namesake to write him a letter detailing his school experiences. Renaming was supposed to draw Indians closer to American culture, to encourage them to emulate their white namesakes.[14]

This process might seem a demeaning, even racist, attempt to erase Indian identity, but students may have seen it in a different light. Unlike white men, both male and female Indians typically had several different names. In many Native cultures, a newborn was given a sacred, secret name, "a protection against danger and talisman of success." This name, however, was almost never uttered; Choctaw husbands, for example, often went a lifetime without learning their wives' birth names. Everyday names, the ones actually used, changed over the course of one's lifetime. In childhood, one might be named after one's family (the mother's side of the family, in matrilineal societies), or become known by a circumstance of birth or a personality trait. Such nicknames might be purposely peculiar or slightly embarrassing, motivation for the bearer to want to overcome it and earn a new name, which normally happened as one transitioned to adulthood. As the story of the Nameless Choctaw suggests, young men traditionally earned their names through feats in war, and oftentimes these were not personal names at all, but rather war titles that might change as one advanced in age and experience. Peter Pitchlynn's uncle, for example, was called Mushulatubbee, meaning "Determined Warrior," with the suffix "ubbee" (sometimes rendered "abi") a marker of military rank indicating that he had killed another warrior in battle. For Indians, one's everyday name was dynamic, not permanent, something to learn from, something to live up to.[15]

Native naming practices changed over time, and by the era of Choctaw Academy, many Indians already had European-sounding names. Some, like Peter Pitchlynn, had white fathers or grandfathers who introduced European naming practices into Native families. Others, like Choctaw teen Okelumbee, redubbed "Samuel Worcester" by missionaries, retained their mission names at Choctaw Academy. A few Native families even created Anglicized names for their children before sending them off to school. Miko Mushulatubbee, for example, drew on his political title to craft a family surname. Although whites usually translated the Choctaw word *miko* as "chief," Mushulatubbee chose the lesser-used cognate "king," which also helpfully invoked the idea of hereditary succession. Thus, in the Choctaw Academy records, Mushulatubbee's sons appear as Peter, Hiram, Charles, and James King. Such names reflected centuries of cultural exchange among Indians and Europeans.[16]

Indian youths came to Choctaw Academy to earn new names. A replacement for the war titles they might have earned a generation earlier, these scholarly names served as markers for a new kind of Indian man. Most of the students did not abandon their sacred names or Native nicknames, but rather added their school names to a short list charting their evolving identities. Drawing on a practice common to both Americans and Indians, the students looked for meaning in their newest names. According to an article in the *Daily National Intelligencer*, probably supplied by Richard M. Johnson, "they like best the names of those whose names are most familiar to them," while those less familiar with their namesakes sought to learn about what made them "*great men.*" Even those dissatisfied with their new names tried to find meaning and dignity in them. Shortly after his arrival at Choctaw Academy, a Potawatomi with the unfortunate school name Andrew Jackson told his teachers and peers that he would thereafter be known as "General Jackson." This young man probably knew enough to loathe Jackson's politics, but he could find some redemption in his namesake's high-ranking war title. In a similar move, some of General Jackson's classmates insisted on being called "Colonel McKenney" and "General Hughes." In adapting their new names, both boys highlighted military service, a marker of masculinity for white and Indian men alike.[17]

Upon waking each morning, boys who had dreamed as Wahyahtubbee, Jack Two Wings, and Topash rose to a drumbeat shortly after dawn and began preparing for another day as Thomas Colbert, Jack C. Williams, and John T. Sprague. This transition might have been slow, for the students woke up surrounded by fellow tribal members, sometimes their own brothers and cousins. Each Indian nation had its own lodging space. The Choctaws lived in the largest dorm, a handsome three-story stone building. Creeks occupied a hewed log house, though in the hot summer months, they sometimes dragged their mattresses outside and slept on raised platforms they had constructed in imitation of their porches back home. As years passed, slaves would build more and more of these sixteen-foot-square log houses to accommodate swelling numbers of students, whose tribal sleeping quarters offered a respite from the multinational, multicultural world of Choctaw Academy.[18]

The only students who did not sleep in dormitories were the monitors. They were older students, young men really, appointed by Johnson and Henderson to enforce the rules: no cursing, swearing, or profane language; no gambling, cards, or games of chance; no drinking; no trading, selling, or giving away clothes; no fighting; no dirty rooms, dirty faces, or dirty clothes. At mealtimes, each monitor sat at the head of a table of his fellow tribal members, where he attempted to tamp down noise and break up food fights. Monitors' duties even extended off-campus, for they were expected to help administrators track down runaway students. In exchange, monitors received several perks. They got nicer rooms, usually in a building that housed the teachers but sometimes in Richard Johnson's own home. Monitors also wore better clothes, similar to the other boys' military-looking gray pants and coats (wool in the winter, cotton in the summer), but made of softer, more expensive material. Perhaps the most notable external marker of a monitor's status was the silver medal suspended from his neck. Stamped with an image of the current US president—the earliest at Choctaw Academy depicted John Quincy Adams—these medals were modeled after the shell gorgets that had distinguished Native leaders since pre-colonial times. The medals were supposed to be reserved for important chiefs allied to the United States, but Johnson wheedled the secretary of war into giving him a few every so often. The students, understanding the symbolism of these silver medals, "expressed great anxiety to have this badge of honor to carry home."[19]

As the silver medals suggest, the student body was divided by rank, often in ways that replicated hierarchy back home. Richard Johnson, no stranger to Indian affairs, had some understanding of Native politics and intentionally chose monitors from leading families. When Choctaw Academy expanded to include students from all three Choctaw districts, Johnson chose one or two from each: for the Western, George Harkins and Forbes LeFlore; for the Northeastern, Daniel Folsom and Peter Pitchlynn; for the Southern, Pierre Juzan. All five were the nephews of district chiefs, successors according to the rules of matrilineal descent. Over the years, other monitors included Potawatomis Anthony Navarre (or Muquadgo) and Joseph N. Bourassa as well as Choctaws August Buckholts and Wall McCann, all of whom came from politically connected trading families. Certainly, students misbehaved, but they probably had greater respect for authority figures who, in some sense, represented power structures back home.[20]

The institution most frequently invoked as a model for Choctaw Academy was West Point, the only other school directly controlled by the War Department. Because it was associated with martial leadership, West Point was highly regarded in Indian country, especially when the end of intertribal warfare meant that US military service was the only viable option for eastern Indians who wanted to become warriors. The first person of color at West Point was a Creek Indian named David Moniac, who was admitted in 1817 and went on to become a major in the US Army. Many Indian families, including Peter Pitchlynn's father John, wanted their sons or nephews to follow in Moniac's footsteps, but admission required the kind of political connections that few Indians possessed. To Native leaders, War Department officials pitched Choctaw Academy as a substitute.[21]

Richard Johnson favored West Point because of its "rigid military discipline," which he and Thomas Henderson believed was beneficial for all boys but especially necessary for "uncultivated sons of the forest." Henderson did not believe in corporal punishment, but rather sought to reform students' "manners, customs, and habits" by disciplining their bodies and minds to keep strict schedules, which the monitors helped enforce. Each weekday, the monitors marched the boys from their dorms to breakfast, to morning classes, to recess, to the midday meal, to afternoon classes, to supper, and, finally, back to the dorms. Saturdays and Sundays featured more time for recreation, but also enforced study hours. This demanding schedule was punctuated by a handful of American holidays, including Christmas, New Year's Day, Easter, Whitsunday, Washington's Birthday, and the Fourth of July. School remained in session during the summer. With rare exceptions, students were not allowed to visit home until they graduated.[22]

Approaching the beginners' classroom, one could hear the students recite, "I am/I rule/I am ruled." Though the students spoke together, their pronunciation was not uniform. Upon opening the door, it became clear why. Sitting on benches in neat rows were dozens of students, whose appearances varied wildly. Most striking to the modern observer would be their ages. Boys as young as six sat next to married men of twenty. Most were Indian, but there were a few white boys, the sons of neighboring planters. The dissonant sounds of their recitation resulted from their varied accents. Potawatomis had a difficult time pronouncing "l," rendering an "n" sound instead: "I am/I runed/ I am runed." Their Miami classmates had no "r" sound in their native tongue and probably replaced it with "l": thus, "I am/I lule/I am luled."[23]

The emphasis in this beginners' class, always the largest at Choctaw Academy, was on mastering the basics of English literacy. At the outset of the Academy, federal Indian agent William Ward suggested that Thomas Henderson learn a bit of Choctaw to ease his labors, but it does not seem that he ever did so. Moreover, the school soon grew to be so diverse that learning one Native language would have done teachers little good. Unlike mission schools, which often promoted literacy in Native languages as a gateway to spreading the gospel, the War Department demanded that Choctaw Academy prioritize English as a means to erode tribal differences and assimilate Indian students. Similar policies targeted other ethnic and linguistic minorities. During this era of massive immigration, American legislators and educators, fearing that multilingualism might lead to political and cultural disunity, pushed newcomers, especially children, to learn English.[24]

They began with spelling, first a syllable or two, then three or four. First, the scholars repeated after the teacher, and later, using their chalk and slates, formed the letters themselves: "h-e-a-t-h-e-n; h-e-r-a-l-d; h-o-r-s-e; h-u-s-b-a-n-d." Advanced orthography was more challenging, with a dizzying number of rules; there were mute consonants, consonants that sometimes acted like vowels, plus verb conjugations that, though fewer in tense than in many Native languages, were nonetheless very foreign. The next step was basic reading and writing, with the aid of Noah Webster's famous textbook: "Washington was not a selfish man. He labored for the good of his country, more than for himself." Over time,

Superintendent Henderson noted that it was the little boys, more than the older students, who proved the best learners in the first class because they mastered English more quickly.[25]

Intermediate students moved on to more advanced English grammar, which included perspicuity, meaning the art of speaking and writing well, the mastery of a "fundamental quality of style" not merely free from defect but exhibiting "a degree of positive beauty." The Academy's students practiced English grammar, in part, through elocution. Such exercises were common during this era, "the golden age of American oratory," when oral speech, intimately associated with republican virtue, was nearly as important as writing. Native Americans, however, had a much longer history of studying elocution, which they considered a key component of male education. Children might pass a winter of long nights by listening to elders recite, from memory, a story cycle that explained the origins of the world or the history of their nation. Boys with a taste or talent for politics might listen to the political speeches of their chiefs and headmen, just as Peter Pitchlynn had done in his youth. By adulthood, Indian leaders excelled at the art of elocution. Of the Choctaws, one white observer declared, "I have never seen orators more easy in manner or more graceful in action."[26]

A second exercise intended to improve grammar was letter writing. "A student can never be better employed than writing letters," claimed Richard Mentor Johnson. No skill, he believed, was more essential for learned men, for those who "exhibit poorly upon paper," even if smart and sensible, would never be taken seriously. Ever the pragmatist, Johnson also saw letter writing as a cheap public relations campaign for the school. He and Thomas Henderson encouraged the students to write their families, friends, tribal leaders, officials in the War Department, congressmen, even the president. Providing ample stationery, Johnson asked his daughter Imogene to keep track of more expensive supplies, including wax and seals.[27]

Although Indians were less practiced at written than oral speech, the skill was not alien to them. For centuries, Indians had used pictographs, maps, calendars, and other graphic art to capture abstract ideas and to send messages over long distances. As a Cherokee leader explained to a British audience, "This is our way of talking which is the same to us as your letters in the book are to you." For his people, belts of beaded wampum contained images that commemorated messages spoken in council. Meanwhile, teachers in the Ojiwbe Midewiwin, a society of healers and religious leaders, used long birchbark scrolls with colored symbols that served as mnemonic devices during lectures. When introduced to European methods of writing during the colonial era, Native people identified alphabetic literacy as "a parallel form of record keeping." Abenakis, for example, used the term *awikhigan* to describe birchbark scrolls and wampum as well as books and letters. After they held councils and made treaties with European powers, some Indian nations began to save copies of documents in tribal archives, storing them alongside wampum belts and medicine bags. Still, though, Indians regarded books and letters as a novel form of communication. Though some regarded literacy as alien and harmful, many others sought to harness its power. Indeed, mastery of foreign knowledge or skills—especially dangerous ones—had long been a pathway to power among Native people. Indian prophets, including the Delaware Neolin and the Creek Hillis Hadjo, claimed that the Creator taught them to read and write. Their communities and many others associated literacy with high status and political sophistication. By the early nineteenth century, increasing numbers of Indians would seek out literacy so that they could communicate more efficiently with one another and with the world.[28]

Choctaw Academy students became avid letter writers. Away from home for several years, students found that letters enabled them to virtually visit family and keep up with friends. Even if the addressee was not literate, she could take the letter to a friend or even the federal Indian agent, who could voice the words of a loved one hundreds of miles away. Graduates of Choctaw Academy wrote to current students, apprising them of news and gossip. Once he returned home to the Cherokee Nation, Timothy Walker updated his friend Ellis Falling on a mutual acquaintance's love life: "You wish to know what, man? Bety married, she married a Volunteer." "Volunteer" was a nickname for white men from Tennessee, after two thousand of them eagerly volunteered to fight under Andrew Jackson during the War of 1812. Walker thought that a pretty Cherokee girl like Bety could have done better: "I think she made a bad choice." The students' correspondence with friends and family was, by turns, eloquent, hopeful, sarcastic, indignant, and funny. Contrary to Johnson's naïve expectations, however, the letters sometimes critiqued the school. Just over a year after Choctaw Academy opened, Johnson's brother-in-law, Indian agent William Ward, warned him that the students sent home some letters that were "not so pleasing." Because the boys' letters seemed to gratify his Washington colleagues, Johnson cooled only slightly in his enthusiasm for the exercise, instructing Henderson "to see that no letter put into the Post office goes without [you] knowing its contents." Although Henderson doubtless succeeded in censoring hundreds of letters, the students still managed to slip the occasional explosive missive in the post, either at Great Crossings or nearby Georgetown.[29]

In addition to composing letters, intermediate students learned geography and arithmetic, while advanced scholars studied moral philosophy, history, astronomy, surveying, and Italian bookkeeping. Beginning in 1833, when Johnson hired a classically trained teacher, some advanced students added Latin and Greek to their studies. As at other antebellum schools, Choctaw Academy lacked a grading system; instead, teachers met at the end of term to determine a student's class standing and future coursework.[30]

In many ways, Choctaw Academy fit into broader American educational trends. Access to higher education expanded dramatically in the first half of the nineteenth century. The number of colleges, for example, increased from 20 schools with a total enrollment of 1,000 to more than 200 schools enrolling 16,000. Adopting new notions of education that emerged from the Scottish Enlightenment, these new schools were mostly secular, run privately or by state or local governments. Formerly the province of a privileged few, education opened to a much broader sector of society, including non-elites, girls and women, and people of color. Many first-generation students expected to use education to enhance their status in a country that was becoming more industrial and more urban. What they learned differed dramatically because there was no educational standardization before the late nineteenth century. Academies were particularly diverse, teaching a wide variety of subjects to students whose ages might span a generation. In terms of curricula, academies were somewhere between common schools and colleges.

Like common schools, they offered spelling, reading, writing, grammar, arithmetic, geography, and history, but academies also prepared advanced students for college.[31]

With the dramatic growth of higher education came new demands. In addition to traditional subjects like Latin, Greek, classical history, and moral philosophy, American schools increasingly added "practical courses" that helped students develop skills in law, business, politics, and science they would need to join a growing middle class. As was true at other antebellum schools, Choctaw Academy students—or their families—had already formed notions about their future and made curricular demands based on those assumptions. Among the more "practical courses" at Choctaw Academy was Italian bookkeeping. Developed by Italian merchants during the Renaissance for keeping track of large amounts of credit and capital, this method of bookkeeping taught students how to keep accounts, balance ledgers, draw up bills, write invoices, and more. Although such a course would be useful to anyone living in a capitalist economy, few antebellum schools taught it. Richard Johnson offered the course at Choctaw Academy because Native families demanded such training for youths who were expected to become planters or merchants.[32]

Another of the most "practical" subjects was surveying, in which students learned geometry and trigonometry in the classroom before hauling their sectors, chains, compasses, and protractors out into the surrounding fields and forests to take measurements and make maps. Unlike most Americans, Choctaw Academy students did not intend to use this skill to mark off and sell individual plots of land, for their nations held land in common. Instead, they sought to use these tools to protect what land they had left, to measure every inch, and to combat shady land speculators and their corrupt surveyors who would, doubtless, continue to pay unwelcome visits to Indian country.[33]

Choctaw Academy students were, for the most part, taught like other Americans. In the early years, their books, like those of other American schoolchildren, were written by British authors and reflected an Anglocentric worldview. In elementary composition, their sample sentences included, "He sailed down the river Thames in the Britannia," and "The Druid priests claimed great powers." By 1830, however, a robust domestic market had emerged, and authors worked to distinguish their books as uniquely American. Noah Webster, who wrote the most popular spelling book of the era, sought to overcome Americans' regional and ethnic cultures by creating a uniform—and distinctly American—lexicon. It was Webster who dropped the "u" from words like "honor," deeming this one among many absurd British extravagances. But American educational reformers like Webster advocated more than cosmetic revisions of British texts. Their textbooks portrayed the United States as the perfect embodiment of republicanism and therefore exceptional in world history.[34]

Protestant values, including industry, moderation, sobriety, and justice, were championed in schools as core values, the source of American distinction and greatness. Although more secular than contemporary mission schools, the curriculum at Choctaw Academy, like that of every American school, was suffused with Christianity. Their superintendent, after all, was an ordained Baptist minister, and he likely amplified the Christian ideology found in their textbooks. From Noah Webster's spelling book, Choctaw Academy students read: "Good men obey the laws of God," and "God will destroy the wicked." More advanced students read Jesse Torrey's moral philosophy textbook, which fused Christianity and republicanism. An overwrought Torrey explained his young readers' role in global history: "You constitute the only insulated *Ararat*, on which the olive branch of peace, and the *'glad tidings'* of freedom and happiness, can be deposited and preserved to a *groaning* world *drowned* in tears!!" To the "sons and daughters of Columbia," Torrey instructed, "Prove yourselves, then, deserving of the exalted office which Providence has assigned you."[35]

As these Indian students sat alongside their white classmates, they must have wondered if they, too, were the favored sons of Columbia. Of course, Choctaw Academy students were American in the broad sense; indeed, as original inhabitants, they were the most American Americans. But English was not their mother tongue, the United States was not their nation, and though both culture and citizenship could change, the future was far from certain. Though the content and form of their education was similar to that of other young Americans, Choctaw Academy students likely experienced it in a different way.

Unfortunately, the authors of the textbooks used at Choctaw Academy assumed that Indians were objects of inquiry rather than scholars. "Did you ever see a Buffalo? An Indian?" "Can savages read? What benefit would come to them from learning to read?" One history book wondered at how Pocahontas had managed to rescue John Smith, seeing as how "Indians delight in torture and blood." Imagine a student's reaction as he sat at a small table in his dorm room, reading by candlelight: Did he snort derisively? Summon a roommate and, speechless with incredulity, point to the offending passage? Or was he familiar enough with American culture to merely shake his head?[36]

Back home, each student learned tribally focused stories exploring millennia of American history, but at Choctaw Academy his lessons ignored and even denigrated perspectives that detracted from US greatness. Thomas Henderson told them that America "was discovered by Christopher Columbus, in the year A.D. 1492." Previous events could be ignored because, as one of their textbooks explained, Indians lacked any "authentic history." The first English settlers "found neither towns, nor pleasant fields, nor fine gardens; they found only woods, and wild men, and wild animals." American history truly began when Europeans brought "the civilization of thirty centuries" to a dark land. What happened subsequently, the means by which Europeans and their descendants gained greater swaths of North America, was not called "imperialism" but rather "expansion," a bloodless term that called to mind natural, geological processes recounted in their geography text—the way prairie fires spread on the Plains, how the Mississippi River widened at its mouth.[37]

Despite their obvious ethnocentrism, many of the texts lauded the accomplishments of non-European peoples. As one of their basic history texts noted, North Africa and the Middle East had highly developed civilizations "while Europe yet remained a savage wilderness." The Egyptians, according to the author of their surveying textbook, "were the first who measured the heavens and the earth." Tytler's *Elements of General History* informed Choctaw Academy students that Mayan hieroglyphs and Incan knot-tying were sophisticated forms of nonverbal communication and could even be used as legal contracts, and that the Aztecs had created "a flourishing empire" where the elite were "polished" and "refined." Tytler, who was British, lavished special praise

Figure 3.1 "Indians Attacking White Settlers," in a textbook used at Choctaw Academy. S. Augustus Mitchell, *Mitchell's Primary Geography, An Easy Introduction to the Study of Geography* (Philadelphia: Thomas, Cowperthwait & Co., 1840), 51. Courtesy of the American Antiquarian Society.

on the more recent artistic and scientific accomplishments of Mexicans and found the achievements of Americans "rather slow and partial" in comparison. The publisher of the US edition felt compelled to add an annotation: "The writer must be under a mistake. Is it not acknowledged throughout Europe, that the United States of North America are not only farther advanced, but faster advancing, in the discoveries of science, and that their progress in literature is more rapid, than any other nation of the new world?"[38]

Some of their texts even offered more nuanced portrayals of Native Americans. Authors of history and geography texts sometimes found it impossible to ignore Native Americans' deep past and ongoing presence. Jedidiah Morse, a geographer who had personally toured dozens of Native nations, informed his readers that whites occupied just over a quarter of North America, while "the Indians still own all the northern part of Spanish America, the western part of the United States, and nearly the whole of British America [Canada]." A few textbooks even acknowledged the sovereignty of Indian nations. Explaining King Philip's War, in which a Wampanoag chief and his allies tried to reverse colonial expansion in New England, author Charles Goodrich conceded that the war's namesake "was a king, and had a just claim to the country."[39]

Most of the geographies used over the years at Choctaw Academy praised Indian nations who had acquired some degree of "civilization." Jedidiah Morse, a strong advocate for Civilization Policy, noted of the Choctaws, "Within a few years, they have made great advances in agriculture, and the arts. They now raise cattle, corn, and cotton, and some of them spin and weave. They are beginning to leave off the wild and savage life, and are becoming civilized." Superintendent Henderson upheld his view, noting that in addition to southeastern nations, the Indians of New Mexico and California were "measureably civilized," notable for their maize agriculture and viticulture, respectively. Such images contrasted sharply with other, more stereotypical portrayals, which sometimes co-existed uneasily in the same volume.[40]

On occasion, texts invited critical perspectives on American history. Their moral philosophy book included a famous speech by the Miami chief Little Turtle. At a Quaker Convention in Baltimore, Little Turtle denounced whites for introducing liquor, "what we think may be justly

Figure 3.2 "Choctaw Village." Used at Choctaw Academy, this geography textbook offers a less exoticized portrayal of Indians. Jesse Olney, *A Practical System of Modern Geography; or a View of the Present State of the World. Simplified and Adapted to the Capacity of Youth*, 34th ed. (New York: Robinson, Pratt & Co., 1841), 123. Courtesy of the American Antiquarian Society.

called POISON," into Indian country. Little Turtle's message resonated with Protestants who upheld temperance as a core American value, but Indians likely understood it as a critique of colonialism. Little Turtle castigated "this evil liquor" as a weapon more deadly than warfare "that destroys our reason, that destroys our health, that destroys our lives." Native Americans also appeared as US history texts cataloged a litany of wars, usually blaming Indians as the aggressors, but occasionally wavering. After recounting the First Seminole War, author Charles Goodrich admitted that Andrew Jackson "was thought by many to have been unnecessarily severe." Addressing the students, Goodrich wrote, "You can judge for yourselves when you are older."[41]

As head teacher, Thomas Henderson advocated this kind of critical thinking. Because Henderson wrote a geography textbook, *An Easy System of the Geography of the World*, we have a strong sense of what and how he taught. At that time, most teachers relied on rote memorization, urging students to repeat after them or to learn passages from their textbooks, but Henderson, following British philosopher Isaac Watts, championed the Socratic method as a more active and engaging way of learning. Henderson was a more capacious and radical thinker than many educators of his day. Telling his students that "a thousand millions of human beings" lived on earth, Henderson introduced them to diverse global cultures: the golden mosque at Mecca; the "rich, populous, and remarkable empire" of Japan; the famed gold and silver mines of the Incas. Henderson reasoned that there might even be life on other planets; humans should not be so egocentric as to think that God made the sun for earth alone. In his corner of the universe, Henderson taught that North America was big enough to hold many nations, Indian and European alike. The United States, in any case, would never want the arid Plains, which were "unfit for cultivation"—best to leave them to "wandering" Indians. "Civilized" Indians, he implied, might find a home in the United States.[42]

By late 1827, the student body had grown to one hundred students, more than Thomas Henderson could personally supervise. Casting about for a solution, Richard Johnson decided to introduce the Lancastrian method of instruction. Developed by Englishman Joseph Lancaster in 1798, the system was subsequently adopted in several American cities, including Washington, where Richard Johnson saw it in action. During the summer of 1828, Johnson invited Robert Ould, who had been trained by Lancaster himself, to implement this system at Choctaw Academy. Delighted with the project, Ould hoped that the Academy, newly reorganized, would banish "the musty idea that our sons of the forest are incapable of civilization." Thomas Henderson remained at the apex of the instructional pyramid, instructing the smallest class—the most advanced students—while also supervising three or four assistant teachers who maintained their own classrooms. Within each classroom, more advanced students (who were usually monitors as well) tutored their peers. What most appealed to Johnson was the system's economy. He believed that Henderson, along with a few lesser-paid assistants, would be able to "teach 500 Boys." The War Department dashed that hope, stipulating that there should be one assistant for every twenty or so students.[43]

Though never as cost-saving as Johnson hoped, Lancaster's method did have another, unanticipated consequence. In tutoring junior students, Natives inevitably filtered the curriculum through their own cultural lenses. The Lancastrian system unconsciously mimicked some aspects of Indian learning, which tended to be more group-oriented and collaborative. Missionaries in the Choctaw Nation noted how older students, having learned to read, immediately began to instruct younger ones, without any prompting from the teachers. At Choctaw Academy, Native students tutored members of their own nations, and, by the mid-1830s, some of them became assistant teachers. Unlike Thomas Henderson, these Native educators could translate words and concepts into Indian languages. In fact, Henderson thought that some of them translated too much, creating a kind of hybrid curriculum, but delaying their pupils' mastery of English.[44]

Outside of the classroom, several student groups provided space for creative, critical thinking. Shortly after the school was founded, Choctaws formed the "General Council of Students," similar to their legislative bodies back home. As other nations joined the school, they welcomed new students into the council, excluding only "the small boys." Led by the monitors, who played a role similar to that of the Choctaw chiefs, the council addressed students' concerns, then proposed and voted on various resolutions. The monitors acted as liaisons, presenting these resolutions to administrators. Several years later, in 1832, some of the students formed a debating society to improve their skills in composition and elocution. A kind of student-run school within the Academy, the debating society, like others throughout the nineteenth-century world, collected books and debated topics ranging from history to morality to politics. Ultimately, student societies, like the Lancastrian system and Henderson's Socratic method, provided another tool for independent thinking, which helped students challenge the American bias and reinterpret their textbooks.[45]

Despite Johnson's emphasis on "order & industry" at Choctaw Academy, the schedule left time for recreation. Each weekday before dinner, the students poured out of their classrooms and into the schoolyard, where they shot marbles, played a version of tag then known as "prisoner's base," and, when the monitors weren't looking, wrestled. Great Crossings and its surrounding area was famous for sulfur and mineral springs and, each spring and summer, the students joined local whites and vacationers at these nineteenth-century health spas, where they swam and bathed. Weekends and, for the intrepid, cut classes left time for less supervised entertainment. The students led their own swimming parties to nearby Elkhorn Creek, fished for log perch and sunfish, and took long, rambling excursions in the woods. They probably played stickball or gambled on games of chance. They certainly took part in another popular Indian pastime—dancing. Each Native nation had distinctive dances, held for all kinds of reasons: celebrating harvests, honoring warriors, remembering the dead, and marking the seasons. Though we have few details about these secret student dances, it is clear that they made Richard Johnson uneasy. Distinctively Indian, such dances expressed the pride and power of Native traditions, sometimes leading hysterical whites, who associated them with war, to retaliate violently, as Americans would fifty years later at Wounded Knee. Luckily, Johnson concluded that the students' dances were an "innocent amusement" and so popular that "to prevent them this enjoyment by force" might result in a rebellion.[46]

When Choctaw lawyer James L. McDonald visited the Academy, he noted, "I was gratified to observe that the utmost harmony prevailed between the Choctaws and the Creeks, and that they all acted together as brothers of one blood, and not as individuals of once hostile nations."

Tribal ties remained strong, of course. The students roomed with fellow tribal members, sometimes even with family. Tribesmen often stuck together during recess, and each nation tried to best the others during examinations. In a foreign country, familiarity was comforting, allowing students to travel back home, even if momentarily, to drop the strain of conversing in English and revert back to a shared mother tongue. But, as McDonald noted, the scholars, bound by a common purpose, could overcome troubled histories—even if their nations, like the Creeks and Choctaws, had warred throughout much of the eighteenth century— and build a peaceful path to the future. Superintendent Henderson noted that this "common feeling of brotherly affection" was widespread among the students. Together, they struggled through lessons in the classroom and, out in the schoolyard, learned one another's games and dances.[47]

Choctaw Academy was a truly international experience that introduced students to other Indians from across the continent and, more intentionally, to white American society. This immersion extended to the classroom, where Indians sat next to white children. During the early years of Choctaw Academy, whites comprised 20 to 30 percent of the student body. Probably holdovers from Henderson's Great Crossings Academy, these young men were, in Johnson's words, "the sons of the most wealthy and respectable families in the county." According to Choctaw Academy's regulations, white boys could be admitted, "provided their number shall not exceed that of the Indians and provided also that they shall be subject to the same rules and be placed in every respect on an equality with them." The school's trustees noted that Indian students "mingle with the whites in a free and unembarrassed manner." In primary subjects, the Indian students equaled and sometimes surpassed the achievements of their white peers; in 1826, the annual examination revealed that the best speller was a Choctaw boy. Aided by their native English, older white students often took more advanced classes, but, as the superintendent noted, this merely "fired the Indian boys with an uncommon zeal to attain similar knowledge."[48]

Choctaw Academy students were also part of the broader community. On weekends, they traveled into town, Great Crossings or nearby Georgetown, strolling the streets, shopping, stopping for an illicit dram at the tavern. They joined the crowds who gathered to enjoy parades, militia musters, and political speeches. The presence of so many Indians, of varied appearance and speech, aroused great interest among the locals. Some whites, having heard of Indians' legendary martial abilities, invited them to take part in shooting contests. "People used to put up a five-cent piece for the Indians to shoot at," one Georgetown resident recalled. "They could most always hit it." Because few local whites had ever met an Indian, they doubtless drew on stereotypes to fill in the blanks. Perhaps the usual stereotypes were so far afield from the well-heeled young gentlemen before them, they had to be discarded. Most locals were more curious than frightened. Especially in the early days of Choctaw Academy, many local planters invited students to visit their homes on weekends. The students turned up in their dark gray suits, scraped off their boots, and spent pleasant afternoons in conversation. If invited to dinner, a student may have drawn on what he learned at the school's Napoleon Society, which instructed young men "in all the peculiarities of etiquette observed in the polite circles of society." Hosts marveled at the scholars' seemingly exotic backgrounds, but they also had plenty in common. Many shopped at the same stores, bathed at the same mineral springs, and hunted and fished in the same woods.[49]

Many of the students also met white and black neighbors at church. Richard Johnson promoted Choctaw Academy to Indians as a secular school, but that was a half-truth. In exchange for a donation of several hundred dollars per year, Richard Johnson loosely affiliated the Academy, for its first few years, with the Baptist General Convention, promising to encourage students to attend Sunday services. In practice, however, Johnson admitted, "The Sundays have been more neglected generally speaking than any school in Christendom. . . . The Boys let loose to spend the whole day as they please." Johnson, never a regular churchgoer himself, did not force the students to attend. Many students, however, were already Christian, and so Johnson and Henderson encouraged them to choose whichever church they wished. Several Potawatomis, having been reared Catholic, went a few miles down the road to St. Francis de Sales, where they worshipped alongside Kentuckians of French and German ancestry. Creeks, more recently exposed to Christianity by Methodist riders, went to First Methodist in Georgetown. Most popular among the students was Great Crossings Baptist Church, nearest to

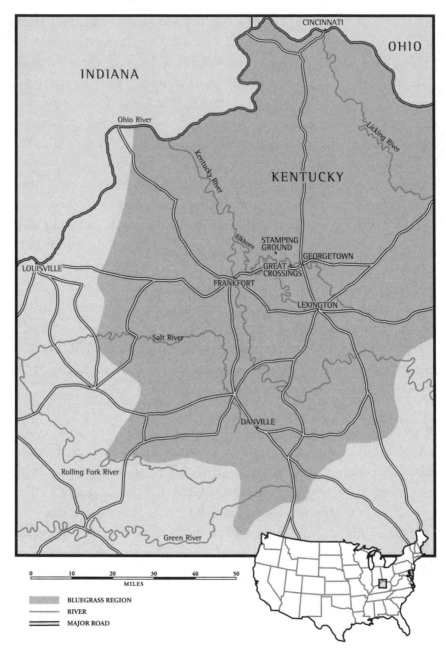

Figure 3.3 Great Crossings and the Surrounding Region, circa 1830.
Map by Ian Byers-Gamber.

the school and most closely tied to the Johnson family. In 1828, following a popular revival, at least twenty students joined a congregation that included familiar faces—Thomas Henderson, Julia Chinn—as well as planters, merchants, and slaves from the surrounding area.[50]

Those who wanted to hear the gospel did not necessarily have to leave campus. In addition to Thomas Henderson's occasional sermons, a few of the students preached. Samuel McIntosh, a Creek student, had already converted to Methodism by the time he came to Kentucky at the age of seventeen. Preaching in English and the Creeks' native Muskogee, McIntosh beckoned fellow students out into the schoolyard to sing and worship on Sundays. A Choctaw named Sampson Birch arrived on campus at about the same time and undertook a similar, bilingual approach. The timing of their ministries suggests that McIntosh and Birch probably inspired the wave of conversions that swept the school in 1828. Their influence went beyond the school, however. In December of 1828, a committee at Great Crossings Baptist Church, which celebrated Sampson Birch's religious joy and eloquence, made him an ordained minister. In subsequent years, some Great Crossings residents worshipped at Choctaw Academy, rather than the local Baptist church, because they were so keen to hear the Native students preach.[51]

Every year, in fact, thousands of whites—men, women, and children from "all classes of society"—visited the Academy. Most were from the Bluegrass region and came in for the day, but others traveled from distant counties or neighboring states, and some incorporated Choctaw Academy as a featured stop on a national tour. The biggest attraction was the annual exhibition. A public demonstration that followed each year's final examinations, the exhibition showcased students' achievements in elocution, composition, mapmaking, and other skills. Always eager to gain patrons and political supporters, Richard Johnson welcomed visitors, offering a free barbecue dinner and encouraging those whom he considered "distinguished" to speak to the students. The annual exhibition, a standard ritual at American academies, was much more popular at Choctaw Academy than at white schools. While crowds at white academies typically numbered in the hundreds, Choctaw Academy, by the late 1820s, boasted an attendance of 2,000 to 3,000.[52]

Americans from across the country could visit Choctaw Academy through the medium of newspapers, which, for the first time in history, had become affordable and widespread. Ranging from the nationally prominent *Niles Weekly Register* to smaller weeklies like the *New Hampshire Observer* to radical firebrands like *The Emancipator*, papers all over the country picked up stories on the Academy. Johnson noted with glee how his Washington colleagues, who could follow the Academy in the *National Daily Intelligencer*, discussed his school "in a public capacity as well as in private circles." The tone of the early articles was laudatory and optimistic. "We rejoice to see such a spirit of improvement among our red brothers," one article noted, exclaiming at the considerable endowments each Native nation put forth. The author expected that the school would "prepare some of the most promising to graduate in Transylvania University," alongside the elite sons of the South.[53]

Choctaw Academy transformed a quiet crossroads into a path that was truly "great," in the sense that it was shared by many peoples. On the schoolgrounds, students, for the first time, met Indians from many different nations, an experience that afforded a continental perspective on the American past and present. Similarly, their textbooks introduced them to distant people, separated by space and time, yet knowable and relevant. At school and in town, students met neighbors who were, variously, free, enslaved, Catholic, and Protestant. Some were very rich—planters with racing tracks, china sets, two-story big houses. Others were clearly poor, much poorer than the students' own families: the Irish immigrants, who spoke a strange English and spent their days building the stone fences that enclosed the plantations; the slaves who did not own even themselves. The students discovered that Americans were of all sorts and that the world—the universe—was wide and full of possibility. Many paths converged at Great Crossings, but when these fellow travelers shared a meal or bowed their heads together in prayer, the way ahead seemed peaceful. Maybe they could live together after all. The defining characteristic of the United States, according to Superintendent Henderson, was that it always welcomed "merit," which was "not confined to any one class of men."[54]

4

Indian Gentlemen and Black Ladies

The trouble began, as it often did, in the dining hall. Students complained bitterly and often of the inferior coffee served there. Peter Pitchlynn characterized it as "mixed with rye" and "badly prepared." To save money, Johnson ordered his slaves to make this weak brew, "believing that it was as good for them as all coffee." That is, Johnson thought that Indians would not know the difference. But they did. Coffee was a common commodity across Indian country—white visitors, perhaps surprised, often commented on this—and many students were used to having a strong cup every morning.[1]

These caffeine-deprived students complained to the dining hall staff. At that time, six or seven enslaved people worked in the two-story structure. A woman named Lucy and her two children served students in the upper room, while twenty-eight-year-old Patience Chinn, Julia's sister-in-law, managed the lower room with the aid of an elderly woman named Fanny and, if they needed additional help, another enslaved boy or young man. Every day, the staff served three hundred meals, which were prepared by the head cook Jerry, and between shifts they tidied the hall and cleaned the serving ware. On the students' side, the monitors were supposed to keep the boys in line, but something broke down that day. One or more of the boys probably made a rude comment. Peter Pitchlynn, himself a monitor, once wrote a letter describing the dining hall staff as "insolent" and "dirty" in appearance. Such slights must have rankled. The waitstaff wore neat country dresses, just like other respectable women in rural Kentucky. If anything, they "dressed too fine," according to white observers. These whites thought that Adaline Johnson, who had taken over some of her mother's duties, was dressing enslaved women in clothes above their station. As for their supposed insolence, Richard Johnson claimed that slaves rarely reacted to students' insults. However, bearing the brunt of students' protests over the quality of the food and dining facilities, slaves did sometimes challenge students, whom they may have perceived as uppity or abusive. Unnamed in the documents, one woman transferred from another area of the plantation to help out temporarily in the dining hall and, perhaps taken aback by the students' behavior, got into an argument with Choctaw John Riddle. Other staff, according to one Creek student, were "very impudent to the scholars." On several occasions, Richard Johnson ordered his slaves whipped "severely for insolence to the students." We do not know exactly what happened that day, but it is clear that complaints about coffee escalated to physical attacks. The students began to riot, "dashing coffee" and "throwing stones" at the dining hall staff.[2]

Incidents like the coffee riot were not unusual at Choctaw Academy, where students and slaves lived and worked in close proximity. Johnson relied on slaves to build dorms and classrooms; make furniture; sew bedding; clean, launder, and mend clothing; maintain the fields and pastures that produced food; and staff the dining hall. Throughout the school's history, anywhere from ten to twenty African Americans, mostly women, worked directly for the students. Miserly with the school budget, Richard Johnson tried to avoid hiring extra laborers. School records document only two instances when Johnson purchased additional slaves specifically to work at the Academy. Instead, he assigned more duties to slaves who already worked long hours on the plantation and in his mills. Even in the school's infancy in the mid-1820s, caring for a few dozen students would have increased slaves' workload considerably. As enrollment grew to nearly two hundred by 1836, the labor associated with school upkeep was tremendous.[3]

Given the students' frustrations and the mounting workload of slaves, perhaps discord was inevitable. On a deeper level, however, cultural crossings fostered convergence as well as conflict. The coffee riot reflected the students' anxiety about their uncertain place in the United States as well as slaves' desire for greater control over their daily lives. Asserting their own elite backgrounds, students like Peter Pitchlynn insisted on parity with whites and deference from blacks. Meanwhile, African American families like the Chinns sought to enhance their status by embracing middle-class values like respectability, self-discipline, and sexual morality. In their separate ways, each group drew on notions of class to challenge racial prejudice.

The economic and social transformations of the early nineteenth century had changed American notions of status. In the urban northeast, the rise of mass manufacturing heralded the downfall of the artisan class, but it also created a greater demand for labor, which spurred a new wave of European immigration. In fact, Richard Johnson owed much of his political success to newly organized working-class whites, who appreciated his efforts to abolish imprisonment for debt, expand veterans' benefits, and bring western land into the public domain. In the South, the introduction of the cotton "gins" facilitated the spread of short-staple cotton production inland, encouraging the growth of plantation agriculture and slavery across Georgia and Mississippi Territory, then called "the Southwest." Some planter elites acquired vast estates, but in doing so they squeezed out white smallholders, who were forced to work as tenants or seek out land elsewhere. Contrary to the hopes of many who thought that the expanding western frontier would eliminate poverty, speculators and powerful families like the Johnsons often seized the best land, leaving limited opportunities for poorer whites. While the gulf that divided rich and poor endured in the West, a middling class developed in America's growing cities, where they filled new roles in education, medicine, law, and government. Meanwhile, the industrial revolution and improved transportation opened a world of manufactured goods to eager American consumers. Once restricted to the well born, refined taste and the status that generally accompanied it became available to anyone who could afford to buy luxury goods.[4]

Indians and African Americans took part in that era's transformations as laborers, consumers, and entrepreneurs—some even became wealthy—which prompted anxious whites to debate the relationship between race and status. Most American intellectuals still upheld the theory, popularized during the Enlightenment, that variations among humans came from growing up in different environments. Though they idealized European society as the pinnacle of civilization, environmental theorists argued that all people could progress through education. A competing and increasingly popular school of thought held that biology determined people's behavior and that racial categories should be fixed and hierarchically ranked. This view had the support of many southern slaveholders, working-class northern immigrants who competed with blacks for jobs, and frontier whites— groups that were gaining a larger share of national political power. Rejecting Old World class divisions, those who stressed biological differences among the races sought to create a distinctly American model of social relations by embracing democracy and egalitarianism among whites (at least rhetorically) while further marginalizing people of color. In popular practice, a mixture of both theories prevailed: Americans determined a person's status by evaluating his appearance, ancestry, social circle, wealth, education, and behavior. It was not a simple calculus, especially when contemporaries looked at people like Imogene, Adaline, and Indian students at Choctaw Academy. With their multi-racial ancestries and privileged backgrounds, they confounded racial theorists who tried to pigeonhole complicated people into orderly boxes.[5]

In the face of mounting racism, people of color drew on notions of status that translated across cultures to stake their place in society and articulate their own hopes for the future. In the words of one white visitor to Indian country, "Indians have classes as well as white men." Most Native Americans lived in ranked societies long shaped by inequalities in social, political, spiritual, and even economic power. Certain lineages dominated chiefly and religious offices, and those same lineages often controlled access to resources such as trade networks or community granaries. Throughout the colonial period, Native Americans had participated in the global economy, producing beaver pelts made into hats and fur coats in Europe, China, and Russia; deerskins that European manufacturers turned into gloves, breeches, and bookbindings; and everyday household supplies like pottery, baskets, honey, meat, and grain, sold to neighboring communities. All of this trade contributed to wealth disparities that by the early nineteenth century became pronounced in many Native societies, especially among the Cherokees, Creeks, Choctaws, and Chickasaws. These nations had roughly the same wealth distribution as did the United States, and their economies mirrored those of their southern neighbors. Most southern Indian householders lived as subsistence farmers, though they still participated in the market economy, and the top 7 percent to 10 percent were wealthy slaveholders who owned plantations, ranches, or trading posts. In the Great Lakes region, many Indians had transitioned from trappers to traders, and some lived the life of frontier gentry. Indian country was also home to an emerging Native middle class, families who might own a few slaves, produce cotton or beef for the market, work for their tribe or for the federal government, preach, teach, or operate an inn or ferry. Choctaw economic growth prompted one white Mississippian to ponder, "Why may they not become the manufacturers of the south and the carriers for the remote west?"[6]

Like many elite Indians, Peter Pitchlynn embraced the privileges that recent economic changes afforded. In 1824, when Peter married Rhoda Folsom, his father sent several slaves to build the couple a new house. Like many masters, Peter also composed shopping lists and sent his slaves to the store to buy household provisions, including luxuries. The young master drank coffee and Madeira wine. He and his family dressed in ordinary clothes made of Irish linen and hemp, but their wardrobes also included cashmere scarves and silk dresses. Rhoda's well-stocked cabinets held a dozen full place settings of china, plus fancy serving dishes, a glass pitcher, and brass candlesticks. When Peter needed to settle accounts, his father forwarded $70 or $100 to him, an impressive sum of money at a time when the average Mississippi farmer made only $10 a month. Peter was also a member of the Freemasons, a fraternal order whose members included George Washington, Benjamin Franklin, John Jacob Astor, and Andrew Jackson. Joining a lodge in Columbus, Mississippi, whose members included whites and Indians, Peter mingled with other elite planters and traders. As a young man, Peter began to travel, and he found that white society sometimes lacked civility when compared to his own.

He sneered at a frontier Christmas ball, writing, "The manners of the people in this country are to me more uncivilized than among the Choctaws; people go to balls without being invited. No regularity in dancing. Everything looked more like dissipation and rowdiness than gentility and so forth. Among all the girls I did not see but one that had anything like manners about her."[7]

As Peter's account of the Christmas soiree suggests, Indian notions of status were about more than money. Power flowed through certain families, and heredity often played an important role in determining rank. Among southern Indians, the office of chief usually passed from uncle to maternal nephew. In accord with the rules of matrilineal descent, Mushulatubbee took a special interest in Peter, helping his nephew become acting secretary of the Choctaw General Council in 1826 when Pitchlynn was only twenty years old. Thus did young Pitchlynn join the ranks of Choctaw leaders, known in their own language as *hatak holitopa*, or "the nobles."[8]

That August, representatives from all three Choctaw districts met to create their first body of national laws. Pitchlynn took on the kind of role that James Madison had played during the US constitutional convention; he took notes of the proceedings, wrote and edited various drafts, and produced a final copy of the constitution. Pitchlynn was, in many respects, a logical choice for such an important position. Despite his youth, he was among the most literate Choctaws, had effectively enforced the temperance laws as a lighthorse captain, and came from a prominent family. Moreover, as a relative of both Mushulatubbee and David Folsom, Peter was likely a consensus choice that helped heal the rift in the Northeastern District. Although Pitchlynn fulfilled his role as secretary without incident, he was stretching his common-school education to its limits.[9]

After the constitutional convention concluded, Pitchlynn began looking for more advanced education. At Peter's behest, the Choctaw attorney James L. McDonald wrote a letter to his former benefactor Thomas L. McKenney, head of the Office of Indian Affairs, calling Peter "a young man of excellent natural endowments." According to McDonald, "the share of education which he has already received, has only given him a higher relish and a more ardent thirst for knowledge." Pitchlynn's desire to better serve his people prompted him to enroll at Choctaw Academy on February 15, 1827.[10]

Pitchlynn's ambitions exceeded the course options available at Choctaw Academy. His initial plan was to attend Transylvania University in nearby Lexington, then continue studying law under Richard Johnson at Choctaw Academy. He proposed to visit Choctaw Academy regularly even while studying at Transylvania, offering Johnson "my assistance in regulating and giving the boys good advice." Johnson agreed and wrote a glowing letter of recommendation to the faculty at Transylvania, calling Peter "a young man of amiable manners and disposition ... more devoted to study than is usual; he will pursue his studies with an ardor and zeal which will do honor and credit to any student."[11]

Pitchlynn's application to Transylvania fell in line with tribal leaders' goal of sending promising students to college in the United States. Chartered in 1780, Transylvania was the first college west of the Allegany Mountains. (Although the name now calls to mind Bram Stoker's vampire country, educated early American audiences grasped its Latin-derived meaning: "beyond the forest.") Initially located in Danville, Kentucky, Transylvania moved in 1789 to Lexington, where residents eager to overcome stereotypical representations of primitive frontier life sought to establish their city as a place of culture and learning. By the early nineteenth century, it ranked as a top American university. In 1820, when Thomas Jefferson tried to garner support for his proposed University of Virginia, he lamented that Virginians "must send our children for education to Kentucky or Cambridge." As Jefferson suggested, many elite southerners attended Transylvania. Among its alumni are the founder of Texas Stephen F. Austin, emancipationist Cassius Clay, and Confederate president Jefferson Davis. Famous faculty included law professor Henry Clay as well as Renaissance man Constantine Rafinesque, who enhanced his knowledge of natural history by birding with fellow Kentucky resident John James Audubon. Rafinesque also studied Indian languages and archaeology. Although Rafinesque left Transylvania the year before Pitchlynn applied, his interest in Native Americans may have influenced his colleagues.[12]

Transylvania owed much of its excellence to its early president Horace Holley, who was at the vanguard of the modernization of higher learning. Since the medieval period, European colleges, the models for American institutions of higher learning, had been religious in orientation and stressed classical coursework in Greek and Latin, but Holley was among those influenced by the Scottish Enlightenment who advocated more practical, secular education, adding the sciences, modern languages, and natural history to the curriculum as well as professional training in medicine and law. Most colleges in the United States denied admission to women and discriminated against men of color, but Holley liberalized enrollment by supporting the admission of Indian students and allowing women to take courses, though women could not formally matriculate.[13]

Unfortunately, Peter Pitchlynn's bid for admission to Transylvania ended in frustration. Horace Holley, accused of being too liberal by Transylvania's conservative board of trustees and too elitist by Kentucky governor Joseph Desha, resigned just before the spring term of 1827, causing turmoil within the college and leaving Peter Pitchlynn's admission status unclear. Under the circumstances, Peter opted to remain at Choctaw Academy for coursework, though disappointment over Transylvania left him "in a melancholy mood." His friend James McDonald wrote him a heartening letter that spring: "Chin up, look forward to brighter prospects, study hard." McDonald had accompanied Pitchlynn up to Kentucky, and then went to Ohio, where he was studying for the bar exam. McDonald lived close enough—three days' ride—that he could make regular visits to Great Crossings, and together he, Peter, and other Choctaws pushed Richard Johnson to facilitate Indian access to education usually reserved for elite white men.[14]

Pitchlynn remained at Choctaw Academy throughout 1827. He and other students respected Superintendent Henderson as a capable teacher, but they discovered that he had little free time to tutor students one on one. To master advanced subjects, ambitious students needed more individual attention. Although Richard Johnson listened to students' concerns, this demand hit him in a particularly sensitive place— his pocketbook. He talked of turning "over a new leaf as to the teaching department," but stalled, not hiring a classical teacher proficient in Greek and Latin until the appointment of Isaac Gardner in the summer of

1833. Johnson did, however, attempt to compensate by tutoring select students in US politics and law. During the congressional recess of 1827, he likely mentored Peter Pitchlynn.[15]

Despite Johnson's attempt at mentorship—or perhaps because of his personal experiences with the congressman—Pitchlynn soured on Choctaw Academy. Just before the winter quarter, Peter decided to transfer to Tennessee's University of Nashville, which was smaller and less prestigious than Transylvania but superior to Choctaw Academy. Although the University of Nashville did not have a law school, the faculty incorporated professional training into the regular curriculum. Among Pitchlynn's courses was moral philosophy, taught by university president Phillip Lindsley, who likely played a role in Peter's decision to relocate. Trained at the College of New Jersey by Samuel Stanhope Smith, one of the foremost American proponents of the environmental (rather than biological) theory of race, Lindsley favored higher education for Indians. According to Lindsley, all men could be "molded into any form and character, and exalted to any degree of intellectual excellence, by suitable instruction and discipline." Outside of the university, Pitchlynn made new friends by joining the local Masonic order, which, unlike his first lodge in Columbus, had few if any Indian members. Nonetheless, Pitchlynn thrived in his new environment and performed well in his courses. Peter's new friend J. Herron, who was probably a fellow Mason, offered him a piece of advice on balancing his intellectual and social life in Nashville: "Arcum intentio frangit, animum remissio," or, roughly, "don't work too hard, don't play too hard."[16]

In early July 1828, Peter returned to Choctaw Academy to pick up a group of graduating Choctaws that included his brother Silas, his nephew Jacob Folsom, and two close friends, Robert M. Jones and Thomas Wall. The week-long stagecoach ride back home gave the five comrades plenty of time for reflection. Shortly after the young men returned to the Choctaw Nation, Peter, likely drawing on their conversations, wrote a critical account of Choctaw Academy and then presented it to the General Council. Intriguingly, Pitchlynn did not include his original critique of the school—its curriculum—but rather focused on material concerns and conflicts with slaves. The first serious challenge to Choctaw Academy, Peter's account opens a window into the darker side of a school where conflicts over race and class constantly simmered and sometimes erupted into violence.[17]

In response to Pitchlynn's dissatisfaction with the clothing provided, Johnson asserted, "I say upon honor that they are not surpassed by the children of the best farmers in the country." This was precisely the problem. For these sons and nephews of chiefs, the garb of country farm boys simply would not do. Generations ago, these boys' chiefly ancestors had worn copper and shell jewelry from hundreds or even thousands of miles away as evidence of their powerful trade connections. Accomplished warriors' tattooed bodies graphically told of their feats—the capture of prisoners, the conquest of enemies—while the skins and feathers of sacred animals in their regalia communicated a special connection with the spirit world. Throughout the colonial era, Indians demanded European clothing—not firearms—over all other trade goods. Over time, Indian men and women incorporated more and more European-manufactured clothes into their wardrobes, but kept aspects of Native dress, especially in ceremonial contexts. And, like their ancestors (as well as most other people across time and space), they still associated exotic or costly articles with high status. Choctaw chiefs disagreed with Johnson's suggestion that "plain dressing is best" and instead demanded clothes worthy of gentlemen. They requested not only the requisite shirts, pantaloons, and coats but also fur hats, silk handkerchiefs, waistcoats, matching jackets, and cravats to tie at the neck. Although Johnson complained that "they set their hearts too much upon dress," he expended several hundred dollars beyond what he had budgeted for clothing to accommodate the students' demands.[18]

Food provoked similar clashes. For millennia, Indian and European elites alike had used the control and distribution of food to claim political power. When colonialism brought these cultures together, translation was initially difficult, so food, as a shared medium, became weighted with additional symbolic importance: a joint Thanksgiving might result in alliance, while theft from corncribs often led to war. Quantity and quality mattered, too. A generous host demonstrated respect by honoring guests with an abundance of good food, including choice cuts of meat, while a stingy one might insult visitors.[19]

Like their forebears, Choctaw Academy students read meaning into food. Choctaw Academy, which followed a "Bill of Fare" prescribed by the federal government, did not match the expectations of Indian students, particularly those of elite students. Breakfast and supper included "Tea or Coffee, or Milk, & Sugar, with Bread and Butter." Compared to today, nineteenth-century notions of appropriate breakfast food are recognizable (with a few exceptions, like the pickles regularly served during the morning meal at Choctaw Academy), but the evening meal—supper—was much lighter. Dinner, served at midday, was the largest meal, featuring more variety and much greater helpings of meat and vegetables than other meals. At Choctaw Academy, dinner might include bacon, beef, pork, or mutton, plus cornbread or hominy, as well as white potatoes, sweet potatoes, cabbage, beans, beets, peas, and other seasonal vegetables. Students from the Plains tribes, who relied to a much greater degree on wild game, found this menu exotic. They, like the other students, complained that it featured too little meat. Responding to this concern, Richard Johnson added fried or stewed meat to breakfast and cold meat or soup to supper. The students also helped themselves by hunting or fishing in their spare time, sometimes enjoying their spoils with friends in the nearby woods but also contributing them to communal meals in the dining hall. Partly, the students were homesick. The hominy prepared by the head cook Jerry, though nearly identical to Choctaw *tomfulla*, could not quite match grandmother's recipe.[20]

In general, however, the students' demands had to do with quality rather than cultural preferences. In his critical letter, Peter Pitchlynn first complained of the school's fatty bacon and inferior cornbread. Pitchlynn disliked the fact that the breakfast menu, in particular, was nearly identical to the cheap food that Johnson gave his slaves. Other students wanted "sweetmeats," meaning pastries, cakes, and candy. Sugar, however, was an expensive commodity, and Johnson claimed he could afford only enough for each student to indulge in a spoonful in his coffee or tea. The food the students hated above all was mutton. Certainly, they were not used to it, but neither were most Americans. Kentuckians, still famous for their mutton barbecue, were unusual in their taste for sheep. Other Americans, including Indians, much preferred pork or beef. Mutton, tough while somehow still greasy, was not considered a polite food. After writing home about how often the dreaded mutton appeared on the table, one Cherokee boy's father sent him cash so that he could occasionally dine out at the local tavern or buy food from nearby farmers or storekeepers.²¹

The students of Choctaw Academy came from distinguished families in Indian country, and they sought to preserve their status in the United States. One Choctaw Academy student, a Chickasaw named Frazier McClish, boasted to Richard Johnson that his nation was "rich" and his parents were "influential." Some aspects of Indian status, like high birth or a prestigious family history, were difficult for US audiences to read, but food and clothing translated more easily across cultures. After seeing Choctaw Academy students breakfasting civilly in their neat uniforms, a visiting white preacher named Walter Scott conceded that "a better behaved and more respectable looking population it would be very difficult for any one to conceive of." Three-piece suits and refined table manners impressed American audiences. Scott conceded that these Indian students might be, in some ways, "superior to white children." Given their power to shape perceptions of status in a changing America, it's little wonder that wardrobes and table settings provoked heated battles over race and place.²²

Mounting racism carved out dividing paths, but Americans of varying backgrounds prized other status markers—family connections, wealth, education, and manners—that suggested they still shared common ground. To enhance her family's standing, Julia Chinn reared her daughters to embrace middle-class values favored by blacks, whites, and some Indians. In the 1810s, Julia began attending Great Crossings Baptist Church, a multiracial congregation that Richard's parents had helped found. Richard sat with Julia and the children in the "Negro section" of the church, but Julia went to services more regularly than did Richard. She also embraced Christian standards of temperance and morality. Her pastor called Chinn "one of the most exemplary and pious women." Julia was certainly industrious and, like middle-class women, her labor supported her husband and family. Richard asserted that Julia was "as irreproachable as any member" of the Great Crossings community "and as much respected in her place as a woman could be." Julia Chinn's literacy and promotion of education also accorded with middle-class values. Chinn passed these values on to her daughters, while seeking to preserve their chastity by preventing illegitimate sexual activity. Imogene, later in life, was noted as "an exemplary member of the Christian church, a devoted mother, faithful wife, and a woman of rare intellectual attainments." By cultivating respectability, Julia Chinn sought to enhance her own status and that of her daughters.[23]

When Adaline and Imogene were in their teens, they began to take on a portion of their mother's administrative responsibilities. Imogene, a few years older, handled some of the accounting, keeping track of checks from her father, paying laborers, and doling out petty cash for expenses. Perhaps Imogene possessed a special talent for organization and inventorying, because she also kept charge of Choctaw Academy's more expensive school supplies. Imogene must have stored these items under lock and key in the big house where the students—and even the schoolmaster—could not get access to them. When Thomas Henderson wanted paintbrushes for the younger boys or a wax seal for the students' homebound letters, he had to ask Imogene for them. Adaline, like Julia, took on a leadership role. Perhaps because her health was delicate, she worked mostly within the big house, supervising and directing enslaved laborers and reporting to her father. Richard wrote Adaline, "I have no instructions to give you. It is your duty my dear Child to think and reason and exercise your best judgment and discretion, and manage to the very best advantage. . . . Everything looks well and I give you very great credit." So great was Richard's confidence in Adaline that in 1828, when she could not have been more than sixteen years old, Richard told Superintendent Henderson, "Do not wait for me" to make decisions regarding student misconduct, but rather "advise with Adaline."[24]

Adaline spent much of her time caring for the clothes and linens of the Chinn family and the dozens of boys and young men of Choctaw Academy. To manage this daunting task, she took charge of a team of four enslaved women who constantly washed, mended, and sewed. Adaline's chief assistant on this team was her cousin Parthena. When the seasons changed and the Choctaw Academy students needed new clothes, Adaline sometimes hired young white neighbors, including one "Miss Margaret," to help out as well. Adaline sent regular updates, including evaluations of the others' work, to her father in Washington. These updates, including one that detailed the production of fifty-six garments in one week, prompted Richard to praise Adaline's ability to promote "industry in those around you."[25]

Although it required a great deal of work, Adaline's management of clothing production had its advantages. African Americans, like Indians, used clothing to express individual taste as well as status. In some areas of the United States, sumptuary laws barred African American women from wearing fancy materials like silk, sewing silver into their clothing, displaying pearls or gold, or dressing their hair in certain "ladylike" styles. In a world where color was not a reliable index of wealth or status, such well-dressed women of color would have upstaged most whites. Luckily for Julia, Imogene, and Adaline, Kentucky had no such sumptuary laws. The Chinns' control over the purchase and tailoring of clothing enabled them to cultivate individual taste as well as a refined style that facilitated mingling with elite visitors to the Johnson plantation, people who, in Richard's words, were "of the highest respectability."[26]

Julia, Imogene, and Adaline may have found their work empowering, but they could never challenge Richard Johnson's ultimate authority, for his role as patriarch underwrote their status. Johnson proclaimed, "Whether I leave black or white to keep my house in my absence it is as sacred by the Laws and the Constitution as if I was in it myself." In the antebellum era, lawmakers were reluctant to limit men's authority as heads of household in any way, even if masters used that authority to empower slaves. Thus, with Richard Johnson's support, the Chinn family could buy silk dresses and good food, take on middle-class work roles, pursue education, even direct the labor of others—black and white. But this same patriarchal power meant that Johnson could withdraw his support at any time for any reason; in Johnson's words, he could have, without penalty, "cut their throats, or treated them as slaves or sold them to Negro buyers." At the time he wrote this, Johnson was not seriously considering any of these acts, but rather vilifying his "enemies" who would have preferred any of these horrific outcomes to the loving manner in which Richard raised and educated his daughters. "Treating these two children *as a Christian* has been the whole of my offending."[27]

Fellow planters would not challenge Richard Johnson's rights as a patriarch, but the social order he fostered at Great Crossings disturbed some. Like most Americans involved in interracial relationships, Johnson and Chinn were never prosecuted, for interracial sex was commonplace. But critics typically grew more antagonistic when black partners or the children of those unions publicly enjoyed class privileges usually reserved for whites. Particular resentment arose from the fact that the Chinns received an education that "was equal, or superior, to most of the females in the country." These critics feared that Adaline and Imogene would demand equality from whites because they were "as well educated as any lady." Others complained that they "dressed too fine." A few Indian students and visiting chiefs agreed, or at least thought that students' clothing should be noticeably better than what the slaves were wearing. Imogene and Adaline, in particular, were targeted by critics, for they attempted to brave America's deepest chasms, crossing from slave to free, property to propertied.[28]

Richard Johnson and Julia Chinn preferred to keep their daughters close, using their power to protect them from harm and ridicule, but Imogene and Adaline inevitably ventured into the broader world. On July 4, 1831, Adaline Johnson prepared to attend a nearby barbecue. Her father was elsewhere delivering "an address on the glories and virtues of the hallowed day" and was unaware of Adaline's plans. Julia may not have known either, for surviving records suggest spontaneity and peer pressure: "some white females" came to the house and "carried Adaline" to the party. The teenager was likely excited by this opportunity to leave home and mingle. It was a huge affair attended by "everybody" in Scott County "bond and free." Around that time, a white man employed by the Johnsons began courting Adaline, and perhaps this party gave them an opportunity to spend time together away from her watchful parents.[29]

Some attendees, however, objected to Adaline's publicly mingling with whites. When Adaline went to the dancing pavilion and took a seat, a group of white women "displayed considerable agitation," as a local newspaper reported, and moved away from that part of the pavilion. The women's actions alerted the party's hosts, who reportedly forced Adaline to leave the party. During her walk home, Adaline must have contemplated whether the invitation had been genuine, whether those "white females" who carried her away were truly her friends. Or had the whole thing been a cruel joke, manufactured to ridicule her family? These were miserable but fitting questions to ask on Independence Day, as Americans of diverse backgrounds contemplated the meaning of freedom.[30]

⤙ ❧ ⤚

The Indian gentlemen and black ladies of Great Crossings both drew on notions of class to preserve or enhance their status in a changing America. Their aspirations often put them at odds, not only with whites but also with one another. Their clashes reveal what is often hidden in histories of antebellum America—a social world shared by whites, blacks, and Indians, one shaped partly by the intimacy created by slavery.

The behavior of Choctaw Academy students ranged broadly, having much in common with that of planter elites like Richard Johnson. Some abused African Americans while others struggled to deal with people who were legally property but actually family. It's not surprising that they behaved this way, considering that many of these students were the sons or nephews of southern slaveholders. Most of those who clashed with slaves at Choctaw Academy, including Peter Pitchlynn, Pierre Juzan, Peter King, and Isaac Folsom, grew up in slaveholding households. By the 1820s, the enslavement of African Americans was a well-established practice protected by law in the nations of the Choctaws and Creeks who then dominated the school. As secretary of the General Council, Peter Pitchlynn himself had recorded the first written Choctaw slave codes, which, besides protecting slavery, outlawed marriage between Choctaws and black slaves and restricted free black immigration from the United States or other Indian nations to the Choctaw Nation. The elite boys and men of Choctaw Academy were replicating behaviors learned at home—privileged access to political and economic power, even control over the bodies of African Americans.[31]

The first recorded relationship between an enslaved woman and an Indian student involved the Choctaw monitor Pierre Juzan. From a prominent family in the Southern District of the Choctaw Nation, Juzan was the son of a white trader of French descent, a nephew of Southern District chief Tvpenahumma, and a grand-nephew of the famous chief

Pushmataha. Owners of a successful trading post at St. Stephens, the Juzans were wealthy and politically well connected. About twenty African American slaves worked in their household. Pierre's father Charles Juzan partially financed a mission school near his home, which Pierre had attended alongside his brothers, sisters, cousins, and aunts. By the time nineteen-year-old Pierre left for Choctaw Academy in the summer of 1826, he was fluent in English, wrote well, and had completed coursework in math and English grammar. Pierre Juzan's early prominence at Choctaw Academy is suggested by the fact that he gave the 1826 invocation speech, reassuring incoming students that they would find friends and opportunities in this "land of strangers."[32]

Juzan himself had found a companion in Dicy. Dicy's background is much less well documented than Pierre's, although circumstantial evidence suggests that she served within the Johnson household rather than on the plantation, and like most household servants, she was probably related to Julia Chinn. She is almost certainly the same Dicy who joined Great Crossings Baptist Church, where Julia Chinn and other enslaved people worshipped alongside students and local whites. Pierre did not belong to the church, but his position as a monitor gave him freedom to move around the school and plantation so that he could keep order among the students. Certainly, Pierre had the time and autonomy to pursue Dicy, though surviving documents reveal few details about the development of their illicit relationship.[33]

In late December of 1827, Pierre decided—or was perhaps forced—to inform Richard Johnson about the affair. The letter reached Johnson in his Senate chamber on the verge of one of the greatest triumphs of his political career. For the second time, Johnson had introduced a bill abolishing imprisonment for debt, which the rising Democratic star considered essential to the expansion of liberty for white men, and this time he knew it would pass. Such a victory should have been cause for celebration with his colleagues in Washington, but instead Johnson fumed over this unwelcome news from home. Although Johnson complained of his "great mortification" over the "fuss" back home, he drafted a letter forgiving Juzan. Pierre and Dicy may have quarreled, but it is likely that the relationship continued, perhaps until Pierre's graduation in the fall of 1828. Thereafter, Pierre Juzan entered Choctaw politics, becoming chief of his district and consulting the Choctaw General Council on matters of education until his death in 1841. In the latter capacity, he corresponded with Choctaw Academy officials and even visited Richard Johnson in Washington during Johnson's vice presidency. It is likely, though, that Pierre Juzan had more than just professional reasons to keep in touch. In 1829, a girl named Malvina Juzan (or Jusan) was born. Twenty-one years later, the 1850 census recorded Malvina Jusan as a free mulatto living in the Johnson household, along with her children Adelaide and Headon Jusan. This surname, along with the timing of Malvina's birth, is highly suggestive. It is likely that Malvina's mother chose to acknowledge Juzan's paternity by using his surname, and Pierre himself may have facilitated Malvina's freedom.[34]

About the same time that Pierre disclosed his relationship with Dicy, a group of students attempted to force their way into the big house. The students involved were Peter King, son of Mushulatubbee and the cousin of Peter Pitchlynn, and David Wall, who had formerly lived with the Pitchlynns while he attended a nearby mission school. The teenagers were possibly reeling from the excesses of a party. Although administrators prohibited alcohol on the campus of Choctaw Academy, students sometimes traded their clothes or other possessions to locals in exchange for bootleg liquor. Whatever the case, young King and Wall broke into the big house "after the Girls." Julia, Imogene, Adaline, and the household servants fought the assailants, trying to push them back into the yard. The defenders prevented assault, but the students remained in the house and damaged some property. Someone managed to slip out and alert the local magistrates, who finally succeeded in subduing King and Wall.[35]

It was this attack that finally prompted the Johnson family to employ an overseer, a white neighbor named Edward Pence. For years, Johnson had relied on Julia Chinn to perform this job, and he reluctantly hired Pence, only caving because he feared for his family's safety. Johnson told Pence that he had to enforce order not just in the fields but throughout Great Crossings, among "black and white and red" alike. Although outraged by an incident that would haunt him for years thereafter, Johnson was loath to punish Wall and King too severely because he could not afford to alienate their politically prominent families. He relied in particular on the patronage and political support of King's father, Mushulatubbee. The students got away with a verbal reprimand and quietly concluded their educations in September 1829. Wall even returned to Choctaw Academy a few years later and took up a position as an assistant teacher. Even as the Johnsons settled back into the routine of everyday life, the memory of the attack lingered. Wall does not seem to have attempted further violence, but Adaline later revealed that she felt uneasy about him.[36]

Despite their concerns, the Chinn-Johnson family and the staff could not control students' behavior. One of the main school buildings was only forty paces from the big house, and other classrooms and dorms were only slightly farther away. In doing their work, the Chinn-Johnson family and the slaves regularly walked from the house to the school buildings. When released from classes (or when cutting classes), and especially on weekends, students moved freely across the plantation, fished in nearby Elkhorn Creek, attended cockfights alongside slaves, and went to town, besting the local white boys in shooting contests. Even during the school day, monitors like Pierre Juzan could roam the grounds under the pretext of rounding up wayward boys. At times, some of the elite young men refused to be crowded into the dorms with the younger boys and demanded to board in the big house. Henderson, a softer touch than Johnson, acquiesced at least a few times. Johnson, writing from Washington, reprimanded his schoolmaster: "You know my family is no fit place for them to mingle."[37]

Other students followed in the footsteps of Peter King and David Wall. An unnamed Creek forced his way into the Johnson house and raped an enslaved woman named Rose. By assaulting Rose, this Creek boy invoked the wrath of several others on the plantation, including Rose's husband Lewis and Julia Chinn, who went to church with Rose. Another student, Peter Pitchlynn's nephew Isaac Folsom, pursued a household servant named Lucinda, and eventually the two were discovered in Richard Mentor Johnson's bed. We do not know whether Isaac forced Lucinda or if she participated willingly, but ultimately "her back paid for it," in Johnson's words.[38]

Johnson fumed, "If the Boys find women or any body outside of *my* yard I would say nothing to them—but to permit them to go into *my* Brick House & get into *my* beds with *my* Negro wenches or to permit any of them to be dogging into *my* house or cellars after the Girls are things which I cannot and will not bear." Making a clear link between his material possessions and his slaves, Johnson regarded these assaults as a serious trespass on his property rights. The congressman never supposed that the students should practice abstinence, nor did he ever claim responsibility for policing their sex lives. Rather, he focused narrowly on keeping control of his own fiefdom. Also telling is Johnson's distinction between "Negro wenches" and "the Girls." A degrading term for low-status women, "wenches," in the eyes of powerful men, lacked honor and were thus sexually available; according to Johnson, some of these "abandoned wenches" were "a disgrace to City Brothels." Johnson used this term for many of his female slaves who worked in the fields and at the mills he owned nearby on Elkhorn Creek. The "Girls," in contrast, included his own daughters as well as Julia Chinn's relatives, including her niece Parthena, sister-in-law Patience, probably Lucinda, and Julia's other nieces and sisters-in-law. Richard clearly favored his own daughters, but in claiming kinship to them, he also acknowledged a relationship with other African Americans, his girls' aunts and cousins. Some of them were women in their twenties or thirties, and in calling them "Girls," Johnson reminded everyone of the grossly unequal power relations at Great Crossings. But with kinship came obligation, and Johnson saw himself as honor-bound to protect his "Girls." The sexual assault in the big house had left "my family disgraced," in Richard's words.[39]

Richard Johnson worried most of all about Julia and his daughters. He expressed concern that the students did not respect Julia Chinn. Because Julia was the eyes and ears of the school, reporting back to Richard through her regular letters, troublemaking students resented her and attempted to discredit her authority. In referencing his family's "disgrace," Richard may also have read Isaac Folsom's bedding of Lucinda as a sarcastic mockery of his own relationship with Julia Chinn.[40]

Along with Richard, Julia and her family fought to preserve the relative privilege they enjoyed at Great Crossings. Julia still kept a close watch over the behavior of slaves and students, judging "who acts well and who acts ill." She identified problems to the overseer Edward Pence and the schoolmaster Thomas Henderson, who then meted out punishments to their respective charges. Chinn's managerial role gave her a power rare among enslaved people: the ability to keep her family close, so that they could offer one another more comfort and greater security. When Peter King and David Wall broke into the house, the Chinns banded together, prevented sexual assault, and called on the local magistrates to protect them. Though enslaved field hands and mill workers faced similar threats, they did not have this kind of recourse. The magistrates came out that December night because they recognized Julia Chinn's authority, her legitimate role as caretaker of Johnson's property, and the fact that she and her family belonged in the big house. Chinn was a woman, an African American, and still legally a slave, but also a plantation mistress, business manager, trusted helpmate, and a mother.[41]

The Indian students, particularly those of privilege, threatened the social order at Great Crossings. They came from the apex of separate nations where status was predicated on heredity as well as political and economic power, societies where whiteness held no special purchase. Demanding the food, clothing, deference, and even sexual prerogatives of gentlemen, the students translated their notions of status to the new context of Kentucky. And, unlike the Chinns, they refused to accept the ultimate authority of Richard Mentor Johnson.

In Choctaw Academy's twenty-three-year history, one of the only students formally expelled was a Choctaw named John Riddle. So great was Johnson's desire to retain the goodwill (and tuition money) of the Choctaws that he did not dismiss Peter King, David Wall, or even Isaac Folsom, making Riddle's departure a telling index of what most unnerved Richard Johnson. Arriving in 1825, Riddle was in the first group of students, and he, like his peers, came from an elite family. Johnson recognized Riddle's privilege, calling him "a Chief." Riddle, then in his late teens, was no chief, but he was politically well connected and would soon serve on the Choctaw General Council. Like several of his classmates, Riddle repeatedly broke the rules at the academy: he drank, he swore, he quarreled with an enslaved waitress in the dining hall, and, according to Richard Johnson, engaged in "orgies" of the "sober" and "drunken" variety. But Riddle went a step further than the other students.[42]

In the early spring of 1828, following the discovery of other affairs between students and slaves, superintendent Thomas Henderson and overseer Edward Pence prepared to mete out the usual punishments. The students got away with a tongue-lashing, while the young black women prepared for the sting of the cowhide on their backs. As Edward Pence uncoiled his whip on that spring day in 1828, however, Riddle restrained him. His motive for protecting the enslaved women is unclear. Certainly, John Riddle had encountered the women on campus before, and his brother William did have a relationship with one of the female house servants. Whatever his reasons, John Riddle incited a revolt on campus. He intimidated the overseer, threatened to beat Superintendent Henderson if he interfered, and called on the other students to disobey school authorities and rally around the enslaved women.[43]

Riddle, master of another plantation in another country, rejected white supremacy. This, in Johnson's mind, was what made Riddle so threatening. In a letter to Thomas Henderson, Johnson raged against Riddle's conduct. "If he can disobey your just order; if he can threaten to fight you; if he can order the little Boys to disobey your order; if he can interfere with my manager in chastising a parcel of outrageous strumpets whose disgraceful conduct deserves almost hanging . . . if he can do all this with impunity, then of course he is your Master and my master, and superior to the laws of our State." Breaking his usual protocol, Johnson asked Henderson to publicly horse-whip Riddle, though Henderson, disinclined toward violence, did not comply. On Johnson's orders, however, Henderson did turn Riddle out on foot, without the usual aid of horses and supplies that sustained returning students on their way home. Nonetheless, Riddle made his way to the Choctaw Nation, where he began a public relations campaign against the Academy. Resentful of Julia Chinn's authority, John Riddle told everyone back home that Chinn was the one who had dismissed him. Riddle claimed that, in a dangerous inversion of the power relations that prevailed in the Choctaw Nation, "Black Masters and Negro mistresses" ran Choctaw Academy.[44]

Richard Johnson identified John Riddle as the first member of a group he called the "gentlemen." Certainly, some Indians proudly claimed the mantle. When the Miami chief Little Turtle was diagnosed with gout, a white acquaintance expressed some surprise, saying that he had thought the disease "belonged to great folks and gentlemen." Little Turtle, peeved, responded, "Well, I always thought that I was a gentleman." At that time,

Americans used the term to describe respectable men who were well born, courageous, honorable, polite, and generous. But Johnson applied the term to Indian students sarcastically. According to Johnson, the top 10 percent of the student body were "too elevated ever to live like ordinary white men." In a word, they were "spoiled." Moreover, their privilege, according to Johnson, made them "insolent" and "disturbers of the peace." While Richard Johnson confidently defended Adaline as a "lady" after the Fourth of July barbecue, he suggested that Indians had no business aspiring to genteel status.[45]

Behind Johnson's whispered insults lurked the anxiety that Indian gentlemen threatened to usurp his authority. He prided himself on the notion that "No man in the United States keeps a more orderly house." Seeking to reclaim his power, Johnson sent home some of the most troublesome students. Still, he did not want to alienate Indian leaders and so explained that they had not been expelled, but rather had graduated. He also resolved to "prevent the mixture of the students with my people." Due to the close proximity of the big house, slave quarters, and school grounds, however, overseer Edward Pence found this edict impossible to enforce. The following autumn, Johnson moved the Academy a short distance, near White Sulphur Spring, and relocated his own family about two miles from the school.[46]

Blaming the move on a lack of firewood rather than his own loss of control, Johnson concealed the students' misconduct from most of his colleagues in the federal government. He explained that President John Quincy Adams was "a dangerous man—if he gets the least impression that an officer is incompetent in any respect he hurls him out." After John Riddle's expulsion, Johnson did visit the Office of Indian Affairs and confided in its director, Thomas McKenney. McKenney responded by writing an ominous letter and instructing Thomas Henderson to read it aloud to all the Choctaw Academy students: "We have the truth of everything here and know everything about it. The Government has got eyes in the Choctaw Academy, and ears too. . . . *Let the youths beware!* . . . I tell them as their friend, their business is to study, to be sober, honest, and obedient to you as their head and preceptor. . . . Order shall be maintained, cost what it may."[47]

The students failed to heed McKenney's warning. It is doubtful that they regarded administrators' only recourse—dismissal—as a real punishment. Moreover, the two-mile walk did not prevent determined young men from trekking down to the slave quarters "to go into the House of black people" and drive away "their husbands if they have no pass and then get into their places." Nor did distance dissolve the threat to the big house. Sometimes drunk young men broke down the kitchen door or hid beneath the stairs during the day and emerged at night to seek out "the Girls." Adaline, who still managed the clothes and linens at the school, complained that the older boys who acted as monitors abused their authority, making themselves "obnoxious" to her.[48]

When Peter Pitchlynn wrote his critical review of Choctaw Academy, he detailed the minutiae of everyday life—food, clothing, housing, personal quarrels. But in the minds of those who fought them, these seemingly mundane battles symbolized a much broader struggle. As students, slaves, school administrators, and the local community debated whether the Indians and African Americans of Choctaw Academy "dressed too fine," bigger questions lurked beneath: Was it even possible for North America's diverse people to forge a shared path, a great path? If so, what roles would people of color play? Would race, in fact, determine place— or might wealth, education, and respectability figure more prominently?

Richard Johnson's mercurial attitudes reveal the diverse and even contradictory views that white Americans held regarding people of color. When Johnson heard about Pitchlynn's negative review of the school, he read it as a betrayal, recollecting "the ties which bound us together not only as friends but as Masons." Invoking their membership in the elite fraternal organization, Johnson acknowledged a shared class identity that cut across racial lines, much as he embraced the kin ties that bound him to his daughters and the Chinn family. At the same time, however, he regarded other African American women as "wenches," fit for sex, whipping, or sale. And, while Richard Johnson publicly courted Indian chiefs, he privately castigated their sons and nephews who acted the part of "mighty gentlemen."[49]

But the Indian gentlemen and black ladies of Choctaw Academy did not submit passively while powerful white men like Johnson judged them. Drawing on her intellect, skills, sexuality, and shared history with Richard, Julia Chinn used all the tools at her disposal to win a better place for her family. She, and later her daughters, espoused middle-class values such as piety, temperance, and sexual morality as a means to demonstrate their respectability. Ultimately, the privilege of Julia, Imogene, Adaline, and the entire Chinn family rested on Richard Johnson's patronage and goodwill. They could not, without risking grave consequences, openly challenge the slave society in which they lived or the mastery that gave Johnson his power over them. Through careful diplomacy, however, Julia did gain more privileges for her family and a route to freedom for her daughters. Indian students had much greater resources at their disposal than Chinn did. Free beyond question and supported by formidable nations, they refused to be subordinated in the United States. Accustomed to power and privilege at home, the Indian gentlemen of Choctaw Academy demanded the same treatment in Kentucky. In their everyday lives—going to barbecues, wearing fancy clothes, studying Latin, and fighting back—these Indian men and African American women asserted that they were not savages or wenches, but rather gentlemen and ladies.

5

Rise of the Leviathan

In the fall of 1827, James McDonald quit his law practice, packed the last of his books and clothes, and swung his traveling cloak around his shoulders. As McDonald waited for the stagecoach that would carry him from Hamilton, Ohio, on the first leg of his long journey southward, perhaps he reflected on the past nine years, all the effort he had poured into achieving his current position: he had learned Latin at a Georgetown prep school, studied law with soon-to-be Supreme Court justice John McLean, moved back to Ohio despite his mother's reservations, and passed the bar. Recently, however, disturbing reports of Mississippi's mounting anti-Indian racism had turned McDonald's attention homeward. In a letter to Peter Pitchlynn, McDonald described how a sense of duty to his people forced him to relinquish his personal aspirations, including "the idea of practicing law." The first accredited Native American lawyer prepared to exhibit himself as an emblem "of Indian capacity," in the words of a white contemporary. By now, this was a familiar mantle for the twenty-six-year-old, who, with his graceful manner, was mostly successful in concealing the strain.[1]

Back home, McDonald sought to maintain the peaceful, collaborative path he had worked hard to build. He moved to Jackson, a Choctaw settlement renamed in honor of the "Hero of New Orleans" and recently incorporated as the capital of the state of Mississippi. McDonald took up a new profession as a small planter. As a child, he had watched his mother manage their family farm and imagined that he would follow in her footsteps, but now, used to a very different kind of work, the occupation bored him. Relying on the labor of his mother's four slaves, McDonald, in his words, acted "the farmer in a lazy way." In his leisure time, he returned to the life of the mind, reading and composing short stories based on Choctaw history and culture. But the Native lawyer focused most of his energy on networking with politicians and other influential white Mississippians. McDonald's white neighbors thought so highly of the young Choctaw that they elected him justice of the peace, an office that authorized McDonald to judge minor civil and criminal cases in Hinds County.[2]

Drawing on his own experiences, McDonald argued that whites and Indians could live peaceably side by side, just as they had for centuries. McDonald himself claimed dual citizenship, addressing members of the state legislature as "Fellow Citizens" while acknowledging his Choctaw identity "without a blush." Turning his attention to Indian removal, McDonald characterized the proposed policy as both illegal and immoral. Any violation of the many treaties that guaranteed the Choctaws' right to remain in their homeland "deserve[d] the attention of every patriot," for such a move would violate the precepts established by that most beloved founding father, George Washington, and handed down to subsequent administrations. Treaties, according to McDonald, were more than binding legal contracts between sovereigns; they constituted sacred obligations that the United States, as a Christian nation, should uphold. He asked these southern legislators, who claimed to love their country so well, to consider the people who had inhabited that land for thousands of years: "Think you . . . their heart-strings do not quiver at the thought of taking a last adieu of the land of their fathers? Think you, that the tear will not start unbidden from the eye of the aged warrior, and that the cries of desolate women will not rise on the gale? Ah! Imagine not that they are without feeling, because they speak in a strange tongue."[3]

McDonald asserted, "There are many fine and gentlemanly men in the Legislature" who "must certainly become advocates of our cause," but privately the lawyer was given to moments of despair and bouts of depression. In a candid letter to his friend Peter Pitchlynn, McDonald confided that "the prospect before me has so little promise in it, that I feel at times exceedingly unhappy." The alcoholism that had plagued McDonald for years intensified during this period of stress, and he fretted, "I now see more clearly than ever that indulgence in the social glass (under feelings of disappointment) will prove my destruction." McDonald tried to avoid gatherings that featured alcohol and buoyed himself through the repetition of his personal motto, *"nil desperandum*—let us never despair." No matter how determined, eloquent, intelligent, or passionate, however, one lawyer could not drown out the gathering chorus of American voices calling for Indian removal. McDonald lamented, "To my mind it looks like a bitter and endless presentation."[4]

McDonald was prescient in his reading of the ominous signs that Americans increasingly favored the relocation of all Indians to the territory west of the Mississippi River, but he also knew that his people had powerful white allies willing to defend Native rights. In the late 1820s and early 1830s, removal emerged as the most divisive political issue in the United States. Two nascent political parties used the debate to articulate different visions of the nation's future. Those who would come to be called Whigs emphasized social progress and economic diversification over territorial expansion. At the core of this group were evangelical reformers who believed that Americans, as God's chosen people, could bring on the millennium by perfecting their society. They echoed McDonald's argument that Indian removal would both violate treaty obligations and stain the soul of the nation. Anti-removal sentiment was strongest among northern evangelicals like missionary Cyrus Kingsbury, who pled, "It is our earnest prayer, that as a nation we may never forget our high and peculiar responsibility to the Sovereign of the Universe, how we discharge the trust committed to us as the guardians of the Indians." Even in the South and West, where white residents had the most to gain from Indian removal, constitutional nationalists and Whigs like Congressman David ("Davy") Crockett defended "the native Indian tribes in this country as a sovereign people," asserting that they "had been recognized as such from the very foundation of the Government; and the United States were bound by treaty to protect them; it was [our] duty to do so."[5]

In the opposing camp stood a diverse coalition of nascent Democrats and a few evangelical leaders, including the prominent Baptist Isaac McCoy. A missionary among the Potawatomis and Ottawas, McCoy had come to believe that lowly frontier whites had cheated, bullied, and corrupted Indians so badly that only removal to a more distant locale would "rescue them from extinction." Most advocates of removal were more self-interested. Showing less enthusiasm for reform, they argued that Indians should be moved to make way for the expansion of their agrarian republic. The movement was strongest in the Deep South, where large Indian nations owned some of the richest cotton land. The Indian population of Mississippi, which claimed dominion over the Choctaw and Chickasaw Nations, stood at 24,000—the largest of any state, and more than all the northern states combined. Back in 1802, the state of Georgia had agreed to cede to the federal government land that later became Alabama and Mississippi in exchange for a promise to remove the Indians. When that promise remained unfulfilled decades later, one resident of Georgia reported, "the popular cry is—exterminate the savages." Joel Chandler Harris, author of the Uncle Remus stories, recorded a folk song that captured the aspirations of many white Georgians:

> All I want in this creation
> Is a pretty little wife and a big plantation
> Away up yonder in the Cherokee Nation

This simple verse explains popular support for Indian removal: whites wanted land, of course, but also the considerable capital and other resources that Indians had accumulated—plantations, big houses, mines, schools, churches, meeting houses, and even slaves. Like the poor of Georgia, thousands of frontier whites imagined how Indian wealth might transform their own fortunes. By the late 1820s, thanks to Democrats' efforts to extend suffrage to all white men, poorer whites exerted unprecedented political power, and their demands began to shape national Indian policy.[6]

Even Commissioner of Indian Affairs Thomas McKenney, once the greatest champion of the federal government's Civilization Policy, began to consider the possibility of removal. Persuaded by Isaac McCoy's argument that frontier whites corrupted and impoverished Indians, McKenney also drew conclusions from his deteriorating relationship with his adopted son, James McDonald. When the two reunited in Washington during treaty negotiations in 1824, McKenney marveled at McDonald's hard-nosed bargaining, but also worried that the strain pushed him to intemperance.

One evening, after inviting McDonald into his office, McKenney privately confronted him about his alcohol abuse. McKenney did not hide his disappointment: "I had looked to you as the crowning of my hopes, and trusted to see, from your continued good example, a day-star arise for the enlightening of your race." Over the years, as McDonald's addiction persisted, McKenney interpreted the disease as a "conflict between his Indian caste and his hope of overcoming it." Unfortunately for McDonald, his status as an emblem of Indian progress also invited scrutiny of his flaws. By 1826, McKenney had washed his hands of McDonald. "I have the kindest feelings for McDonald, and he knows it. But I abominate his late habit. I have done all I could to save him." McKenney maintained his belief that Indians could assimilate into American society, but he decided that they needed more time and greater distance from whites.[7]

Choctaw Academy students, elite sons of Indian country who resided in the United States, were uniquely positioned to take notice of the changing political and cultural climate. Plus, the English they learned in school helped overcome language barriers, enabling students from different tribes to compare notes about recent events. A young Creek boy dubbed "Richard Mentor Johnson" at Choctaw Academy was the son of the great chief Opothle Yahola, and he may have told his peers how his father had successfully lobbied Congress to overturn the fraudulent Treaty of Indian Springs, though his people still lost millions of acres. Other Creeks at the Academy were among those forced by that treaty to leave their ancestral homelands in Georgia and crowd in with distant relatives in Alabama. Their Potawatomi classmates had probably overheard their elders describe the "rough talk" of frontier whites like Illinois governor Ninian Edwards, who spun lurid, apocryphal tales of Potawatomi "depredations" against local whites in the hopes that federal officials might remove them.[8]

Students from a variety of tribes knew about Thomas McKenney's tour of Indian country during the fall of 1827, during which the commissioner of Indian affairs had tried to persuade their families to consider removal. Potawatomi chief Senatchewane offered a typical response, explaining that the suggestion that he and his people "be driven off from the home of our ancestors, leave here the bones of our wives and children . . . is calculated to break our hearts." Peter Pitchlynn trekked down from Choctaw Academy to reclaim his role as secretary of the General Council when McKenney addressed the Choctaws in mid-October. Although Pitchlynn and the Choctaws warmly greeted McKenney with a feast and a dance, they, like every other nation McKenney visited, rejected his proposal. Privately, some Choctaw leaders confided to McKenney that to "even to *seem* to approve it" might lead to angry tribal members "shooting them by the way-side, or cutting their throats."[9]

McKenney's stance also made him unpopular at Choctaw Academy, where students, like their families, overwhelmingly opposed removal. Richard Johnson tried to tamp down what he described as students' "prejudice" against the highest-ranking official in the Indian Affairs department. In a speech to the students prepared by Johnson, schoolmaster Thomas Henderson explained McKenney's position: "This is his idea, that so long as a tribe of Indians lives within the boundary of a state they will be subject to imposition, more and more as the whites increase till they are rooted out, even if the [federal] government tries to protect them." Although most students remained opposed, some found truth in McKenney's argument. Perhaps another of McKenney's statements regarding the federal government ran through the students' minds: "The Government has got eyes in the Choctaw Academy, and ears too.... *Let the youths beware!* . . . Order shall be maintained, cost what it may." Despite the efforts of school administrators to quiet dissent, the scholars speculated and worried over the fates of their nations.[10]

Richard Johnson quietly supported removal, though he never gave the students or their nations "a hint of my opinion." Johnson was chief among the congressmen who authorized McKenney's 1827 tour of Indian country, and, when that failed, he led the motion to appropriate $15,000 so that tribal delegates could visit Indian Territory on an expedition led by removal advocate Isaac McCoy. Johnson explained, "I am extremely anxious to see these Southern tribes fixed upon a basis that never can be shaken by the white people of the states in whose limits they now reside." Johnson, however, also had a financial stake in the matter; he knew that removal would force tribes to negotiate new treaties with the federal government and reasoned that they might use resulting funds to enroll their children at Choctaw Academy, which would help him "conquer and melt" his long-standing debt.[11]

Johnson, rather than Thomas McKenney or other Indian Affairs officials, proved the most effective promoter of the US-sponsored trip to Indian Territory, framing it as an exploratory expedition with no strings attached. Some leaders, drawing on relationships developed with Johnson through Choctaw Academy, welcomed his mediation in their increasingly fraught relationship with the federal government. Ultimately, five tribes, the Chickasaws, Choctaws, Creeks, Ottawas, and Potawatomis— all of whom knew Johnson through Choctaw Academy—agreed to send delegates to explore Indian Territory. A Creek headman consented after reflecting that Johnson had "done much more for [our children] than I expected." Choctaws, meanwhile, asked Johnson if he might be willing to accompany them on the expedition. Johnson demurred, but suggested that perhaps "2 or 3 of the smartest students" might "see a little of the world by going with the exploring party." The Choctaw General Council selected a total of six delegates, including Peter Pitchlynn. Proud of "an English education equally good or better than most of my countrymen," Pitchlynn enthusiastically accepted his role as interpreter.[12]

Peter's family begged him "not to go explore the new world." For most of the past two years, Peter had been away at school, first at Choctaw Academy, then at the University of Nashville. His young wife Rhoda had needed help managing the couple's estate and caring for their infant daughter Lavinia. Peter's kin and his mother-in-law supported Rhoda, but everyone felt his absence. Likely repeating a comforting line offered by her father, three-year-old Lavinia told the others, "Pappy is gone to the Ball Play and will bring me home beads." In addition to practical concerns for Peter's health and safety on such a long journey, his family worried that other Choctaws would see Peter's participation on the expedition as a tacit endorsement of removal, which remained extremely unpopular. Undeterred, the twenty-two-year-old packed his journal, clothes, rifle, and a few books. On September 26, 1828, Peter and his personal servant "Black Peter" left the Choctaw Nation en route to St. Louis, where they joined forty-one other chiefs and tribal officials for a three-month tour of Indian Territory.[13]

Pitchlynn regarded the trip as a grand adventure. He met Indians from many different tribes, exchanged tobacco and words of peace, flirted with a beautiful young Osage woman, and met the Shawnee prophet

Tenskwatawa, who, with his brother Tecumseh, had spearheaded a powerful anti-colonial movement two decades earlier. Tenskwatawa's group of Shawnees were among several thousand eastern Indians who, escaping white encroachment, had moved to the trans-Mississippi west during the last few decades. Peter regarded these eastern Indians as "long separated brothers" who were "pretty much like ourselves."[14]

Overall, however, Peter could not imagine living in Indian Territory. Plains Indians who inhabited the region had little in common with the Choctaws. In his journal, he recorded meeting the Kansas Indians: "You never saw such a people in your life. Their manners and action are wild in the extreme. They are in a perfect state of nature and would be a curiosity to any civilized man." The Sioux he found "a rude and uncultivated race, and from every appearance a miserable set." Pitchlynn had a more agreeable experience at an Osage village, where he tasted buffalo for the first time. Never an important part of eastern Indians' diets, buffalo had disappeared from that region the previous century, and, like Pitchlynn, most Choctaws had never seen one before. Although he publicly played the role of diplomat, Pitchlynn recorded in his journal that encounters with such alien people left him frequently shocked and sometimes contemptuous. For thousands of years, the Choctaws had been farmers who lived in settled communities, and, of late, they had become increasingly literate, politically centralized, and market-oriented. To Pitchlynn's mind, the Choctaws were civilized, a distinction that had nothing to do with race. Many other eastern Indians used similar rhetoric to distance themselves from Plains peoples and assert that they, like US citizens, lived in "civilized nations."[15]

Turning his attention from the people to the land, Pitchlynn found that it, too, was strange, and large portions of it "good for nothing, and never will be, for it is all prairie and nothing in them but rock and gravel; a tree in that country is a perfect curiosity." Incredulous, Pitchlynn wrote, "Notwithstanding that these things are all true, the white people with us have been presumptuous enough to tell us that it is a fine country." He and the other Indian delegates rejected the idea of settling there.[16]

In early December 1828, as Pitchlynn and his colleagues neared the end of their expedition, Andrew Jackson was elected president of the United States. By then, citizens, rather than their state legislators, voted directly for the president in all but two states—Delaware and South Carolina—and they offered overwhelming support for Democrats, giving Jackson 56 percent of the popular vote and both houses of Congress, including a large majority in the House of Representatives. In Georgia, where support for Jackson's pro-removal platform was strongest, John Quincy Adams did not receive a single vote. Buoyed by this popular enthusiasm, Jackson was determined to please his constituency and enact his own vision for North America's future by removing all eastern Indians. Jacksonian democracy would empower white men by colonizing Indian country and redistributing its resources.[17]

Andrew Jackson believed that Indian treaties, many of which he had negotiated, were a relic of his nation's birth, when the United States had been too weak to conquer Native nations. But now, "circumstances have entirely changed" and to continue to acknowledge Indians' rights to territory or self-government was, in Jackson's words, "an absurdity." Rather than sovereign nations or even potential citizens of the United States, Indians were, according to Jackson, merely "subjects" of a growing empire. Perhaps more legitimately, Jackson feared that Indian nations, like European empires that claimed land in North America, represented a challenge to US sovereignty, one that might prevent territorial expansion.[18]

To support such a radical change in Indian policy, Jackson and his Democrats needed more than legal and political rationales: they needed ideological buttressing. The solution came in the form of a more virulent strand of American racism, supported by "scientific" evidence and conveniently deployed to achieve slavery's expansion and Indian dispossession. The concept was pioneered by physician Charles Caldwell, a graduate of the University of Pennsylvania who began to challenge his former mentor Benjamin Rush's environmental theories of race. In the 1810s, Caldwell, drawing on pseudo-scientific evidence gleaned from the shapes and sizes of skulls, argued that Indians and African Americans were innately, biologically inferior to whites and could not achieve progress through white efforts to civilize them. In 1819, Caldwell accepted a position at Transylvania University, just down the road from Choctaw Academy, where, throughout the 1820s and 1830s, he refined and publicized his view of a "natural" hierarchy of the races, helping to popularize biological racism among intellectuals and policymakers. This was a bottom-up movement, in which scientists "discovered" evidence to support the racist diatribes of poor squatters and self-interested planters, making hard-line racism seem legitimate, even natural. In response, one Choctaw citizen lamented, "Above all scoundrels, deliver me from the intelligent and well educated scoundrel!"[19]

Lewis Cass, a territorial governor of Michigan who wanted to relocate that area's considerable Indian population, used Caldwell's theories to justify Indian removal in a highly influential article published in the *North American Review* in January of 1830. Characterizing the Civilization Policy as "unsuccessful and unproductive," Cass declared, "there seems to be some insurmountable obstacle in the habits or temperament of the Indians, which has heretofore prevented, and yet prevents, the success of these labors." Cass used the article to convince the educated public that Indian removal was an inevitable consequence of the march of progress, even divinely ordained, for "the Creator intended the earth should be reclaimed from a state of nature and cultivated," not merely "traversed . . . by wandering hordes of barbarians." It was even best for Indians: "A removal from their present position and from the vicinity of our settlements, to the regions beyond the Mississippi, can alone preserve from final extinction the remnant of our aboriginal population." Andrew Jackson agreed with Cass's humanitarian justification, saying that Indians could not survive "in the midst of another and superior race." In 1831, after a scandal forced his friend John Eaton to resign, Jackson appointed Lewis Cass secretary of war to lead the department that handled Indian Affairs.[20]

Indians and their white allies were incredulous. In response to the characterization of Choctaws as "nomadic," Horatio Cushman, a son of missionaries who resided in the Choctaw Nation, retorted, "There certainly never has a greater error been promulgated about any people." Choctaws had farmed the same fields for a thousand years; surely the whites, who restlessly pushed west with each succeeding generation, more closely resembled "wandering hordes of barbarians." A Scottish visitor to the United States agreed, claiming that Kentuckians, not Indians, most closely resembled "Tartars" because they were constantly moving "in search of fresh pastures." Indians also entered the public debate.

In a letter to the *Arkansas Gazette*, a Cherokee named Nu-Tah-E-Tuil asked, "What is civilization?" Nu-Tah-E-Tuil ventured a few guesses: "a practical knowledge of agriculture," "good and comfortable buildings," "morality and religion," "school and the education of youth." Cherokees, he argued, would beat common whites in every category.[21]

Contrary to Cass's characterization of the Civilization Policy as a failure, the reforms undertaken by Indians during the early decades of the nineteenth century had actually succeeded too well. Many Indian nations walked the same path as the United States, intensifying economic production and developing centralized national governments. Frustrating US imperial ambitions, Native nations refused to cede land, relinquish their sovereignty, or "amalgamate" into disappearance.

Once the darlings of the Civilization Policy, these achievers, in the eyes of the Jackson administration, had become problems. Cass had a ready answer: "the progress made by these Indians in civilization" was "exaggerated," largely confined to "the *half-breeds* and their immediate connections." Resistance to removal, imagined the Jackson administration, came from "white Indians": "the great body of the people . . . in a state of helpless and hopeless poverty" would be delighted to resettle in the west, where they could resume their barbarous, wandering lifestyle. In this view, Indian luminaries like James McDonald were not really Indians at all. Rather, their exceptionalism derived from their partial white ancestry. Never mind Mushulatubbee, the plantation-owning education reformer, or the "full blood Choctaw girl" who impressed missionaries with her composition on logician Isaac Watts's *The Improvement of the Mind*. Ignoring inconvenient evidence, Americans invented a language of blood born of scientific racism—of "full" and "half" and "mixed"—and imposed it on Indian country in an attempt to discredit and silence some of the most outspoken critics of the federal government. In this rhetorical strategy, the empire discovered a powerful tool of dispossession. By redefining the nature of Indianness—away from a primarily political identity based on membership in a sovereign nation and toward one based on racial purity and adherence to an unchanging culture—Indians and their nations could be erased over time. It was a catch-22: those who failed to adapt would be crushed by the march of progress; those who adapted would not be counted as Indians.[22]

Although previous leaders had entertained the possibility of removal, Jackson differed in that he was determined to make it the cornerstone of his presidency. According to his vice president Martin Van Buren, "There was no measure, in the whole course of his administration, of which he was more exclusively the author than this." Jackson inaugurated the spoils system in American politics, replacing long-serving officials with party loyalists, and his purge of the Office of Indian Affairs was particularly thorough. One agent who managed to hang on to his job called the new recruits "grossly immoral, incompetent and ignorant." Thomas McKenney, who remained sympathetic toward Indians and endorsed voluntary (rather than forced) removal, expressed shock when he was fired. The secretary of war responded, "Why, sir, everybody knows your qualifications for the place, but General Jackson has long been satisfied that you are not in harmony with him, in his views in regard to the Indians." Choctaw leaders, who had long loathed their drunk and incompetent agent William Ward, actually hoped for a replacement and suggested a few candidates, but Jackson was satisfied with Ward's allegiance. Even more important than Jackson's use of the spoils system was his signal that in violation of the US Constitution and federal law, he would respect state sovereignty over Indian sovereignty. Anticipating Jackson's inauguration, states with large Indian populations began to extend jurisdiction over Indians residing within their borders through a series of laws passed in the late 1820s.[23]

The extension of state jurisdiction alarmed Choctaw Academy students, who understood the consequences: "We as a nation can no longer live upon our present soil and enjoy those liberties and those laws of our own making." Mississippi would not recognize the territorial claims or government of the Choctaw or Chickasaw nations. Furthermore, Mississippi laws would categorize Indians as people of color, "as miserable as free negroes," in the students' estimation. As students at the academy discussed the extension of state law over Indians, a group of Choctaws argued that the consequences would be "most shocking": "We cannot but dread them." In Mississippi, as in most states, free people of color could not vote, hold office, or testify in court. The extension of state law would transform Indians from citizens of a sovereign nation into subjects of an increasingly racist empire.[24]

Indian leaders protested that such a loss of autonomy would render them slaves in their own homeland. In a petition to Congress, Creek chiefs asserted, "We have never been slaves—We have been born free." In fact, the Creeks reminded their audience, Indians were the original Americans and, until recently, *masters* of the entire continent. European immigrants had come to "our country few in number and feeble in strength," and Indians had given them "land on which to live," "food to supply their hunger," protection "under our own roofs." Now that the roles were reversed, with the United States gaining strength as Indian nations weakened, the chiefs wondered, "For which of our services to you are we condemned to slavery? For which of them are we subjected to the penalties of forfeiture?"[25]

Despite the lobbying efforts of James McDonald, the Mississippi state legislature voted in February 1829 to extend its jurisdiction over the Choctaw and Chickasaw nations, effective the following January. Mississippi outlawed Indian self-government, annulled tribal laws, and set a fine of $1,000 to anyone presenting himself as a chief. The three Choctaw district chiefs, echoing the vast majority of their people, continued to oppose removal, but Mushulatubbee was not so sure. Since losing his district election to David Folsom two years earlier, Mushulatubbee sought a way to reclaim political power, which is probably what provoked his visit to Choctaw Academy in October of 1829. Recognizing that the students' residence at Johnson's plantation and their American education offered them privileged insights into US politics, Mushulatubbee asked Choctaw scholars what they thought of removal. The majority of students continued in their opposition, but fourteen out of a total of fifty-five Choctaw students urged Mushulatubbee to consider it. To leave their homeland and the remains of their ancestors would be a terrible fate, "but the time has come when it appears that we must do something to better our condition and the question now arises in what to do, whether it is more honorable to provide for the living or the dead." Remaining in Mississippi, they argued, would destroy the Choctaw Nation—if not literally, then at least politically.[26]

This group of fourteen Choctaw students, led by Robert M. Jones, summarized their arguments in a letter addressed to their "friends and countrymen," which Mushulatubbee carried back to the Choctaw

Nation. Mushulatubbee promptly called citizens of the Northeastern District to a council and ordered interpreter Middleton McKee to read the letter aloud. The elders listened to the words of their faraway children who urged them to make a treaty, soon, before the tyranny of Mississippi worsened their situation. The petitioners advised their leaders to seek a just price for their eastern lands as well as protection from the US military against hostile Plains tribes whose territory they would invade.[27]

Although the petitioners acknowledged the troubling logic of removal, they still tried to imagine routes to co-existence and collaboration—this, after all, was the mission of their school. In their petition, the scholars addressed Indian Territory, a fuzzy geographic and political space whose future had been ill-defined by US policymakers. The students argued that the United States should guarantee that the Choctaws' western territory would one day be admitted to the union as a Choctaw-dominated state. Drawing on their knowledge of US history and politics, these petitioners understood that states and federal government shared power in a realm of divided sovereignty. They believed that a Choctaw state would both empower Indians and preserve a measure of autonomy.[28]

While Mushulatubbee's political rival David Folsom denounced the letter as a product of Richard Johnson's meddling, the crowd found some truth in it. Although the majority did not necessarily endorse the students' plan, they rewarded Mushulatubbee for his foreign policy intelligence by re-electing him chief of the Northeastern District that November.[29]

Like the student body at Choctaw Academy, citizens of the Choctaw Nation divided over the best course of action. Tvpenahumma, former chief of the Southern District, decided to emigrate voluntarily in the fall of 1829; he asked his nephew Pierre Juzan, a Choctaw Academy graduate, to help organize and act as interpreter for one hundred Choctaws who followed him. Perhaps Tvpenahumma was persuaded by Juzan's view that Indian Territory might become a permanent home where the Choctaws could reassert their sovereignty. Others argued that "in a few years, the Americans will also wish to possess the land west of the Mississippi should we remove." Such a sobering thought gave way to hopelessness in some. A Chickasaw chief lamented to Peter Pitchlynn that so great was the power of the rising American empire that "it is almost a farce for [Indians] to say whether they will or will not go." Most, however, counted on their tribal leaders and even the US federal government to protect the homeland. George Harkins, a Choctaw Academy graduate who had recently visited Congress with Richard Mentor Johnson, argued that Indians should wait out Jackson's presidency; surely the next administration would restore sanity.[30]

Despite the opposition that Harkins noted while in Washington, Andrew Jackson continued to push his removal agenda. The central piece of legislation underlying this policy shift was the Indian Removal Bill, the object of fierce debate in Congress. New Jersey senator Theodore Frelinghuysen, in a six-hour speech, proved the most passionate defender of Indian rights: "Our ancestors found these people, far removed from the commotions of Europe, exercising all the rights, and enjoying all the privileges, of free and independent sovereigns of this new world. . . . They have nothing to do with State sovereignty, or United States sovereignty. They are above and beyond both." To make the bill more palatable, Jackson's supporters had to denude it, framing removal, in the words of Mississippi senator Robert Adams, as "a free and voluntary choice of the Indians themselves." Passing the House by a very slim margin—102 to 97—the Indian Removal Act, signed into law on May 28, 1830, merely gave the executive branch the authority to make treaties with individual Indian nations that wished to exchange eastern lands for western ones "that the United States will forever secure and guaranty to them." To achieve his objective, Jackson would rely on common whites and local authorities to make life for Indians as unpleasant as possible, saying condescendingly to "my red Choctaw children," "their father cannot prevent them from being subject to the laws of the State of Mississippi."[31]

The Choctaws were first on Jackson's list. Choctaws were outraged, regarding this as a deep betrayal by Jackson, their ally during the War of 1812 and, in 1820, a treaty-negotiator who had guaranteed their lands "forever." However, several of the Choctaw Nation's most powerful politicians, including district chiefs Greenwood Leflore and John Garland as well as recently deposed David Folsom, decided that removal was inevitable and sought the best possible treaty terms. Garland and Folsom ceded power to Leflore, claiming to US officials that he was the Choctaw Nation's sole chief, and Leflore sent Jackson a list of demands. Leading a rival political faction, Mushulatubbee and Peter Pitchlynn denounced Leflore as " his royal highness," a traitor who had unilaterally bargained away their country "without the consent or knowledge of the people of this Nation." Pitchlynn also castigated his uncle David Folsom, rightly pointing out that the former chief had used government kickbacks to send his children to school in the United States "at the very time he was recommending the missionary school to us": "Does this look like he had the interests of his constituents at heart?" As the Choctaw Nation neared civil war, Jackson rejected the original Leflore proposal, with its $50 million price tag, and sent two of his most trusted foot soldiers, Secretary of War John Eaton and longtime friend and business partner John Coffee, to draw up a new treaty.[32]

In mid-September of 1830, six thousand Choctaws gathered at Dancing Rabbit Creek to observe the negotiations. Under arbors shaded by towering pines, oaks, and mulberry trees, families set up camp and shared meals of bread, venison jerky, and *tomfulla*. The atmosphere was loud and rowdy, for the Indian families were joined by about one thousand enterprising, if seedy, whites who beckoned Choctaw men to saddle up to makeshift bars and gambling tables, or invited them to join prostitutes for an hour in the tents they had converted into brothels. The Christians in David Folsom's camp sang and prayed instead, assiduously avoiding vices which they knew to be gateways to poor earthly judgment and hellfire alike.[33]

The atmosphere quieted on the morning of September 18, when representatives of the Choctaw Nation—three chiefs and sixty captains—met the US commissioners in council. They formed a circle, in the middle of which sat seven beloved women, representing the kin groups or *iksas* who technically owned all Choctaw land in accordance with tribal tradition. Over the course of several days, Secretary of War John Eaton did most of the talking on behalf of the federal government, claiming that "the treaty would be in every respect eminently beneficial to them." Early in negotiations, only one Choctaw leader, a captain named Killihota, spoke in favor of removal, glowingly describing the lands they might acquire in the west. Waves of disgust reverberated from the crowd, and one of the *iksa* mothers leaped to her feet. Bearing a knife, she warned, "Killihota, I could cut you open with this knife. You have two hearts." Killihota responded, "I have only one heart and that for my people," but he failed to sway those assembled.[34]

As the Choctaws persisted in their resistance, the US commissioners grew increasingly desperate and angry. Eaton rose to make a speech characterized by "brutal roughness," in the words of one witness. If the Choctaws did not remove, the United States would beat a red path of war. The president "would march an army into their country," and should the Choctaws resist, "it would be just as foolish as it would be for a baby to expect to overcome a giant." Outraged by Eaton's comments but also satisfied with the chiefs' rejection of the proposed treaty, most of the crowd went home. Eaton, however, approached Choctaw leaders with a final, terrifying statement. If they did not sign a removal treaty, the United States would usurp all the Choctaws' homeland as well as their proposed western territory. Eaton said "that their country would be overrun by the whites, who would come among them like flocks or blackbirds and swarms of locusts; that they and their children would become paupers and beggars; that they would be broken up and utterly destroyed as a nation . . . that they would soon have no country and no home." Should the Choctaws come to the president, "he will turn a deaf ear to your lamentations and laugh at your calamities." Finally, Choctaw leaders acquiesced and proposed treaty terms. Eaton and Coffee deemed these too extravagant and offered a counter-proposal. On September 27, 1830, 171 of those assembled—less than 3 percent of the original crowd—signed the treaty under what one white witness described as "the controlling influence of fear, coercion and duress."[35]

The resulting Treaty of Dancing Rabbit Creek, the first Indian removal agreement, ceded the last of the Choctaws' eastern lands, about 11 million acres, in exchange for 15 million acres in Indian Territory, roughly the southern half of what is now Oklahoma. Although the overall acreage was greater, the quality of the land was poorer, and Kiowas, Comanches, Caddos, and Wichitas still claimed dominion over portions of it. Additionally, the treaty provided a total of $400,000 over the course of twenty years for the collective use of the tribe, a figure that fell short of Choctaw leaders' expectations. To persuade the small group who remained at Dancing Rabbit Creek, the federal government offered them lucrative perks, including land, cash, and other goods. While chiefs, captains, and their families considered these payments prerogatives of the tribal elite, others decried them as bribes. Less controversial articles of the treaty reflected the Choctaws' ongoing commitment to education: leaders secured $50,000 for schools and teachers' salaries (though they had hoped for $200,000), plus a pledge from the United States to fund higher education for forty Choctaw youths for a period of twenty years. Indeed, citing their "rapid advancement in education," Choctaw leaders championed one of the proposals recommended by the Choctaw Academy students, asking for "a delegate upon the floor of Congress who shall receive the same pay and enjoy the same privileges as a delegate from one of the territories of the United States ... with the ultimate view of being admitted a member of the Union as an independent state." Tribal leaders, like their children, held out the possibility that Indian polities might share a measure of power within the US federal system. The treaty, however, stated, "The Commissioners do not feel that they can under a treaty stipulation accede to the request, but at their desire, present it in the Treaty, that Congress may consider of, and decide the application." Though disappointed in aspects of the treaty, the chiefs believed in its central promise: to make the Choctaws' lands in Indian Territory a permanent home where "no territory or State shall ever have a right to pass laws for the Government of the Choctaw Nation of Red People and their Descendants."[36]

Other Choctaws, upon hearing of the Treaty of Dancing Rabbit Creek, "expressed the utmost astonishment and indignation." After obtaining copies of the treaty and reading its scandalous contents, Choctaw citizens urged the US Senate not to ratify it. Peter Pitchlynn's nephew James Folsom, then away at school, wrote that such perfidy would cause the United States to "go down to future eyes with scorn and reproach on her head. . . . It will never be eradicated from her history." Angry with their elected representatives, the Western District deposed Greenwood Leflore in favor of his nephew George Harkins, a twenty-two-year-old graduate of Choctaw Academy who promised "not to do what my uncle did," while Joel Nail, a captain of the Lighthorse police force, replaced Nitakachi in the Southern District. Mushulatubbee remained in power, though his nephew Peter Pitchlynn would win the next election. A nationwide protest movement, seeking to nullify the treaty, nominated James

McDonald and Peter Pitchlynn to travel to Washington. In response, Agent William Ward called out the Mississippi militia, who broke up public meetings and prevented McDonald and Pitchlynn from leaving the state.[37]

The protesters took solace in one article of the treaty. Article 14 promised that all Choctaw families who wished to remain in Mississippi would be granted hundreds acres of land and, if they remained for five years, US citizenship. Reflecting the influence of James L. McDonald, this article preserved the possibility of peaceful coexistence as well as dual citizenship, for it stipulated that claimants "shall not lose the privilege of a Choctaw Citizen." At a national meeting in June of 1831, in accord with Article 14, William Ward announced "that all who did not wish to emigrate had a right by the Treaty to stay, and hold lands, and that he was then ready to receive their names, and register them in his book." A queue of hundreds of well-prepared village leaders from throughout the Choctaw Nation stood ready. They carried bundles of sticks, explaining "that these sticks represented a number of Indians who were unwilling to go away, and who wish to remain, become citizens and hold their lands, and that they would give in the names of each head of a family, the number, and sizes of their children." When the interpreter relayed this message, William Ward, according to a number of eyewitnesses, "took up the sticks, and threw them away, and said there were too many of them, and told the Interpreter to tell them that they must move West of the Mississippi." In the end, Ward completed the paperwork for only a few dozen of the ten thousand Choctaws who wished to remain.[38]

Despite Ward's behavior, many Choctaws "said they would go home and live on their lands," proclaiming their "confidence that the [federal] Government would not drive them off." They would be sorely disappointed. After the Treaty of Dancing Rabbit Creek was ratified in February of 1831, Choctaws were exposed to an orgy of white theft and violence. According to Grant Lincecum, neighbor and friend of Choctaws, Ward's sub-agents "used all kinds of threats, and told them that if they did not go the soldiers would soon come with their muskets, and bayonets, and drive them off." Choctaw families sought refuge in nearby forests or swamps, and returned to find white families farming their fields, occupying their homes, even eating at their tables. State and federal officials turned a deaf ear to Choctaws who, citing treaty articles guaranteeing US protection, pled with them to remove "all persons acting as intruders" and "prevent further molestation and destruction of [our] property."[39]

Elites, especially those who had paved the path of peaceful co-existence, still believed that they might remain in Mississippi. They continued to plant crops, raise livestock, and ship cotton and beef to market in Mobile and New Orleans. As the mission schools closed in preparation for removal, some sent their children to local white schools. Peter Pitchlynn, nominated to serve as justice of the peace in Lowndes County, turned down the offer, but other Choctaws with political experience considered running for office. "To the voters of Mississippi," Mushulatubbee declared his candidacy for Congress: "Fellow Citizens: I have fought for you, I have been by your own act, made a citizen of your state; . . . I have always battled on the side of this republic. . . . I have been told by my white brethren, that the pen of history is impartial." In the minds of white Mississippians, a more serious candidate for office was James McDonald. A gentleman, slaveholder, and the third-largest landowner in Hinds County, McDonald, in the words of a contemporary, was "generally and justly admired both by white and red men." Urged by white friends to consider a run for the state legislature, McDonald attended a number of political gatherings, but, on several occasions, drank "rather too much *wine*—and shouted rather too lustily for Henry Clay." McDonald worried that his "objection to Genl. Jackson" in a heavily Democratic state nullified any possibility of election. He decided not to run.[40]

Removal, however, sought to create a stark divide between whites and Indians. Soon, even those whose ancestry or education might have given them a foot in US society discovered that they had been far too optimistic about remaining in the state. Local whites were determined to push *all* Choctaws out of the state, but not before they acquired as much property as possible. Calling Mississippians "the damnedest people in the world," John Pitchlynn fumed, "the white men is stealing our horses, cattle, and hogs, and whipping some of the Indians for claiming their [own] property." When removal confronted him with a racial crossroads, John Pitchlynn, like many intermarried whites, chose to identify with his Indian kin. "The longer I stay the worse

I despise white people," John declared. "I find that [neither] Indians nor Indians' friends can live with white people." Moses Foster, a well-educated Choctaw who had served as national secretary before Peter Pitchlynn, hoped to use the courts to recover Choctaw property. When Foster filed charges against white thieves and con men, however, he discovered rampant racism in the courts: "What kind of justice has an Indian, or what chance has he for success—none!" Peter Pitchlynn's brother described the onslaught of anti-Indian violence as biblical, saying that whites "bred lice, frogs, and turn[ed] river[s] into blood. . . . The white folks bred difficulties of every description in order to prevail in setting the Indians to move out of the country." After witnessing the horrors that befell his family and friends, James McDonald decided, "I would urge no Indian to take the five years stay" lest he "be swindled out of his property by some cunning avaricious white man." Writing to Peter Pitchlynn, he urged, "Let your advice, therefore, be to them to remove—and to remove speedily. Tell them they cannot stand the laws."[41]

The Choctaws were the first nation to endure the new removal policy, and their experiences laid out a pattern that would be replicated many times over the course of the next decade. As states extended their jurisdiction over Native nations and exposed Indians to white avarice and vigilante justice, the federal government, under the influence of Jackson's strong executive branch, turned a blind eye. Protesting this violation of constitutional principles and treaty terms, the Cherokee Nation brought two cases before the Supreme Court. The second case, *Worcester v. Georgia* (1832), was an overwhelming victory for the Cherokees—even John McLean, Jackson's recent appointee (but also James L. McDonald's law professor)—concurred with the majority opinion that states had no jurisdiction over Indian nations, and that Indian nations retained all the sovereign rights that they had not explicitly ceded in past treaties. Jackson, however, ignored the decision and empowered treaty commissioners to single out Indian leaders—even leaders of minority factions—who might be willing to consider removal, sweetening the pot by promising payoffs. These shady agreements, called by one US official "mock compacts" made by "a few minor chiefs," tore at the fabric of Indian nations, leaving those outside the treaty councils to wonder: Which lands had been ceded? Had mineral rights been sold also? Hunting rights? Who signed and how much were they paid?[42]

Meanwhile, Indians reported that "they could scarcely ever show their faces in the neighborhood of the white settlements without being reviled and maltreated. . . . They beheld themselves hemmed in on all sides— they saw the graves of their fathers ploughed up." In Alabama, planters used a combination of kidnapping and debt slavery to compel Creeks to labor on their plantations. In the Midwest, land cessions and the growth of Chicago resulted in lower crop yields and game shortages, producing a famine exacerbated by an outbreak of cholera. Life in the East became so unpleasant that removal began to seem like a more attractive option. However, some Indians, including the Creeks, Seminoles, and Sauk and Mesquakie, refused to comply, and, as Eaton had promised in his threatening speech to the Choctaws, the United States "march[ed] an army into their country." The United States ultimately removed most eastern Indians, about 100,000 souls, using violence against the recalcitrant. One historian noted how, after capturing the Sauk and Mesquakie war chief, "The government exhibited the prisoner Black Hawk around the country, as the imperial Romans did with captive monarchs."[43]

Removal, ultimately, was not a single act of Congress, or a lone experience endured by Cherokees on the Trail of Tears; it was a thousand betrayals, a series of dispossessions, an ethnic cleansing designed to radically restructure North America. The nature of US empire, long debated, began to take definite shape under Andrew Jackson's leadership. The Tennessean echoed the hard-line racism of his core constituency, but also elevated this discourse by marrying it to recent "scientific" discoveries from phrenology. Born of debates over Indian removal, this wicked alchemy produced a new brand of racism that would empower a core republic of whites, including commoners and even new European immigrants, to claim dominion over a continental empire where people of color could be marginalized as perpetual subjects or, worse, chattel.

～⋇⟳～

In early September of 1831, the body of James L. McDonald washed up on the banks of the Pearl River near his home in Jackson. Perhaps it was foul play, for McDonald was an avowed Whig and a champion of Indian rights in a state where neither was popular. But even McDonald's close friends who mourned the loss of his "talents and genius" discounted that possibility, deeming his death a suicide, or perhaps an accident. McDonald himself did not record his thoughts that day, but for some time they had been dark and clouded by drink. McDonald's former patron Thomas McKenney later blamed this particular bout of melancholy on a white woman who had spurned McDonald's marriage proposal, but McKenney may have been eschewing what he saw as his own culpability in his ward's decline. In any case, McDonald's correspondence does not mention a white belle. Instead, James McDonald told his friends that he had been "on the point of losing all hope": he wrote of his crushed professional ambitions, crippling alcoholism, and concern for the future of his nation. He excoriated himself for his weaknesses and failures, counting his participation in the Treaty of 1825 as one of the only accomplishments "to which I can look back with any thing like unmingled satisfaction." It seems that the demons that had hounded James McDonald for years finally caught him that night: he could not call to mind his motto, "nil deperandum." Just prior to his death, he looked out from his high bluff perched above the Pearl, a river that, originating at the sacred mound Nanih Waiya, had sustained countless generations of Choctaws. Now, she served ever-increasing numbers of strange masters whose prayers, spoken in a strange tongue, were not meant for her.[44]

The Land of Death

Terror seized central Kentucky long before cholera arrived. The disease was new to Americans, having originated in the Ganges Valley of India in 1817, then carried via tall ships, steamers, railroads, stagecoaches, and dirt paths around the world, finally arriving in the United States in 1832. Traveling speedily along the same trade routes, the news detailed cholera's grisly symptoms: fever, cramps, spasmodic diarrhea, and black vomit. In some places, more than half of those infected died: two thousand deaths in New York, four thousand in New Orleans. At least the disease was often mercifully brief; those who fell ill in the morning frequently expired before midnight, their dehydrated corpses having taken on an unearthly shade of blue. Rising up like a deathly miasma, cholera claimed five hundred victims in Lexington before arriving at Choctaw Academy in early June of 1833.[1]

The first to fall ill was the academy's head cook, an enslaved man named Jerry. According to a subsequent medical report, "The greatest mortality prevailed during the first 6 or 7 days and in almost every case which terminated fatally, little or no warning was given and in a very few hours the patient expired." Thomas Henderson and his family, all struck by the disease, sequestered themselves at home, and the other teachers fled. Operations at the school were suspended and classrooms converted to makeshift hospitals. Richard Johnson sent sixty uninfected students away to board at another plantation. Samuel Hatch, a physician who inspected Choctaw Academy a few times a year, had left medicines and instructions in anticipation of the epidemic. After cholera arrived, however, Hatch could not leave his practice in Georgetown, and so care of the sick and dying fell to the academy's usual doctor, Julia

Chinn. Praising Chinn for having lost only one patient in the last several years—a student with a tubercular inflection of the lymph nodes called scrofula—Hatch was confident in her abilities. With so many sick, Chinn drafted Richard Mentor Johnson as well as two Indian students, John Jones and Joseph Bourassa, to act as nurses. Dr. Hatch credited Choctaw Academy's ad hoc medical team with saving many lives, and he singled out John Jones "to whom great praise is due."[2]

Ultimately, cholera affected all groups at Great Crossings, but slaves, who endured the worst diet and toughest working conditions, suffered the highest mortality rate—fourteen individuals of a total population of about sixty. Of the 129 students, only nine died: 6 Choctaws, 2 Seminoles, and 1 Miami. As cholera finished its course at Great Crossings, it claimed a final victim. Julia Chinn, worn down after weeks of caring for the sick and dying, succumbed to the disease. On July 6, fellow members at Great Crossings Baptist Church mourned the death of Julia Chinn, "one of the most exemplary and pious women," according to her former pastor. They likely buried her in the church cemetery that same day.[3]

Great Crossings Baptist Church set aside Saturday, July 13, as a day of fasting and prayer for the souls of cholera victims, but also for the soul of the nation. They, like other evangelicals across the United States, worried that the plague might be divine retribution for America's sins. The Indian members of Great Crossings Church may have agreed, for many Native cultures saw disease as either punishment for spiritual transgressions or the creation of twisted humans and other evil beings. These diverse believers located blame in different places: some pointed to intemperance, others to greed or pride or poverty or violence. But the will of God and the mysteries of the spirit world remained opaque. Even fellow humans were hard to read, though many scrutinized their neighbors and countrymen for the source of their suffering. Peter Pitchlynn did not consider himself a Christian, but he found wisdom in a passage from the Book of Jeremiah: "Thus saith the Lord; Cursed be the man that trusteth in man. . . . The heart is deceitful above all things, and desperately wicked: who can know it?"[4]

❧❧

On January 29, 1832, the day before Peter Pitchlynn's twenty-sixth birthday, he awoke early, an hour and a half before dawn. As Pitchlynn lit his campfire, he began to sing and whistle, as usual. Pitchlynn was a morning person, plus he was "remarkably fond of travelling." A good friend once explained that Peter loved adventure and even danger, that he had "an astonishing memory of places," and that he was "never lost in a city, woods or prairie." On that cold January morning, however, Pitchlynn's cheer vanished as he reflected on recent events: "My mind in spite of everything would turn towards home. I thought of my wife, then came the children, each one in turn. I thought of everything around my long abandoned home." Peter was leading one of the first groups of Choctaws to Indian Territory. During removal, the devastation of the cholera epidemic would be visited tenfold on emigrating Indians.[5]

The previous May, Mushulatubbee, aware of Choctaws' anger over his role in the Treaty of Dancing Rabbit Creek, had stepped down as district chief, and Peter Pitchlynn had been elected to replace him. This election took place after Mississippi had dissolved the Choctaws' government and was not acknowledged by US officials, who feared that a shift in power would undermine the removal treaty. People of the Northeastern District nonetheless respected Peter's authority. According to the federal government, Pitchlynn had consented to the removal treaty, yet only an "X" appears where his signature should be. Perhaps he never actually signed. Or maybe Pitchlynn, fearing the wrath of his countrymen, wanted to make it appear as though he had not signed. In any case, he had been willing to protest the treaty to the federal government. In explaining his enduring popularity, one acquaintance wrote that Pitchlynn was so charismatic that it was difficult to dislike him, "however conscience might compel conclusions on matters of mutual consequence unlike those he had reached." Fellow Choctaws trusted the young chief to conduct them "across the Mississippi to our new country."[6]

The US government planned to remove the Choctaws, who then numbered about 20,000, over the course of three years, forcing about 6,300 westward each fall during 1831, 1832, and 1833. It did not work out so neatly. Many Choctaws were determined to remain in Mississippi and claim land under Article 14 of the treaty, and others, when federally appointed enrollment officers came calling, hid out in the forests and bayous. But that first fall, almost four thousand readied themselves to leave. They had to abandon their homes, farms, churches, and schools, all of which would be sold to whites. Most painfully, they had to leave behind Nanih Waiya and all their other sacred places, including the graves of their ancestors. For generations, the Choctaws practiced a multi-stage burial attended by ritual at every step: they built scaffolds on which they placed the bodies of the recently deceased; then they allowed the flesh to decompose; finally, specially trained bone-pickers cleaned the bones, then bundled and interred the remains in mounds or other communal graves. One army general who oversaw Choctaw removal remembered that his group insisted on properly burying those who had recently died, remaining in their villages for several weeks, until the last funeral rites had been completed.[7]

Pitchlynn's party consisted of 406 fellow residents of the Northeastern District. They gathered at the house Peter shared with his wife Rhoda and their three young children. With the aid of their slaves, Peter and Rhoda acted as hospitable hosts, providing the visitors with beef, corn, and fodder for their horses, and converting their plantation into a temporary campground as they waited for all the emigrants in Peter's party to arrive. Although under the charge of a white civilian agent named Thomas McGee, the emigrants took some comfort in the fact that some of their own young men, recently educated at Choctaw Academy, would help them on the journey. In addition to Peter, there was John Riddle, who would drive a wagon and team of horses, and Thomas Wall, who would interpret for them.[8]

The emigrants could bring only what they could carry on their backs. For this first large-scale effort at Indian removal, the federal government did not make provisions for the emigrants' baggage, leaving no room in the supply wagons for personal possessions. As they prepared to leave their homeland forever, Choctaws must have agonized over what to bring for a three-month trip and their new life in Indian Territory. As residents of the Deep South, few Choctaws had winter clothing suitable for the harsher environment of the midcontinent. But those lucky enough to own extra shirts, leggings, moccasins, or dresses packed them, and some Choctaw women, anticipating camping out during the trip, spun and wove yards of coarse cloth and made tents. Others carried religious regalia, books, flutes, or other precious things small and light enough to carry. Choctaws were not allowed to bring tools, and they had to turn over their horses and cattle to US government agents who were supposed to drive the livestock to Indian Territory. They were not sure what to do with their dogs. When it came time for Peter's wife and children to emigrate, his little son, Lycurgus, left his dog with his grandfather John, who would try to stay in Mississippi. Those without friends in Mississippi let their pets trot alongside them.[9]

More than five hundred slaves accompanied their masters to Indian Territory. An 1831 census counted 521 enslaved people in the Choctaw Nation, but in the months before removal, the wealthiest Choctaws sold some of their cotton, livestock, or allotments and used the proceeds to buy more slaves. Enslaved people helped pack and prepare, and then carried many of their masters' possessions on the long journey. US officials issued slaves the same rations as Indians, though they demanded that many slaves perform extra work. Some acted as translators, easing communication between white agents and Choctaws, while others drove wagons, piloted boats, or repaired equipment.[10]

Setting out from the Choctaw Nation in groups of a few hundred, sometimes up to a thousand, these motley emigration parties sometimes stretched for miles, making slow progress toward a dreaded destination. Choctaws and their slaves walked most of the 550 miles to Indian Territory. The US government provided a few extra wagons—about 5 for every 1,000 emigrants—but given such limited space, only the elderly and the very ill could ride in them. Even for wagon passengers, the journey was rough, punctuated by jolts from the crude dirt roads.[11]

Pitchlynn reported that the first 150 miles of the journey went fairly well, until his party reached Memphis, Tennessee. The US emigrant agent had neglected to book them a steamboat to cross the Mississippi River, and so they had to wait for one, camping out in unseasonably cold weather amid bouts of sleet and snow. Without enough blankets to go around—the US government issued only one per family—Choctaws and enslaved people shivered in their cotton clothing, and many trudged through the icy slush barefoot. Finally, two weeks later, on December 1, 1831, they were ready to board a steamer called the *Brandywine*. By chance, the famous French historian and political theorist Alexis de Tocqueville happened to be in Memphis, and he saw Peter Pitchlynn and his party of Choctaw emigrants: "It was then the heart of winter, and the cold that year was unusually bitter. The snow on the ground had frozen, and enormous chunks of ice floated on the river. The Indians traveled in families. Among them were the wounded and the sick, newborn infants, and dying elders." Tocqueville watched the Choctaws crowd onto the steamboats, but noted that their dogs were not allowed on board. "When the animals finally realized that they were to be abandoned for good, they began to emit the most terrifying howls, then leaped into the icy waters of the Mississippi and swam after their masters." The miserable scene left a profound impression on the French traveler, who celebrated America's democracy while condemning its racism. He wrote, "The memory of that solemn spectacle will stay with me forever."[12]

Although most emigration parties only rode on steamboats to cross the Mississippi River, Peter's group remained on the *Brandywine* much longer. Torrential fall rains had created vast swamps west of the Mississippi River and left many of the already poor roads impassable. The party's leaders decided to try to get as far west as they could aboard the *Brandywine*. Alternately plagued by small icebergs and low water, the journey was painfully slow. Nearly a month later, they had made it only 150 miles. To make matters worse, in the cramped, dirty quarters of the steamboats, most of the group got sick. Low water forced the ailing party to disembark at Arkansas Post, where they waited, alongside two thousand other stranded Choctaws who had come up from Vicksburg, for the water to rise. Due to poor planning, emigration officials had little food and only sixty tents for the 2,400 people who remained exposed to the elements throughout one of the coldest winters on record. To pass the time, Peter and some of the other emigrants sang a song they had composed during the trip:

> Jackson sent the Secretary of War
> To tell Indians of the law
> Walk oh jaw bone walk I say
> Walk oh jaw bone walk away
>
> On my way to the Arkansas
> God damn the white man's law,
> Oh come and go along with me
> Oh come and go along with me.

It snowed, it hailed, I do you tell
And I thought it would pelt us all to hell,
Oh the hard times we did see
Oh the hard times we did see.

The salted pork and damned poor beef
Enough to make the devil a thief
This is hard times I do say
This is hard times I do say.

We have gone to the West
You will say tis for the best,
We shall never think it so
We shall never think it so.[13]

By late January, after three weeks of miserable camping, another steamer, the *Reindeer*, picked up the emigrants, but low water stopped them again in between Little Rock, Arkansas, and their destination, Fort Smith, just over the Arkansas line from Indian Territory. At this point, the US emigration agent hired a crew to man a shallow, open-air cargo vessel called a keelboat to carry women, children, and the elderly the rest of the way to Fort Smith, while most of the men, including Pitchlynn, would drive the wagons overland. Peter spent his twenty-sixth birthday on that trail, recording in his diary the bitter cold and his loneliness. As he rode, Peter also must have reflected on his party's misfortunes so far and worried about his compatriots on the keelboat.[14]

Pitchlynn's party arrived in Indian Territory in late February of 1832, four months after leaving Mississippi, but this first round of Choctaw removal went so poorly that the federal government revised its removal procedures. Stipends for those who took charge of their own emigration were raised from $10 to $13 per person. About 1,000 Choctaws took advantage of this provision, as did the entire Chickasaw Nation— 5,200 people—and they experienced much lower death rates than government-organized emigration parties. After 1832, regulations for federally removed parties also changed, allowing emigrants baggage up to thirty pounds per person. This wasn't much, but it allowed emigrants to take a bit more from home. The War Department placed most of the blame for the disastrous 1831 Choctaw removals on the civilian agents it had hired to oversee the process and replaced them with army officials, who, the government reasoned, had greater experience with the logistics of mass movement.[15]

Removal conditions, however, remained deplorable, and most parties suffered as much as or more than Peter's initial group. The federal government hired independent contractors—those who offered the lowest bids—to provide the emigrants with food, but, like so many other US agents in Indian Affairs, they were usually self-interested. One contractor who received $20,000 to provide provisions to a group of southern Indians bragged to a colleague that "he had never issued a single ration." A Seminole chief reported only a marginally better experience: "Rations [were] issued irregularly; when due, not delivered; and when delivered but half issued." Potawatomis said that removal agents forced starving women to trade sex for food. A lieutenant in the US Army testified that Alabama militiamen hired to help capture Creeks in preparation for removal raped several women, sometimes after beating or shooting them.[16]

Extreme weather and disease compounded the misery. Robert M. Jones, who drove his fellow Choctaws' cattle to Indian Territory in 1831, called it "the severest winter I ever saw." Half of the herd froze to death. By the following winter, cholera had migrated up from New Orleans to infect weakened emigrants waiting to cross the Mississippi River. In November of 1832, the disease broke out among a Choctaw party camped at Vicksburg; in one day, forty men died, in addition to an unrecorded number of women and children. After the infected party crossed the river, they kept on walking, though "death was hourly among us, and the road lined with the sick." The wagons had space for only the most gravely ill. As one US agent reported, "Fortunately they are a people that will walk to the last, or I do not know how we could get on."[17]

As the emigration parties passed through towns, white residents gathered to gawk as though the Indians and their slaves were, in the words of one eyewitness, "as great a rarity as a travelling caravan of wild animals." More sympathetic Americans gave them tobacco or food. One Louisiana farmer was so shocked and outraged by the treatment of the emigrants that he wrote a letter to the secretary of war in which he explained that he allowed a party of Choctaws to gather pumpkins on his property. The farmer reported that although the Choctaws were starving, they would not enter his fields until he had invited them. They ate the pumpkins raw "with the greatest avidity." Choctaw emigrants, the first to suffer the consequences of the Indian Removal Act, were also the first to call their journey the "Trail of Tears."[18]

The tears did not stop once the emigrants reached Indian Territory. By spring of 1833, the second major wave of Choctaw emigrants had arrived, bringing the population up to about 9,000. The recent arrivals had managed to plant their first crops in their new fields and looked forward to their first harvest. That June, just as the corn began to ripen, a massive flood surged through the Arkansas River valley. It swept away the Choctaws' newly constructed houses and government buildings, hundreds of acres of corn and other crops, and livestock. In its aftermath, rotting cattle carcasses littered the wasted fields, mosquitoes bred in the stagnant water, and the people became sick with cholera and malaria. About 600 Choctaws died, and the survivors, their farms ruined, soon grew hungry.[19]

The Choctaws' emigration agent William Armstrong, far more competent than William Ward, reprimanded the federal government for exacerbating the emigrants' suffering. Armstrong, who later became the Choctaws' federal Indian agent, reminded his government that the United States was bound by treaty to provide provisions for emigrants for one year. Armstrong reported that the barrels of flour, corn, and bacon, if they arrived at all, were often rotten. Finally, Armstrong argued that medicine should be among the necessary provisions, though none arrived.[20]

Survivors of the flood suffered tremendously in the months that followed. According to Armstrong, "The women and children ... have been from 4 to 6 days without anything to eat; *anything.*" Corn—if it could be found—cost nine times as much as it had before the flood, the price skyrocketing from 42 cents to $3.75 a bushel. Starving Choctaws accepted rations that had been rejected by the US army, including barrels of spoiled bacon three or more years old. The famine intensified the following spring and summer, this time due to a drought that lowered the level of the Arkansas so drastically that supply-bearing steamboats could not descend the river. One of Peter Pitchlynn's uncles told him that the drought had "dried up all the lakes and ponds, and caused all the turtles and other amphibious animals to die with thirst." Choctaws perished from want, too. Armstrong reported that more than 1,200 were starving, surviving on one pint of corn per day.[21]

Before removal, federal officials told Native leaders that Indian Territory was "a fine country," even "the best in the world," but since 1804, when Lewis and Clark labeled that country part of the "deserts of America," federal officials had known that Indian Territory was more arid than the East and had more extreme weather. Stephen H. Long, the leader of several expeditions of the Corps of Topographical Engineers, went even further in a report reprinted as an exposé in the Indian newspaper *Cherokee Phoenix*: "In regard to this extensive section of country, we do not hesitate in giving the opinion, that it is almost wholly unfit for cultivation, and of course uninhabitable by a people depending upon agriculture for their subsistence." Recent climate studies show that removal forced Native peoples to Indian Territory during one of the region's most extreme droughts—even worse than the 1930s Dust Bowl. Such dry conditions nurtured vast, nightmarish fires on the prairies. As a white observer who visited Indian Territory in the removal era noted, "Huge waves of flame with a roaring sound like that of the ocean . . . rush[ed] onward with fearful rapidity." Sometimes propelled by tornadoes, prairie fires outran men on horseback and swallowed entire villages.[22]

Choctaws marked each death by firing shotguns or blasting loud notes from cow's horns. Loud noises, Choctaws believed, helped jolt the spirit from the body and start it on the journey to the afterlife. During and after removal, the shots and blasts came with terrible frequency. Peter's wife Rhoda, delirious from two weeks without proper sleep during one epidemic, lamented, "This country is sickly . . . full of diseases— all kinds you can mention." Peter agreed, saying, "I am certain there is no country in the world where strong constitutions are more broken up than this." The Pitchlynns, like other families, especially feared for the lives of their children. In 1832, during the second year of Choctaw removal, they lost an infant. After the flood of 1833 destroyed all of their crops and much of their livestock, the Pitchlynns decided to move away from the Arkansas River to the southern portion of their new nation, along the Red River. Calling the settlement "New Hope," the Pitchlynns prayed it would prove a healthier place. They could not, however, escape the waves of disease that rolled through Indian Territory. The Pitchlynn children Lycurgus, Leonidas, and Peter Jr. all contracted whooping cough, but they escaped with their lives. Rhoda reported that it "killed most all [the] children [in the] neighborhood."[23]

Enslaved people suffered alongside Choctaws, just as they had during the Trail of Tears. They, too, had to adjust to a foreign and frequently hostile place, where famines and other privations were frequent. Just a few months before the whooping cough epidemic, many slaves in the Choctaw Nation caught an unidentified fever. Enslaved children were probably among those who died of whooping cough, since Rhoda Pitchlynn indicated that it struck nearly every child in the surrounding area. Rhoda also lamented that many enslaved children on her own plantation "got influenza very bad." Rhoda enlisted the aid of missionaries to care for the sick and dying, while Solomon, an enslaved man who acted as the Pitchlynns' overseer, kept the farm running so that everyone could eat.[24]

Between 1836 and 1840, a smallpox epidemic raged on the Plains, killing over 15,000 Indians, including 500 to 600 in the Choctaw Nation. Among the victims was Peter's uncle Mushulatubbee. After emigrating to Indian Territory, he was briefly reinstated as chief, taking a prominent role in intertribal councils that cultivated peace between Plains Indians and removed easterners. In 1834, when Mushulatubbee was in his seventies, he stepped down as chief and lived his last four years among his kin who came from the Northeastern District, which, in Indian Territory, was renamed the Mushulatubbee District.[25]

Choctaws tried to make a strange land into a homeland, but in doing this they usurped the land of others, including the Kiowas' most sacred place, Rainy Mountain. The Caddos and Wichitas also claimed portions of the Choctaws' new country, and other nations skirted the Choctaws' borders: to the north, the Osages; to the west, the Comanches and Apaches. By the time that Choctaws arrived in Indian Territory, they found, in the words of Chief Nitakachi, "that their hunting grounds were very much occupied by other nations." Plains Indians led hunting expeditions and war parties into the Choctaw Nation, and other displaced

Figure 6.1 Indian Territory, circa 1840. Map by Ian Byers-Gamber.

eastern Indians—the Cherokees, Shawnees, Delawares, Kickapoos, and Piankashaws—had created farms and small settlements within Choctaw territory before the Choctaws actually arrived in 1831.[26]

During removal negotiations federal officials told eastern Indians not to fear Plains tribes "because congress has passed a law authorizing your Great Father to protect all Indians moving there from all trouble or molestations from other persons. All the Indians who have moved are at peace among themselves and at peace with the Indians of the country." Although US troops were sent to Indian Territory, they offered little protection to eastern Indians. It soon became plain to tribal leaders that US authority was weak at best in the region. At an inter-tribal council in 1834, Indian leaders told William Armstrong and other US representatives "that neither the Pawnees, the Comanches or Kiowas have a country within the bounds of the United States." In fact, many of their enemies' villages were within territory claimed by Mexico or the Republic of Texas, where the US military had no authority.[27]

More troublesome than foreign Indians were frontier whites, especially Texans, who enjoyed a great deal of autonomy even before they gained independence from Mexico in 1836 and founded an independent republic that lasted until 1846. Choctaws shared a border, the Red River, with the Texans, who opened rowdy bars and ran bootleg liquor into Indian Territory. Choctaws complained that their white and Indian neighbors squatted on their territory, poached game, and stole guns and horses. The bodies of Choctaw hunters, scalpless, were sometimes found at the site of their last campfire. Young men went down to the Red River bars and got into bloody, sometimes fatal, brawls with the Texans. Hardly a virgin wilderness, Indian Territory was a crowded, hostile, and sickly place.[28]

The violence of removal spread from colonizer to the colonized, finding its way, like an infectious disease, into the bodies of Choctaws. Rates of alcohol consumption surged during the removal era, as Indians sought relief—however temporary—from their waking nightmare. During removal, when Mississippi extended state jurisdiction over Indians, the Choctaw Nation lost the power to enforce its own prohibition laws, and white bootleggers seeking a quick buck capitalized on the vulnerability of the depressed. A missionary reported that in less than a year, thirteen Choctaws drank themselves to death.[29]

Whiskey poisoned the Pitchlynn family as well. In late spring of 1831, Jack Pitchlynn, Peter's older half-brother, traveled from his Chickasaw wife's home down to the Pitchlynn house near Columbus, Mississippi. It was a small group that afternoon—probably just Jack, his half-brother Silas, and their father John. Jack showed up to the dinner table drunk and got into an argument with Silas. The brothers quarreled, then Jack pulled a tomahawk on Silas and struck a fatal blow. Silas bled out on the dining room floor, killed by his own half-brother. Jack fled back to the Chickasaw Nation to seek protection among his wife's family. Silas's death was mourned throughout the nation and beyond. Robert M. Jones, who had gone to Choctaw Academy with the Pitchlynns, sent Peter a condolence note. Peter rarely wrote about Silas's death—maybe it was too shameful or too painful—though his later speeches on temperance make it clear that he dwelled on the tragedy. Probably no one grieved for Silas the way that his mother Sophia did. She had been away from home at the time of the incident, perhaps visiting relatives, but her tears must have been bitter. Sophia had never pretended to love the children of John's first marriage the way that she loved her own. The Pitchlynns—under the direction of Sophia herself, according to family recollections—decided to deal with matters the traditional way. The Choctaws' law of blood demanded that life must pay for life. The matrilineal relatives of the slain were obligated to kill either the murderer himself or a relative of the murderer to compensate for the life lost. After Silas's death, Sophia's male relatives did their duty; they tracked Jack down and executed him.[30]

Other Choctaws turned the violence of removal against their neighbors by accusing them of witchcraft. Choctaws, like most other people throughout history, had long believed in witches, malevolent men or women who summoned spiritual forces to attack innocent people. During the drought of 1834, as fevers raged and the people starved, rumors circulated that witches were to blame. Despite the US agent's attempt to suppress the witch hunts, two alleged offenders—a man and a woman in separate villages of Mushulatubbee's district—were identified and killed by mobs in April of that year, and subsequent accusations surfaced in other times of stress.[31]

Kiowas called 1833 "the Winter that the stars fell," after a meteor shower that November, but their new Choctaw neighbors interpreted the celestial event in a less matter-of-fact, more ominous way. They thought of their origin story, which described the West as a land of disease and death, a land they had escaped eons ago. In one version of the story, after the Choctaws settled in the southeast near Nanih Waiya, a holy man told them that if they ever left, they would die. Nanih Waiya was more than a sacred mausoleum for the dead; she was the anchor of their nation, a place set aside for them by the Creator. By laying their dead to rest at Nanih Waiya, Choctaws became part of the Beloved Mother, and they part of her. Was all of this suffering the fulfillment of the holy man's prophecy? Could the nation survive so far from Nanih Waiya?[32]

Whether or not the Pitchlynn family believed in the prophecy, they took to calling Indian Territory "the Land of Death." Peter's sisters Mary and Rhoda and his brother Thomas relocated to Indian Territory, but, by early 1834, they had all returned to Mississippi. The Pitchlynns were not alone. In defiance of federal policy, thousands of other removed Indians came back to the East: some resettled in or near their former homelands even though they lacked land titles; many in the Great Lakes region crossed the border into Canada; others joined different tribes that managed to avoid removal altogether. In all, about 100,000 Indians were removed or killed, while 30,000 remained in—or returned to—the East, including 5,000 to 6,000 Choctaws. Peter Pitchlynn moved back and forth several times to aid with removal and settle family business. After the flood of 1833, Peter considered moving back for good. His delighted father responded, "We can make a settlement all in a few miles of each other and when any of us is sick we can visit each other and be a help to one another." Peter ultimately decided against returning to Mississippi, though he did ask his parents to take care of his youngest children—Lycurgus, born in 1830, and Leonidas, born in 1833—until he, Rhoda, and their older children, daughters Lavinia and Malvina, got settled in Indian Territory.[33]

After many discussions, Peter's parents John and Sophia decided to remain in the East, asking leaders of the neighboring Chickasaw Nation (which would not remove until 1837) to help protect them. They were elderly, John's eyesight was failing, Sophia already had tuberculosis, and they worried about catching cholera and other diseases. Sophia told Peter that as he was her oldest living son, she loved him more than she could "tell in words," but that she could not "go and leave her dead children behind her," referring to Silas and those she had lost in their infancy. John's health deteriorated throughout 1835, and he died on May 20. In his final weeks, John spoke of Peter often and wrote him letters detailing continued harassment and theft by white newcomers. John lamented, "I have lost all my stock of horses, cattle, [and] hogs." It had been a mistake to remain in Mississippi.

In his last letter to Peter, John voiced a dying request: "I do not wish for any of my children to stay in this country after I am dead." The family honored that wish. Sophia was eager to go, citing her fear that white villains might steal the family's remaining property. She and the rest of the Pitchlynns soon relocated to Eagletown, near Peter's New Hope settlement in the southeastern part of Indian Territory.[34]

⇝✒⇜

Although the cholera epidemic disrupted classes for a month during the summer of 1833, Choctaw Academy continued to operate normally throughout Indian removal, even though many tribal elders worried over why the federal government would move parents one way and their children another. Families and tribal leaders struggled over the best course: Should they send students before or after removal? After all this, could they even trust whites with their children?

Hearing of "the terrible disease that scourged Kentucky" the Quapaws, recently forced from Arkansas into Indian Territory, wanted all of their boys returned, but some other tribes reasoned that the outbreak was an isolated incident and that during removal their children would be safer and healthier at Choctaw Academy. After the Cherokees learned of the horrors that befell emigrating Choctaws, their agent reported that they "became clamorous . . . to send their children to the Academy; pressing and urgent applications were constantly made to me from all quarters." Fractured into pro- and anti-removal political factions, Cherokee leaders argued over whose children should be selected. The Miamis, after two years of crop failures and violence from Indiana settlers, also became desperate to place children at the academy. Choctaws continued to send students throughout the removal crisis, sometimes going to great lengths. During the drought of spring 1834, more than one thousand Choctaws were starving and the Arkansas River was too low for steamboats, but sixteen determined Choctaw boys outfitted canoes and paddled the first portion of their journey. They all made it to Kentucky, though some were sick with pleurisy, and one boy died a few hours after arriving.[35]

During removal, however, most Indian families took the opposite route, insisting on keeping their children close during their journey and relocation to Indian Territory. Creek leaders explained, "We have so much on our minds at this time": they feared that Choctaw Academy was too far from Indian Territory, that death or distance might prevent them from seeing their children again. Moreover, Creeks, like Choctaws, had been promised land if they decided to remain in the South, and, as the chiefs explained, "We have not got our reserves yet." Now distrustful of the federal government, Creeks made no effort to fill the Choctaw Academy slots. In 1834, though the Creek Nation had already paid tuition for twelve students, only one boy, Ned Crowell, went. Crowell "was himself extremely anxious to go on, and his parents did not object." As conditions worsened for Creeks in Alabama, where speculators and con men cheated Indians out of their lands and property and the state denied their civil rights, the tribe relented and resumed sending their children to the Academy.[36]

On October 31, 1837, however, the Creek Nation suffered a horrific tragedy. Commissioned to take Creeks from New Orleans to Arkansas en route to Indian Territory, conductors crammed 611 Creeks onto the *Monmouth*, a steamboat described as "rotten, old, and unseaworthy" by a New Orleans newspaper. Headed north in the dark of night, the *Monmouth* crossed the Mississippi River into the lane reserved for southbound ships and collided with another boat. The *Monmouth* tore in half, dumping most of its passengers into the river, then sank. In all, 311 Creeks died. Survivors helped one another to the riverbanks, then combed the shore, nursing the living and crying over the dead. Choctaw Academy mourned, too. Two of the students, Thlobote and Robert Blue, lost both parents, and Ishomiye and Daniel Barnett learned that their siblings had drowned. In May 1838, chiefs Jim Boy and David Barnett, who both lost children on the *Monmouth*, visited Choctaw Academy and withdrew six students, including their sons, explaining that "their surviving friends are anxious that they should now return to their homes again." The Creek chiefs, who had written several times, had to show up at the school and make their demand in person to get their sons back.[37]

Richard Johnson, who hated to lose students, tried to release as few as possible. In fact, the Academy grew during removal, benefiting from a new round of treaties in which several tribes set aside education funds. Enrollment increased from 95 students in 1829 to 175 by the first quarter of 1835. Richard Johnson's joy at hearing about the Creek removal treaty was apparent in his letter to Thomas Henderson: "40 scholars to be sent to our school. We learn that the chiefs from the nation will . . . sell out bag and baggage for the West!!"[38]

Although Choctaw Academy remained open during removal, operations were hardly smooth. In December of 1830, when "eight fine looking" Seminole boys arrived at the academy, Thomas Henderson told Johnson that he did not have enough rooms with fireplaces to accommodate all of the boys in cold weather. Johnson, eager to admit as many students as possible, crowded them into already full dorms and asked overworked slaves to clean up after them. The boys' rooms and clothes were particularly dirty after the cholera epidemic, which left Johnson's entire estate in disarray. Julia Chinn must have been an effective manager, for after her death the students' complaints about their clothes, rooms, and linens multiplied. And, amid the confusion and stress of removal, the students themselves were jostled about. After admitting that he had accidentally sent too many students to Choctaw Academy, agent William Ward frantically scrawled, "I am a great hurry as the mail is weighing and the House and yard full of Indians and Indian Agents etc etc preparing for the removing many of the Indians."[39]

The students probably found it difficult to concentrate on algebra or enjoy a Saturday ball game when they thought of their families, far away and likely suffering. Timothy Walker, a Cherokee who had graduated from Choctaw Academy, tried to keep his friend Ellis Falling, a current student, apprised of events back home. Falling knew that in 1835, a minority faction of the Cherokee Nation had signed a removal agreement, the Treaty of New Echota. Over 15,000 Cherokees out of a total population of 18,000 signed a petition protesting the treaty and refused to leave their nation. By 1838, however, school officials tried to shield students from what was going on. It was probably Thomas Henderson who intercepted a letter from Walker to Falling written in September of 1838, while the US army was rounding up Cherokee citizens into prison camps, preparing to force them west, and Tennesseeans were claiming the Falling family's property. Walker wrote the letter on behalf of Falling's illiterate mother, who beckoned him home, saying, "Be sure and come—and come as quick as you can." In considering the behavior of Americans, one wonders if Walker thought back to an essay he had written at Choctaw Academy condemning theft as uncivilized behavior: "I consider that stealing is one of the lowest and most degraded habits that a man can get into. . . . A person that steals will never be contented."[40]

Although Thomas Henderson likely kept that letter from reaching Ellis Falling, the tumult of removal still touched him and other students. The experiences of a group of Seminole boys, in particular, demonstrate how Choctaw Academy students were affected by the upheaval. Although most Seminoles opposed schooling, these students hailed from a distinctive region of the Seminole Nation called Apalachicola, and their families attempted to assimilate some aspects of American culture into their own. In December of 1830, the Apalachicola chiefs sent several of their sons and a few other boys, eight in all, to Choctaw Academy. They were a bit younger than average, aged nine to eleven, and spoke no English. An African American man who served Chief Vacca Pechassie (probably his translator Jim Walker) escorted the boys from Florida to Kentucky, translated for them for several days, and helped them get settled. They all received new names, even though some, like Billy Blunt, already had Anglicized names. Thus did Seminoles redubbed F. C. McCalla (after a school trustee) and Charles Caldwell (the Transylvania professor who proposed scientific racism) begin their studies.[41]

Two and a half years later, in May of 1833, the Apalachicola chiefs were preparing for removal, and they wanted their children back. Chief Blunt, in particular, was adamant that he would not leave without his son Billy. If the Seminole children had left immediately, two of them might have avoided an early death from cholera that June. But as Chief Blunt's anxiety mounted, Richard Johnson stalled. Thomas Henderson did not pursue the matter seriously until that October, when he summoned the remaining Seminole boys. As usual, school officials had failed to write down the students' Native names when they arrived, and now Henderson had to determine who was Blunt's son.[42]

While Henderson insisted that the boys could now "speak good English," not one "could tell the name of his father, nor even the Indian name by which he was called himself before he left the nation." Eventually, Henderson wrung additional information out of them: "Two of the boys say their fathers died before they left the nation; One says he knows nothing of his father, and the other two say their fathers were hunters and not chiefs, and that neither was named Blunt." Part of the problem was translation. For Seminoles and other matrilineal tribes, their closest male relatives were their mothers' brothers—"uncles" in English— and the boys may have confused the terms "uncle" and "father" during Henderson's questioning. Furthermore, Indians did not always call their leaders "chiefs." For example, the title of Vacca Pechassie, father of Jack Vacca and Orsler, was usually translated into "king" in English. Later, one of the boys told his father that he did not want to leave school, so some of the boys may also have feigned ignorance. Even allowing for these miscommunications and omissions, the students probably did not have a firm grip on English, even after three years of schooling.[43]

Richard Johnson figured that Blunt's son must have died in the cholera epidemic, but he was not sure. Johnson decided to bring George W. Hord, the one boy who said his father was a chief, to Washington for questioning at the Office of Indian Affairs. Secretary Elbert Herring talked to the boy, learning that he was actually Jack Vacca, the son of Vacca Pechassie, and that his brother Orsler was the one who had died of cholera along with an orphan named Aaron from Osaa Hadjo's town. Blunt's son Billy was alive and well at Choctaw Academy, where he was called Charles Phillips. Herring wrote to Chief Blunt, letting him know that his son was alive.[44]

Doubtless, Blunt was relieved, but he and the other chiefs had some idea of the federal government's negligence with their children, and they refused to remove until all Seminole students were returned. Faced with this ultimatum, the federal government forced Johnson to comply. Finally, in February of 1834, the six Seminole survivors returned. Chief Blunt was happier than his son Billy, who cried, asking his father if he could return to school. Perhaps this was why Billy kept silent all those months. Blunt refused and the family prepared for their journey west. All the boys' families had heard rumors that "some were dead," but ultimately the mourning fell to Vacca Pechassie and his family. Although their servant had implored Choctaw Academy staff "to take special care of this boy," Orsler was dead—nine months gone—his body buried among strangers.[45]

⁓℮✳↩

In the fall of 1839, several Potawatomis graduated from Choctaw Academy. They loaded their parting gifts, including clothes and books, into their new saddlebags and rode northward in the direction of their villages along the Yellow River in northern Indiana. Although some students, like Billy Blunt, wanted to remain at Choctaw Academy, many others leapt at the chance to return home. These Potawatomis were almost certainly ecstatic about seeing their families for the first time in years and taking on new roles at home. Fellow Potawatomi graduates had become schoolmasters, translators, or entrepreneurs; one had opened a shoe and boot shop. These Potawatomis, too, probably wanted to do something useful for their people, who hoped to remain in Indiana. Just a few weeks earlier, their chief Red Bird had once again refused to remove, telling a US Indian agent, "We say again, we will not go. We wish to die where our forefathers died." The agent claimed that Indian Territory was "better than this country" and "very healthy." Red Bird retorted that he had heard contrary reports from his countrymen who had already removed: the Plains tribes were hostile, the land was arid, and the government rations inadequate. "When we get there we are left to our own destruction, and there is not one of us that is so daring as to go." Red Bird believed that his people could continue to walk the path of peace along with his white neighbors, many of whom were friendly: "They hunt with us and we divide the game. . . . We wish to be connected with them, and therefore we will not go." Up to half of the Potawatomi population remained in the East, evading the government's attempts to remove them, but the Choctaw Academy graduates' families were not among them. When the students reached the Yellow River, they found white strangers occupying their former homes. Their families had already emigrated, and no one had told them.[46]

Most graduates knew of their families' relocation to Indian Territory and prepared themselves to come "home" to a strange place. But even they were not ready. One Creek graduate told an acquaintance, "I often fancied, while on my journey home, that upon arriving [in Indian Territory] I will seek employment there in some public capacity where I may have an opportunity to making known all that I have learned, that will be of service to my people." When the Creek scholar gave a similar talk to his chiefs, they scoffed at his clothes, speech, and manners, saying, "You advise us? You are a White man!"[47]

With removal, the United States abandoned the collaborative spirit that had forged Choctaw Academy and carved a bloody, divided path. The Creek chiefs suggested that, given their new situation, such schooling was no longer worthwhile. When Choctaw Academy alumni rejoined their families, some of them struggled to translate their skills to Indian Territory or felt overcome by the pain and misery there. The Creek graduate who was ridiculed by the chiefs recounted, "My plans had failed, my means were failing, my relations were poor, I had no means of profitably employing my time, [so] to disperse care and trouble, I turned to drinking Whiskey." This young man, so full of promise, was killed in a drunken accident by one of his friends. Two other alumni committed suicide shortly after arriving in Indian Territory. One found his family living in extreme poverty. Another graduate's mother had died while he was away, and his father, full of bitterness, no longer seemed to love him.[48]

However estranged these young graduates may have felt in their final days, in death they joined more than 25,000 other Indians—about 20 percent of the total Native population east of the Mississippi—who died during removal or in the epidemics, famine, and violence that followed. The overall population loss was even higher than this total suggests. One US official who visited the Choctaw Nation explained that for two years after removal very few children were born, for "the suffering and broken health of the women reduced the women past conception."[49]

Removal forever altered the relationship between Indian nations and the United States. Not so long ago, Indians had considered their nations peers of the United States. The Choctaws and many other Native nations had conducted peace treaties and contributed valuable military service during their ally's time of need. A refutation of such collaboration, Indian removal sought to transform sovereigns into subjects. Bound like captives to a rising empire, Native nations were both insiders and outsiders, central to the nation's growth yet pushed to the margins. Even more deadly than the rationale of removal was the lived experience, called by one contemporary "a process of coercion, fraud and tyranny unsurpassed in the annals of man."[50]

7

Rebirth of the Spartans

George Washington Trahern was not popular at Choctaw Academy. Nicknamed "Wash," he had arrived in 1831, joining his cousin William Trahern. Continuing the family's reputation for high-handedness, Wash quarreled with enslaved people and annoyed Adaline so badly that she wrote her father several times about his misbehavior. Even other students complained about young Trahern, a rare break in group solidarity. Thomas Henderson considered expelling him. Richard Johnson had a theory that Wash figured he could act insolently because his older cousin always protected him.[1]

Wash's conflicts likely came from his own insecurity. Although Wash, like his cousin William, was well connected in the Choctaw Nation, the younger boy was an orphan. Wash's mother Delilah died giving birth to him. His white father, Wesley, was a trader and planter who passed away a few years later. All that Wash remembered of him was his broad-brimmed black hat and the occasional spankings he delivered. As removal approached, the family's slaves and property "all went to the devil," according to Wash. Fortunately, the Choctaw Nation had set aside funds in their removal treaty to support Wash Trahern and other orphaned children.[2]

Trahern's saving grace was his "intellectual power." According to an acquaintance, his black eyes shone with "the activity of his mind." Back at Elliot Mission School in the Choctaw Nation, he had been the most outstanding pupil, and soon after coming to Choctaw Academy he was placed in the top class, excelling in several subjects. He particularly enjoyed geography, which foreshadowed his later love of travel, but Trahern's chief ambition was to become "a great orator."[3]

At the height of Indian removal, Wash Trahern argued that the skills he was learning at Choctaw Academy were still worthwhile, an argument that redeemed him in the eyes of administrators and peers alike. By then, Choctaw Academy was dangerously out of step with national politics. As the only Indian institution directly controlled by the federal government, Choctaw Academy had always been an experiment watched with interest, but now it had become the object of close scrutiny. As US Indian policy shifted from assimilation to exclusion, many white Americans asked why Native children should be educated at all. Before the board of trustees and hundreds of local whites, Trahern gave a speech later circulated to Congress that challenged the United States to live up to its promises: "We, the youths of the forest, look upon you as friends; your Government has told us you were such, and shall we be disappointed? Shall a youth of the forest apply in vain for that necessary instruction which the white man possesses? I hope not. We hope for better things."[4]

～✦✦～

Richard Johnson knew that Andrew Jackson and his secretary of war Lewis Cass had considered closing Choctaw Academy. Commissioner of Indian Affairs Elbert Herring, however, argued in favor of maintaining the school, linking its continued existence to the honor of the United States. A nationally visible symbol, Choctaw Academy was a form of redemption for the nation, providing a means to "discharge the mighty obligation we owe [Indians] for all the injuries they have sustained, and all the sufferings they have endured." Choctaw Academy, argued Herring, should be "the boast and not the reproach of our country." Lewis Cass was more skeptical about the utility of Choctaw Academy, which, he argued, would "produce few salutary results." As secretary of war, Cass was the mouthpiece for Jackson's Indian policy, and he argued that Native Americans were uncivilized people who had little use for intellectual pursuits. But Cass did favor a certain kind of education for Indians. Instead of Latin and algebra, Indian schooling should focus on the "wholesome truths" of Christianity, "the ruder handicraft arts," and "a proper mode of agriculture."[5]

The battle between Herring and Cass was part of a broader national debate over education. Since the Middle Ages, upper-level schooling had consisted almost entirely of coursework in Greek and Latin and was designed to improve the wisdom and moral character of elite men. But in the mid-nineteenth century, other groups—women, people of color, and middle- and working-class whites—demanded access to education. At the same time, the United States, Great Britain, and Western Europe were industrializing, and many leaders in those nations argued that their citizens needed more practical educations to fill roles in the new economy. Some educational reformers believed that physical labor should play an important role in practical education. Jesse Torrey, author of a popular textbook used at Choctaw Academy, argued that students should spend no more than eight hours per day studying; at least two or three hours should be devoted to laboring on a farm or in a workshop. Inspired by Swiss and German schools whose coursework included sports and outdoor labor, Harvard professors Joseph Cogswell and George Bancroft opened the Round Hill School in Northampton, Massachusetts, in 1823. Round Hill, however, was unpopular and closed after eleven years. Most whites figured that their children could learn to labor at home, and that higher learning, which was time-consuming and expensive, should be focused on intellectual and moral education only. While they shunned manual labor for their own children, white educators and politicians figured that it might suit those of supposedly inferior ability or prospects, especially lower-class whites, Indians, and African Americans.[6]

Reactions from people of color varied. African Americans debated whether certain kinds of manual labor were inherently degrading. Most middle-class blacks, including Frederick Douglass, argued that fellow African Americans should not work as domestics, waiters, or barbers because those jobs smacked of the servility of slavery. Meanwhile, a dissenting group led by James McCune Smith, a blacksmith who later earned a medical degree at Glasgow University, argued that all forms of labor could bring self-improvement. Wherever they fell in this debate, most African Americans supported manual labor schools that taught the mechanical trades because they regarded these occupations as solidly middle class.[7]

US officials were fond of calling Indian men lazy—"averse to any kind of manual labor," in the words of one agent— but Indians certainly saw the value in skilled labor. Blacksmiths, in particular, were in high demand in Indian country. In 1828, trying to attract an American black-smith to work in their town, one group of Choctaws built a smith shop and adjoining house, purchased tools, iron, and steel, and raised hundreds of dollars for his salary. But even as they set aside resources for this position, Choctaw leaders declared, "The Indian people will teach themselves metalworking." Indians were delighted when they could hire fellow Natives instead of foreigners. But their sons did not need to go to a fancy boarding school to learn to make horseshoes or repair guns. The Choctaw General Council resolved that boys "who will not or cannot learn" should be removed from Choctaw Academy and "bound out to good useful trades" nearer their homes "so that the money of the Nation may not be expended in vain."[8]

Beyond financial considerations, Indian leaders feared that Jacksonian officials like Cass sought to turn the elite sons of Indian country into an underclass of American servants, or worse, slaves. If manual labor was introduced at Choctaw Academy, Choctaw leader Israel Folsom feared that students would acquire "all the vicious habits of the lower orders of the whites, with negro labor & notions."[9]

Richard Johnson hoped to appease federal officials and Indians alike. Certainly, the manual labor proposal held financial appeal. For years, Johnson had cajoled students into doing odd jobs around the plantation, helping his slaves plaster the dining room or replace shingles, but now he developed a grand scheme to expand the students' workload. He proposed to hire four master craftsmen—a blacksmith, a tailor, a shoe-maker, and a wagon-maker—who would teach the students their trades. Johnson could then sell the fruits of their labor at the store he owned in Great Crossings. He estimated that each shop would generate $1,000 in profit annually. A politically savvy move, the introduction of these trades would save the school and swell Johnson's bank account at the same time. Such a curricular change, however, violated the school's founding principles. Avoiding manual labor was a chief reason that Choctaw Academy appealed to tribal leaders in the first place, and the school still depended on Indian nations for money. Seeking support for the shops,

Johnson leaned on Indian students and teachers at Choctaw Academy to endorse his plan.[10]

Between 1832 and 1833, a student-teacher named Joseph Napoleon Bourassa wrote a series of letters to top US officials, including Secretary of War Lewis Cass, Commissioner of Indian Affairs Elbert Herring, and N. D. Grover, an army general in charge of Potawatomi removal. Bourassa argued, "a young man with a trade will be more beneficial to his tribe than he would be with a first-rate education; because the savage or wandering tribes are not capable to support a schoolmaster." A blacksmith would be more welcome than a Latin scholar because "an old Indian would be more pleased to get a knife or a tomahawk from his son than ten well ordered philosophical or historical lectures; for he will say, these lectures do not feed me nor clothe my children." This was especially true in the context of removal, Bourassa explained: "In the first settling of a country . . . we see that it was not by the use of the pen and the book, but the use of the axe and plough."[11]

Bourassa was an ideal messenger. A Potawatomi, Bourassa also had Ottawa and French ancestry, and he grew up speaking all three languages. Successful traders, Bourassa's family supplied pelts for John Jacob Astor's American Fur Company. In September of 1820, Bourassa, then ten years old, entered Isaac McCoy's Carey Mission School in Michigan Territory, where he added English to his repertoire and worked on his skills in writing and arithmetic. In 1827, at the age of seventeen, Bourassa was one of the first Potawatomis to transfer to Choctaw Academy, where he studied for two years. Reared in a wealthy family, Bourassa disdained the dining hall food and refused to eat there. Although Johnson privately complained about Bourassa's insistence on privilege, he made arrangements for the Potawatomi to dine with a neighboring white family. Although annoyed, Johnson relied on the leadership and academic accomplishments of top students like Bourassa. The two even developed a personal relationship, and Bourassa's later correspondence makes it clear that he regarded Richard Johnson as a mentor. In his old age, the Potawatomi recalled that when he was at Choctaw Academy, Richard Johnson had regaled him with stories from the War of 1812. Bourassa left after the spring term of 1828 but returned in October of 1831, telling Johnson that he wished to study advanced mathematics, then law. When Bourassa told federal officials that "some students . . . cannot learn their books, but could trades," he spoke with some authority, for, by that time, he was a teacher—the first Indian teacher at Choctaw Academy. Bourassa taught English and spelling to beginners, started a choral society, and was paid an extra $25 annually to keep order in the dining hall. Perhaps drawing on the medical knowledge he had gleaned from his uncle Shabbona, an Indigenous practitioner who treated whites and Indians, Bourassa distinguished himself as a capable nurse during the cholera epidemic. By the time Joseph Napoleon Bourassa wrote letters to federal officials in support of the workshops, he'd had a long and distinguished career at Choctaw Academy.[12]

Johnson wanted to reach out to Indian nations as well. In particular, he needed the support of the Choctaw Nation, which still sent the most students to the Academy, and he enlisted the help of another Indian teacher hired a few months after Bourassa, William Trahern. The cousin of Wash Trahern, William was an advanced student who taught intermediate reading and writing. Trahern and Bourassa were close friends, having bonded as classmates years earlier. In fact, during their school days, Johnson identified them as partners in mischief: "It is ruinous to the school to have many such students as Trahern & Bourassa" who were "too much elevated ever to live like ordinary white men." As a student, Trahern joined his friend Bourassa to dine with neighboring whites, and when he became a teacher, Trahern demanded that he live at Richard Johnson's big house rather than an inferior boarding house. Like Bourassa, Trahern came from a wealthy trading family and Johnson tolerated his insistence on privilege because he needed young Trahern to draw on the connections that empowered him in Indian country.[13]

William Trahern composed several eloquent letters to tribal leaders, including Peter Pitchlynn. Like Bourassa, Trahern lauded the importance of the "mechanical arts," but his argument was more nuanced. Trahern explained that Choctaw Academy's one-size-fits-all approach to schooling was not working. "It has been exemplified beyond all doubt, that there are some minds which will not take [book] learning, and at the same time have a very great mechanical genius." Those who did not do well in school "will have no education, no profession of any description, and be a nuisance to their country." The Choctaws needed to create different kinds of education to prepare their children to take on a wide variety of roles in their new homes in the west. They needed shoemakers, blacksmiths, teachers, doctors, and lawyers, all of whom would be "useful to their people" in different ways.[14]

Joseph Bourassa and William Trahern had complicated motives for writing these letters. Both made practical points about the utility and value of learning a trade. In fact, Bourassa claimed that two of the students in his class had told him that they wanted "to learn the tailor's trade." It is also clear that many students, especially those who came to Choctaw Academy without knowing English, never progressed beyond basic literacy, so it is easy to imagine that top scholars like Bourassa and Trahern grew exasperated with—or merely pitied—those who struggled with the curriculum.[15]

While there may have been an element of truth in their letters, Bourassa and Trahern were driven by personal and financial motives as well. Richard Johnson had long relied on elite students to act as spokesmen in Indian country. Sometimes, as with Peter Pitchlynn, the plan backfired, but often the Indian gentlemen of Choctaw Academy painted a favorable portrait of the school and recruited new students from their respective tribes. Johnson sometimes bribed them to do so. A few years earlier, when the Choctaws were slow to fill their enrollment quota, Johnson told Thomas Henderson to enlist William Trahern's help: "You might offer him a contract to give him 30 or 40 or 50 dollars to send on from 6 to 10 . . . children." Johnson quipped, "Trahern loves money." It wasn't much of an insight. By then, Choctaws were thoroughly enmeshed in a capitalist economy, and Johnson's bribes were particularly attractive during the lean times of the removal era. Even privileged families lost many of their assets, and the federal government never compensated most Indians for the houses they were forced to leave behind or the cattle and horses who died or "disappeared" on the way to Indian Territory. When confronted with the diseases and disasters that struck Indians in their new western homes, a few extra dollars for an overpriced barrel of corn might make the difference between life and death. Several other students, as the scions of elite families or important leaders in their own right, received money from removal treaties, but because they were away at school they had difficulty accessing it. At least four Potawatomis named Richard Johnson their legal trustee and authorized the federal government to pay him their share of treaty money. Others asked Johnson to help them hire attorneys or to pressure his federal colleagues about their financial claims. Johnson readily used his political capital to help them, but such favors entangled students in a web of obligation.[16]

When Bourassa and Trahern wrote to federal and tribal officials, they did so at Johnson's behest, but they also expected to get something in return. Even though the Potawatomis had filled their quota at Choctaw Academy, Joseph Bourassa wanted the school to admit some of his male kin. This was managed easily enough. Lewis Cass approved the idea, saying that some of the Potawatomis who had completed four-year terms could be sent home. On November 8, 1832, Joseph's brothers Mark and Stephen as well as his cousin Benjamin Bertrand arrived at Choctaw Academy.[17]

Bourassa and Trahern both had another request, more expensive and complicated than influencing admissions at Choctaw Academy: they wanted to earn professional degrees. Joseph Bourassa chose law, saying, "I could prove more useful to my people and country with a knowledge of law." Friends had loaned him law books, which he had been studying in his spare time for the past year. Now, he wanted to attend Transylvania University, the same Lexington school that Peter Pitchlynn had applied to several years earlier. In his letter to Pitchlynn, William Trahern shared his own ambition: "I am extremely anxious to study medicine, and I cannot conceive that there is anything in which I could gain a proficiency, which would be more to the advantage of our people." In rationalizing their requests, Bourassa and Trahern disagreed with Lewis Cass that there was "little use" in teaching Indians "abstract principles," and instead asserted that, while basic literacy and trade education would suffice for many Natives, others—including themselves—were "capable of studying" medicine, law, and other advanced subjects.[18]

Overall, Lewis Cass was "highly gratified" with Bourassa's letters, which echoed many of his own views on Indian education. He and other federal officials even agreed to comply with his and Trahern's requests to attend professional schools, though the commissioner of Indian affairs reassured his colleagues, saying, "It is not to be expected that many will be [as] ambitious of intellectual culture and progress." In fact, many

Choctaw Academy students hoped to attend professional school, but few received as much help as Bourassa and Trahern. When Henry Folsom asked the War Department for funds to attend medical school, he was rejected. Folsom was a top student, but he had done no special favors for Richard Johnson. In contrast, six months after Bourassa wrote his letter to Lewis Cass, he was studying law at Transylvania University. Bourassa's self-preparation must have been impressive, for he managed to earn his law degree and graduate from Transylvania in just one year.[19]

William Trahern joined his friend Bourassa at Transylvania. Perhaps even more important than the money Trahern received from the War Department was the support of Transylvania faculty member Benjamin W. Dudley, one of the most renowned surgeons of the early nineteenth century. After graduating from the medical college of the University of Pennsylvania and traveling to Europe for additional training, Dudley pioneered new methods of brain surgery and bladder stone removal, losing only 3 patients in 225 surgeries, a shockingly low fatality rate for that pre-antiseptic era. Dudley disagreed with Lewis Cass's characterization of the intellectual abilities of Indians: the professor had met Trahern sometime around 1830—perhaps he attended one of the annual exhibitions—and he championed the Choctaw's application. Under Dudley's mentorship, Trahern completed his coursework in 1835.[20]

As Bourassa and Trahern pursued their professional degrees, Richard Johnson moved ahead with the introduction of manual labor into the curriculum. After receiving the secretary of war's approval and $500 from the US Treasury, Richard Johnson instructed his slaves to construct four new outbuildings. By September of 1833, Choctaw Academy's classrooms included not just those supplied with desks, paper, globes, books, compasses, and protractors but also workshops containing hammers, anvils, forges, leather, needles, rope, saws, and planes. Henderson found a tailor, a shoemaker, a wheelwright, and a blacksmith, though he admitted that the salary Johnson had authorized—a cut of the proceeds from the shops—did not attract the most "steady and sober" bunch.[21]

Next came the problem of placing students in the workshops. Commissioner of Indian Affairs Elbert Herring stressed that working in the shops should be voluntary, but Johnson found few willing candidates. The most enthusiastic was perhaps Thomas L. McKenney, a Potawatomi

Figure 7.1 Joseph N. Bourassa in 1837, shortly after graduating from
Transylvania. Sketch by George Winter, Courtesy of Tippecanoe County
Historical Association, Lafayette, Indiana.

who aspired to open a clothing and shoe store after he returned to his
nation. McKenney quickly distinguished himself as an accomplished
workman, making "first rate boots and shoes." Later, McKenney studied
European styles and learned to make "beau monde" clothing, according to delighted white visitors. An approving Johnson sent samples of
McKenney's work to the secretary of war. McKenney, however, proved
the exception. Fewer than one in ten students signed up despite the fact
that Johnson offered each student a $5 signing bonus if he agreed to work
in the shops part-time for two years, plus a small portion of the profits.[22]

The students' shunning of the workshops was certainly a form of
resistance, but it paled in comparison to the firestorm of protest that
erupted from their families in Indian country. The first time that William
Trahern wrote to Peter Pitchlynn, Pitchlynn did not even respond.
Trahern chose to believe that the letter had gotten lost in the chaos of

removal. Perhaps it did, but Pitchlynn would have rejected Trahern's proposal anyway. In fact, he and his friend Henry Vose had recently discussed how the Choctaws needed even more advanced coursework than what was available at Choctaw Academy, especially in math and science. Resisting the introduction of manual labor at Choctaw Academy, many leaders in Indian country upheld their demand for higher education.[23]

Chief Richardville of the Miami Nation was furious when he learned that his grandson Maankoonsa, called, insultingly enough, "Lewis Cass" at Choctaw Academy, was working in the tailor shop. A shrewd politician and successful trader, Chief Richardville wanted his grandson trained in bookkeeping and mathematics so that he could work as a clerk in the family mercantile business. Thomas Henderson, however, judged Maankoonsa's intellectual abilities merely "ordinary," and, after four years, kept the boy confined to the lower classes. When Maankoonsa was not learning the basics of reading and writing, he was measuring and sewing clothes for local whites. When Richardville finally found out about Maankoonsa's tailoring work in 1835, he demanded the return of his grandson. Maankoonsa rode the stagecoach back home alongside his tribe's agent A. C. Pepper, but, unfortunately, in the middle of the night something spooked the horses, and they threw the driver, then ran wildly for two miles. Frightened that they might crash, Maankoonsa leapt from the stagecoach, cutting his right kneecap to the bone. Finally, Maankoonsa, after five years away, returned to the Miami Nation injured, in tattered clothing that made his grandfather "ashamed" of him, with an education that had prepared him to be a humble tradesman rather than an entrepreneur or a leader of men. It was a sight Chief Richardville never forgot. Thereafter, Richardville "very frankly confessed that he was opposed to sending more boys to the Choctaw Academy."[24]

Chief Richardville's outrage was shared by other Indian leaders. Funds resulting from the Treaty of Dancing Rabbit Creek allowed forty additional Choctaws to attend school in the United States each year, and the War Department, with Richard Johnson's encouragement, had assumed that all forty would be educated at Choctaw Academy. But after learning about the workshops, the Choctaws sent their first official memorial of protest against the school to the president, insisting that twenty of those students be educated at more elite colleges, universities, and professional schools. Across Indian country, families grew more reluctant to send their children to Choctaw Academy. William Armstrong, the Choctaws' federal agent, explained, "They consider the promises and arrangements heretofore made, with Colonel Johnson, have not been compiled with." Armstrong warned Commissioner of Indian Affairs Elbert Herring, "These people have their prejudices, and they have their rights; and there are very many among them who know them; and will not be neglected."[25]

Several Cherokee leaders withdrew their sons under the conviction that boys at the Academy did not receive "the intellectual improvement" they needed "to make them eminently useful and competent to the performance of the highest public duties." Miamis, led by Chief Richardville, demanded the return of all their students, saying that they wished to send them to school closer to home. Some Miami families were wealthy enough to hire private tutors for their children, but for most Indians, this was not an option.[26]

Because of removal, Indians and missionaries were forced to leave behind the mission schools they had worked so hard to build back east. The Choctaw Nation and the American Board of Commissioners for Foreign Missions invested a total of at least $150,000 (about $4,000,000 today), and neither party recovered the cost of the schoolhouses, teachers' houses, farms, and other property associated with the missions, or the untold labor costs. Following these financial losses, the missionary board became reluctant to invest heavily in new western missions and directed its missionaries to focus on evangelization and circuit-riding instead of schooling Indians. For Indians, removal further complicated their feelings toward missionaries. Across Indian Territory, people from many different tribes suspected that missionaries had been complicit with removal. In consequence, Mushulatubbee tried to prohibit missionaries from settling in his district, and the Cherokees required all preachers to obtain a license from their National Council before entering.[27]

Despite the qualms of many Choctaws, their federal agent reported, "the anxiety of the Indians for a school is so great" that they created makeshift schools in half-built churches, chiefs' houses, or underneath oak trees. Mission schools did slowly rebuild in the west, but the challenges were immense. There was little money for schoolhouses, much less for desks, books, and other supplies. One teacher reported that several of his pupils had mastered reading, and might have moved on to writing "had they stationery provided." The schools themselves were few and far apart, and families who did not live within walking or riding distance had to pay for their children's room and board; few could afford to do so in the poverty that followed removal. A schoolmaster lamented the poor fare his charges endured: "Relative to their food and clothing, it is of the most miserable kind; their whole costume consisting many times of a single shirt." Because of the students' poor diet, many contracted scurvy. Malnourished children in crowded schoolhouses were also particularly susceptible to the epidemics of smallpox and whooping cough that repeatedly struck Indian Territory in the 1830s. Teachers also died from these diseases. Between 1836 and 1837, the Choctaw Nation lost six teachers, which forced the closure of half of their schools. Because they had difficulty recruiting eastern teachers, the Choctaw Nation offered an extravagant salary of $833 annually, more than twice as much as Choctaw Academy teachers and most other educators in the United States earned. One William Stierman of Lancaster, Kentucky, received a year's advance salary to support his relocation to Indian Territory, but he took the money and disappeared. Teachers who did show up were sometimes "without talent," in the words of one missionary. Indeed, the literacy skills of Choctaw Academy's better students surpassed the abilities of several of the new mission schoolteachers.[28]

Indian families were upset about the curricular changes at Choctaw Academy, but Indian Territory offered no attractive alternatives. By 1834, the Cherokee and Creek nations were again sending children to Great Crossings. Choctaw chiefs had never had any trouble filling their slots. According to their agent, "I may safely say of the Choctaws that in every way in which an opportunity for education is offered, they are ready to avail themselves of the benefit." Many families and tribal leaders resolved to make the best of Choctaw Academy until they could create an alternative.[29]

Acknowledging the concerns of tribal leaders, Lewis Cass hoped that the federal government and Indian country could "meet upon a middle ground," and agree on a curriculum that united manual with intellectual education. Commissioner of Indian Affairs Elbert Herring told Thomas Henderson that learning trades in the shops should "not only be voluntary, but also secondary to the ordinary branches of education, and must be auxiliary to, and not a substitute for, the common education."[30]

In response, Richard Johnson and Thomas Henderson created a two-tiered system of education at Choctaw Academy. Thomas Henderson claimed that some students "manifest quite a taste for literature and refinement" but most "could be sent home with good trades and a sufficient education for mechanics and farmers." The majority would learn basic skills, spelling, reading, writing, and arithmetic, while school administrators attempted to coax and cajole them into working at the shops. Even with the inducement of pressure and bribes, few boys signed up. Despite the students' lack of enthusiasm, Johnson continued to promote the shops, giving the shirts, shoes, and tools produced there as gifts for colleagues in Washington or selling them at his general store in Great Crossings. Johnson even planned to expand the students' workload by making them farm fifteen or twenty acres. This scheme never came to fruition because students, who believed that farming was the work of Indian women (especially, in some nations, non-elite women) and slaves, forcefully rejected it.[31]

Meanwhile, those who had mastered the basics of English literacy took up advanced coursework in grammar, geography, astronomy, natural and moral philosophy, Latin, ancient Greek, law, and medicine. To accommodate the students' demand for these subjects, Richard Johnson had to hire two new faculty members. In the summer of 1833, Isaac Gardner took over the top class of students. A former lawyer, Isaac Gardner was fluent in Latin and Greek and had taught at academies in Virginia and Washington, DC. The following spring Johnson hired Dr. John Cotton, the academy's first physician-in-residence. Since Julia Chinn's death, slaves and students had acted as ad hoc nurses, and doctors were called in for serious cases, so Cotton's medical expertise was welcome. Cotton, like Gardner, was a classically trained scholar, but he taught subjects, including grammar and geography, to second-level students and spent the rest of his time caring for the sick and mentoring a few Indian scholars in medicine.[32]

Few would question the utility of Dr. Cotton's instruction in medicine, but classical education was more controversial—not just for Indians, but for all Americans. Reformers like Benjamin Rush asked, "Do not men use Latin and Greek as the scuttlefish emit their ink, on purpose to conceal themselves from an intercourse with common people?" Because Americans from all walks of life believed that education might enhance their social, political, and economic standing, they eagerly sought out opportunities to learn. Alexis de Tocqueville noted, "There is hardly a pioneer's hut in which the odd volume of Shakespeare cannot be found." Yet few had the opportunity to study classical languages. Of his childhood in Indiana, Abraham Lincoln recalled that the expertise of schoolteachers rarely extended beyond basic "readin, writin, and cipherin": "If a straggler supposed to understand Latin, happened to sojourn in the neighborhood, he was looked upon as a wizard." While some, like Rush, argued that ancient languages were of little value in a new empire, others prized classical learning precisely because it was rare. Greek and Latin were associated with high class and history's great civilizations, a combination that proved compelling to Indian scholars. Centuries earlier, Native leaders had sought out knowledge that was restricted to political elites and religious specialists, sometimes traveling to distant centers of learning. Though the form and content of esoteric knowledge changed over time, Choctaw Academy students retained the hope that they might deploy it to enhance power.[33]

By insisting on advanced coursework, the students and their families had forced the federal government to compromise its position on Indian education. Though Choctaw Academy administrators succeeded in introducing manual labor into the curriculum, participation remained voluntary and few students enrolled. The conflict exposed the power of Indian students like Joseph Bourassa and William Trahern. As the school grew from a few dozen students to nearly two hundred in the mid-1830s, Richard Johnson increasingly depended on them to act as spokesmen, monitors, and teachers. In return, these gentlemen insisted that Indians possessed intellects equal to those of whites, and they demanded access to upper-level and professional subjects.

But this victory was not without consequence. Of the federal government Richard Johnson wrote, "They are looking with open eyes at our school." Beginning in 1834, President Andrew Jackson made several changes. He insisted on more regular and thorough reports, and began sending an officer from the War Department to make annual inspec-tions of the school. In an attempt to prevent future protests from the families of Choctaw Academy students, the War Department declared that Indian parents, whom they declared "incompetent judges," could no longer visit the school or pull out their children at will. Arriving stu-dents were declared wards of the federal government, and they could not leave unless they graduated or received permission from the Academy's trustees. After Lewis Cass chided Thomas Henderson as "too easy, too indulgent," Richard Johnson heightened disciplinary measures, telling Henderson "the more military you can make it the better."[34]

No one at Choctaw Academy spoke more eloquently about Indian abili-ties than Wash Trahern. His 1838 speech, in which Trahern challenged the federal government to uphold the founding principles of Choctaw Academy, was part of a special exhibition attended by trustees, local clergy, and other guests. Dr. Benedict, who taught English grammar, asked his class to write essays, and then selected the best students to give speeches. Several students decided to use this public forum to challenge the stereotypes about Indians popularized during removal. These essays must have been particularly impressive, because they were among the few that Thomas Henderson and Richard Johnson sent to high-rank-ing officials in Congress and the War Department, and three of them were published among the papers of the House of Representatives. These essays, which ultimately reached a wide and politically important audi-ence, offer revealing insights into how Indians conceived of their place in the American past, present, and future.[35]

Several students wrote outstanding essays, but the trustees agreed that young George Washington Trahern showed the most talent as both a speaker and a writer. His essay, "On History," demonstrated the uses of history and focused largely on ancient Greece. While it might seem a surprising choice for a Native teenager, Trahern's topic was a clever choice and one that appealed to his audience. Trahern wanted to explain his point of view as an Indian and sway the crowd while being careful not to openly insult Andrew Jackson, Lewis Cass, or other popular American political leaders—a tricky proposition. By using historical allegories, stories drawn from safely remote classical antiquity, Trahern could subtly critique the American present. This technique would have been familiar to American audiences, who considered themselves the inheritors of Greek and Roman culture. According to a popular American textbook that was used at Choctaw Academy, American colonists had brought "the civilization of thirty centuries" to a savage land. Americans were also taught that history was not merely a chronicle of events, but rather a source for important moral lessons, which might prove especially instructive at a time of such great change. Those looking for a model of republican virtue quoted the eloquent speeches of Cicero, and, when critics like Henry Clay or David ("Davy") Crockett wanted to critique Andrew Jackson's concentration of power in the executive branch, they likened him to Julius Caesar, reminding Americans of how the Roman general had destroyed a republic and made himself emperor.[36]

By the 1830s, however, Americans looked more to Greek than Roman history. It is ironic that they did so at the dawn of their own imperial history—perhaps the parallels were uncomfortably close—but, during an era in which all white men gained the vote, the democratic city-state of Athens appealed more than the aristocratic Roman republic lionized by their forefathers. Athenian culture, too, appealed to Americans, who sought to emulate its art and architecture as well as the prosperity and widespread influence Athenians had once enjoyed.[37]

Indians were not excluded from Americans' reimagining of the classical past. Ancient Greeks and American Indians were both known as master orators. The trustees of Choctaw Academy claimed that some of the students' "native eloquence" called to mind "the ancient days of Greece," while Thomas Jefferson compared the speeches of Chief Logan favorably to those of Athens' greatest orator, Demosthenes. Usually, however, Americans designated themselves modern Athenians and likened Indians to Spartans. Alexander Tytler, whose *Elements of General History* was used at Choctaw Academy, explained that since Sparta was founded by invading Dorians from Thessaly, "the most barbarous of all the Greek tribes," many intellectuals thought that they "bore the nearest resemblance to the rude Americans." Spartans, like contemporary Indians, were best known as great warriors. As in many Native societies, male Spartans trained for war from early childhood, becoming inured to pain and physical exertion, vying for public war honors and titles, learning about heroism and honor through the stories of venerated elders. By the time they grew into well-formed and brave men, "all other nations appeared but children in the art of war."[38]

The students, too, favored the comparison. Unlike many of the representations of Indians in their textbooks, this one was useful, even empowering. They were proud of their ancestors' prowess in war, and other facets of Spartan culture may have resonated with them as well. Spartans embraced a communal spirit and were said to have divided their land and food equally among all free families, much like Native nations, where people held land in common and the chiefs redistributed food and other resources. Finally, and perhaps most usefully for those who protested the workshops at Choctaw Academy, Spartans deemed the mechanical arts "much beneath them." With slaves and servants to do such work for them, Spartan citizens and Indian gentlemen could concentrate on higher pursuits.[39]

Figuring prominently in Wash Trahern's essay was the ancient Spartan lawgiver Lycurgus. Upperclassmen like Trahern had encountered Lycurgus in Plutarch's *Lives*, which some read in Greek or Latin. Less advanced students also met Lycurgus, who appeared regularly in illustrated readers for beginners. Dialogue among the different ranks of scholars was facilitated by the Lancastrian system, in which advanced students instructed more junior students. Students who were bilingual or multilingual also translated for those who struggled with English literacy. Such tutoring facilitated comprehension in two ways: it helped beginning students understand course content while also inevitably framing that material through a Native lens.[40]

The members of the Choctaw Academy Debating Society likely discussed Lycurgus as well. While the original minutes do not survive, a group of students founded the Eagletown Debating Society in the Choctaw Nation shortly after they graduated, and that society's records suggest strong similarities with counterparts elsewhere in America. Dedicated to "moral and intellectual improvement," the Eagletown society provided a space for members to improve their rhetorical skills; discuss literature, law, history, current events, philosophy, and the sciences;

and facilitate "social, friendly, and instructive intercourse." Throughout
Europe and America, a very popular topic among debating societies was
who best served the interests of his country, the Athenian Solon or the
Spartan Lycurgus. Their approaches to law and education differed, but
both were seen as foundational figures in great societies. Appealing to
young men who saw themselves at the helm of evolving nations, this
topic was almost certainly debated at Choctaw Academy. And, signifi-
cantly, the way in which students engaged the topic differed markedly
from the read-and-recite pedagogy that dominated nineteenth-century
classrooms. The student-run debating society, like the mediation process introduced by the Lancastrian system, encouraged students to
think independently, in this case to use knowledge gleaned from texts to
make critical arguments.[41]

Said to have descended from Hercules, Lycurgus belonged to one
of Sparta's two royal families. After his elder brother Polydectes died,
Lycurgus inherited the throne, though his rule was short, for the royal
family discovered that Polydectes' widow was pregnant. The queen gave
birth to a male child, and Lycurgus abdicated in favor of his nephew.
Many Spartans urged Lycurgus to stay on as king regent—or even to
kill his infant nephew—for he possessed, according to Plutarch, "abilities from nature to guide the measures of government, and powers of
persuasion, that drew the hearts of men." But, seeking a peaceful transfer of power, noble Lycurgus left his city. For ten years, he traveled to
foreign lands: Crete, Egypt, Spain, Africa, and India. In these distant
lands, Lycurgus learned about their customs, laws, and politics, and he
thought about which ones might prove useful to Sparta. While visiting
Greek colonies on Asia Minor, Lycurgus collected the poems of Homer,
which had been carefully preserved by the Eolians and Ionians but lost
to other Greeks after two centuries of war. Combining the ancient wisdom of Homer with new lessons adapted from foreign cultures, Lycurgus
returned home on a mission to reform and strengthen his own society.[42]

While retaining Sparta's traditional monarchy, Lycurgus established a
senate of popularly elected representatives to balance the power between
commoners and elites. Lycurgus further restricted privilege by redistributing land, rationing food, abolishing specie in favor of a local currency that
could not circulate outside of Sparta, outlawing banking or moneylending,

and prohibiting the production of luxury goods. Through these reforms, Lycurgus hoped to extinguish the greed that led to "ambition of distant or excessive conquest." Lycurgus, however, is best known for the realm of reform he considered to be most important: education. It was Lycurgus who turned Sparta into the classic military state by establishing a rigorous program training all men for war. Under Lycurgus's reforms, Sparta overcame centuries of instability and soon rivaled Athens as one of the most powerful city-states in the ancient world.[43]

Out of the dozens of biographies in Plutarch's *Lives* or the hundreds of historical figures who populated the pages of their ancient Greek history textbook, it is easy to see why this particular story resonated with Wash Trahern and other Choctaw Academy students. Descending from their nation's ruling families, they had traveled to a foreign country in pursuit of new knowledge which they might use to reform their own societies and enact a new vision for a stronger future. Like Lycurgus, who carried Homer back to his people, they would not forget the wisdom of ancient traditions but rather combine them with new customs that proved, in one student's words, "good or useful." Another admirer of the ancient Spartan lawgiver, Peter Pitchlynn named his first son "Lycurgus" and, when the boy turned sixteen, urged him to read Plutarch's biography of his namesake. But most people actually called the boy "Push," a nickname taken from his middle name "Pushmataha," after the Choctaw Nation's most famous and revered chief. In naming his son, Pitchlynn combined respect for tradition with an expanded worldview, neatly capturing the aspirations of many Indian leaders of his generation.[44]

In referring to Lycurgus, Wash Trahern alluded to one of the foundational principles of Choctaw Academy: that Indians might improve their own societies by selectively adapting American ways. Trahern argued that by studying ancient and modern history, the students "could learn their mode of government, and their military exploits, and their customs, and copy after them; or, if they are not fashionable at the present day, learn lessons from them." Such cultural borrowing was normal and need not be seen as a sign of Indians' weakness, for many of the students' textbooks reported how the barbaric Britons had learned from their Roman conquerors, who merely imitated the Greeks, who had imported the customs of still more ancient civilized states like Egypt and Phoenicia.[45]

Trahern's American audience would have agreed that they were help-fully extending the blessings of "civilization" to Indians, but young Wash had a more challenging message as well. Subtly invoking a shared assumption that Indians represented modern-day Spartans, while the United States was Athens reborn, Trahern contrasted the two societies. Spartans, "frugal," "hardy and strong," were content to govern their own city-state, while Athenians, in pursuit of "luxury" and power, conquered much of the eastern Mediterranean. Going back to the ancient lawgiver, Wash Trahern wrote, "Lycurgus told the Spartans not to go to war too often with the same nation, lest they should learn their mode of warfare, and conquer them from their own lessons." Spartans, after all, had used new knowledge not only to revitalize their own society but to challenge and eventually conquer their old rival, Athens.[46]

To its critics, the United States, like ancient Athens, represented the perils of popular democracy. Peter Pitchlynn favored British author John Gillies, who noted, "The people of Athens, successful in every enterprise against their foreign as well as domestic enemies, seemed entitled to reap the fruits of their dangers and victories." They "adorned their capital with the richest spoils of their vanquished enemies." Observed Gillies, "It is of little consequence whether a country be governed by one tyrant or a thousand; in both cases alike the condition of man is precarious, and force prevails over law." Like Choctaws who came to regret their aid to the United States dur-ing the War of 1812, the Spartans realized that they had erred in defending Athenians against enemies and would-be tyrants. By 500 B.C., according to the Academy's textbooks, Spartan leaders asserted that the ambitions of the Athenians threatened the liberties of all Greeks. Peter Pitchlynn named his third son Lysander, after the admiral of the Spartan navy who defeated Athenians at Aegospotami in 405 B.C. and forced them to surrender their colonies and city-state the following year. Thereafter, Lysander destroyed Athenian democracy and instituted a puppet government controlled by Sparta called the Thirty Tyrants. Deplored by nineteenth-century American and European intellectuals as a villain, Lysander probably appealed to Indians' anti-colonial ambitions, wherein they, too, might humble their oppressors and "conquer them from their own lessons."[47]

Wash Trahern was one of several students who used the 1838 exhibition to critique US imperialism. Twenty-three-year-old August Buckholts, a Choctaw scholar who also taught beginning students, thundered, "White man, remember that the soil on which you now tread was once the Indian's free, sacred, and unbounded home. But O! How changed!" Another senior Choctaw student, Adam Christie, surveyed colonialism's damage. "The aborigines of North America have been imposed upon, have been cheated, have been destroyed, since the white men first trod their shores and soils; they have been driven from the shores of the Atlantic to the Rocky mountains. . . . Now they have hardly one foot to call their own."[48]

Adam Christie accurately captured popular American thought regarding Indians when he wrote, "Many are led to believe that they will never become enlightened or civilized; and in the course of half a century, they will be extirpated." The students' textbooks distilled this bleak view, stating that "the savages are every year becoming less numerous and formidable." These authors, unlike the students, laid no blame on European invaders. Jesse Olney, author of their geography textbook, glossed over Indian removal, explaining, "Most [Indians] prefer their own modes of savage life to those of the whites, and as the latter have extended their settlements, they have removed farther and farther back into the wilderness: and at the present time but a small number of them are found east of the Mississippi river." Some authors lamented the loss. One of the students' reading textbooks contained a fictitious story about "Powontonamo," an elderly Mohawk who returned to the village of his birth so that he might die beside an oak tree he had planted as a child. But instead of a stout oak tree in his Mohawk village, Powontonamo found that whites had settled in his town and chopped down his tree. The bodies of his family were still there, lying in their graves; their souls had departed. Crying, Powontonamo "broke his bow-string, snapped his arrows, threw them on the burial-place of his fathers, and departed forever." According to American thought, the disappearance of Indians was an inevitable, if sad, consequence of the march of progress.[49]

This view came from dominant American understandings of the relationship between time and history. Most cultures viewed history as cyclical, a repetitive process analogous to the life cycle of an organism:

societies were born, grew, peaked, declined, and died. It seemed the natural order of things. But, beginning in the early nineteenth century, Americans declared themselves exempt from this cycle. Americans believed that not only could they match the achievements of Greece and Rome, but that they could also surpass the ancients and all other civilizations by breaking out of the circle of history altogether. Influenced by millennial ideas popularized during the Second Great Awakening, Americans started to think of themselves as exceptional, as the chosen people of Providence, and to see their history as linear, moving upward at a forty-five-degree angle toward perfection. "We are the nation of human progress," wrote journalist John O'Sullivan, "who will, what can, set limits to our onward march?" O'Sullivan, who later coined the term "manifest destiny," declared, "Providence is with us, and no earthly power can." This hubris captured the zeitgeist of a young nation flush with victory over Indian and imperial rivals and powered by technological and transportation achievements that helped them seize the wealth of a continent.[50]

While they were destined to outshine all other civilizations, Americans believed that Indians dwelled outside the great drama of human progress. According to a popular textbook, before Europeans' "discovery," America "was overrun by a few hordes of wretched savages, who existed in a state little advanced above the irrational creation." And, due to their racial inferiority, Indians had gained nothing from being in contact with "civilized" people. In the words of Lewis Cass, reprinted in a Choctaw Academy textbook, "We have taught them neither how to live, nor how to die."[51]

Not everyone endorsed the theory of American exceptionalism. Where Jacksonian Democrats celebrated progress and expansion, others saw corruption, excessive materialism, and social upheaval—unmistakable foreshadowing of decline. John C. Calhoun, Jackson's former vice president, became one of his leading critics, reminding Americans that "Augustus Caesar did not change the forms of the Roman Republic, but exercised a most despotic power over the laws, the liberty and the prosperity of the citizens." The founder of the Hudson River School, painter Thomas Cole, affirmed the cyclical view of history, predicting that the United States would share the fate of Rome. In a five-part series called

The Course of Empire, he depicted the transformation of a pastoral paradise into a decadent empire, followed by a violent fall, and then desolation. Some Whigs worried that Indian removal would play a pivotal role in their nation's denouement. Reverend Cephas Washburn argued that removal left "a foul stain . . . upon our national escutcheon, which is now indelible. . . . It will not be washed away in all time, nor all eternity." Even critics of removal, however, fixated on Americans' agency, casting Indians as victims who lacked a serious role in the great drama of history.[52]

The students of Choctaw Academy engaged in these debates, supporting some critiques made by British authors and American Whigs, but they also used their 1838 exhibition to voice Indigenous perspectives, reframing the American story by placing Indian actors at the center of a sweeping history. Like other Americans, the students' perspective was geographically capacious, surveying the entire continent, but they also encouraged their audience to add greater temporal depth to their analysis, to consider an American history that was much more ancient than generally acknowledged. Choctaw Adam Christie reminded his listeners that his people built and ruled civilizations for eons before Columbus arrived: "The Indians once stood like lords over this continent." It was "the white man," not some faceless force of progress, that "brought them low." Christie pinpointed Indian removal as the nadir, lamenting that "in casting our eyes over North America, we find many of the tribes of Indians immersed in obscurity—yea, in destruction." "*But*," Christie continued, "such has been the fate of all nations which have existed, and the fate of which now exists . . . such is the revolution of nations and cities, empires and kingdoms, that they cannot exist in their splendor, remain firm and immoveable to the end of time, without their destruction, or wavering to their centre."[53]

The students also added a Native twist to their interpretation of cyclical history. Influenced by the fourteenth-century scholar Ibn Khaldun, most Western intellectuals thought that societies enjoyed only a single life cycle, but Indians believed they might continue to ride the great wheel of time for multiple revolutions. Rebirth and world renewal were at the core of many Native religions. From Tecumseh and Tenskwatawa to Wovoka's Ghost Dance of the later nineteenth century, a belief in revitalization motivated Indian activists. Theirs was not a call to rep-licate the past but rather to incorporate new ways—new dances, new prayers, new ideas, new practices—to make a better future.

Like Cherokee intellectuals who compared their society to a phoe-nix rising from the ashes, Choctaw Academy students imagined themselves Spartans reborn. Wash Trahern argued that in the after-math of removal, Indians were on the upswing: "The favorable reports from the War Department ought to give [pleasure] to all friends of civilization; it states that several of the Indian tribes are progressing in the arts and sciences; that they have schools among them, and they are daily increasing." And Adam Christie promised, "So long as the blood flows and circulates in our hearts and bodies, we will contend, at all times . . . to evince the world that the Indian race is not obliter-ated." Referring to their shared future in Indian Territory, Christie concluded, "May this institution produce members who shall resem-ble pillars of marble—strong, well polished, fit to decorate and sup-port the temple of union in which our various tribes shall hereafter assemble."[54]

8

The Vice President and
the Runaway Lovers

In June of 1835, Great Crossings was abuzz with the news that the Democratic Party had just selected local son Richard Mentor Johnson as its vice presidential candidate. As Johnson's kinfolk and supporters proposed toasts in his honor, Whig antagonists launched a fresh round of assaults on his personal life and professional abilities. Meanwhile, a drama of a different sort unfolded at Johnson's home.

Taking advantage of the upheaval created by the celebrations, a young Anishinaabe man named John Jones and seventeen-year-old Miami George Hunt (or Waapipinšia) left the Academy. Commandeering Richard Johnson's carriage and two horses, they loaded their own trunks full of clothing and supplies, plus two additional trunks for companions who would join them shortly. The two young men had occupied quite different stations within the school: Hunt was a student, while Jones was part of a small group of young Indian men who worked as teachers. Jones had attended Carey Mission School in his youth and, at some point, had become a Baptist minister himself. In addition to his teaching duties at Choctaw Academy, Jones was engaged in post-graduate work, reading law under Johnson and attending lectures at nearby Transylvania University. Richard Johnson, before Jones's departure, called him "a very worthy young man and very promising."[1]

Three days after Jones and Hunt left, two young African American women, under the pretext of going to gather strawberries, saddled their horses and took off after the Indian men, meeting them at a prearranged spot. In a letter to federal officials, Johnson stressed that they were "valuable servant girls," but there was much more to the story.[2] Both women were nieces of Julia Chinn and cousins of Adaline and Imogene, slaves who worked within the Johnson household and who had likely been educated alongside Johnson's daughters by Thomas Henderson. One of the young women was called by the newspapers "*Miss* Chinn" in faux deference. We do not know her first name. The other woman was Parthena Chinn. The daughter of Julia's brother Daniel, Parthena worked under the direction of her cousin Adaline, making and mending clothes for the Choctaw Academy students. Parthena was also Richard Johnson's concubine following Julia Chinn's death. Her father, Daniel, later expressed outrage at Johnson's actions, and the fact that Parthena chose to flee suggests that she did not participate in the relationship willingly. When Parthena escaped, she carried $300 in cash, which, according to the *Lexington Observer*, she took out of Richard's drawer—"she having possession of his keys." Because of the positions of authority they held, the Chinns had greater freedom of movement within the household, on campus, and throughout the plantation, a circumstance that helped them plan and prepare for their escape.[3]

After they joined their accomplices, one of the Chinns posed as a free woman and George Hunt acted as her husband, while the other woman and John Jones, who had a darker complexion, took on the role of their servants. Together, a lady, a gentleman, and their two "slaves" traveled north toward Anishinaabe country. The runaways' decision to leave the school hinted at the undercurrents of resistance that would eventually surface to destroy Choctaw Academy, while media coverage of their escape reflected hardening racial politics in the United States.[4]

Before he turned rebel, John Jones was one of the Academy's most accomplished scholars. By the time that he arrived in Kentucky, he was already fluent in English, French, Ottawa, Potawatomi, and his native Ojibwe. He had acquired this multilingualism as a youth in his homeland, Anishinaabewaki, the diverse Great Lakes region dominated by loosely confederated Anishinaabe communities bound by kinship ties. Jones's mother, according to missionaries, was Ojibwe, but at the Carey

Mission School John associated mostly with Potawatomis, a pattern he maintained at Choctaw Academy and in his post-graduate life.[5]

By the time Jones came to the Academy in November of 1832, he was already in his early twenties, and he quickly distinguished himself as a leader. The following summer, during the cholera epidemic, Jones nursed many students and slaves back to health, prompting attending physician Samuel Hatch to single out him out for special praise. Once classes resumed, he continued to excel, becoming a teacher for the beginning students and managing the Academy's choral society. As a Baptist minister, Jones may have preached on Sundays; although the documents do not speak directly to this, other students, including Choctaw Sampson Birch and Creek Samuel McIntosh, preached in their native tongues to receptive audiences. While Christianity remained controversial in Indian country, some saw conversion—or at least familiarity with gospel teachings—as essential for civilized nations. In any case, Jones's multilingualism would have been an asset at this diverse school, enabling him to communicate with nearly everyone.[6]

Given his abilities and influence, John Jones quickly become part of the group of Indian monitors on whom Richard Johnson relied to run the school. In 1833, Jones told Johnson that he wanted to return home for a few weeks to help his people negotiate a treaty, and Johnson offered to pay his expenses—and then some—if he would recruit additional students to Choctaw Academy. Over the next year, Jones made several trips back and forth to Indiana, escorting graduates home and bringing back new Miami and Potawatomi students. At the same time, the War Department began to pay for John Jones's law education, which included tutoring under Johnson and supplemental lectures at Transylvania University. The timing suggests that this support was contingent on Jones's performance as a teacher and recruiter. For six months leading up to his departure, from winter to spring of 1835, John Jones began to ask the War Department for more. For his fellow students, he requested an expanded library with more law books. For himself, he wanted to go to Transylvania Law School full-time for two years. "If the appropriation is not extended," Jones explained, "my object in view will be entirely frustrated."[7]

We will never know all the reasons behind John Jones's departure. Perhaps the War Department denied his request to attend law school.

Certainly federal officials moved slowly with such decisions and could be capricious in their patronage. Maybe Jones grew tired of recruiting, monitoring, and disciplining fellow Indians. During the week of Christmas 1834, John Jones visited the workshop where Anishinaabe Thomas McKenney turned out expertly crafted suits and shoes, but McKenney told Jones that he wanted to quit the shop so that he could fully concentrate on academic coursework. In his subsequent report, Jones called McKenney "flighty in his course," but did he sympathize with his fellow Anishinaabe who aspired to greater intellectual achievement? He must have, on some level, for he wished McKenney well on this new path.[8]

Jones must also have considered the plight of enslaved people who did the majority of work on campus, though the origin of the collaboration between Jones, Hunt, and the Chinn women remains a mystery. We cannot hear their whispered conversations in the fields or read their surreptitious notes passed in the dining hall, though such things must have happened. Perhaps John Jones formed a relationship with one of the enslaved women he had nursed during the cholera epidemic. Richard Johnson believed that Jones had seduced and corrupted one of Julia's nieces, presumably his lover Parthena, for he later stated, "His course is doubly dishonorable towards me, after my distinguished friendship to him." Certainly, sexual relationships between students and slaves continued despite Johnson's disciplinary measures. Johnson complained that "profligate young men," especially monitors like Jones, continued to sexually assault enslaved women. But the fact that Julia's nieces voluntarily—and at great risk—ran away with John Jones and George Hunt indicates that more consensual relationships, perhaps merely friendships, developed among students and slaves as well. Doubtless, many factors figured into Jones's decision to leave and to help the enslaved women escape. His later actions suggest that he continued to believe in education, but Minister Jones had lost his faith in Choctaw Academy.[9]

Richard Mentor Johnson became a national candidate during a period that marked the beginning of modern American politics. For the first time, national elections were dominated by two well-defined parties,

Democrats and Whigs, who inaugurated a period of intense partisan-
ship, extended campaigning, and nasty media debates. Seeking a head
start on the presidential election of 1836, the Democrats decided to
hold their convention a year early, in late May of 1835, at the Fourth
Presbyterian Church of Baltimore.

Going into the convention, Richard Johnson was at the peak of his
career. After talking to other cadets at West Point, former Choctaw
Academy student Jacob Holt asserted, "I think he will be a prominent
candidate for President," adding that there were many in New York
state "who would vote for him in preference to Van Buren." Indeed,
enthusiasm was strongest among New Yorkers, but Johnson's popularity extended nationwide. Supporters lauded Johnson's defense of
Sunday mail service as a major victory for religious freedom. Also popular was the congressman's "untiring zeal" in favor of veterans' benefits.
Who could argue against rewarding "the revolutionary soldier for toil
and blood expended in establishing our liberties"? Johnson's greatest
achievement in Congress, however, was the abolition of imprisonment
for debt, an issue for which he continually lobbied until it finally passed
both houses of Congress in 1832.[10]

Behind the scenes, Richard Johnson was known as an amiable bridge
builder who helped heal personal rifts. In 1832, for example, Johnson
stepped in to mediate a conflict between President Andrew Jackson and
his predecessor John Quincy Adams. Back in 1827, when the two men
were campaigning for the presidency, Adams supporters had uncovered
a sex scandal and published the story in the *Cincinnati Gazette*: nearly
forty years earlier, Jackson had lived in sin with a woman named Rachel
Robards, who was still legally married to another man. Rachel managed to get a divorce and secretly marry Andrew four years later, but
still, Adams supporters argued, this scandal exposed Jackson as an adulterer who was ruled by passion rather than reason. Soon after the story
broke, Rachel grew ill and died, leading her husband to attribute her
death to distress over the scandal, which he fervently denied (though
it was almost certainly true). Richard Johnson informed John Quincy
Adams that Jackson "had been led to believe that [Adams] was the cause
of those publications against his wife." Although Adams was a gossip
who had, for example, composed lewd ballads about Thomas Jefferson

and Sally Hemings, he denied an active role in fomenting the scandal. With Richard Johnson acting as mediator, the two presidents managed a grudging truce, one of many such reconciliations managed by Johnson, whom many on Capitol Hill considered a "warm friend."[11]

While his personal and political achievements in Congress were considerable, the bedrock of Johnson's popular appeal remained his reputation as an Indian-fighter. Recommending Johnson for the presidency, newspapers in Kentucky and New York dwelled on his military accomplishments, his red badges of courage, his slaying of Tecumseh in single combat. Calling Johnson "the people's choice," one proponent claimed that Johnson had "saved the women of the west" from all manner of barbarous violence—"from the savage scalping knife" to "the brutality of the British soldiery." Johnson himself regaled audiences with his tale of the Battle of the Thames; at Choctaw Academy exhibitions, he sometimes trotted out relics related to the battle, like the drum captured from British troops or a tomahawk presented to him by a fellow officer as a war trophy. Johnson's friend Richard Emmons, drawing on an epic poem he had written about the War of 1812, created a short musical called *The Death of Tecumseh*, which was performed at theaters in the lead-up to the election. Richard Johnson attended a performance in Washington, where he was delighted to receive a standing ovation: "a very crowded audience huzza'd to the death of Tecumseh and I have *more* friends ever by a *hundred*!" Emmons, bolstered by the musical's popular success and Johnson's patronage, created a longer version of the play, *Tecumseh; or, The Battle of the Thames, a National Drama*, which was performed in New York, Philadelphia, and many other cities in 1836, the year of the election. It was Emmons who composed Johnson's longtime campaign slogan, "Rumpsey Dumpsey, Colonel Johnson killed Tecumsey."[12]

Many voters considered Choctaw Academy another of Johnson's important achievements in Indian affairs, the next step in the conquest of the continent. An editorial in a Kentucky newspaper neatly linked Johnson's wartime service to his role as schoolmaster, asking, "Who is it that after the long arduous toil of a Congressional session retires to his own peaceful sequestered retreat in Scott Co. to instruct in the arts of peace, the children of those Indians whom his valor subdued in war?" In an endorsement of Johnson printed in the *Kentucky Sentinel*,

Reverend Walter Scott lauded the colonel's labors "for the elevation of the Aborigines and their children" as a positive good for the United States, "if the nation owes a spark of pity to the race of men whom we have dispossessed and driven from their native lands." Well-connected newspaper editor and politician John Norvell summed up Johnson as "a favourite with the country as a patriot, a soldier and a friend of tolerant and liberal principles."[13]

At the 1835 Democratic National Convention in Baltimore, Martin Van Buren, Jackson's handpicked successor, was the unanimous choice for the party's presidential candidate, but Richard Johnson remained popular. At that time, the party, not the presidential candidate himself, selected vice presidential candidates, and the majority caucus put forth Johnson as the nominee. But Johnson's support was not as universal as Van Buren's. Several southern states threw their support to William C. Rives from Virginia, and Rives's fellow Virginians protested Johnson's nomination the loudest. One member of their delegation explained that Virginians "had no confidence in [Johnson's] principles nor his character." Nonetheless, most northern states and the West, which then included Tennessee, Kentucky, Ohio, Indiana, Mississippi, Louisiana, and Missouri, voted in favor of Johnson, giving him the two-thirds majority he needed to secure the nomination. In response to Johnson's victory, the Virginia delegation "hissed most ungraciously."[14]

For critics, Johnson's past provided plenty of fodder. Snobby East Coasters thought him a country rube who was only "slightly educated," and a British visitor who attended a dinner party with Johnson called him "as strange-looking a potentate as ever ruled." She elaborated, "His countenance is wild, though with much cleverness in it; his hair wanders all abroad, and he wears no cravat. But there is no telling how he might look if dressed like other people." Doubting the intellectual acumen of such a specimen, many Whigs claimed that someone else had written Johnson's most famous speeches, perhaps Johnson's friend Obadiah Brown, a high-ranking postal official. Others derided Johnson's work in Indian Affairs, lamenting the death of Tecumseh, whom some dubbed "a much greater man" than Johnson, and calling Choctaw Academy a moneymaking scheme. One reporter suggested that as compensation for writing Johnson's congressional speeches, Obadiah Brown received part of "the spoils of the Choctaw Academy." But all of these charges could be attributed to meaningless partisan slander; Whigs often depicted their Democratic opponents as unsophisticated social and intellectual inferiors. It was Washington insider Alfred Balch who put his finger on the real hot-button issue. In a letter to Andrew Jackson, Balch explained, "I do not think from what I hear daily that the nomination of Johnson for the Vice Presidency will be popular in any of the slave holding states except Kentucky on account of his former domestic relations."[15]

～✺～

Richard Johnson emerged as a vice presidential candidate as mainstream whites embraced an exclusionary vision of America. Indian removal pushed Native people to the margins, while states mounted obstacles to emancipation and enhanced restrictions on free people of color. Instead of a diverse empire of liberty, the United States was emerging as a white-or-black society where the only people of color tolerated could be legally classified as property. Linking Johnson's interracial relationships to his candidacy, one Massachusetts newspaper remarked, "Well does he deserve to govern others, who knows not how to govern himself—to be a ruler over freemen, himself a slave!" A slave to his passions, that is. Far worse than Andrew Jackson's peccadillo with Rachel Robards, Johnson's transgression was a sin of a different color, according to contemporary critics.[16]

Johnson's critics used his candidacy as an opportunity to vent racial anxieties of every sort. The most radical Whigs—those who favored the abolition of slavery and women's suffrage—said that Johnson was a rapist, "the violator of the virtue of his female slaves." They argued, as do many modern scholars, that the power dynamics in master-slave relationships were so skewed that consensual relationships were impossible. These radical Whigs speculated that through his extensive "slave-breeding" Johnson was selling his own children at the auction block; certainly, they argued, he was perpetuating the institution of slavery.[17]

Most white Americans, however, showed little concern for the basic human rights of enslaved women and instead worried that Johnson might try to empower his family and other people of African descent. A Maryland newspaper reported that Johnson "has for more than twenty years lived in open connection with a *negro slave*—who has recognized her offspring as his children, educated them and endeavored to force them upon society as in all respects equal to those of his free white neighbors, and who now boasts that his black or *yellow* daughters, are as accomplished girls as any in the immediate vicinity." At a town hall meeting in Albany, New York, Whigs asserted that Johnson's actions were "an insult to the community of which he is a member, a disregard of the feelings of our southern fellow citizens, and a precedent which must lead to the most fatal consequences in the slave holding states." In Kentucky, Johnson's political enemies stoked the fire, claiming that he would take his "family of colored boys and girls" to the "white-house should he become President." As this media coverage demonstrates, Richard Johnson's great transgression was not interracial sex, but rather his public acknowledgment of his mixed-race family, an act that blurred the color line and threatened white supremacy.[18]

Whig antagonists claimed that Johnson would rule the country much as he managed his household. "We learn that Col. R.M. Johnson's nomination is received with ecstasy by the colored population," the *Louisville Daily Journal* sneered. "They think that when he comes to be President, they shall all be white folks." Attempting to influence recent immigrants, whose place in America's racial hierarchy was uncertain, a Whig newspaper in New York City claimed that Richard Johnson threw a lavish ball with "elegant wooly-headed managers" but neglected to invite the "wild Irish." Whigs and some pro-slavery Democrats characterized Johnson as an abolitionist. The *Lexington Observer and Kentucky Reporter* asked: "Richard M. Johnson is offered to the Northern Fanatics as a man after their own heart. . . . What more would they have than a man whose life illustrates, whose practice carries out the maxims of their school? A man who has never had any wife but a negress? Who has reared up a family of mulatto children under his roof? Who has recognized their mother as the mistress of his household? Who has endeavored to force them into the highest circles of fashionable society?" In a series of stories that ran in the weeks after Johnson's vice presidential nomination, the *Cincinnati Daily Gazette* claimed that his candidacy emboldened free blacks, leading them to riot and even to rape white women: "When the official influence and power of the Nation nominates an open practical Amalgamationist

Figure 8.1 An Affecting Scene in Kentucky, by Henry R. Robinson, 1836. This cartoon lampoons the Johnson family as well as Richard's vice presidential bid. His daughters attempt to comfort him with kind words and their mother's portrait (note the African head-wrap), while an abolitionist and a free black man offer support. A Democratic supporter marvels that the "slayer of Tecumseh" could be "overcome by a summer cloud." The man on the far left is a postmaster who pledges to "stick to you; if you promise to keep us in office," likely a reference to Johnson's former friend Amos Kendall, postmaster general, and certainly a jab at his political cronyism. Courtesy of the Library of Congress.

for the second office of the Government, it is in the order of things that a new spirit should go abroad among the *'people of color.'*"[19]

Writing to newspapers, Thomas Henderson and other allies defended Johnson. Few denied Johnson's relationship with Julia Chinn—the evidence was simply overwhelming—though some tried to characterize it as a youthful indiscretion. But Henderson also suggested that people who lived in glass houses should not throw stones. Reminding his audience that Imogene and Adaline were blameless in this scandal, "the children of God" who "had no agency in bringing themselves into the world," Henderson argued that Johnson in "admitting that they are his children" was "certainly entitled to more credit in the sight of Heaven, for raising them as he did, rather than to have turned them into a negro quarter or sent them to a cotton farm." Many masters, Henderson lamented, condemned their children to a still "more degraded condition" than fieldwork; some masters sold their own daughters into prostitution in the notorious "fancy girl" brothels of Lexington or New Orleans. Henderson operated under "a conviction that those who are so ready to heap sin and guilt upon the heads of others are commonly the most profligate and guilty persons."[20]

William Henry Harrison and, later, John Tyler, were rumored to have fathered children with enslaved women, but, in this case, Henderson was probably referring to Henry Clay, a fellow Kentuckian and the nation's most prominent Whig politician. Kentuckians whispered about fair-skinned slave children at Ashland, Clay's plantation. A story circulated that Clay's wife caught him in bed with his favorite mistress, "attending to the yellow girl more lovingly than suited her feelings." To pacify his wife, Clay supposedly sold his lover and their children "down the river" to the cotton plantations of the Deep South. A white Mississippian reported that he heard the whole story from one of Clay's enslaved children and observed, "Much as has been said about Col. Johnson's 'Negro Wife,' but he did not sell his Children as Mr. Clay has done."[21]

Johnson's relationship with Julia Chinn was most commonly compared to that of Thomas Jefferson and Sally Hemings. In Louisville, Kentucky, two gentlemen got into a heated argument that led to a duel because "one of them happened to blame Col. Johnson and approbate Mr. Jefferson for the same act." Most of the fighting, however, was verbal and played out in the pages of newspapers. In many ways, Johnson's defenders appreciated the comparison. Not only did it liken him to one of the United States' most capable statesmen, but the overblown newspaper coverage also called to mind the dirty little ditties that John Quincy Adams had written about "Dusky Sally." These poems, intended "to prostrate" Jefferson, instead produced the opposite effect, and, in the words of Johnson's supporters, "now stands as a monument of reproach to the author."[22]

The difference between Johnson and Jefferson, however, was explained by one Cincinnati newspaper: "Like other men, the author of the Declaration of Independence had his faults, but he was at least careful never to insult the feelings of the community by an ostentatious exhibition of them." If Jefferson was obsessively secretive, Johnson, by comparison, was brashly open. A British visitor named Frederick Marryat, who met Richard Johnson shortly after this scandal broke, found Americans' hypocrisy—not to mention their "unjust prejudice against any taint of the African blood"—ridiculous. Johnson, in the words of Marryat, had acted in a more honorable fashion than Jefferson: he educated Imogene and Adaline "and received them into his house as his acknowledged daughters." In doing so, "he has outraged society; and whenever they want to raise a cry against him, this is the charge, and very injurious it is to his popularity—'that he has done his duty as a father and as a Christian.'"[23]

Johnson himself was publicly silent on the matter, allowing his defenders to speak for him. Privately, he expressed shock at the "vile trash" printed in the papers. Johnson believed that such prying into his family life violated his privileges as a patriarch. Blaming the fuss on "a few political zealots," Johnson defended the honor of his daughters, affirming that they pursued quiet lives as respectable women—"they injure no one." He admitted that the sudden firestorm of controversy took him by surprise and now raged so furiously that it would be difficult to control. Ever the optimist, Johnson hoped that "the more they abuse me the greater the indignation of our friends and honorable men of all parties."[24]

To keep the Democratic ticket viable, Johnson did have to clarify his stance on slavery. During the Missouri Compromise debates, Johnson had championed abolition societies. He also linked slavery with his crusade to end imprisonment for debt, lamenting both as "involuntary servitude." Still, Johnson voted in favor of the Missouri Compromise, framing slavery as a states' rights issue. When he became a national candidate, Johnson cooled some of his earlier emancipationist rhetoric and toed the party line, maintaining his stance on states' rights while claiming that abolitionists threatened national security by agitating the South. One wonders, though, about the veracity of a story printed in the abolitionist newspaper the *Emancipator,* which claimed that when Johnson visited New York City "he took much pains to express to some of the gentlemen of color his deep interest in the question of their rights and prospects, as all he should leave behind him at death (his two daughters) were identified in destiny with him." Nineteenth-century newspaper articles cannot be taken as fact, but this one certainly contained a measure of truth. Richard Johnson was deeply anxious about his daughters and their future prospects in an increasingly racist society.[25]

⁓≪≫⁓

On June 6, 1830, when Imogene Johnson was nineteen, she married a white man named Daniel Pence. The two had known each other since childhood, Daniel having grown up on a neighboring farm. The pastor at Great Crossings Baptist Church, where her parents were members, performed the ceremony, and the couple recorded the special date in their new family Bible. The Bible was not their only wedding present—Richard Johnson also gave Imogene and Daniel a nearby farm. Two and a half years later, on November 8, 1832, Imogene's sister Adaline married another local white man, Thomas W. Scott. The day after the ceremony Richard deeded Thomas and "Adaline J. Scott his wife" the entire Blue

Figure 8.2 Imogene Johnson Pence, early 1850s. Courtesy of Brenda Brent Wilfert.

Springs estate, site of the former school, "an equal and joint interest to each in fee simple and their heirs forever." Likely attending the wedding of Thomas and Adaline was the infant son of Imogene and Daniel. He was named Richard Mentor Johnson Pence, after his grandfather.[26]

Existing documents do not speak to whether Imogene and Adaline chose their partners or dutifully conformed to the wishes of their parents, but whatever the case, their marriages to white men had undeniable advantages. Men had access to a much greater range of jobs and received higher pay for their work, so having a husband often enhanced women's economic security. This was especially true for white men, who also enjoyed easier access to credit as well as legal recourse in troubled times. As Richard Johnson knew, the wills of white men who attempted to leave property to their mixed-race children were often contested by disapproving white relatives. In deeding houses and farms during his lifetime wholly or partly to white sons-in-law, Johnson sought to ensure that his daughters had the means to live comfortably. It is unclear what assets Daniel Pence and Thomas Scott brought to their marriages, but by 1836, the two jointly owned a dry goods store. Among their best clients was Richard Johnson, who contracted with them to purchase clothing and other supplies for Choctaw Academy. By 1841, Daniel and Imogene had earned enough to increase the size of their farm by purchasing a large tract of land from Imogene's father for $875. Their ownership of slaves helped to finance this purchase. Imogene brought at least one slave to the marriage, a woman named Mariah given to her by her father. Over the decades, Daniel and Imogene Pence continued to accumulate wealth, and they eventually owned thirty or more slaves. In the antebellum South, ownership of land and slaves provided the surest path to economic security, a circumstance that encouraged free people of color to perpetuate the institution of slavery. In a tragic paradox that was replicated across the region, the Pences' autonomy was built on the enslavement of others.[27]

As Imogene and Adaline entered adulthood, their father gave them one final gift of immeasurable worth: their freedom. Throughout their daughters' childhoods, Richard and Julia had prepared Imogene and Adaline for emancipation. Richard saved and planned for his daughters' manumission, actions that suggest that he was a willing and even eager participant in the process. Julia surely lobbied behind the scenes, for she, like all other enslaved women, knew that slavery passed through the maternal line. If Richard and Julia had not acted, their children, grand-children, and, for all they knew, their descendants forever forward would remain enslaved. Richard Johnson did not file a formal deed at the Scott County courthouse, nor did he write their manumission into his will—a risky strategy that relied on the compliance of white relatives. Instead, he did so informally. This was a common practice among slaveholders, who merely had to communicate their intention, verbally or in writing, to set someone free. In fact, Richard had always treated his daughters as family, rather than property, and a formal legal act of manumission would only have called the community's attention to their peculiar domestic arrangement. In the case of the Johnson family, freedom was not a single act but rather a process that required careful planning on the part of their parents and culminated in the girls' marriages. In Kentucky, and indeed throughout the South, slaves could not marry whites, nor could they legally own property. When Imogene and Adaline married Daniel and Thomas and simultaneously inherited farms, houses, and slaves, they demonstrated to the community that they were not slaves, but rather well-to-do free women.[28]

Indeed, Richard and perhaps Julia may have wanted fellow Kentuckians to acknowledge their daughters not only as free, but also as white. Although enslaved people were never regarded as white regardless of their appear-ance or ancestry, free people with one-fourth or less African ancestry were, legally speaking, white. Borrowed from the Virginia legal code, this was the case in Kentucky and several other southern states. Although the southern economy was based on racial slavery, antebellum Americans did not think of racial groups as discrete and stable. Lawmakers in antebellum South Carolina, that cradle of plantation culture, found race so slippery that they refused to set criteria for whiteness, ultimately using circular logic to conclude that "whites" were those accepted by their communities as white. Richard wanted his children to take advantage of Kentucky stat-utes that regarded his daughters as white, not necessarily to denigrate their African ancestry but rather to maximize privilege for themselves and their children and grandchildren.[29]

Many local whites, however, rejected the status aspirations of Imogene, Adaline, and their families. A few weeks after Adaline's marriage, a critical editorial in the *Lexington Observer and Kentucky Reporter* deployed both biological and cultural theories of race, reminding readers of the Johnsons' African ancestry while pointing to Thomas Scott's marriage to call his own racial identity into question. The editorial claimed that the whites of Scott County "have been shocked and outraged, by the marriage of a mulatto daughter of Col. Johnson to a white man, if a man, who will so far degrade himself; who will make himself an object of scorn and detestation to every person that has the least regard for decency, for a little property; can be considered a white man." In most states, including Kentucky, whites could not legally marry blacks, leading these critics to suggest that Scott and Pence were themselves closeted people of color. The same logic applied to Johnson. Of the vice presidential candidate, newspapers asked: Was Johnson "a *White* or a *Black* man"? Was he "*free* or a *slave?*"[30]

꘎

After leaving Choctaw Academy, John Jones, George Hunt, and the Chinn women headed north, tracing one of the major routes of the underground railroad. Great Crossings was only seventy miles from the border of the free state of Ohio. Newspaper reporters supposed that the two couples were bound for Canada, and they were likely correct. Two years earlier, in 1833, Canada had abolished slavery, joining Gran Colombia, Chile, Uruguay, Bolivia, most northern US states, and much of Europe in banning the institution. In 1834, the rest of the British Empire followed suit, liberating nearly one million slaves in the Caribbean, Mauritius, and South Africa. By the time the two couples escaped from Choctaw Academy, slavery had begun to look less like a ubiquitous practice and more like a peculiarly American evil. In response, defenders of slavery lashed out against calls for black liberation and even pushed for slavery's expansion far into the West. Key to US imperialism, slavery provided not just a source of labor but a racial ideology that shaped legal, political, and social culture across an increasingly large swath of North America. Even within free states, US law allowed owners to pursue and capture runaway slaves. As long as the Chinn women were in the United States, they were not safe.[31]

Canada was also a beacon of freedom for Native Americans during this era. Rather than face removal, many joined Native communities across the border. This prospect was especially appealing to Anishinaabeg like John Jones. Americans tried to parse out Anishinaabe communities into tribes—Potawatomis, Ojibwes, and Ottawas—but Indians themselves usually resisted this label. Anishinaabeg of different "tribal" affiliations often intermarried, lived in the same village, and held councils together. In the words of Chief White Cloud, "You see people here apparently of different nations but we are all One. . . . We have but one council fire and eat out of the same dish." Extending into Canada, Anishinaabewaki territory, in Indigenous eyes, predated and superseded all colonial claims. Better to live with Anishinaabe cousins, they reasoned, than to face strangers and an unknown fate in the West. In the United States, Jones and Hunt confronted different prejudices and policies than the Chinns, but they all looked north for a measure of liberation.[32]

The couples' decision to join forces was an unusual one, even for a place as diverse as Choctaw Academy. Most of the students came from the South, and their nations, like the rest of the region, depended on African American slavery. In the 1830s, the slave populations of southern Indian nations ranged from a low of 3 percent among the Choctaws to a high of 20 percent among the Chickasaws, a figure that rivaled that of Kentucky, where 23 percent of the population was enslaved. These numbers grew during the removal era, as elite Indians scrambled to liquidize their assets and buy slaves. Peter Pitchlynn, for example, owned ten slaves in 1831, but he then sold nearly everything he owned and used the proceeds to buy additional slaves. By the next year, Pitchlynn held forty-five slaves, all of whom were destined for Indian Territory. Removing Indians had to give up their land, houses, and even livestock, but the federal government allowed them to keep slaves, a policy that encouraged the spread of African American slavery among Indians in the West. The entrenchment of black slavery among the Cherokees, Chickasaws, Choctaws, and Creeks was reflected in increasingly stringent legal codes. Had John Jones and George Hunt "publicly take[n] up with a negro slave" in the Choctaw Nation, for example, they could have been punished with fines or whipping.[33]

Northern Indians like Jones and Hunt did not come from egalitar-
ian societies—their own nations, in fact, had a history of holding war
captives from other tribes in bondage—but they had little experience
with African American slavery: their economies did not depend on it;
their leaders did not practice it; their laws did not speak to it. In fact,
several Wyandot leaders spoke out against the enslavement of African
Americans, denouncing it as a foreign practice that violated their cultural
sensibilities. Other northern Indian chiefs sometimes refused to comply
with US requests to return escaped slaves. In Anishinaabewaki, kinship
mattered more than race, and outsiders who managed to get adopted or
marry in could become valued members of society. Even in some Indian
communities in the South, as Peter Pitchlynn disapprovingly reported,
"people of my own color" and "Negroes" sometimes "mingle together in
society upon an equality." Peter's own father, John, working with other
influential citizens of the Choctaw and Chickasaw nations, was involved
in a lawsuit that succeeded in protecting a free black family who lived
among them, William and Medlong Cooper and their five children,
when a white American woman tried to illegally enslave them. Indian
attitudes toward African Americans and slavery ranged wildly from one
region to the next, or even within a single community or family. This
diversity of opinions on race and slavery was reflected within the student
body at Choctaw Academy, where some posed as masters while others
acted the part of liberators. In collaborating with the Chinn women,
John Jones and George Hunt presented the most overt challenge to slavery in the school's history.[34]

～✢～

Twenty-four hours after the runaways crossed the Ohio River at
Maysville, a posse sent by Johnson did the same. Leading the posse was
Edward Pence, Johnson's overseer and brother of Daniel Pence, who had
married Imogene. At Columbus, Ohio, Pence offered a $500 reward for
the return of the two enslaved women, and he persuaded the Franklin
County sheriff to join his posse. The runaways guessed that Pence was
riding hard on their heels, so they aimed for breakneck pace, covering
three hundred miles in about five days. Still, their stagecoach and trunks

slowed them, while Pence and his posse gained ground. Unfortunately, just shy of the Canada border, about thirty miles south of Lake Erie, Johnson's men succeeded in overtaking the runaways near Medina, Ohio. A local magistrate examined the Indian men and released them, but turned the enslaved women over to Edward Pence. Relieved and doubtless weary, Pence turned southward at a slower pace. He stopped to spend the night in Columbus, Ohio, where he rented several rooms for the group. Unknown to Pence, however, John Jones and George Hunt had followed the party back to Columbus. Around daybreak, Richard Johnson's nephew, who had been guarding the Chinns, went downstairs to wash and locked the women inside of their hotel room. The Chinns launched a daring escape, jumping from their second-story room to rejoin Jones and Hunt in the nearby woods. The runaway lovers were off again.[35]

By this time, newspapers across the United States had picked up the story. The *Vermont Phoenix* breathlessly reported the women's escape from the Columbus hotel, while the *New York American* informed readers that love drove the couples' flight and that they both planned to marry. Indeed, most coverage sensationalized the interracial aspect of their story—two enslaved, mixed-race women, one the "colored paramour" of the vice presidential candidate, and their Indian beaus—as subversive and dangerous. The *Lexington Observer* called Jones and Hunt "savage marauders" who had kidnapped two unwilling "captives." The Indians violently fought off would-be saviors, "unwilling to yield their rich and beautiful prizes." This was a captivity narrative, related to the audience as a farce in which the "savage marauders" were a pair of scholars in suits. The victims, rather than white women, were slaves who could never aspire to the status of ladies. With mock sincerity intended as humor, the author hoped that "Mrs. Johnson" would soon be "restored to the *fond embraces* of her distracted husband."[36]

The lovers' connection to the vice presidential candidate, of course, drove the media's interest in the story. Another Lexington newspaper argued that the students were "but following the example of their superiors." The *Louisville Journal* elaborated, claiming that instead of teaching Indians the "arts of civilization," Johnson "has set them the example and been their practical tutor in all the mysteries of the most low, brutal and degrading licentiousness." The editorial continued, "Under such circumstances, it is no matter of surprise that his pupils should take possession of his wife or daughter, whenever the whim or fancy led them to prefer these favored personages to other wenches of the neighborhood." The story of the runaway lovers provided an opportunity for Johnson's critics to keep his interracial relationships in the public eye, demonstrating that the congressman, far from a virtuous patriot, was an infectious cancer whose immorality might corrupt the whole republic.[37]

After the Chinns' escape from the hotel, the whole city of Columbus was on alert. Johnson's posse prioritized the capture of Parthena, and they managed to seize her, though the rest of the party escaped. Parthena was locked away, this time in the Columbus jail, as Edward Pence arranged for her transport. The posse might have continued their search for Miss Chinn, but sympathetic citizens of Columbus pressed for a writ of habeas corpus to release Parthena from jail. Hearing this, the posse paid a stagecoach company an express fee and guarded Parthena on the way back home. She must have endured a miserable ride. Surely Parthena Chinn dreaded what awaited her in Kentucky.[38]

What few comforts Parthena had previously enjoyed depended upon her master's goodwill and could vanish in an instant. Certainly, the threat of sale or separation from family must have played a major role in the decision of Parthena's aunt, Julia Chinn, to act as a loyal partner to Richard Johnson. But Parthena chose a different course, and the outcome illustrates just how swift and terrible a master's vengeance could be, even for one of "the Girls" whom Johnson previously acknowledged as kin. First, Parthena was tied to the whipping post. According to another slave, Johnson had a standard punishment for runaways: his overseer lashed the offender until her skin split, then treated the wounds with salt. Thereafter, Parthena and her children were sold to a slave trader. Her father, Daniel, later told a reporter from the abolitionist newspaper the *Liberator* that the buyer was James Peak. Although there is no record of the transaction, other evidence backs up Daniel Chinn's claim. Richard Johnson previously sold women who had affairs with Indian students "down the river," a solution that both punished the women involved and alleviated Johnson's debt. Peak was one of Johnson's creditors. He had supplied textiles used at Choctaw Academy, but, like many Kentucky merchants with New Orleans connections, his trade likely included slaves.[39]

Indian removal had paved the way for a parallel African American experience, in which 750,000 enslaved people were sold down the river to the notoriously harsh slavery of the expanding cotton frontier. Rather than dying out, as many Americans had hoped, slavery boomed in the Jacksonian era. The opening of Indian land led to greater demand, which doubled and even tripled the value of slaves. Fair young women like Parthena, sold as "fancy girls," sometimes fetched the highest price of all. Kentucky was at the heart of this noxious commerce. Beginning in the 1830s, Kentuckians sold 2,300 slaves south annually, and thousands of others—mostly slaves but also kidnapped free blacks—from elsewhere in the Upper South passed through the state. Parthena was captured during the peak of the slave-trading season and likely sent to one of nearby Lexington's slave markets. The largest, owned by Lewis Robards, was a theater that had been converted into a slave jail. Even after Parthena was sold, she might have had to remain in the jail or a slave pen for several weeks, until the dealer filled his quota. Because she was sold in late summer, Parthena probably marched overland in chains into the Deep South, beginning at sunup, walking until early afternoon, eating meals of bread, cheap meat, and coffee.[40]

Parthena's kin felt the consequences as well. No one felt the loss of her absence more keenly than her children, who were likely sold apart from their mother. Parthena also left behind many family members at Great Crossings, and some of them suffered punishments for failing to disclose the plot. However, Parthena's flight and its consequences, rather than subduing the Chinns, only emboldened them. Inspired, other family members sought to emancipate themselves. Shortly thereafter, while acting as Richard Johnson's valet on a campaign trip to New York City, Parthena's brother Marcellus slipped away. Johnson asked prominent abolitionist Lewis Tappan and black minister Peter Williams to help him find Marcellus, saying that he "was very anxious to get the boy, not so much for himself, as for his mother, who grieved at being separated from him." He was even "willing to emancipate" Marcellus if he would return. Perhaps Johnson was serious: he had, of course, freed his daughters and a few other slaves, including a relative of Julia's named Milly Chinn. But no one was convinced, certainly not Marcellus, who fled to New Bedford and became a sailor whose voyages took him far away from American slave country. In a similar move, Parthena and Marcellus's father Daniel escaped a few years later while Richard Johnson was campaigning in Detroit. From there, Daniel Chinn traveled a short distance to Canada, where he would live as a free man.[41]

꩜

Despite the media coverage of the runaway lovers and other scandals that linked him to the Chinn family, Richard Johnson won the vice presidency. But just barely. Regarding Johnson, an advisor to Martin Van Buren complained, "Our Party lost ground by his nomination, he was dead weight." Southerners, in particular, objected to Johnson's interracial relationships, calling him the candidate of "Amalgamationists, Abolitionists, and Irreligionists." Embarrassingly, Johnson and Van Buren lost Kentucky. Virginia's reaction was even more shocking. Although Richard Johnson won the popular vote in that state, Virginia's electoral delegates refused to cast their ballots for him, leaving Johnson one vote short of the majority he needed to win. For the first and only time in US history, the election of the vice president fell to the Senate, and they supported their old colleague Richard Mentor Johnson. Despite the narrowness of his victory, Johnson exalted. In Washington, he moved from the simple boarding house on E Street where he had lived for decades to a large and fashionable house on Capitol Hill. Contrary to popular fears, he did not invite his family to join him. They stayed behind in Great Crossings, continuing to manage his estate, including Choctaw Academy.[42]

When the runaway lovers story broke, Richard Johnson told his old acquaintance Amos Kendall that "his habit of his younger days had been abandoned." Kendall was not sure about this claim but reasoned that if Johnson continued to have relationships with black women he would do so secretly. Soon thereafter, however, Kendall was forced to conclude, "It seems that I was entirely mistaken." According to Kendall, Johnson was heartened by his triumph in the election, "as if it were real public approbation to his conduct in that respect." After selling Parthena, Richard took up with another Chinn, another of Julia's nieces—Parthena's sister—an eighteen-year-old, possibly named Dinah, whom locals described as fair and handsome, with freckles and shapely curves. When Johnson went home during the summers, he, according to Kendall, "openly and shamefully" carried on a relationship with this woman. They could be seen together at Johnson's tavern at Great Crossings, where Dinah, like her cousins Adaline and Imogene, played the piano. In a private letter, one visitor claimed that she "calls him my *dear Colonel* and is called *my dear* in return." As they had years earlier, when Richard had coupled with Julia, some called the woman "Mrs. Johnson."[43]

Johnson might have fathered children with Parthena, her sister, or possibly other enslaved women, but of all the women in his life, he favored Imogene and Adaline. He continued to offer them financial support, helping Imogene and her husband Daniel buy additional land to add to their plantation. When away from home, Richard worried over Adaline's delicate health, urging her not to overwork herself.[44]

In late February of 1836, Richard received the news he had dreaded: Adaline had died. About twenty-two at the time of her death, Adaline left behind an infant son named after her grandfather, Robert Johnson Scott. Richard grieved the loss of his "lovely and innocent child," writing, "She was a source of inexhaustible happiness and comfort to me." Sweet and wise, Adaline had never "done an act that even ruffled my temper." Johnson compared his grief to that of King David, who prayed that God would take his own life in place of that of his child. Johnson wrote that, like David, he knew that he ultimately had to accept the will of Providence. Unspoken, but perhaps present in Johnson's mind was the reason behind David's loss: God had punished David for his illicit relationship with Bathsheba. Had Adaline, "lovely and innocent," paid for Richard's many sins? Did Richard, like King David, remember sexual misdeeds born of lust and callousness? Did he see something in the expressions of Parthena's father and brother that reminded him of his former lover, of her flight and his brutal retaliation? Others in the region wondered—they wonder still—if the public shared the blame, if the strain of nasty assaults on her family contributed to Adaline's frailty.[45]

After Parthena's recapture at Columbus, the rest of the runaway party vanished from the public eye. John Jones and George Hunt returned home: Jones to Anishinaabewaki, Hunt to the Miami Nation. Both spoke out against Choctaw Academy, urging their chiefs not to send any more boys. They advocated a new kind of education, a departure from Choctaw Academy, arguing that Indian students should attend schools close to home and learn from Indian teachers who could offer bilingual instruction. George Hunt became a translator and diplomat for his nation, which fought removal throughout the 1830s and 1840s. In treaty negotiations, he demanded that education annuities go directly to schools within Miami country. Meanwhile, Jones continued to teach and preach, putting his principles into practice, lecturing to students in English, Ottawa, and Potawatomi at a Baptist school in Anishinaabewaki. As for Miss Chinn, she disappeared from the historical record, a sign that John Jones and George Hunt might have succeeded in introducing her to a world of different possibilities. Richard Johnson believed that Chinn had made it to Canada, but she also might have remained in the Miami or Potawatomi nations, finding sympathetic or at least accommodating friends in Indian country. Chinn's English literacy would have appealed to those who advocated Western education, while her youth, strength, and familiarity with hard work would have made her a productive member of society or an attractive wife. John Jones later married an "excellent woman," whom local missionaries assumed was "white": Could this "white" woman have been the fair-skinned Miss Chinn?[46]

Americans' response to the story of the vice president and the runaway lovers demonstrated the degree to which racism had triumphed in their new empire. Some public figures had once touted amalgamation as a great path that might unite all Americans, but by the mid-1830s, critics from across the political spectrum decried interracial sex as a national menace. In a letter to President Martin Van Buren, one of Johnson's former friends predicted that he would bring "lasting disgrace to our party and our country." That country was, by this time, firmly dedicated to white supremacy, and Johnson's actions threatened it with unwanted diversity—the proliferation of people who blurred the color line, possibly even free, privileged people of color. Increasing intolerance pushed some who objected to the new racial order to seek refuge outside the

United States, in the borderlands of Anishinaabewaki, on the free soil of Canada, or across the high seas.[47]

Those who remained behind had to survive in a society shaped and circumscribed by the politics of race. Imogene must have felt the barbed arrows that targeted her and her family. Petty toasts from planters and politicians made their way into the papers: "Richard M. Johnson: Free negroes are not allowed to emigrate to Tennessee; who will support their daddy against the law?" Although surviving documents do not preserve Imogene's thoughts, this must have been a dark period. What did she think of her cousin's escape and the terrible reckoning that followed? Certainly, she knew that Parthena was gone down south, never to return. The sensationalized media coverage must have disturbed her sister Adaline's final days. But Adaline likely dwelled, too, on the loss of Parthena. For a decade, the cousins had spent nearly every day together, washing and mending clothes for Choctaw Academy students. To pass the time, they must have shared a thousand stories, jokes, and private thoughts. That intimate bond was severed when Parthena, scarred from the whipping post, left Great Crossings in chains. Obscuring Americans' complicated ancestry and interconnected lives, racism poisoned morals, broke families, and framed a narrowed vision of the continent's future.[48]

9

Dr. Nail's Rebellion

Prior to February 1839, everyone at Choctaw Academy agreed that Adam Nail was an exemplary student. Perhaps not surprisingly, he came from a family of scholars. His grandfather Henry was prominent among those who supported the introduction of mission schools into the Choctaw Nation in 1818, the same year Adam was born. In his youth, Adam attended a mission school, Emmaus, near his home in the Southern District. His kinswoman Susannah and his uncle Joseph both taught at mission schools. Yet the Nails, like many other Choctaws, found the mission schools lacking. Two of Adam's uncles, Robert and Morris, were among the first students at Choctaw Academy. Robert would go on to become superintendent of the entire Choctaw school system, while Morris, after returning from Choctaw Academy, was chided by other Choctaws for having "swallowed the dictionary." When Adam was seventeen, he followed his uncles' path to Choctaw Academy, where he, too, excelled. Immediately placed in the highest class, Adam soon began to study medicine under the direction of the school's physician Horace Benedict, who commended Mr. Nail's "attention and acquirements," asserting "his assiduity and morality have been of the most praiseworthy kind, and have gained the full confidence of his superior, and bid fair to make him an ornament to the profession." By October of 1837, Benedict felt that his student had accomplished enough to be called "Dr. Adam Nail." The following year, Nail wrote the annual medical report; Richard Mentor Johnson had fired Benedict and replaced him with Dr. Nail.[1]

Dr. Nail's position proved short-lived. Adam Nail questioned whether current students got the same quality of education that his uncles Robert and Morris had received a decade earlier. Nail hoped that reforms might restore Choctaw Academy, but he feared that removal had banished the possibilities of the school's early days. Like former teacher John Jones, Nail would use his authority to challenge Choctaw Academy. Unlike Jones, however, Nail's rebellion would take place inside the school, and its effects would prove much more powerful, commanding the attention of the Choctaw and US governments, and bringing about the beginning of the end of Choctaw Academy.

～e ୨←

Citing Nail's "probity, assiduous application to his duties, and increasing skill in the curative art," Dr. Benedict considered the young Choctaw perhaps the most promising medical student—white or Indian—he had ever seen. Nail absorbed Benedict's lessons, assisted the doctor as he cared for other students, and, after exhausting the Academy's library, bought advanced medical textbooks on anatomy, surgery, and botany. Like most doctors in antebellum America, his training took the form of an apprenticeship, though Nail hoped to one day complete a medical degree in Lexington or Philadelphia.[2]

At school, Nail combined Choctaw and Western medical knowledge. His teacher Dr. Benedict praised Nail's "Botanic remedies"—a product of his Choctaw upbringing—writing to the trustees that "Dr. A. Nail has contributed much, <u>very much</u>" to the quality of health care at the Academy. Unusual in that age, when doctors prescribed castor oil laxatives and mercury purges, Benedict preferred botanical medicine, and he encouraged Nail to retain certain Choctaw practices. Benedict's attitude is perhaps less surprising considering that Western and Native medicine had much in common. Seeking to rid the body of disease, Native doctors, like whites, sometimes bled patients or used emetics. However, the harshness of Western "cures" often caused more harm than good, while Native prescriptions were milder. Moreover, Native doctors had the advantage of thousands of years of accumulated knowledge about North American pharmacopeia, which compelled even white patients to seek them out. Choctaws, for example, had thousands of natural remedies: a root decoction to treat gangrene; a snake root poultice for snake bites; wild cherry tea for menstrual cramps; a candy made with Jerusalem oak to cure intestinal worms.[3]

Traditionally, Choctaw medical students learned from experienced Indian doctors, in an apprenticeship similar to that among whites. Even after his or her (for there were many female doctors in Indian societies) initial training, which usually involved paying a high fee to the teacher, a Native doctor might seek out an additional internship under another healer. Native medical education had varied areas of specialization and multiple levels of expertise. The Choctaws, for example, distinguished among *alikchi, apoluma,* and *stahullo.* In contrast to whites, Indians believed that doctors needed spiritual as well as intellectual power, and even the most common type of healer—an alikchi or "physician"—needed to be "thoroughly judicious" and "highly moral."[4]

Despite his people's expertise, Nail still wanted to go to school. He may have believed, as did some Indians, that only whites had special knowledge about how to cure diseases originating from Europe. Christopher Columbus and his successors had brought a horde of previously unknown diseases: smallpox, influenza, the black death, malaria, yellow fever, whooping cough, and more. Colonial invasion and the warfare and slaving that followed propelled these diseases across Native North America, resulting in terrible mortality. To stabilize their populations, Native healers used quarantine, botanical medicine, ceremony, and, starting in 1801, vaccination. But the stresses of recent decades had invited a deadly resurgence of these maladies, while removal compromised the abilities of Indian doctors by separating them from their traditional pharmacopeia and plunging them into a new environment. One Choctaw explained that his people needed more doctors trained in Western ways "in consequence of the sickly climate to which they have removed." He, like generations of Choctaw alikchi before him, sought out knowledge—the right knowledge for the time—by apprenticing under an experienced doctor.[5]

Dr. Nail lost his old mentor and became Choctaw Academy's doctor-in-residence on August 1, 1838. At that time, his most sickly patient was a student who had contracted scrofula, or, as Nail called it, "the King's Evil." Named in remembrance of Edward the Confessor, an eleventh-century English king who used his divine touch to cure sufferers, the King's Evil was a kind of tuberculosis that affected the lymph nodes and often produced lesions on the neck and face. A bacterial infection, the King's Evil was rampant in the packed quarters of many nineteenth-century boarding schools in Europe and America, but rare at Choctaw Academy. Indeed, with the exception of the cholera epidemic of 1833, few students died at the Academy, thanks in large part to the ministrations of Julia Chinn and a revolving team of nurses that included students and slaves. Although Nail occasionally dealt with serious illnesses, most of his cases were colds, fevers, chicken pox, respiratory infections, and wounds. The students, who had sometimes rejected medicine from white doctors, appreciated Nail's botanical cures. Perhaps it was the daily, intimate contact with the students—seeing their bare chests and backs, wondering about the sources of their cuts and bruises—that turned Adam Nail into an activist.[6]

His first protest came in February 1839. Teacher William Venable was about to whip some students who had misbehaved when one of them, Andrew Weir, "made a bold resistance" and called on the other students to help him. Recognizing Weir, Nail rushed over. The two were both Choctaws, and their culture deemed whipping a highly shameful punishment inflicted only on criminals and slaves. Beyond their tribal connection, Nail and Weir had both entered the Academy the same year. When Weir came to school, he could not speak English, so he and Nail were placed in separate classes, but, still, the two knew each other well, having lived on campus for nearly five years. Protecting Weir and the others, Nail and a few of the more senior students at the Academy intervened and "took up the fight." Venable, intimidated to fight "those that are of my own age and size," backed down. No students were beaten that day, but the fact that teachers were so quick to resort to the lash is an index of just how much control Indians had lost at Choctaw Academy.[7]

Venable railed against Nail and the others, but the doctor retained his position at Choctaw Academy. In the months that followed, Nail cataloged the deficiencies and abuses he saw at the Academy, sharing his conclusions with some of the older students. After his bold defense of Andrew Weir and the other students, Nail had earned a reputation as a leader, one that was probably bolstered by the position he held on campus. Doctors were the renaissance men of the Indian world, at once healers, professors, and tribal historians. All had some degree of religious power, and those of great ability could even transcend the mundane to commune with the spirit world, to foretell events and shape the future.

At twenty, Nail was still a novice, but he had accomplished enough to impress Indians and whites alike.[8]

It was from this position of authority that Nail, in October of 1839, wrote a petition protesting conditions at Choctaw Academy. As Peter Pitchlynn had done ten years earlier, Nail chose to attack the Academy with pen and paper, weapons well suited to his abilities. Whereas Pitchlynn wrote a letter of complaint to fellow Choctaws, Nail composed a formal petition and acquired the signatures of thirty-two students. Nail mailed the document not only to the Choctaw General Council, but also to the US secretary of war, whom he invited to Great Crossings to see "the true state of the school."[9]

Nail and his collaborators leveled a series of charges that fell into three categories. They complained that material, moral, and academic standards had all declined in recent years. First, they cataloged material deficiencies: "Our shirts are scarce—one for summer and one for winter—no suspenders"; "Our bed-clothes are very indifferent"; "Our rooms we are constantly patching." Ten years earlier, Peter Pitchlynn asserted that Choctaw Academy could not provide for gentlemen, but material conditions had declined much further since then. Even Richard Johnson admitted it: "I feel confident that the charge of dirty boys and ragged boys to a certain extent and dirty houses or rooms is correct." To accommodate the growth of Choctaw Academy's student body, Johnson told Thomas Henderson to "crowd many of the little boys together" in the dorms. He also sought to economize on clothing. Although students continued to receive finer outfits for their journey home, they wore cheap clothes at school—mismatched cotton and denim pants and jackets rather than smart wool suits. By 1839, one white observer described the students' clothing as "coarse," noting that it was "such as are generally used by the poorer classes of country people in the Western States." Twice a year—winter and summer—teacher Daniel Vanderslice was supposed to hand out clothing. This had always been the custom at Choctaw Academy, but whereas Adaline had once overseen regular mending and laundering, Vanderslice made no such provisions, and he was often late or careless in supplying the students. Moreover, whenever students asked for a repair or replacement, Vanderslice would "speak very cross to us." Vanderslice, probably with Johnson's permission, developed a system whereby students had to work off the cost of replacing clothing, either in the shops or on the plantation.[10]

White and Indian visitors noted the increasingly shabby appearance of both the school and the students. When Cherokee Charles Webber dropped off his little brother, he worried about conditions there, later telling the chiefs that "the scholars were dirty and ragged, and appeared more like slaves than otherwise." A white visitor, one Mr. Joyce from Louisville, used even stronger language. Expecting the pomp and polish of the school's early days, Joyce reported that the students, instead of living in brick or frame houses like their white neighbors, slept in shoddy log cabins in a "more degraded state than the most neglected 'negro quarters' I ever saw." Ten years earlier, Peter Pitchlynn asserted that Choctaw Academy could not accommodate the needs of gentlemen; he feared, as did many other Indians, that if white society failed to accept his people as equals, Americans would start to see them as akin to slaves. Those fears, seemingly, had been realized.[11]

After the deaths of Julia and Adaline, both of whom had worked hard to maintain order at the Academy, Richard—especially in the busy aftermath of his vice presidential election—increasingly relied on several teachers who, in the words of one War Department official, were "*a set of worthless bloodsuckers*." Before his career as a penny-pinching tyrant at Choctaw Academy, Daniel Vanderslice had been involved in Chickasaw removal, overseeing the journey from Memphis to Indian Territory. Several of the Chickasaw students remembered Vanderslice from those dark days. Another teacher, O. P. Rood, had taken part in an equally inglorious aspect of US Indian affairs—the Second Seminole War, in which the United States had undertaken a scorched-earth campaign in an effort to starve the Seminoles out of Florida. Obsequious and spineless, Rood was passive to the abuses he saw at Choctaw Academy. Even more detested was Robert Evans. The overseer of Johnson's plantation following the departure of Edward Pence, Evans became a teacher in 1837, at which point he also began to administer the food supply at Choctaw Academy. The students found that they now had bigger problems than weak coffee and tough mutton; Evans sometimes gave them spoiled meat, and, in a move similar to Vanderslice's solution to the clothing problem, he refused to replace broken silverware or soiled tablecloths and insisted that the students go without. "We all hate him," Choctaw Academy students reported. According to the students, Evans was a drunk who swore at and whipped them as well as an adulterer: "He is so mean that he lives with one of Col. Johnson's negro women when he has got a woman for his wife at home." Sleeping with slaves was taboo in respectable white society and illegal in a few Indian nations, including among the Choctaws.[12]

Indians and whites alike agreed that teachers should possess not only the right knowledge, but also strict moral standards, which they could pass on to children. Protesters asserted that the opposite was happening at Choctaw Academy, where profane teachers corrupted the students. Adam Nail and the other petitioners argued that "the students contract bad habits" not only from their supervisors at school, but also from the tavern at Great Crossings. Owned by Richard Mentor Johnson, the tavern offered accommodations and amusement to "sportsmen, that is gamblers," explained a local named Americus Hay. The Choctaw Academy students, according to Hay, "are there at all times," exposed to "card playing, cock fighting, horse racing, and swearing."[13]

Like parents in the United States, Indian families worried about the vices that their boys learned while away at school, and a paramount concern for both groups was alcoholism. Evangelist Lyman Beecher launched an anti-drinking crusade in 1812, and by the 1830s, local temperance societies were widespread across the United States. Temperance had an even longer history in Indian country. Choctaws had temperance laws dating back to at least 1770—seventy years before Maine became the first "dry" US state—when the chiefs prohibited Spanish Louisiana from importing liquor into their nation. Since then, leaders from many different Indian nations had attempted to control or prohibit the flow of alcohol. Although there is some archaeological evidence for alcohol production in the pre-colonial era, most Indians were unfamiliar with hard drink until the arrival of Europeans. It was the ills of colonialism— warfare, land loss, poverty, and hunger—that induced Indians to over- indulge, a trend that traders and treaty officials, eager to impair Native judgment, often encouraged. Peter Pitchlynn lamented, "We have made a beloved thing of the worst thing the white man has." For Pitchlynn, who as a young man on the Lighthorse police force had enforced the

Choctaw temperance laws, the crusade was a personal one. He blamed "the disasters that befell my brothers"—the murder of Silas at the hands of Thomas and Thomas's subsequent execution—on drink: "The drunkards' road is full of dead men's bones—There is blood at the beginning and to the very end. All along, it is full of sorrow, wailing and deep misery." Alcoholism, Pitchlynn worried, would push Indians further along the red path forged by removal. Linking education and temperance, Pitchlynn argued, "If this nation ever comes to ruin it will be by ignorance and whiskey."[14]

Uniting movements coming out of both the United States and Indian country, the students of Choctaw Academy formed a Temperance Society over the 1834 Christmas break, and more than one hundred students and a handful of local whites joined. The Great Crossings Temperance Society required members to make pledges and even set up a system of self-governance that punished backsliders. Despite these inducements, many students, driven by depression, boredom, or bad company, began drinking. They sometimes traded food or clothing to slaves for whiskey or took a short walk down to the tavern to sneak an illicit dram. Echoing an increasingly popular sentiment in Indian country, one resident of the Choctaw Nation wondered if graduates of Choctaw Academy were "injuring their people more by the vices which they have introduced, than improved them by the knowledge they have acquired."[15]

Nail and his fellow petitioners concurred, pointing out that in addition to material conditions and morality, the quality of instruction had also declined. They concluded their petition by writing, in perfect English, "Excuse our ungrammatical sentences—we do not learn much here."[16]

The petitioners identified one major cause for the decline: "Our superintendent is about fifty miles from here, and has been away for one year; comes a few days to each quarterly inspection." In 1838, Thomas Henderson told Richard Johnson that he wanted to resign and move with his family to a new farm. Burned out from years of overwork, he had also earned enough money from Choctaw Academy to pay off his debts. Panicking, Johnson talked Henderson into staying, assuring the superintendent that he could split his time between the school and his new farm. If always Johnson's creature, Henderson was deemed even-handed and competent by most students—Johnson would call him "indulgent." Certainly, Henderson had been the steadiest presence since the founding of Choctaw Academy. In his absence, disorder and abuse flourished.[17]

Henderson's departure gave Daniel Vanderslice and Robert Evans much greater authority. The Indian petitioners charged that Vanderslice and Evans were "profane" men, who privileged discipline over education. More and more students returned from Choctaw Academy claiming, as Peter Folsom had, that they "could learn nothing at that school of any importance." In the teaching department, Native instructors and Isaac Gardner remained the only bright spot. Classically trained, Gardner taught the most advanced students, who "highly esteemed" him on account of his "profound education" and "devotedness to their improvement and happiness." Years later, Choctaws would "mention his name as a token of our grateful remembrance of the kindness he bestowed upon our sons in that distant land," where, in the school's later years, "they received nothing but injustice and oppression." The unevenness in the teaching department meant that the gap between advanced learners and ordinary students, always present, grew in the school's later years.[18]

Class placement depended not on intelligence but rather on the ability to speak English, the only language of instruction at Choctaw Academy. A minority of students arrived at Great Crossings with some command of English, usually because they had attended a mission school back home or because they had a family member fluent in the language. Most were not so lucky. They sat, bewildered, as teachers babbled incoherently for hours on end. Luckily, aided by the Lancastrian system in which advanced students tutored newcomers, those with elder tribal members at school found ready translators. This helped new students understand lessons, but not necessarily speak English. John Page, for example, was a bright eleven-year-old, but a monolingual Choctaw speaker when he came to Choctaw Academy in 1834. Growing up amid the chaos of removal, he never had the chance to attend a mission school and none of his relatives spoke English. It took about two years before Page could express himself in English. But Page was determined to excel and he remained at Choctaw Academy for a total of seven years, by which time he could read, write, and speak not only English but also Latin. But most monolingual students never matched John Page. Certainly, Page had an exceptional intellect and work ethic—he would later become a pastor, teacher, judge, and, finally, treasurer of the Choctaw Nation—but another, more happenstance factor worked in his favor: his age. Page, coming to the Academy at age eleven, retained the language-learning abilities of youth, but, especially after removal, most Indian nations were reluctant to send boys so young. By 1839, the year of Nail's protest, the average age at entrance was fourteen, by which time, as Thomas Henderson noted, their "habits, customs, and . . . disposition [were] settled." And so, because the majority could not speak English, students struggled for three, four, even five years without learning much, as they later reported to their tribes.[19]

The students' academic progress was also stymied by administrators' continued efforts to force them into manual labor. Trying to compensate for the students' apparent lack of academic progress, Thomas Henderson claimed "that these boys can learn any mechanical art as easily as white boys and indeed it is thought that they learn *more rapidly* during the time they remain in the shops." In other words, Indians were particularly suited to physical rather than intellectual work. This logic, in line with the racist thinking of the day, appealed to new commissioner of Indian affairs, Carey A. Harris, who decided in 1838 to come up with a plan to make labor in the shops compulsory. But Harris stepped down shortly thereafter and his successor, T. Hartley Crawford, refused to force the boys into the shops, which remained highly unpopular. In October of 1839, just a few weeks before Nail's petition, the quarterly report revealed that of a total of 125 students, only 3 worked in the smith shop, 3 in the shoe shop, and none in the wagon shop. The students had so overwhelmingly rejected manual education that the trustees were forced to conclude, "We think it would be proper to discontinue the shops entirely."[20]

Even as the students rejected working at the shops, they increasingly found themselves compelled to toil elsewhere in Great Crossings. As meals became sparse under Evans's harsh rule and Vanderslice demanded that students pay for much of their clothing, they had to work to supply their basic needs. A neighbor reported that at any given time, he could see up to twenty Indians laboring on Johnson's plantation. For years, students had resisted farming, but finally some—compelled, perhaps, by hunger—began to tend patches of sweet potatoes, cabbage, and melons.

Alongside slaves, the students hauled wood to the sawmill, mixed mortar, and laid brick. A visitor to Johnson's tavern reported that the students were "employed in the most menial offices about the hotel." They eagerly picked up tips, small change, from the boarders.[21]

The dramatic changes at Choctaw Academy mirrored shifts in US Indian policy. Given the school's political and symbolic importance, it had to be "consistent with principle," in Richard Johnson's words. In the school's early days, whites and Indians worked together to create a shared path toward coexistence, but removal represented a crossroads. The United States chose exclusion and separation, forging a bloody western course. Indians who had not yet walked the Trail of Tears—or even traveled the trail back eastward—found that neglect had rendered the old, shared path nearly invisible. The protesters at Choctaw Academy perceived that the only course remaining to them at Great Crossings was an education for second-class citizenship, if not servitude, and this they refused to accept.[22]

The petitioners led by Dr. Adam Nail represented about one quarter of the student body—mostly elite Choctaws and Chickasaws—but many other students, those who were not so advanced or socialized outside of that circle of upperclassmen, protested in other ways. Two Quapaw students, called Rufus King and Gilbert Lafayette at Choctaw Academy, had arrived in 1830 not knowing a word of English and were still stuck there nine years later, even though the usual term was four years and the stipulated maximum was five. Without elder tribal members there to tutor and translate for them, they had not made much progress in coursework. They did, however, learn enough to write a series of letters back home "inflaming the minds of the Quapaws against the institution" and begging the chiefs to bring them back home. The chiefs ordered both of the boys home, though Johnson, scheming to retain as much tuition money as possible, only allowed Lafayette to depart. Rufus King learned of Johnson's decision at the last minute, after he had already prepared to leave. As he stood in his smart new suit—the going-away clothes that all departing students received—King must have been outraged. But he took action, freeing himself two years later by running away.[23]

Even those who could not permanently escape from the school took short leaves of absence. Under the pretense of skipping class to work on

Johnson's plantation, they went hunting or fishing in the surrounding countryside or visited the slave quarters, where they traded their clothes or stolen silverware for whiskey. To assuage their hunger, they killed and ate hogs from Johnson's farm or another nearby plantation. In the woods and pastures, they practiced their tribal ways, singing, dancing, and playing Indian stickball. As the curriculum deteriorated and order crumbled, more and more students skipped class. Between the absconders and those who labored for Johnson, classrooms were sometimes only half full. A federal official named Joshua Pilcher stopped by Choctaw Academy for an unannounced visit one Sunday afternoon. Expecting to see students engrossed in a sermon by a visiting preacher, reading books in their dorms, or engaged in wholesome play in the yard, Pilcher was astounded to learn that 100 of the school's 125 students were off campus, their whereabouts unknown.[24]

Resistance sometimes took the form of arson. In 1838, students set fire to several buildings in Great Crossings, burning down Thomas Henderson's house, a multistory boarding house where the other teachers lived, and the post office. This must have influenced Henderson's decision to move away. The following year, arsonists targeted the main academic building, which sustained severe damage. In a thousand ways, large and small, official and anonymous, intellectual and physical, the students of Choctaw Academy protested conditions there. Some thought the school could be reformed; others believed it should be destroyed.[25]

Returning students related horror stories to their families and tribal leaders: "We can't tell you half the bad treatment we have received." Of course, many of these graduates (or escapees) were "leading young men," whose words carried a great deal of weight with the chiefs, who were often their kin. Within the relatively close confines of Indian Territory, word about Choctaw Academy spread like prairie fire, resulting in "great opposition and prejudice" against the school.[26]

Nail's petition confirmed the worst suspicions of critics in Indian country. Choctaw Israel Folsom found it laughable that his people had once believed that Choctaw Academy might "improve and better the condition of our people." Based on what he had observed from Choctaw Academy alumni, who included his nephews, Folsom asserted, "having received only the smatterings of education . . . when they come back to us they make bad Indians and bad white men." Leaders of the Miami Nation sent a petition to the president, arguing that the youths they sent to Choctaw Academy gained "habits of shameful dissipation and profligacy" and that many "destroyed themselves by their vices, discrediting the institution and the tribe to which they belong." Shortly after returning from Choctaw Academy, the son of Creek chief Opothle Yahola, dubbed "Richard Mentor Johnson" at school, stabbed a fellow Creek, then fled west to avoid punishment. The Indian Dick Johnson was later murdered in Texas. Reflecting on the tragedy, the Creek chiefs concluded, "The boys that have come from [Choctaw Academy], have not turned out generally well, and many of them rather badly." Expressing a widely shared sentiment, Choctaw chief Thomas Leflore lamented, "When I sent my son to that school, I expected him to get an Education, and to learn how to conduct himself with propriety—But I am sorry to think that I have sent my son to such a base place."[27]

Moreover, because they spent so long at that "nursery of vice," students at the Academy missed out on the knowledge and morals they would have acquired at home. Cut off from the rituals, ceremonies, and epic storytelling that were at the core of Indian education, they failed to learn—or incompletely learned—the values esteemed by their nations, especially the generosity and hard work necessary to foster a communal ethic. Indeed, some Native communities believed that those who spent their youths among whites could not be considered men in the fullest cultural sense because they had missed traditional coming-of-age ceremonies. During their first summer after puberty, for example, Potawatomi boys, having received instructions from elder kinsmen, undertook a vision quest, each one going to the woods alone to pray and fast for days, until a guardian spirit appeared to give him his personal medicine. If not initially successful, the boy repeated the ritual until he acquired the medicine that made him a true man. Even those who valued Western schooling began to argue that education needed to be more holistic, that students need to learn not just academics but also cultural values. James Gardner, a Choctaw who had attended the Academy in his youth and retained his school name as an adult, wrote, "We are desirous to educate our sons but experience has taught us that education in books alone is but poorly calculated to improve and better the condition of the red people." Even if graduates were good scholars, they were not always good Choctaws.[28]

White citizens of Scott County also began to turn against Choctaw Academy. Combining their observations of students' resistance with removal ideology, many argued in favor of racial segregation. Formerly, they recalled, "the Indian youths were invited and received into the most respectable families in the neighborhood." The students "conducted themselves respectably and were treated accordingly." But by the time of Nail's petition, neighborhoods considered the students' morals "exceedingly bad." Repeating some of Nail's concerns, local whites deplored how students dressed in tattered clothes raided their orchards and melon patches and stole livestock. Moreover, the students seemed, in the words of one neighboring white planter, "entirely unacquainted with their relative position"—that is, subordinate—"towards their more Christianized white brethren." They refused to be governed by white teachers or administrators and "with stubborn tenacity" clung to their Indian "habits and manners."[29]

A local group of whites decided to write their own petition to the War Department. Led by Benjamin Kenney, a former trustee of Choctaw Academy who had written glowing letters of recommendation for Adam Nail, the petitioners called the students a "set of thieves," who were "debased, below the negroes of the country." Many citizens of Scott County no longer wanted Choctaw Academy students anywhere near their homes; they asked the War Department to close Choctaw Academy or at least remove it from their region.[30]

Other Great Crossings residents remained sympathetic to their Indian neighbors, but they, too, noted that racial harmony seemed less possible than it had a decade earlier. Local whites encountered runaways and, on some occasions, may have helped them. In a telling letter to two nearby planters, Richard Johnson explained that, if captured, the three recent runaways "shall not be punished in any way for the frolic." In fact, they would soon be sent home to Indian Territory "with a good outfit of clothes and money to bear expenses." "Please send them back," Johnson pled—"you will very much oblige me." Another neighbor, John Cabill, wrote to Choctaw leaders about troubling conditions at the school, explaining that a negligent Johnson relied too much on "evil councilors" like Evans. Cabill agreed with the petitioners that Choctaw Academy was problematic, but placed blame on white administrators, not the Indian students.[31]

Despite dissenting voices like Cabill, many white observers argued that education was wasted on Indians. An 1839 editorial published in the *Boston Daily Advertiser* and reprinted in other newspapers claimed that most students learned nothing at Choctaw Academy, though "every few years, a particularly clever boy . . . is, with great boasting, given over to an advocate or a physician, to learn a profession; and then he is said to study law, medicine, moral philosophy, and etc." What, according to the editorialist, was the source of such a boy's genius? He was "chiefly of white descent." Real Indians, according to a War Department official, could not overcome their "original characteristics" and forever retained "idle and listless habits." [32]

A group of Potawatomi and Miami students experienced this racial pigeonholing when they took a leave of absence to attend treaty negotiations. After the treaty was concluded, the students were shocked when federal agents refused to give them their portion of the money and supplies owed to all tribal members. Alumnus Joseph Bourassa recalled how the agent had called them "halfbreeds"—even though some had no white ancestry—and "observed we were not entitled to draw because we wore our dress as the Whites." The Potawatomis appealed to their chief who said, "Of course you may draw for you are Indians as much as ourselves." Many white onlookers disagreed. Segregating "halfbreeds" allowed Americans to use the language of race to suggest that real Indians were incapable of the intelligence, self-governance, and advanced degree of civilization that supposedly characterized whites.[33]

Richard Johnson did not know about the students' petition until the Academy's Board of Trustees found out in early January of 1840. When Johnson received their letter, he rushed from his Senate chamber to the office of the secretary of war. By then, Secretary of War Joel Poinsett had already received a copy of Nail's petition and passed it to Commissioner of Indian Affairs T. Hartley Crawford.[34]

Picking up on an allegation in the trustees' letter, Johnson claimed
that the War Department should view Nail's report as "altogether false
and unfounded . . . entitled to no credit whatever." Having so recently
been informed that Dr. Nail's "morality," in the words of his teachers,
was "of the most praiseworthy kind," Poinsett and Crawford must have
been confused. Johnson clarified: his overseer Robert Evans had recently
forbidden Nail from visiting the "negro quarters," where Nail had "sometimes open[ed] their doors by violence." Nail retaliated, fomenting rebellion out of "mortified pride and self importance." Certainly, Nail would
not have been the first student at Choctaw Academy to sexually assault
enslaved women at Great Crossings. However, in the voluminous correspondence regarding sexual violence or misconduct on the part of students, Adam Nail was never mentioned. How opportune that Richard
Johnson would have discovered it just in time to discredit Nail in front
of War Department officials.[35]

Whites' reaction to Nail's activism demonstrates the degree to which
scientific racism had triumphed in United States. After decades of
intense debate over the capabilities and place of Indians in the United
States, white Americans could safely cast Indians as "immoral, filthy"
and "debased," tainted by their "original characteristics," a nature re-
enforced by their ongoing, willful association with African Americans,
whose influence supposedly led to further corruption. Many white
observers concluded that even the best and brightest of Indians had
proven that they lacked—and could never gain—the virtue necessary to become a citizen of the US republic. It was this shift in popular
opinion that Richard Johnson and other Choctaw Academy administrators believed allowed them to stray from their educational mission
and single-mindedly pursue an underlying, if ever-present goal: making money. Richard Johnson's honor and reputation depended on what
was socially acceptable in society. Removal had turned the bald theft
of Native resources into national policy, while Johnson's authority and
influence gave him license to capitalize on the Indian wards under his
thumb.[36]

But Richard Johnson miscalculated on two accounts. He overestimated his own power and underestimated that of Indian nations. Even
as officials in the War Department told Johnson that they doubted the

truth of Nail's allegations, they quietly began investigating Choctaw Academy. In Indian country, a not-so-quiet revolution was under way. Despite the losses of removal, Native nations refused to be forced on a metaphorical path toward underclass status and instead vowed to chart another course. Adam Nail, as it turned out, was no regular alikchi but rather a more accomplished sort of medicine man, for he had influence over human actions and the power to shape the future.[37]

10

The New Superintendent

In early April of 1842, English novelist Charles Dickens was on a steamboat bound for Louisville, more than halfway into a tour of the United States. He was, as he later recalled in his travelogue *American Notes,* extremely bored. Dickens denigrated the other steamboat passengers as uncultivated rubes: "They travel about on the same errands, say and do the same things in exactly the same manner, and follow in the same dull cheerless round." Among the mouth-breathers and tobacco-spitters, one man stood out, "as stately and complete a gentleman of Nature's making, as ever I beheld; and moved among the people in the boat, another kind of being." A "remarkably handsome man," he had "long black hair, an aquiline nose, broad cheekbones, a sunburnt complexion, and a very bright, keen, dark, and piercing eye." This prince among barbarians, come to rescue Dickens from the "dreary crowd," was Peter Pitchlynn.

It was Pitchlynn, a self-confessed bibliophile, who reached out, sending his card to Dickens. If Dickens was surprised that Indians rode steamboats, he was amazed that they had calling cards. The two talked for hours, dwelling at length on literature. Dickens reported that Pitchlynn "fiercely" analyzed all that he read. The Choctaw, like many Americans, loved the poetry of Sir Walter Scott, especially the beginning of *The Lady of the Lake* and the battle scenes in *Marmion.* Dickens told Pitchlynn that he should come to London, that he would enjoy the antiquities preserved in the British Museum. Pitchlynn returned the favor, inviting Dickens to Indian Territory to hunt buffalo, though the novelist declined, "I should not be very likely to damage the buffaloes much," prompting a hearty laugh from Pitchlynn. Although Dickens swooned over the Choctaw's dark good looks, he confessed some disappointment in seeing Pitchlynn dressed in "our ordinary every-day costume." Pitchlynn explained that he wore Indian dress at home and American attire abroad. He had just spent the last seventeen months traveling back and forth between Great Crossings and Washington as a representative of his nation. Dickens asked him "what he thought of Congress." Pitchlynn "answered, with a smile, that it wanted dignity, in an Indian's eyes."

When Pitchlynn met Dickens, the Choctaw was ebullient, fresh from one of the greatest coups of his career, and he would soon be reunited with his people. As a parting gift, Pitchlynn gave Dickens a lithograph

Figure 10.1 PP. Pitchlynn, Speaker of the National Council of the Choctaw Nation and Choctaw Delegate to the Government of the United States, Charles Fenderick, 1842. Pitchlynn gave Charles Dickens a copy of this lithograph. Courtesy of the American Antiquarian Society.

of himself, recently made in Washington by the famous artist Charles Fenderick. Dickens pronounced it "very like, though scarcely handsome enough," and carefully preserved the lithograph "in memory of our brief acquaintance." With radiant flashes of intellect and charm, Pitchlynn stunned Dickens, defying his expectations of Indians as primitive, war-like, unlearned, and exotic. In his recollections of that 1842 steamboat ride, Dickens remembered the whites as savages and Pitchlynn as the civilized one. As a representative of the Choctaw Nation, Pitchlynn cultivated a worldly and modern image, using it to build bridges in Washington, where he would take advantage of regime change to pursue a goal he had sought these past fourteen years: the destruction of Choctaw Academy.[1]

⋘ ❧ ⋙

Peter Pitchlynn's journey had been set into motion by the petition of Adam Nail. The Choctaw Nation received Nail's petition in January of 1840, and it is likely that Nail, having been fired from Choctaw Academy, presented it to the General Council in person. For years, a rising tide of discontent had mounted in Indian country. With Nail's petition, the wave broke, drowning out what little support remained. The Choctaw General Council created a new position, superintendent of Choctaw schools, and appointed Peter Pitchlynn to the office. "For experience has taught us," the Council explained, "that in general, white men have come among us, whose motives have been entirely governed by money." It was absurd to rely on the leadership of whites "when we have men among us who are fully competent and able to fill all such places." Pitchlynn's first task would be to inspect Choctaw Academy and decide on the best course of action.[2]

Pitchlynn left Indian Territory in early fall of 1840, bound for Great Crossings, which had been set into a flurry of activity by Nail's petition. Johnson blamed the Academy's problems on Henderson's absence and wrote the superintendent, telling him that he should spend as much time at the Academy as possible, going home only on weekends. Henderson agreed, but refused to move back permanently. To ease the minds of federal officials, Henderson claimed that he was devoting renewed attention to the "moral and intellectual instruction" of "the Indian mind." He began to teach Sunday school on a weekly basis and invited ministers to come once a month to lead Christian services. Attempting damage control in Indian country, Henderson sent a series of conciliatory letters to Choctaw officials, including George Harkins, Pierre Juzan, and Peter Pitchlynn.[3]

When Johnson returned home during the Senate recess, he interrogated the Academy's teachers and administrators, desperate to learn more about the rebellion staged on his own property. Eventually, a group of elderly enslaved people cautiously approached white intermediaries (perhaps because they feared retribution from the Indian students) saying that they wished to remain anonymous. After their conversation with the slaves, the white intermediaries filled Johnson in on the students' "infamous conduct that was perpetrated and constantly in action." Johnson told Henderson not to let any of the current students leave and to redouble his efforts to censor students' letters. In Johnson's words, when "left to themselves . . . they tell lies." The lack of communication only made Indian families more anxious; they stormed into the offices of federally appointed Indian agents, demanding information. Exasperated, the leading federal official in Indian Territory complained to the commissioner of Indian affairs: "What information has ever been given me from the school, as their agent that enables me to answer a single question of the many that the parents of the children often ask me about them? Not one."[4]

Peter Pitchlynn would demand answers. Arriving at Great Crossings in the fall of 1840, he informed Johnson and Henderson that, as superintendent of Choctaw schools, he would be conducting a fifty-day examination of the Academy.

Pitchlynn was the first outsider to gain access to Choctaw Academy's financial records—not even federal officials had yet seen them. Perhaps even more revealing than Pitchlynn's physical inspection of the school, these documents detailed fifteen years of financial mismanagement by a man who had taken as his personal maxim "Poverty has no Law." Over the years, Johnson had developed many schemes to maximize profits. While the War Department stipulated that students should be at Choctaw Academy no more than five years, some, like Quapaw Rufus

King, had been there for ten. The school's rolls sometimes listed a student's tribal affiliation incorrectly, meaning that the federal government was billing the wrong Indian nation. If a student ran away or was sent home before the middle of a quarter, his nation was still charged for the entire term—in fact, sometimes for multiple terms thereafter. Most disturbing, this practice extended to those who died at school. Daniel Vanderslice claimed that "the funeral expenses would on average be more than the balance of their time to the close of the quarter."[5]

To cover up his graft, Johnson had appointed a rotating cast of kinsmen and friends to act as trustees; several of them were financially entangled with Johnson. He paid these trustees to conduct biannual inspections and then paid himself for hosting them at his tavern. Johnson contracted with his sons-in-law Thomas Scott and Daniel Pence as well as Daniel's brother Edward to supply the boys' clothing and other supplies.[6]

Indian nations had footed the bill. During the 1830s, they spent a combined total of $40,000 annually (over $1,100,000 today) at Choctaw Academy. The single largest contributor was the Choctaw Nation, which paid between $10,000 and $12,000 each year. Johnson's murky financial records make it difficult to know how much he spent on legitimate school expenses, but profits increased under Evans's harsh rule. By 1840, Johnson and his associates pocketed at least $10,000 each year, in part by cutting corners whenever feasible. This happened at a school more expensive than many elite institutions in the region, such as the University of Virginia and the University of North Carolina. Many years earlier, James L. McDonald had warned federal officials, "The appropriation made by the Choctaws is, to say the least of it, *amply sufficient* for the support of these boys. . . . They ought in no event to suffer."[7]

Peter Pitchlynn admitted that Choctaw Academy had produced a number of fine scholars—indeed, many continued to do well in courses including Latin and moral philosophy—but "as soon as it became the fountain of a large speculation to those who had the management and control of it, it became the nursery of vice in place of knowledge and morals." He found that "a cruel and rigid economy was adopted some three or four years ago towards this school and none has carried out this principle more studiously than Mr. Vanderslice, and that doubtless by positive instructions from Col. Johnson." Most of the students were missing at least one essential piece of clothing—a winter coat or a decent pair of shoes—and Pitchlynn found their bed linens "filthy" and "insufficient for the cold seasons of this country." The monitors, led by John Page, presented Pitchlynn with a petition requesting "more meat on the table" and proper silver and serving ware. Most students professed a "constant desire to go home." Pitchlynn thought the school would be better off if certain groups were sent home: the troublemakers, especially the drinkers, and the seriously ill—surely those suffering from tuberculosis who were too sick to learn. Pitchlynn communicated all this and more to parents back in the Choctaw Nation. Some were "relieved . . . of a load of anxiety," just knowing that their children were safe and well. Others professed sorrow and outrage, if not surprise, figuring that such evils "are of common occurrence in the kingdom of the prince of Darkness." In his report on Choctaw Academy to the Choctaw General Council, Pitchlynn was forced to conclude that "Col. Johnson's fair and liberal promises have never been complied with." He asked, "When shall the Red man receive justice?"[8]

Peter Pitchlynn left Great Crossings in early January of 1841, headed for Washington, where he would demand justice for his people. It was not his first trip to the capital. Back in 1838, Pitchlynn and three other Choctaw Academy graduates, Robert M. Jones, Pierre Juzan, and George Harkins, had been appointed by their General Council to seek redress for property losses during removal as well as the full amount promised to Choctaws under the Treaty of Dancing Rabbit Creek. These Choctaw statesmen were only a few of the dozens of Indian diplomats who came to Washington every year. Some Indian nations, like the Cherokees, supported one or more representatives who lived in Washington while Congress was in session, monitoring the US government, keeping their nations apprised of events, and, when necessary, presenting petitions or requesting meetings with top officials.[9]

Pitchlynn's first order of business was to meet with Commissioner of Indian Affairs T. Hartley Crawford and Secretary of War John Bell. Having read Adam Nail's petition and many other letters from Indian country, both men were familiar with the problems at Choctaw Academy. Pitchlynn asserted that the "students are attentive and show a great anxiety to profit by the labor and money expended upon them."

But Choctaw Academy, Pitchlynn suggested, was broken beyond repair, and his people were wasting their money. For all Indian nations that had contracts with Choctaw Academy, the federal government had automatically transferred the lion's share of their education funds to Richard Mentor Johnson. Although many nations had periodically protested that their money would be better spent elsewhere, Johnson had used his influence to drown out their complaints. The time had come for the Choctaws to reclaim their school funds and take charge of their own children's destiny.[10]

The plan that Pitchlynn unveiled was revolutionary: a system of schools in Indian Territory, controlled by Indians. After reclaiming the Choctaw Academy funds, the Choctaw General Council planned to build and oversee several academies within the Choctaw Nation. In a follow-up letter to Crawford, the Council argued, the "children are ours, and the money is also ours." Looking back on the past few decades, the Council recalled, "Full experiments have been made of the whitemen, and failure has been the result. We wish therefore that the experiment might also be made of our own people in controlling, and managing and teaching our Schools." The United States, the Council argued, also had a moral obligation to the Choctaws: "We have made great sacrifices to accommodate the views and wishes of your Government, and have stood by your side in all your wars." In his conversation with the commissioner of Indian affairs, Peter Pitchlynn made a final argument: Not only did his people have the money, desire, and moral authority to control their own school system, they also had the ability to do so. The Choctaw Nation was home to many brilliant thinkers and accomplished scholars. "We," said Pitchlynn, "know how to appreciate such an institution and . . . are fully able to establish it upon a broad and permanent foundation."[11]

Behind closed doors, Pitchlynn used much stronger language. For years, he and other leaders had considered ways to reassert control over the education of their own youth. Could the General Council appoint teachers at Choctaw Academy? Could more science courses be incorporated into the curriculum? Former Commissioner of Indian Affairs Elbert Herring had stonewalled them. Pitchlynn fumed, "I have seen enough of the avarice of whitemen to convince me that where Indians have much money there will be aching palms to grasp at it—this has ever been the case, they have got our lands, they have got our money, but what good have they done for us?" Pitchlynn asserted, "There are no public funds belonging to the Choctaws which we should prize more highly than our school funds and none which we should watch over with greater care and strictness." It was through education, Pitchlynn contended, that the Choctaw Nation would survive, prosper, and even rival other modern nations around the world. Through the second-rate education offered at Choctaw Academy, the United States was holding them back. General Council member Israel Folsom agreed: "I am going to strike with the largest sledge hammer I have . . . against the Choctaw Academy. . . . I have been waiting for an opportunity these ten years."[12]

There was a reason the General Council had chosen this time to send Pitchlynn to Washington, for, in the words of John Quincy Adams, Richard Mentor Johnson's "Vice-Presidential chair" had just been "drawn from under him." As Martin Van Buren sought reelection, the Democratic convention—for the first and only time—declined to name a vice presidential candidate. Colleagues continued to sneer at Johnson's interracial relationships. Even his old friend Andrew Jackson grew tired of Johnson "pointing to his scars," using a decades-old battle with Tecumseh to suggest that "not rewarding him" was a "cruelty." The press began to depict him as "no longer . . . an active and constructive statesman, but as the westerner obsessed with the desire for office." Some reporters listed "defrauding the unhappy Indians" as chief among Johnson's sins. Still, in the election of 1840, the longest and most expensive presidential campaign yet, Johnson toured the country in support of Van Buren and financed productions of *The Battle of the Thames*. But his efforts were in vain. William Henry Harrison and his Whig Party won the presidency by a huge margin—234 electoral votes to Van Buren's 60—and claimed sizable majorities in the House and Senate. Johnson did nothing for the Democratic ticket. But the biggest issue was the Panic of 1837, the first depression in the country's young history, which had deepened by the time of the election. Blaming the president for his impotency in the crisis, Americans dubbed him "Martin Van Ruin."[13]

Leaders in Indian country were well aware of regime change in Washington. They discussed American politics on the pages of their own newspapers, in the halls of council houses in Indian Territory, in federal offices in Washington, and even with American neighbors. A graduate of Choctaw Academy named Thomas Wall lived near the Arkansas line, where he sometimes chatted with local whites. As an Indian, Wall could not vote in US elections, but he encouraged his neighbors to support the Democrats, saying, "I had much rather the old hero of the Thames was our president than old Granny Harrison, the sham hero of Tippecanoe." A few Choctaw Academy graduates like Wall expressed sympathy for Richard Mentor Johnson, but—whatever their personal feelings about the vice president—they recognized his defeat as an opportunity for policy change.[14]

In Washington, Pitchlynn had several successful meetings with federal officials. Commissioner of Indian Affairs T. Hartley Crawford was receptive to Pitchlynn's proposal, writing, "I certainly have no disposition to uphold this institution against the wishes of the Indians." Pitchlynn lobbied Congress to investigate and audit Choctaw Academy. As a House of Representatives committee began to comb through the tangled web of Choctaw Academy's financial records, interim Secretary of War Albert M. Lea, who oversaw the transition in administrations, considered whom he should appoint for the on-site school inspection. Rather than relying on Richard Mentor Johnson's handpicked trustees, Lea selected someone without connections to Johnson, an attorney from Louisville named William S. Crawford. Inspector Crawford spent a week at the Academy, touring the facilities and interviewing faculty and students. The students told Crawford his visit had sent the staff and slaves into a frenzy of cleaning and repairing in preparation for his arrival: "This is the way they do every time when somebody comes here." Notwithstanding this attempt at polishing, Inspector Crawford found that Adam Nail's charges against the school were "well founded." He cataloged Choctaw Academy's deficiencies in a lengthy report to the secretary of war.[15]

On March 13, 1841, just over a week after the inauguration of President William Henry Harrison, the new secretary of war, John Bell, fired Thomas Henderson and appointed Peter Pitchlynn superintendent of Choctaw Academy. In reality, this move merely confirmed a decision already made by the Choctaw General Council. Commissioner of Indian Affairs T. Hartley Crawford explained that Pitchlynn was appointed "at the insistence" of the Choctaw Nation, "in the hope that, from a better comprehension of the Indian character, he can judiciously manage the pupils at the Academy, give a more beneficial direction of their application to the branches of study they are prosecuting, and a moral tone to their conduct." Crawford continued, "The appointment of Col. Pitchlynn is to be considered in the light of an experiment," the first time that an Indian would have such a strong hand over federal Indian policy. Privately, Pitchlynn exalted, writing his brother, "I do believe that I can fill that station better than any whiteman can, and do more good to my nation." Pitchlynn was more reserved with the commissioner of Indian affairs, telling Crawford that he would accept the position, but that he intended to use his authority to shut down Choctaw Academy in favor in Indian schools in Indian Territory. Crawford agreed.[16]

His mission accomplished, Pitchlynn headed west, stopping only briefly at Choctaw Academy to demote Daniel Vanderslice to "sub-superintendent." Back in Indian Territory, Pitchlynn reported to the General Council, which empowered Pitchlynn to "use your utmost exertions" to close Choctaw Academy by the following spring. Even if Pitchlynn failed in this, the Council instructed, he had to bring home all Choctaw students.[17]

While in Indian Territory, Pitchlynn briefly reunited with his family. They were desperate to see him. Recently, the whole family had suffered from "sore eyes"—probably trachoma. Widespread in Indian Territory, trachoma was a bacterial infection that could cause blindness. In Peter's absence, his wife Rhoda, with the help of kin, had managed to care for their six living children. Everyone recovered, but the ordeal took a toll on Rhoda. Even when she did have time to sleep, Rhoda was haunted by nightmares, worried about her husband. As for Peter, he had missed Mary Rhoda, his infant daughter, the most. Mary Rhoda had black eyes and a dark complexion and, of all the Pitchlynn children, most closely resembled her father. Mary Rhoda could only say a few words at the time, though her older brother, Peter Jr., was more vocal. Among his first sentences was, "Pappy is gone to Kentuck." With heavy hearts, the Pitchlynn family watched Peter depart once again. They could, at least, take comfort in having Peter's picture, the same one Pitchlynn gave Dickens. This high-quality lithograph, a marvel of new printing technology, was probably the most lifelike portrait they had ever seen. Mary Rhoda cried, afraid of the eerie likeness, but Peter Jr. was delighted, kissing it and asking his mother "what reason Papa can't talk."[18]

When Pitchlynn returned to Great Crossings in mid-August 1841, he thought about all the families fragmented by Choctaw Academy. "I know," wrote Pitchlynn, "the feelings of their parents, they expect of me that I will be father to their children in this distant land and that I will take kind care of them when sick." In fact, Pitchlynn was related to several of the Choctaw students; he was particularly fond of his nephew William B. Pitchlynn. Peter may have felt a special responsibility to care for William, since William's father Joseph had died several years earlier. Certainly, William was excited to see his uncle, whom he followed around campus. But even for non-relatives, Choctaw families expected Pitchlynn to act as a surrogate father. One parent explained to Pitchlynn, "I have written to my sons giving advice to be governed by your experience and advice." Pitchlynn called the students "Orphans among Strangers and in a Strange land." The students needed a father, and perhaps Pitchlynn needed a family.[19]

Of the Academy, Pitchlynn vowed, "Its last days shall be its best days." As a surrogate father, Pitchlynn would not only care for the students but also offer them instruction and discipline. In place of Pastor Henderson's Christian sermons, Superintendent Pitchlynn gave lectures on morality and suppressed drunkenness and gambling. The students respected Pitchlynn as an Indian, backed by tribal authority. Teacher Isaac Gardner was impressed, explaining that Pitchlynn "brought the school to order when it would have been difficult for another person to have done it."[20]

Richard Mentor Johnson knew that Pitchlynn wanted to withdraw all the Choctaw students, but he hoped to change the superintendent's mind. Initially, Johnson was delighted to learn of the appointment of Pitchlynn, "who of all men living is best calculated to sustain the school as he is something like the Founder of it." Reminding the Choctaw of his long-standing personal connections to the school as well as the ties that bound them as Masons, Johnson called Pitchlynn "friend and Brother." Johnson invited Pitchlynn to stay at his home rather than in the superintendent's cottage, bought him a new suit, and told Robert

Evans, the teacher/overseer, "to neglect every other business and attend to Col. Pitchlynn and his wishes." Johnson clearly believed that he could bribe Pitchlynn into submission. He implored the Choctaw, "Get scholars from all the tribes in your Country and enable me here to get you an ample salary." Explaining that he could bill the education fund "of each tribe according to the numbers," Johnson promised "compensation I can get as large as you may deem proper." Praising Pitchlynn's "sensible and noble letters" while condescendingly critiquing his grammar, Johnson urged the superintendent to write to a few Washington officials, to recant some of his previous statements and to declare "your intention to remain at the school."[21]

Johnson seriously miscalculated. Certainly, Pitchlynn, in the words of close friend Gideon Lincecum, was "fond of money." The salary he demanded as superintendent was $1,500 per year, nearly twice what Thomas Henderson had made, and much of it came out of Johnson's pocket. But, as Lincecum further explained, "money was never a life motive" for Pitchlynn. And this particular money, the school funding, was blood money, wrung from the earth, "the wails of our native land." Serving a higher purpose, Pitchlynn refused to be bought off at Choctaw Academy, too long governed by the greed of "the whitemen and the rascals." As for his approach to Johnson, Pitchlynn explained, "My plan of whipping enemies has been always to let them alone. Keep very still; keep my own thoughts to myself. . . . Go on with my own ways and with my own plans as though I had no one to oppose me. I never condescend to notice them."[22]

The longtime congressman was mystified by Pitchlynn's distance and incorruptibility, writing, "I believe he is deranged." Johnson leaned on neighbors to write letters discrediting Pitchlynn; for good measure, he forged a few himself. Johnson forwarded these missives, which claimed that Pitchlynn was a drunk who "trampled upon propriety and honor," but they did no good. Johnson was incredulous that federal officials, even those of a different political party, would support an Indian diplomat over their old colleague, the war hero, the slayer of Tecumseh. After overhearing Peter Pitchlynn tell a group of students that Johnson would have to kill him to stop him from closing Choctaw Academy, the former vice president wrote the secretary of war: "I am totally in

midnight darkness as to what has been done at the City of Washington."
Working at cross-purposes, Johnson and Pitchlynn spent several awk-
ward months at Choctaw Academy, sitting together at the faculty table
in the dining hall and exchanging terse words.[23]

The students did not know all the particulars of the cold war brew-
ing between Johnson and Pitchlynn, but they understood its broad
brushstrokes. Many students, especially Choctaws, assumed that Peter
Pitchlynn had come to rescue them. Instead he told them to wait "until
their course of study shall be finished or the time expires when they
may return to their nation with honor to themselves and their name as
Choctaws." Chief among the discontented was Joseph Lancaster, who
had come to the Academy as a boy of eleven in 1831. Ten years later,
he knew Latin, but what he really wanted was to be among his people,
to learn what it meant to be a Choctaw man. Lancaster, who came to
Kentucky before removal, had never seen Indian Territory.[24]

In September of 1841, this miasma of anxiety, hope, and desperation
produced one of the most racially charged battles at Great Crossings.
Engaging in a usual, if now officially discouraged activity, Joseph
Lancaster and a young enslaved man were cockfighting when they began
to quarrel, perhaps over the money that typically passed between hands
at such events. As their shouts attracted a crowd in the schoolyard, the
two came to blows. Administrators, including Richard Johnson, quickly
separated the young men, and neither was seriously injured.[25]

Johnson ordered the slave to apologize to Lancaster, who forgave him,
but Pitchlynn exploded at this lenient punishment. At that time, men
fought others of similar rank. Slaves were supposed to passively accept
blows from their social superiors; the fact that this young enslaved man
fought back implied equality. As other teachers reported, Pitchlynn
fumed, "Kill him! Kill the damn negro son of a bitch!" Coming from
men allied firmly with Johnson, these words must be taken with a grain
of salt. And yet they do sound like the man who, as a student, complained
about the "insolence" of Johnson's slaves and whose "Pitchlynn temper"
was notorious among acquaintances. No further violence ensued, but
afterward Pitchlynn gathered the Indian students and, after the roll call,
lectured them not to associate with slaves, and especially not to suffer
their insults. Indians could not count on whites to protect them because

"the whites had no law among themselves except to punish the poor." Pitchlynn told the students to "be brave" and "take the law in their own hand."[26]

In the aftermath of this fight, the students revolted. Some rioted, breaking their bed frames, shattering windows, tearing their linens and clothes. A few weeks later, teenaged Choctaw Ambrose Sevier followed overseer/teacher Robert Evans out to the smokehouse, where he beat Evans with a bat. Sevier had been at the Academy for seven years, long enough to have grown hungry and hard from Evans's scanty meal provisions and forced labor regime. Another fight, less well documented, involved Napoleon Jackson, a twenty-year-old Quapaw who had learned little English during his three-year stint and was desperate to go home. Taking matters into their own hands, increasing numbers of students had run away—eleven pupils, about 9 percent of the student body, left in August 1841 alone. Many others planned to follow. In the aftermath of the Lancaster fight, about half the student body signed a petition to Peter Pitchlynn: "We the undersigned students . . . are determined to stay here no longer . . . we will not stay here two days longer; a great many of us are now ready to leave and we don't wish you to agree to any thing Col. Johnson says." Pitchlynn, however, urged them to be patient. They agreed—for the time being—noting with satisfaction how Pitchlynn "made those mean rascals about us tremble." In a letter to the Office of Indian Affairs, thirty advanced students vowed to leave if Pitchlynn left: "We will take our little brothers with us; we can't leave them here when they will suffer so much and no one will take care of them."[27]

Indian protests convinced many War Department officials that the school should close. The Office of Indian Affairs confirmed that, at the very least, Choctaw students should be released "so as to prevent" further "commotion and violence." Even Richard Johnson's handpicked board of trustees agreed. Predictably, the loudest dissent came from Johnson himself. If he could retain Choctaw Academy's revenue for a few more years, Johnson felt sure he could finally extinguish his debts. To colleagues in the federal government, Johnson repeatedly suggested that "a sudden winding up and removal of the school might be injurious to all concerned." One federal official replied, "If he knew the great excitement prevailing against the school he would say nothing."[28]

Peter Pitchlynn planned the students' journey home. The Choctaw General Council appropriated $600 to pay for the boys' transport. But Pitchlynn's mandate also extended to the Chickasaws, who had recently hired Pitchlynn as an attorney and given him a list of students to be sent home. Altogether, seventy-four Choctaws and Chickasaws were scheduled to depart. Pitchlynn decided to divide these students into two groups: one to leave that fall, the second the following spring. The first group was supposed to be the smaller, targeting scholars who had served the most time at Choctaw Academy, including nine students over the age of twenty-five. On the morning of November 25, 1841, Johnson looked on in impotent disapproval as thirty jubilant boys and young men left the school grounds, filing out after Pitchlynn.[29]

Thirteen other students had decided that they could not stay at Choctaw Academy, not for one more term, not even for one more day. They probably caught up with the first group as they climbed into stagecoaches bound for Louisville. The stagecoaches probably hummed with happy chatter in the Choctaws' and Chickasaws' closely related language, but talk likely switched to English when they realized that a few outsiders had joined them: a Quapaw, a Potawatomi, and an Iowa. The latter may have told his comrades, as he later told folks in Indian Territory, that he was "heartily sick of his academic pursuits." Pitchlynn welcomed the newcomers, saying, "Had the whole school come on I would have sent them home."[30]

Pitchlynn and the students rode the stagecoach all day, arriving in Louisville that night. Pitchlynn booked several rooms at the Galt House, a riverfront hotel on Main Street that his friend Charles Dickens called "splendid," a place so handsome that it seemed more like "Paris, rather than hundreds of miles beyond the Alleghanies." With easy access to the steamboat docks, lavish meals, and famous cocktails, the Galt House was popular among travelers and vacationing southern planters. Despite its posh reputation, however, the Galt House had a diverse clientele that represented a broad swath of the bustling port city of Louisville. In the lobby, the students would have seen rich couples up from their country estates, wearing the new clothes from their shopping expeditions, attended by African American slaves who were also smartly dressed. The many white men who populated the bar were, on the whole, decidedly rougher in appearance, some with long, greasy hair partially concealed by hats with upturned back brims. They started off with mint juleps in the morning and moved on to harder stuff from there, peppering the bar with chewing tobacco spittle and, occasionally, bullet holes. Even amid such a tableau, the group of Indians probably attracted some attention, but, given their new suits and dignified comportment under Pitchlynn's watchful eye, they were on the more respectable side of the spectrum.[31]

The next morning, from their hotel rooms, the boys watched the steamboats docked along the banks of the Ohio, while Peter Pitchlynn left to book their passage on a westbound vessel. Using funds forwarded from the Choctaw General Council, Pitchlynn purchased tickets for all the students, including those from other nations. Before he could return to the hotel, however, Pitchlynn was intercepted by William Crawford, the Louisville lawyer who had conducted the recent, critical inspection of Choctaw Academy. Crawford told Pitchlynn that Daniel Vanderslice had sent teacher O. P. Rood up to Louisville to fetch the thirteen "runaways" who had left the Academy without official permission. Pitchlynn

Figure 10.2 The Galt House, circa 1845, drawing on stone by John H. Bufford, published by B. W. Thayer & Co., Boston. Gift of Miss Edith Barter, Collection of the Speed Art Museum, Louisville, Kentucky.

agreed to meet with Rood back at the Galt House, and Crawford, as a representative of the War Department, joined them. As Rood later recalled, Pitchlynn met him in the lobby, saying that if any students wished to return to Choctaw Academy he would not stand in their way, "but he could not nor would not force them, and further that he believed it would be folly to attempt to persuade them to return."

Pitchlynn led Rood and Crawford upstairs and asked all of the "runaways" to join them in one room. Upon seeing Rood, some of the younger boys began to cry. Rood started to speak, but Pitchlynn cut him off: "Don't cry, boys. If you do not wish to return, you need not. Do you want to go back to Choctaw Academy?" Thirteen voices responded "NO." Rood countered, suggesting that running away was "disgraceful," that "it would be but a short time before they would get permission and money to return to their homes honorably." The students sat, impassive, resolute in their determination to escape. Pitchlynn turned to Rood— "it is useless to talk, let us go." As Pitchlynn led Rood out of the building, he explained why he could not back down. His actions had nothing to do with his own grievances against the school; rather, Pitchlynn explained, "I had rather fight it out with Col. Johnson than my whole nation."[32]

❦

The Galt House showdown with Rood was but one key battle in the larger war Pitchlynn was waging on behalf of Indian rights. Pitchlynn did not accompany the students on their journey back home. Giving extra money to two of the older students, Pitchlynn told them to take charge, and then boarded a steamer traveling in the opposite direction, toward Washington, DC. Pitchlynn had received a letter informing him that the Choctaw General Council had once again appointed him, this time to seek redress for unfulfilled treaty promises. In a petition to Congress, Pitchlynn reminded the House and Senate that the Choctaws had been "staunch in their allegiance and attachment," even following the "disheartening circumstances of their removal west."[33]

Legally and, as Pitchlynn suggested, morally, the United States was bound to uphold its treaties with Indian nations. Of central importance was the Treaty of Dancing Rabbit Creek. The United States had not fully compensated the Choctaw Nation for its eastern homeland or Choctaw individuals for property lost or damaged during removal. Additionally, Pitchlynn invoked Article 22 of the treaty, in which the Choctaws had requested "a delegate in Congress to watch over their interests." This delegate, Pitchlynn explained, would "be selected by the Choctaw Nation from among themselves, but to reside permanently at Washington at the expense of the United States." People like the Choctaws were unwilling inhabitants of a growing empire, but treaties ratified by Congress explicitly acknowledged sovereign rights retained by Indian nations, giving them a share of power within the US system of divided sovereignty. Pitchlynn was determined to exercise Indians' share of power to the fullest extent, calling on law and honor to guide ethical relations among nations.[34]

The United States did not comply with the Choctaws' request for a delegate, or a similar, ratified article in the Cherokee removal treaty, but Pitchlynn began to act as a de facto delegate. He lobbied for his nation's rights and presented claims from individual Indians and other Native nations for stolen land and property. Pitchlynn's wife Rhoda thought that this mission was dangerous: "White people might kill you," she fretted. But Peter reveled in his mission, putting his education to use for a purpose that Richard Johnson would never have conjured in his worst nightmares. By all accounts, Pitchlynn was a persuasive speaker, "in the foremost rank of orators," according to an *Atlantic Monthly* reporter. Another white writer likened Pitchlynn to one of the most able US politicians of the day, calling him "the Calhoun of the Choctaws."[35]

In addition to his intellect and rhetorical abilities, Pitchlynn used his social skills to draw people in. According to one white acquaintance, "He possessed such sweetness of spirit, such gentleness of manner, such manly frankness, such thorough self-respect . . . that one could not help loving him." From his hotel on Pennsylvania Avenue, Pitchlynn continued to cultivate his relationships with officials in the Indian Office and War Department, but also extended his social network. Alongside other politicians, he attended plays at Ford's Theatre and vacationed at a "splendid hotel" in Washington Springs, where he danced, dined, and played billiards. One unnamed congressman, after hearing Pitchlynn's petition to the House and Senate, wrote that he approved the Choctaws' plan to govern their own school system. "I find, Col., your name is very familiar here at Washington, a number of my friends in Congress have inquired after you, and spoken of you in very high terms." Pitchlynn asked Masonic friends and other prominent acquaintances to write letters of introduction to senators, attorneys, and businessmen. One such missive described Pitchlynn as "a well educated gentleman of extensive connection and has the confidence of 20,000 Choctaws." [36]

Instead of assassinating Peter Pitchlynn, as Rhoda had feared, many white people in the District of Columbia regarded him as a minor celebrity. Perhaps, like Dickens, they were drawn to his charm and wit, or the seeming incongruity of an Indian gentleman. At art galleries and theaters, he rubbed elbows with socialites, one of whom invited Pitchlynn to give a lecture at a lyceum in Georgetown. Part of the expansion of intellectual culture across America in the nineteenth century, lyceums were educational organizations that sponsored public programs. We do not know what Pitchlynn spoke about that day, but his favorite topics included Choctaw history and culture as well as education, temperance, and the law. Whatever the theme, the tables had turned: the Indian was educating whites. Perhaps Pitchlynn told the audience, as he had told others in Washington, that they should visit the popular gallery of George Catlin, an artist whose work featured American Indians, and there behold a portrait of a younger Peter Pitchlynn, head cocked to one side, resplendent in Choctaw regalia (see Figure 1.1). Pitchlynn rarely missed an opportunity for self-promotion, but his major motive was to gain white allies for his people. In Pitchlynn's conversation with Charles Dickens, he praised Catlin's collection as "elegant." His meaning had less to do with the artist's skill and more with his empathy—his portraits, eschewing many of the negative stereotypes of the day, captured Indians' strength, dignity, and beauty. Catlin and other artists, Pitchlynn told Dickens, "had painted the Red Man well; and so would I, he knew, if I would go home with him." Dickens, like the lyceum audience, could be educated by the Choctaws—and then write about it for a global audience. Sensing the Englishman's disdain for their fellow steamboat passengers, Pitchlynn was optimistic about where Dickens's sympathies might lie.[37]

Pitchlynn's education helped him forge ties with a wide range of politicians and intellectuals, but the power of literacy also helped him reach a global community of anti-colonial activists. Native intellectuals like Pitchlynn were particularly interested in another marginalized people who had suffered colonialism and diaspora: the Irish. This fascination might have begun at Choctaw Academy, where Superintendent Thomas Henderson encouraged the comparison. In his geography course, Henderson explained that people in rural Ireland "live in a wretched state of poverty." Henderson continued, "Their huts are much like the Indian wigwams, and one of the principal differences in their mode of living is, the Indian is free, but the Irishman is a slave to his landlord." Another text, meant for intermediate students, asserted that the Irish were a pre-modern people who doggedly held on to their ancient customs, including their backward, thousand-year-old government, and their religion, best characterized as "the cherished fragments of paganism." The conclusion of the chapter on "Adherence to Old Customs," meant to castigate the Irish, probably delighted and inspired the Native students: "After seven hundred years of either nominal or real domination, England has been unable to anglicize Ireland."[38]

The power of print media introduced Pitchlynn to Daniel O'Connell, an Irishman who never stepped foot in America. Known as "The Liberator," O'Connell was a politician who successfully pushed through many reforms that empowered Irish Catholics, though his ultimate political goal—Irish self-governance—remained elusive. A brilliant orator, O'Connell gave stirring speeches in the Irish House of Commons, some of which were later printed and circulated throughout the world. In his journal, Pitchlynn copied part of an O'Connell speech on bigotry: "She has no head, and cannot think; no heart, and cannot feel. When she moves, it is in wrath; when she pauses, it is amid ruin; her prayers are curses—her God is a demon—her communion is death— her vengeance is eternity—her decalogue written in the blood of her victims; and if she stops for a moment in her infernal flight, it is upon a kindred rock, to whet her vulture fang for a more sanguinary desolation." When choosing the eagle as the national symbol, the Continental Congress likened the United States to the Roman empire, and Pitchlynn agreed that the raptor, violent and peripatetic, was an apt avatar.[39]

O'Connell's anti-colonial politics would continue to influence Pitchlynn and perhaps other Native leaders as well. When the Irish Potato Famine struck in the late 1840s, killing one million and driving two million to emigrate, southern Indians gave generously to the victims: Creeks donated 100,000 barrels of corn, while Choctaws collected

$710. For a people still recovering from their own diaspora, these were powerful gestures of support for a fellow colonized people.[40]

⤙ ⤚

When Peter Pitchlynn met Charles Dickens, the Choctaw was headed west to pick up the last Choctaws and Chickasaws from Great Crossings. Pitchlynn had already resigned as superintendent of the school, writing the commissioner of Indian affairs how he was driven by "feelings of duty to carry out the wishes of my people to bring that Institution, which they have long looked upon as the nursery of vice and degradation instead of morals and intellectual improvement, to a speedy termination." The commissioner warned Richard Johnson and other Choctaw Academy administrators not to stand in Pitchlynn's way, which made this second departure easier than the first. Benjamin Franklin was one of twenty-one Choctaws and eleven Chickasaws who had been waiting "in great anxiety" for this day. He had come to Kentucky as a teenager ten years earlier, knowing little or no English, but had committed himself to his studies. Now a man of twenty-five, Franklin was at the top of the first class and head monitor. As one of the oldest students at Choctaw Academy, Franklin should have gone home the previous fall, but Pitchlynn asked him to stay and watch out for the younger children. Franklin did so, contenting himself by writing letters to friends and relatives in Indian Territory, who filled him in on the news he had missed during his long sojourn—Choctaw politics, the whooping cough that killed so many children. On April 10, 1842, Benjamin Franklin put on his new suit, arranged his Latin books inside his trunk, and prepared to see "our own native country" for the first time.[41]

The journey went smoothly at first. Pitchlynn and the students took the stagecoach up to Louisville. Surveying the boys, Pitchlynn noted that, as usual, the clothes Johnson had given them did not measure up to genteel standards. They needed to look smarter, not just for the Galt House crowd, but for their welcome-home celebrations. From a Louisville merchant, Pitchlynn bought summer vests, shoes, and hats. He booked passage on a steamboat owned by a fellow Indian, a Cherokee named Joseph Vann, which took them to Little Rock, Arkansas.[42]

To reach Indian Territory, Pitchlynn had to book another steamer. Pitchlynn encountered the captain of the *Governor Morehead*, who told him that the fee would be $500. Pitchlynn thought that this was too high and moved on to find another vessel. Seeing an opportunity to swindle a group of Indians, Morehead later sued Pitchlynn for breach of contract, persuading an Arkansas judge and jury to award him the $500 he had originally quoted Pitchlynn. Pitchlynn's lawyer was furious; "There never was a more rascally proceedings in a Court of Justice." Sickened by this episode, a repetition of the orgy of theft and injustice that had characterized removal, Pitchlynn comforted himself; "There is a day coming when exact justice will be done to all, and the captain of the Morehead will then receive his due if he does not in this world."[43]

Pitchlynn had received an audience in Congress, acclaim in a Washington lyceum, and respect from Charles Dickens, yet the state laws of Arkansas would not allow him to testify in court. It was a paradox that represented the plight of Indians in the new American empire: they were both sovereigns and subjects; nation builders and persecuted minorities; educated and worldly, and yet, in the eyes of whites, forever savage. But in turning away from Choctaw Academy Peter Pitchlynn and the Choctaws had achieved their objective, a feat made all the more remarkable because Indians had few rights under US law. Indians had to invoke treaty rights and moral authority to seize autonomy wherever they could find it. To Peter Pitchlynn's mind, nothing was more important than controlling their own schools, which held their children, the key to the future—"no nation can become prosperous without them." Upon returning home, Pitchlynn reported to the General Council, "Finally this institution has been so far as we are concerned brought to a close. . . . A new era in the history of our schools is now on the eve of commencing."[44]

11

Orphans among Strangers

In early 1842, Antoine Gokey was in the office of his federal Indian agent, demanding the return of his seventeen-year-old son, John. The Sauk and Mesquakie teen had just completed a four-year term at Choctaw Academy, and his father, excited to see John again, had written to him, sent him money for the return journey, urged him to come home as soon as possible. But Antoine heard nothing in reply.[1]

Fortunately, Antoine's worst fear was not realized. John was alive and well, though Choctaw Academy records indicate that he had probably spent more time in the fields and blacksmith shop than the classroom. John's silence likely resulted from Johnson's censorship, which became more aggressive after Adam Nail's petition. John's classmates David and Augustus Garrett were more successful in sneaking letters out. Pronouncing themselves "sick of Kentucky," the Garrett brothers lobbied the War Department as best they could: "When we arrive at the Scott [County] we was quite Small and now are grown, and wishes to see our father & kinfolks once more before our boddy shall be put in the dust." The Garretts, having attended the funerals of at least fourteen classmates, feared that final silence that would forever separate them from their families. They felt more like captives than students, a sentiment they shared with many other classmates. In fact, Richard Johnson began to use the idea of captive students to justify the school's existence to War Department officials. "Remember the expedition of Black Hawk," Johnson said, referring to Gokey's tribesman who had fought removal. "It makes the tribes more friendly to have their boys with us." He admitted to holding on to the sons and nephews of chiefs, in particular, to encourage Indian politicians to send others to take their place.[2]

New disciplinary measures contributed to the students' suspicion that they were prisoners. Formerly, students had enjoyed several holidays—a week off at Christmas, another after final exams, plus Easter, Whitsunday, July 4, and George Washington's Birthday. As student resistance mounted, Johnson worried that such free time gave students opportunities to plot rebellions, and so he banned vacations, replacing them with "voluntary labor, amusements and study." Daniel Vanderslice, who reclaimed his role as superintendent after the departure of Peter Pitchlynn, introduced new military exercises, forming the students into a battalion and commanding their drills and marches. Such exercises, Vanderslice explained, "habituate the Indian youth to prompt obedience, regularity in their movements, and the restraints necessary to maintain order."[3]

Peter Pitchlynn called the students who remained at Choctaw Academy "Orphans among Strangers." The first students at the Academy had called Great Crossings "a strange land," but they also noted that "our white brethren . . . are friendly and kind to us." Twenty years later, the place seemed less like a crossroads and more like an island, cut off both from US society and Indian homelands. Pitchlynn's allusion was metaphorical, but the students were, increasingly, literal orphans as well, not high-born sons but poor children without relatives to claim them.[4]

John Gokey, fortunately, had an influential father desperate for his return, but even Gokey would remain in Great Crossings for another year. The captivity of John Gokey and other latter-day Choctaw Academy students resulted from a détente between Richard Johnson and Indian nations. In the words of one Indian Affairs official, "There seems to be much repugnance on the part of these Indians to send any of their youth to the Academy." John Beach, agent for the Sauk and Mesquakie, talked to Antoine Gokey and tribal members at length, noting that their opposition to Choctaw Academy came "less from aversion to their education than a dislike to send them so far from home, among strangers, and for an uncertain period." Richard Johnson, desperate to retain tuition money, would not release current students unless others arrived to take their place, so young men like John Gokey were forced to remain at the Academy long after the conclusion of their four-year terms.[5]

Federal official Ethan Allen Hitchcock, who toured the diverse nations of Indian Territory in spring of 1842, remarked, "On one point I found but one sentiment, and that was a most decided opposition to the establishment or continuance of Indian Schools beyond the limits of the Indian country." Inspired by the example of the Choctaws, who had just withdrawn their final students from Choctaw Academy, other Indian nations were determined to follow their lead. For Indians, it was not a question of whether Choctaw Academy should close, but rather how and when.[6]

❦

In the fall of 1845, federal Indian agent Richard Elliott stood before the Potawatomi chiefs who had gathered at Council Bluffs. When Elliott, following instructions from the War Department, requested that the Potawatomis send more children to Choctaw Academy, he "was greeted with a laugh of derision from one end of the council to the other." They had been told that Choctaw Academy would close soon after the last Choctaws left and now, three years later, they demanded the return of all their children. Elliott reported to Washington, "They considered it perfectly absurd in me, as their agent, to ask for more boys for that Academy."[7]

Many leaders in Indian Territory wanted to follow the Choctaws' lead. Creek chiefs told their Indian agent, "Our brothers the Choctaws are allowed their fund at home, where we hear there is a large School underway, and that they have taken away all their boys from Kentucky and put them home." They wanted "to have our whole fund to use here as they have done." Fearful of conjuring stereotypes about Indian savagery, Creeks were careful to state that their protest against Choctaw Academy came from the fact that they "regarded such propositions as schemes for obtaining their money without rendering any equivalent" rather than "any strong prejudice against improvement."[8]

Most of the nations still involved with Choctaw Academy, the Ojibwes, Creeks, Iowas, Miamis, Ottawas, Potawatomis, Quapaws, and Seminoles, declared that they would send no more students. The vehemence of some was such that William Armstrong, the ranking federal agent in Indian Territory, stopped asking them. In their councils,

Indian governments passed resolutions, diverting money away from the Academy in order to plan for their own schools. To make this happen, however, they had to regain control over education funds set aside in treaties. In 1845, representatives of the United Tribes of Council Bluffs, composed of Ojibwes, Ottawas, and Potawatomis, came to Washington to discuss Choctaw Academy with the War Department. As their agent explained, "Their funds have been taken without their approbation or consent—*against their earnest remonstrance*—in bad faith, as they believe, on the part of the Government—and they have determined that no more of their children shall go to that institution."[9]

When representatives of the United Tribes of Council Bluffs came to Washington, Richard Johnson met them. Johnson claimed to be a tour guide for two exceptional Potawatomi youths, Antoine Bourbonnais and Anthony Navarre. Bourbonnais was a top student, while Navarre (or Muquadgo) taught beginning students; both had family at Council Bluffs. During their two-week visit, Johnson did indeed show Bourbonnais and Navarre the sights. The Potawatomis watched Congress in session and shook hands with President James K. Polk. But the timing of this trip was no coincidence: Johnson wanted to remind the chiefs from Council Bluffs that their children were in his hands.[10]

After losing the vice presidency, Johnson ran for national office several times without success. Still, he kept coming back to Washington. To his friend William B. Lewis, an auditor in the Treasury Department, Johnson wrote, "I can save my home estate and disenthrall myself if I can only succeed in keeping up the school for the present—it injures no body." No white body, at least.[11]

As Johnson became politically obsolete, money alone drove his need to maintain the Academy. Johnson had been in debt almost continually since the Yellowstone Expedition of 1819, and he took out additional loans to finance a more lavish lifestyle during his vice presidency. When creditors became insistent, Johnson had to sell his latest plantation, Longview, and move into a more modest dwelling on the White Sulphur property. To the secretary of war, he claimed, "I am working as hard as a galley slave and living upon less comfort to get out of debt." Those actually held in bondage by Johnson suffered much more as a consequence of his debt. After the Choctaws withdrew their students, Johnson mortgaged and then sold twenty-four slaves to pay his most adamant creditors. Johnson attempted to hold on to "my black people whom I have raised or inherited, and who I wish to set free at my death." Among these were his own biological relatives—nieces and nephews, mostly, some of whom had been educated alongside Adaline and Imogene. Though Adaline had passed on, Imogene lived nearby and likely took an interest in the fortunes of her cousins. But even these intimate relations were not safe. In 1847, Johnson admitted that he had to sell ten of his "most valuable slaves," though he claimed that they all chose "their own masters in the neighborhood." This way, families, including his own, could remain nearby. Johnson claimed, it was "the best I could do for them."[12]

In a fevered desperation to retain "the few blacks which remain with me" as well as his mills and a farm, Johnson pled for Choctaw Academy. In the White House, halls of Congress, and offices of the War Department, he reminded friends, acquaintances, and strangers of his war wounds, his old friendship with Andrew Jackson, his financial "embarrassment"—whatever seemed likely to evoke their sympathy. President John Tyler grew so tired of seeing him that he told Johnson to address his concerns to the secretary of war. Tyler, perhaps feeling bad for the secretary, added that Johnson should write letters rather than come in person.[13]

The only office Richard Johnson avoided was the one he should have gone to in the first place: that of Commissioner of Indian Affairs, T. Hartley Crawford. Crawford refused to aid in Johnson's schemes, for, after Peter Pitchlynn's visit, he had come to believe that Indians should go to school closer to home. Hearing of Pitchlynn's success, other nations began to lobby Crawford, who helped them regain control of their education funds and returned children to desperate parents. Crawford also empowered Indian nations by stipulating that only chiefs in council could select new students for Choctaw Academy. Formerly, the process varied from one nation to the next, with chiefs, national councils, or families selecting students. Sometimes teenagers or young men volunteered to go. But this ambiguity could give way to corruption, as agents seeking to curry favor with Richard Johnson sometimes used coercive or deceptive means to convince families to enroll their children. Crawford's new policy enabled the legitimate governing bodies of Indian nations to reassert control. As a result, student enrollment declined from 122 in 1841 to 55 by 1844.[14]

Richard Johnson rejoiced in March 1845 when President Polk replaced Crawford with William Medill, an old friend whom Johnson called "my Brother." Regarding Choctaw Academy, Johnson explained to Medill that President Polk "authorized me to say to you that was his wish that you should do all in your power to sustain it." Whatever Medill thought of this fib, he rescinded Crawford's policy that only chiefs in council could select students, telling Indian agents to press for students, asking only for "the consent of their parents or guardians." In time, though, Medill came to see Choctaw Academy as a failure, an embarrassment to the Office of Indian Affairs.[15]

The American court of public opinion was coming to the same conclusion. Between 1841 and 1848, Congress authorized three separate investigations to "enquire into the manner in which the Choctaw Academy in Kentucky is conducted, whether the Indian youth sent there for instruction are properly attended to in respect to their clothing, boarding, morals and general education." The proceedings of the 1846 and 1848 were printed in several major newspapers, where Americans learned that Choctaw Academy was "a humbug and a public nuisance" and "an abuse against the confidence and rights of the poor Indians." Even Democrats like William Sawyer of Ohio railed against Richard Mentor Johnson, arguing that the $500,000 expended to date at Choctaw Academy was "enough to educate all the Indian children in the United States." Sawyer was incredulous that Johnson requested an additional $10,000 for rebuilding expenses in the aftermath of the 1841 student arson. This cost far exceeded what Johnson had actually spent on replacement quarters for students, according to one widely reprinted report, which called the buildings "rude and nearly dilapidated old cabins, fit only for negro quarters, and in fact far less comfortable and tasteful than those occupied by the Colonel's (Johnson's) negroes a few rods from the place." Kentucky representative Will Thomasson, echoing Peter Pitchlynn, called for the closure of Choctaw Academy in favor of schools in Indian nations.[16]

❧※❧

Students responded to the crisis in complicated ways. They understood that, for the United States and Indian country alike, weighty abstractions like sovereignty, power, and honor were at stake, but Choctaw

Academy was their everyday reality, and it shaped their self-image and vision for the future.

Some, continuing in Adam Nail's path, resisted in overt ways that underscored negative perceptions of the school in Indian country. Kuknahquah was also called Joseph Clymer, after his father, a white trader who sent the thirteen-year-old to Choctaw Academy after abandoning the boy's Potawatomi mother and marrying a white woman. Furious over the white trader's actions, the Potawatomis expelled Joseph Clymer Senior from their nation, then sent his son to school in Kentucky. Given the distressing circumstances of Joseph Clymer Jr.'s arrival at Choctaw Academy, it is not surprising that the Potawatomi teen struggled with coursework and got into trouble. Clymer befriended Baptiste LaFramboise, who was also a Potawatomi and the son of a wealthy trader, and together, they planned to escape. Leaving on June 2, 1846, the day after summer clothing and bedding was distributed, they sold these items and a few books, which afforded only a little cash for a long journey. Thanks to their own resourcefulness and the kindness of strangers, however, the teens reached their respective homes six weeks later. Clymer lived on the Osage River, while the LaFramboise family was at Council Bluffs. Families, desperate to hear about loved ones at Choctaw Academy, gathered about Clymer and LaFramboise. Potawatomis in these two different places—and everywhere in between—repeated the students' tales of misery.[17]

Hot on the heels of Clymer and LaFramboise were two Potawatomis with a very different message. Antoine Bourbonnaise and Anthony Navarre, both monitors, were sent by Richard Mentor Johnson. Each located and questioned one of the runaways. Bourbonnaise claimed, "I made Baptiste weep when I spoke to him about his having run away." To cover their own shame and ward off any attempt to discipline or return them, the runaways trumped up charges against Choctaw Academy, according to Bourbonnaise. He and Navarre traveled Potawatomi country, attempting to counteract the runaways' stories and allay concerns about the school. Conflicting tales of Choctaw Academy triggered debate in Indian Territory. Some believed Bourbonnaise and Navarre, while others were certain that they had been bribed. Johnson's handpicked interlocutors were at least partially successful; that summer, the Potawatomis extended their Choctaw Academy contract for two more years, until their own schools were built.[18]

By this time, Antonie Bourbonnaise and Anthony Navarre were practiced diplomats, having traveled with Richard Johnson to visit the Potawatomi delegation in Washington the previous year. In many ways, they were beholden to Johnson, part of a cadre of monitors who maintained order at the school. In addition to classroom tutoring, monitors made sure that the students cleaned themselves and their dorms. They also broke up fights and reported misconduct. In return, they received upper-level education, authority, and better clothing and food than the other students. As a teacher, Navarre also earned a salary. The two young men must have found the compromise worthwhile. A letter they co-wrote to the commissioner of Indian affairs offers a clue into their rationale: Bourbonnaise and Navarre wanted to use their time in the United States to observe and remember "whatever is good or useful."[19]

Nail's rebellion and the ensuing scrutiny forced some material and curricular improvements in Choctaw Academy's final years. Like Bourbonnaise and Navarre, other students agreed that "good or useful" things could still be learned there. Perhaps the most accomplished student ever to attend Choctaw Academy was a Potawatomi named Arcmuggue. Enrolling in 1837 at the age of sixteen, he was called Joel Barrow, after a federal agent among his people.[20]

Like many who entered in Choctaw Academy's later years, Barrow was an orphan. As elite families increasingly resisted sending their own children, the War Department encouraged Indian leaders to fill their quotas with orphans, "in relation to whom the [US] Government may properly be considered as guardian." Many nations rejected not only the proposal that a foreign government care for their children but also the very notion that any "orphans" lived among them. "Orphan" came into the English language in the 1400s, as Europeans began to prune their extensive family trees in favor of more mobile nuclear families. In contrast, most Indian nations maintained extensive kin networks that were able to absorb parentless children. In trying to define this concept to Indians who had no word for it, Harris clarified, "By orphans, I mean those having neither father nor mother." Miami leaders responded, "Does our father [the president] think us dogs, that we would not take

care of our boys who had not fathers or mothers to take care of them?"
Elsewhere in Indian country, however, the concept was gaining traction,
as nations like the Choctaws and Cherokees instituted new property and
inheritance laws that privileged nuclear families. Additionally, the horrors of removal, with its appalling death tolls, left more and more children without close relatives. In their treaties and governing documents,
some Indian nations began to make provisions for orphans, including
money to pay for boarding school.[21]

Joel Barrow, for one, was grateful for the opportunity to go to school.
According to Richard Johnson, Barrow had no previous Western education, a fact that made his accomplishments all the more remarkable.
By the early 1840s, Barrow studied moral philosophy, read Latin and
Greek, and excelled in elocution. He was also interested in belles-lettres,
the French art of beautiful writing that had become a transatlantic
sensation among the literati. In 1842, after the Choctaws abandoned
Choctaw Academy, Joel Barrow, highlighting the long-term presence
and achievements of his own people, suggested that the school should be
called "Potawatomi Academy." He took a leadership role, assisting Isaac
Gardner in teaching the most advanced students. An active member of
the Academy's Temperance Society, Barrow demonized the ills of drinking and gambling: "It is said that love of play is a demon, which only takes
possession as it kills the heart."[22]

Given the intensity of his intellect and self-discipline, it is not surprising that Joel Barrow became the first student in several years to attend
Transylvania University. Saying that he wanted to "be useful to my people," Barrow aimed to study medicine. The salary he earned as a teaching
assistant was not enough to cover tuition and other fees, so Barrow had
to lobby Secretary of War John Bell for additional money. It is an index
of Barrow's resourcefulness (and perhaps desperation) that he strategi-
cally switched his "school name" to John Bell, hoping that the secretary
would act as a patron. Unfortunately, President John Tyler went through
several secretaries of war, and subsequent secretary James Porter was
unimpressed with Barrow/Bell's new name. Porter also recollected the
alleged misdeeds of Choctaw Academy's last Indian doctor, Adam Nail,
whom he called " a great scamp," but granted the request anyway. Packing
up Adam Nail's medical textbooks, Barrow went to Lexington, where

he boarded with a local white family while the Transylvania Medical School was in session. Handsome and gentlemanly, Joel Barrow had a very successful career at Transylvania, ranking "among the most promising" during his first year and improving thereafter. When he graduated in 1844, Barrow's professors reported that he "surpassed all the white students, law and medicine."[23]

While a medical student, Joel Barrow went back to Choctaw Academy and shared with fellow Indian students a simple but powerful observation: we should select that which is nutritious and avoid whatever is poisonous. This seems to explain Barrow's attitude about Great Crossings. Many vices thrived there—drinking, gambling, idleness—and these Barrow assiduously avoided. But Great Crossings and nearby Lexington also held great promise, the ability to commune "with the soul of *Bacon*," explore the stars with astronomer William Herschell, range "with *Paley*, through the departments of morals," or trace "the footsteps of *Locke* amid the mazes of philology." For some students, Choctaw Academy still had lessons worth learning. As Joel Barrow pointed out, Indian country had no universities, no medical schools, only school systems in early infancy.[24]

A few Indians with firsthand experience in Indian Territory's nascent schools confirmed Barrow's concerns. Jefferson Jenkins was one of the youngest children ever to enter Choctaw Academy, coming there in 1834 at the age of seven. He was one of the forty-three students who left with Peter Pitchlynn in fall of 1841. At the time, Jenkins was delighted, but he voluntarily returned to the school in early 1846, a penitent man. "I was one of the Choctaws who were persuaded to leave here with others before we knew the advantages of an education, and many of us have since much regretted our withdrawal from this school, I have since found out by experience that this is much the best school, having many advantages over the schools in the Nation." The Choctaw Nation refused to pay Jenkins's tuition at Choctaw Academy, and he did not have enough money to pay his own way, so he left again after a few months.[25]

While many in Indian Territory agreed with the chiefs of the Choctaw Nation, who declared, "We loathe and abhor that miserable institution called the Choctaw Academy," others, like Jenkins, thought they might learn something valuable. When his fellow Choctaws departed, John

Page decided to stay in Great Crossings. A Baptist convert, Page prepared for a career in the ministry by studying for a year under a local pastor. Frazier McClish, a Chickasaw from a wealthy family, graduated from Choctaw Academy in 1840, but returned a few years later, asking Richard Johnson to tutor him in American law and political science. Several prominent Creeks from Hillabee Town, including Milly Francis, daughter of the famous Creek prophet Hillis Hadjo or Josiah Francis, sent their boys to Choctaw Academy in open defiance of their chiefs. Some Potawatomi and Miami families made the same choice when the local schools promised by chiefs failed to materialize.[26]

William Barnett, a judge and captain of a district in the Chickasaw Nation, visited Choctaw Academy in 1845 and advised his people to continue supporting the school for a few more years, writing, "The Indians can gain a more general and practical knowledge of all that is useful to them and their different tribes at this than at any other school to my knowledge." In the latter years of Choctaw Academy, Richard Mentor Johnson noted that the Chickasaws were the most favorably disposed toward the school, though he may not have understood the complicated reasons why. Back in the 1830s, when the Chickasaws were negotiating removal, they insisted on a cash settlement, rather than payment in western lands. As the Chickasaws' scheduled 1837 removal date approached, the United States urged them to join the Choctaw Nation. Both initially balked at the suggestion, but eventually brokered a deal: the Chickasaws paid the Choctaws $530,000 for the right to settle in the western part of the Choctaw Nation in Indian Territory. According to the terms of the agreement, the Chickasaw would become the fourth district of the Choctaw Nation. But, after arriving in Indian Territory, the Chickasaws chafed at their minority status. They did not like Choctaw laws, which, as they said, "seem like the white man's laws," and their representatives lacked the votes to overrule decisions of the Choctaw General Council. Chickasaws also hesitated to pool their considerable resources with those of the Choctaws; they wanted to maintain and control their own national budget. In short, they did not want "to part with their name." Chickasaws resolved to remain citizens of their own nation.[27]

The Chickasaws were pushing against one of the major objectives of removal policy. Through removal, the United States had hoped to lump all Indians together, both literally into a place called "Indian Territory" and conceptually into one racial category. By doing so, it sought to compromise the sovereignty of Indian nations and convert them into internal minorities. Although Indians recognized the cultural ties and lived experiences of colonialism that connected them, they resisted US attempts to compromise their sovereignty.

In 1842, after the Choctaws had withdrawn their students from Choctaw Academy, both the Choctaw Nation and the War Department assumed that the Chickasaws would join their Choctaw countrymen. But, in a letter to the secretary of war, the Chickasaw chiefs expressed "some degree of astonishment" upon hearing "that the Chickasaws are willing to put their school funds with the Choctaw funds and have a large Academy in the Choctaw Nation." They concluded, "We are opposed to uniting any part of our funds with the Choctaw funds." Instead, Chickasaw leaders planned to build their own schools. In 1844, the chiefs and captains, including Judge William Barnett, scaled back on tuition to Choctaw Academy—supporting thirteen students rather than twenty—and put the remainder of the funds toward new school construction in their district. Since the Chickasaws were not willing to contribute to the Choctaw school fund, the Choctaw Nation expelled all Chickasaws from its school system. Chickasaw leaders were content to continue sending elite young men to Choctaw Academy until the new schools were ready.[28]

~≈≫~

In a coordinated effort, all Indian nations involved with Choctaw Academy set their contracts to expire in 1848. Richard Johnson, however, struggled desperately to retain the fifty-five students who remained: Could the federal government extend their contracts for a few more years? Even a few months? The largest group, thirty-four Potawatomis, were set to depart on July 23, exactly two years after the Treaty of 1846 was ratified. President James K. Polk, acceding to one last request from Johnson, asked the Potwatomis if their children might stay on a bit longer, until the fall or early winter. In council, the chiefs and headmen unanimously refused. As summer approached, Johnson claimed that the waters of the Ohio and Mississippi were too low to send the Potawatomis home by steamer. This was a common enough occurrence, but Potawatomi leaders decided that this was a final, desperate gamble to squeeze a few more thousand dollars out of their national coffers. Again, they refused.[29]

The Chickasaws' contract was also set to expire in late July. That summer, a Chickasaw delegation was in Washington, where they requested that their children be delivered to them. Commissioner of Indian Affairs William Medill agreed, telling Richard Johnson, "The request is a reasonable and proper one and should of course be complied with." Johnson balked, however, and so the Chickasaws hired Johnson's old adversary Peter Pitchlynn as an attorney, instructing him to pick up the boys in person.[30]

During the summer and fall of 1848, the remaining students set out for their respective homes. On July 23, the last Potawatomis crowded onto the lower deck of a steamboat. Superintendent Daniel Vanderslice had bought the cheapest fare, so they lacked "blanket or bed" and were "exposed to the heat from the steam . . . and the damp and chilly air at night." A Mr. Linsey, who escorted them home, took pity on the boys. He persuaded the captain, for $20, to give them passage in the cabin, bedding, and seats at the table. The last Miami student, John Lasselle, went home alone. His only remaining tribal member, a boy of eleven called Jay Columbia, was the last student to die at Choctaw Academy, a victim of measles. Choctaw Academy's final students were seven Creek boys who left on October 31, 1848. The first students came to Great Crossings from across the continent—from the Florida swamps, to the Osage prairies, to the ice-bound lakes of the far north—but the last, with a few exceptions, shared one destination: Indian Territory.[31]

The final Chickasaw students went east, rather than west. When Peter Pitchlynn arrived at Great Crossings, he was angered, if not surprised, at the students' appearance. "I found the Chickasaw boys at Johnson's School nearly naked—as poor and shabby a looking set as I ever saw." Chickasaw leaders, seeking to avoid the exorbitant fees Johnson charged for outgoing outfits, instead authorized Pitchlynn to buy them new clothes "adapted to the institutions and society which they are about to enter." They were going to college in the Northeast. After making their way via steamer to the eastern seaboard, the Chickasaw students boarded a new technological marvel, a train, that would carry them into the future. The Chickasaw chiefs "congratulat[ed] themselves on the prospect of placing those boys at other, and as they confidently hope, better institutions."[32]

As Peter Pitchlynn withdrew students from Choctaw Academy, Richard Johnson fumed, claiming that Pitchlynn "thinks he has more power than the Government." More accurately, Pitchlynn and other Indian leaders used all the tools at their disposal—including lessons gleaned from their colonizers—to preserve their *own* nations. In this age of loss, Native nations scored a momentous victory, for nothing was more essential to Indian survival than the redemption of their children.[33]

Indian Schools for Indian Territory

Alfred Wade was one of the first twenty-one students who arrived at Choctaw Academy when it opened on November 19, 1825. At seventeen, Wade was the oldest in that first class, and he quickly distinguished himself. Thomas Henderson described Wade as a hardworking student who was "particularly perfect in arithmetic." Satisfied with his progress, Alfred's father recalled him after only two years at school and sent another family member in his place.[1]

It was the school's custom to send students away with a few parting gifts, a suit and new saddlebags containing a book or two of subjects at which they had excelled. Wade took his arithmetic workbook. In this large, leather-bound book, he had copied out problems in neat cursive writing and calculated the answers, displaying impressive skills in long division. When his attention strayed, he filled in blank spaces with doodles, usually the names of his schoolmates in an elaborate script with embellished details. In the fall of 1827, Wade took this arithmetic workbook 500 miles back to the Choctaw Nation. Five years later, the arithmetic book accompanied him for another epic journey, when his people were forced to Indian Territory. The federal government permitted each emigrant to Indian Territory to carry only thirty pounds of baggage. Only thirty pounds to hold memories of their homeland and to make a new life in the West. This arithmetic book was important enough to Wade to make the cut and important enough for his descendants to keep it for ninety years, before donating it to the Oklahoma Historical Society, where it remains today.[2]

When Richard Johnson sent Alfred Wade back home with his arithmetic book, he hoped that the book would act as a mnemonic device, prompting

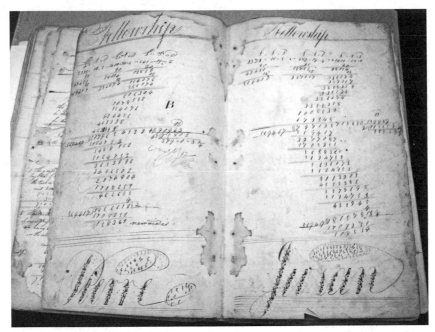

Figure 12.1 Alfred Wade's 1827 Arithmetic Workbook. Note the name of his classmate Pierre Juzan doodled at bottom. Alfred Wade Collection, Courtesy of the Research Division of the Oklahoma Historical Society.

Wade to recall fondly his days at Choctaw Academy so that he might echo federal policy in Indian country. But it is clear that Wade imbued the book with very different meanings. Its pages reflected the social world that Indians constructed at the school, the intertribal connections that would bond them as strange tribes became neighbors in Indian Territory, and the knowledge that Wade and others would use to take the fight against American imperialism away from the battlefield and into the newspapers, courts, lyceums, and halls of Congress. This arithmetic workbook is a seemingly simple object, yet it speaks volumes about the school that produced it, and the unintended lessons it taught to Wade and his peers.

❧❦

In December of 1832, a group of Choctaws gathered under an old oak tree and sang hymns they had learned back home. Recent arrivals in Indian Territory, they summoned the energy to begin building a log

cabin that would become Wheelock Academy, the first Choctaw school
in Indian Territory. Over the next several years, schools appeared in all
three Choctaw districts, but with Choctaw Academy consuming the
lion's share of Choctaw school funds, the new schools struggled and had
to ask severely impoverished parents to pay for their children's room and
board. One teacher applauded his students' progress in reading and felt
confident that they might begin to write "had they stationery provided."
Those who could afford it began to send their children to white schools
in neighboring states.[3]

On November 29, 1842, ten years after a group of weary emigrants
built their first schoolhouse at Wheelock, the Choctaw General Council
passed an education bill that would revolutionize Indian schooling.
Pitchlynn had returned to Indian Territory triumphant, having rescued Choctaw students from their namesake academy and Choctaw
money from Richard Mentor Johnson. Taking control of their education
funds, which then amounted to about $28,500 annually, the Choctaw
General Council created one of the most extensive public school systems in North America, which would serve over 12,000 Choctaws. New
Superintendent of Schools Peter Pitchlynn declared to fellow Choctaws,
"In this let us be united; In this let us be ambitious."[4]

The Choctaws demanded that they should control their own schools.
To the General Council, Peter Pitchlynn argued, "The Choctaws now have
intelligence enough among them to manage their own institutions without
the advice and council of whitemen." As the first superintendent, Pitchlynn
was the ex-officio president of the four-member board of trustees, which
included the Choctaws' federal agent plus one member appointed by each
of the three districts. The trustees created policies, set salaries, hired and
fired teachers, attended annual examinations, and reviewed all expenses
associated with the schools. A separate Building Committee, consisting
of members of the General Council, evaluated bids from Choctaw contractors, then oversaw the construction of the new schools. The General
Council members who wrote the Schools Act of 1842, mostly graduates of
Choctaw Academy, sought to prevent the greed, corruption, and cronyism
they saw in the management of their alma matter.[5]

The board of trustees tried, first, to hire Choctaws as teachers and
principals, but quickly found that they did not have enough personnel or

resources to support their planned school system. Peter Pitchlynn waged an uphill battle when he suggested that the Choctaw Nation might turn, once again, to missionaries. Distrust of missionaries was widespread in Indian Territory because many Indians believed that these outsiders had colluded with the federal government to implement removal. Pitchlynn countered by pointing out only that only a minority of missionaries had supported removal, while many had defended Indian rights, going so far as to "follo[w] us to our new homes," where "they have again established churches and schools among us . . . notwithstanding they have received no aid from our school funds in this country nor from the government of the United States." Ultimately, the General Council decided to contract out the staffing of several schools, so long as the societies agreed to pay the teachers' salaries and, more importantly, abide by the regulations set forth in the Schools Act of 1842. The General Council selected several different mission societies—one for each of the selected schools—so that no one society would dominate. Still, Choctaws were wary. Pitchlynn's cousin Israel Folsom, a fellow member of the General Council, wrote, "Peter, let us be cautious." Referring to the aftermath of the Panic of 1837, the first US depression, Folsom continued, "Times are hard among the whites and they are aching for the money—we will find a great many are wolves in sheep's clothing who have bit more often than we."[6]

Choctaws took the risk because they wanted to dramatically expand schooling, to create a comprehensive educational system that would serve nearly every member of their nation. At the top were six academies, one male and one female institution for each of the three districts. Peter Pitchlynn sent his eldest son Lycurgus to the most prestigious male academy, Spencer, which boasted a handsome campus with three whitewashed wood-frame dorms, one of which was named "Pitchlynn Hall." Lycurgus's coursework, like that of students at the five other academies, mirrored that of white academies, and was very similar to the upper-level coursework at Choctaw Academy: geography, grammar, philosophy, US and ancient history, chemistry, algebra, geometry, trigonometry, and Latin. Peter Pitchlynn told his son to study hard, to read about the laws created by his ancient Greek namesake, for, one day, he expected Lycurgus to "stand by my side in the Council of the Nation."[7]

Pitchlynn and the General Council sought to provide their most promising youth with an education equal or superior to that in Western nations, while accommodating the needs and customs of Choctaws. The trustees set the school term to run from October to early July, so that students could return to their families for summer vacation. This break enabled students to help their families with the summer harvest and to take part in its associated religious festival, the Green Corn Ceremony. Meanwhile, the Building Committee selected academy sites in heavily settled areas so that many students could continue to live with their families rather than board at school. Annual examinations, which at Choctaw Academy had served as a showcase for a white audience, became festive events for Indian families. Each July, kin and tribal leaders arrived the night before, camped out, and then feasted at the dining halls before cheering on their children, who, depending on the exercise, answered questions and recited speeches in Choctaw, English, or Latin. Tremendously popular, the six academies typically had waiting lists that exceeded one hundred students. "Schools! Schools!" was the common cry, "the great subject among the Choctaws," according to one teacher. "Inquiries are often made—'When can you give us a school teacher?' "[8]

Figure 12.2 Wheelock Female Academy, the first Choctaw school established in Indian Territory. Seen here in the late 1880s. Muriel Wright Collection, Courtesy of the Research Division of the Oklahoma Historical Society.

Because the academies could accommodate only about 10 percent of those who sought admission, most Choctaws went to local schools, which came in two varieties. The first, called "neighborhood schools," ran five days a week, while "weekend schools" served adults and children who worked during the week. Typically located in one- or two-room log cabins, these schools were built by local community members, who petitioned the General Council for funding. Soon, every town and most small villages had local schools, which focused mostly on the basics— reading, writing, and arithmetic—but, unlike white common schools or the new Choctaw academies, the teachers were nearly all Choctaw, and they instructed students mostly in their native language. Lavinia Pitchlynn, Peter's eldest child, became a schoolteacher, presiding over both neighborhood and weekend schools near their family home at Eagletown. At the neighborhood school, Lavinia's pupils included her brother Lycurgus and other youngsters bound for the academies as well as local children who would return to their family farms after mastering the basics. Even more diverse were weekend schools. There, thirty-year-olds sat next to small children, helping each other through spelling exercises. Because local schools were widespread and offered instruction in Choctaw, they were particularly instrumental in democratizing education.[9]

With their new school system, the Choctaws became one of the first nations in the world to offer equal access to education for girls and women. As Israel Folsom argued to fellow members of the General Council, "Our Nation have been mistaken in thinking to improve and civilize the people by educating the boys only." The "female school," Folsom argued, "is more necessary for the Nation than the boys— because the girls have been neglected so long." While the old mission system admitted girls, advanced female students had no opportunity to pursue higher education. The General Council, eager to remedy this mistake, overwhelmingly voted in favor of a resolution to offer girls and women equal access to co-educational neighborhood and weekend schools and to create three female academies, a number equivalent to those for males. In part, the Choctaws were influenced by American notions of republican motherhood. In his conversations with the secretary of war, Peter Pitchlynn echoed US rhetoric regarding education for women: "Intelligent mothers rear up enlightened and intelligent children, they are the first to plant good seed in the minds of the young, and make impressions the most indelible." Choctaw leaders believed that female education was key to maintaining their status as a "civilized" and "enlightened" nation. But the empowerment of women also resonated with traditional Choctaw values, which helps explain the popularity of female schooling even among cultural conservatives. Since time out of mind, Choctaw women had been heads of household, clan mothers, farmers, political advisors, and bearers of culture. To a matrilineal people, educating women simply made sense.[10]

Mary Rhoda Pitchlynn attended the most prestigious of the female academies, Wheelock. Site of the first Choctaw Christian service after removal, Wheelock boasted a handsome white chapel, newly constructed sandstone dorms and classrooms, and fresh spring water, a rarity in Indian Territory. Mary Rhoda, "sassy" and beautiful, was Peter's favorite child, a fact that he made no effort to hide. "Rhoda is better than all of you—and smarter, too," Peter wrote to his son Lycurgus. "I know she is." His father and sister so infuriated Lycurgus that he vowed to visit Wheelock to watch their annual examinations. Lycurgus never recorded the results—this fact, itself, may be telling—but others were astonished by what they saw at Wheelock. "I have never heard any Indians speak and pronounce the English language so correctly as they do," the Choctaws' agent wrote to the commissioner of Indian affairs. Mary Rhoda Pitchlynn was singled out for special praise, as Peter Pitchlynn, in his capacity as superintendent of schools, discovered when he inspected Wheelock: "the most outstanding examination," "the most talented girl that has ever been at Wheelock"! Peter delighted in recording Mary Rhoda's accolades and in passing them on, relentlessly, to Lycurgus. Obviously, Peter intended this as a motivational technique, but for Lycurgus, the sting came from knowing that much of it was true. Lycurgus never excelled the way that Mary Rhoda did, and, with the exception of some womanly arts—spinning and weaving, needlework— the curriculum at Wheelock matched that at Spencer.[11]

The new school system also catered to all classes of Choctaws—not just the rich or well connected. While most schools in the United States were still private academies, too costly for the majority of white families, the Choctaw Nation developed a modern public school system, which charged nothing for tuition or books. The Choctaw Nation, drawing from its education annuity, could cover everything except boarding. While local schools were within walking or riding distance for most Choctaws, fewer could easily reach the six national academies. Poor children often worked to pay for boarding, and determined groups of students sometimes banded together and built a cabin where they could live together during the school week. To further aid poor and middling families, the General Council took several steps to democratize access to the six academies, decreeing that each family could send no more than one child at a time to the national academies, that the two flagship institutions should admit students from across the Choctaw Nation in numbers representing the relative population of each district, and that all the academies should reserve one-tenth of their slots for orphans whose board would be paid by the Nation. While not perfectly implemented—the Pitchlynn example demonstrates that elite families often sent more than one member to the academies—the new school system came very close to achieving the General Council's aim to ensure that "every Choctaw shall enjoy the blessings of education."[12]

Choctaw Academy graduates, noting the difficulty with which their monolingual peers had struggled back in Kentucky, ensured that their new school system would teach in Choctaw as well as English. Neighborhood and weekend schools, which catered to beginners, focused largely on reading and writing in Choctaw, which took monolingual speakers only a "little labor" to learn. Even the academies, however, attracted many monolingual speakers, so they included several bilingual courses to help beginners ease into English. In contrast to both Choctaw Academy and the old mission system, most of the teachers under the new system were Choctaws who were proficient in their native language, English, and sometimes a third tongue like Latin, Greek, or French.[13]

Before the Civil War, the Choctaws produced eleven million printed pages, a publishing boom supported by the expansion of literacy. The movement began in the 1820s, when missionaries partnered with bilingual Choctaws to create spelling books and a hymnal. In the 1840s, demand rose dramatically, as teachers sought out texts for the monolingual Choctaws they taught at neighborhood and weekend schools.

Newly printed works included the Bible and other religious tracts, plus original hymns composed by the Choctaw preacher Allen Wright. Other, more secular works catered specifically to the new schools and included grammar and arithmetic textbooks. Initially, such books were published in US cities like Boston and Cincinnati, but by 1848, the Choctaws had established their own press at Doaksville, which also turned out copies of the first Choctaw newspaper, the *Choctaw Telegraph*. Edited by Daniel Folsom, who had been a monitor at Choctaw Academy, the bilingual weekly featured local, continental, and global content, plus financial coverage, literary sketches, and more.[14]

As Daniel Folsom's editorial career demonstrates, the expansion of education led to new job opportunities for Choctaw graduates of Choctaw Academy and the mission schools. Teachers included women like Lavinia Pitchlynn, who was only seventeen when she began to teach at neighborhood and weekend schools in Eagletown and Mountain Fork, near her family's home. Nearby, in the Kiamichi Mountains, Choctaw Academy graduate Alfred Wade taught a class of sixty-two at a popular neighborhood school. Like most other Choctaw teachers, Wade employed the Lancastrian system, which resonated with Choctaws' appreciation of collectivism and group learning, while enabling Wade to address the diverse skill set of his class. Teaching in both English and Choctaw, Wade focused on bilingual literacy as well as his favorite subject, mathematics. Wade was one of dozens of Choctaw Academy graduates who taught in the new school system. Other teachers included Samuel Worcester, known as Okelumbee in his youth, who sought to prevent the corporal punishment he had witnessed in Kentucky. Thompson McKinney, who got a jump start on his career by serving as an assistant teacher at Choctaw Academy, explained that he relished the opportunity to come back to his own nation "to improve the rising generation."[15]

Because the Choctaws were the first Native nation to implement a comprehensive school system, they became educational leaders in Indian Territory. Peter Pitchlynn was fond of explaining to white and Indian audiences that by producing "schools and educated men," "we have acquired a name and character abroad and are now placed in advance of all the nations of red people in point of civilization." Before 1842,

Pitchlynn had to add a caveat: "the Cherokees only excepted." In the early nineteenth century, boosted by their mission schools, newspaper, constitution, famous intellectuals, and victory before the US Supreme Court, the Cherokees were widely regarded as the most "civilized" Indian nation. After a minority faction signed a removal treaty in 1835, however, the Cherokee Nation plunged into a decade-long civil conflict marked by violence, suspicion, and widespread unrest. Although the Cherokee Nation passed a Public School Act in 1841, the plan was not implemented until the 1850s. One elite Cherokee explained, "In my own country there is a continual excitement that is a great check to education." Preferring to send his son to an Indian school rather than a white institution where he would surely face racial prejudice, this Cherokee father negotiated with Peter Pitchlynn so that his son could attend Choctaw schools. Some families from neighboring tribes followed this path, paying the Choctaw Nation small fees for tuition and board.[16]

Drawing inspiration from the Choctaw public school system, other Native nations began to plan their own. As the Choctaws' federal agent told the commissioner of Indian affairs, "The idea of creating schools themselves, in their own country, under their own control and supervision, has had great effect upon the adjoining tribes." Soon after Choctaw Academy closed, all the tribal nations that had sent children there sought to redirect their education annuities to develop their own schools. The last to do so were the Seminoles, who, in the past, had repeatedly and emphatically told their agent, "We don't *care* if the Government will put a school among us as once was *promised*, it will be for the *mothers* to say, if they can *spare their children*." In 1848, the Seminole clan mothers finally allowed missionaries in to teach and, the following year, they built a school of their own. Even nations that had previously shown little interest in schooling, like the Kansas and Mdewakanton Dakota, began to build academies.[17]

Although the Choctaw educational system remained the most extensive, other nations adapted aspects of the Choctaw model, negotiating contracts with one or more mission societies and using their education annuities as leverage to command influence. A typical contract stated, "These schools shall be subject at all times to such directions and control as the National Council may see proper to exercise." In defiance of the US government, which preferred Protestant missionaries, Native nations including the Potawatomi, Osage, and Miami partnered with Catholic religious societies. Even before their contract with Choctaw Academy expired, Creek chiefs began to interview and hire teachers for their new schools. As the Osage planned their national academy, they set the school term to allow for a break long enough to allow children to accompany their families on summer hunts. Native nations were determined to ensure that the schools of Indian Territory served Indian interests.[18]

Many Choctaw Academy alumni helped shape these schools as trustees, parents, and teachers. Among the Miamis who fought to regain control of their nation's education annuity was George Hunt, who had escaped Kentucky with the Chinn women in 1835. His co-conspirator, the Potawatomi John Jones, became an influential teacher. A strong advocate for "the New System," Jones traveled throughout the Great Lakes and Indian Territory, encouraging bilingualism and the recruitment of Native faculty. In 1849, with the help of John Jones, John Tipton, Joseph Bourassa, and other Choctaw Academy alumni, the Potawatomis opened two national academies.[19]

In creating their new educational system, Choctaws were not merely imitating their American neighbors but rather positioning themselves at the vanguard of a worldwide movement to democratize access to education. Even in the United States, which gained an international reputation for liberal, co-educational schooling, only three states, Massachusetts, Delaware, and Pennsylvania, established free public schools before the Choctaws. Peter Pitchlynn studied the reforms of Horace Mann, educational innovator and secretary of the board of the most highly regarded American school system, the one in Massachusetts. While Pitchlynn and other Choctaws kept track of their US neighbors' educational developments, they ultimately took a more global view. One instructor at Koonsha Female Academy declared that he looked forward to developing "a school that will not be inferior to institutions of the same kind in New England or any other England." In a speech to fellow Choctaws on patriotism, Peter Pitchlynn attempted to cajole rural farmers to send their children to school by citing the example of Prussia, where the law dictated that all children must attend. In that country, Pitchlynn noted, recalcitrant fathers could be imprisoned for failing to comply. Foreign educators and missionaries watched the Choctaw experiment with interest. Some predicted that the Choctaws would soon "vie with the most enlightened nations on our globe."[20]

Eventually, the General Council endorsed Pitchlynn's plea to make schooling compulsory, one of many signs that their education system had more in common with progressive nations like Prussia than nearby US states. Kentucky, for example, did not establish public schools until 1850. During the years of Choctaw Academy, only one in ten white children in Kentucky had attended primary school, a statistic common throughout the South and West. Schooling provided by the Choctaws and other Indian nations was markedly better than what Arkansas, Texas, and, later, Oklahoma Territory could offer. Reluctant to turn away the dozens of white children who kept turning up at their schools, but unwilling to pay for the education of foreigners, the nations of Indian Territory developed a policy: non-citizens could attend Indian schools, but they had to pay a small fee for tuition and books, generally a dollar per month. A senior army officer who toured Indian Territory noted that the pupils' English was "free from many prominent defects among our border people, West and South." Their literacy, he noted, was deeply impressive—"I mean for any school."[21]

The fact that Choctaws admitted white children to their schools demonstrates that they had not entirely severed educational ties with their US neighbors. Some in Indian Territory had dreamed of creating a "Choctaw University," but the proposed institution never materialized. Instead, under the Schools Act of 1842, the General Council decided to use some of the funds formerly expended at Choctaw Academy to send forty of their most promising youth abroad to college or professional schools. Superintendent of Schools Peter Pitchlynn helped place students at a broad range of institutions. After excelling at Delaware College, Allen Wright went to divinity school at Union Theological Seminary and later became a renowned teacher and minister in Indian Territory, offering instruction in Latin, Greek, English, and Choctaw. Although Lycurgus

Pitchlynn never matched Wright's grades, he, too, went on to professional school. While studying law in Tennessee, Lycurgus learned, among other things, "The greatest recommendation in Tennessee for any public office is the man that has the most children and can tell the nastiest anecdote." In 1854, Joseph Pitchlynn Folsom became the first Choctaw to graduate from Dartmouth; he then returned to the Choctaw Nation to practice law. Women, too, were among the Choctaws who went away to college. Pitchlynn's daughter Mary Rhoda attended Southern Masonic Female College in Covington, Georgia, where she earned many demerits for mischievous behavior, but also high marks in moral philosophy, chemistry, and rhetoric. From the mid to late nineteenth century, Choctaws could be found at colleges throughout the United States, including Wesleyan Female College in Georgia, Roanoke College in Virginia, the Arkansas School for the Deaf, Georgetown in the District of Columbia, and Yale in Connecticut.[22]

Despite prevailing racial attitudes, many institutions accepted Indian students. Responding to booming American demand for higher education, hundreds of colleges sprang up in the mid-nineteenth century, though, having overestimated the market, many would not last. Many college deans knew that many Indian nations possessed a wealth of resources, including capital especially reserved for education. As Superintendent Pitchlynn visited various campuses, considering where to place Choctaw scholars, college officials competed with one another, touting their virtues and offering fee discounts.[23]

Many institutions clamored for Indian money, but actual Indians were not always greeted with the same degree of enthusiasm. Zach Colbert, a Chickasaw who needed to improve his Latin before entering college, enrolled at the Alger Institute in Connecticut and was astonished when the school would not place a white roommate with him. Lonely and bored, he left school shortly thereafter. Choctaw Lewis Garland noted that "friendly feelings" abounded at the Marietta Institute in Ohio, though when local residents discussed a nearby mound site, they maintained that an "unknown" race, some "people more civilized than the Indians," built it. Peter Pitchlynn Jr., a self-proclaimed ladies' man and hell-raiser, generally enjoyed his brief stint at Oxford College (now Emory University), though he did tell his father about a bizarre incident with his peers. When young Pitchlynn first arrived, before he found a boarding house, he stayed in a hotel with some other students. Having heard that an Indian had enrolled, the students speculated as to "where that Indian was." All the while, Peter wrote, "I was sitting in the room." Like other elite Choctaw men who traveled abroad, Peter was probably "perfectly at ease in black coat, pants, vest, polished boots." Such an out-fit, a white contemporary noted, was so at odds with American stereo-types about Indians that it would have enabled Peter to walk "unnoticed through any of our streets."[24]

In their quest for higher education, Native Americans endured rac-ism, homesickness, even the possibility of death far from home, costs that they bore to improve their own prospects or enhance the power of their people. They were not seeking to become more "white" but rather to embrace modernity, to survive and even thrive in a changed world. The commissioner of Indian affairs noted that Native people had embraced "the progressive spirit of the age . . . which it seems is confined to no particular race." Choctaws took advantage of a communications revolution made possible by improvements in transport and technol-ogy, subscribing to American periodicals like the *New Orleans Picayune*, *North American Review*, and *National Intelligencer*, and reading famous American authors like Daniel Webster and Washington Irving. In 1848, Sampson Folsom reported that "everyone in the [Choctaw] Nation" was anxious to learn the outcome of the Whig convention, even though none could vote in the upcoming presidential election. Torn between two candidates, the warrior, "Rough & Ready" Zachary Taylor versus "the Great Pacificator" and consummate statesman Henry Clay, Folsom suggested that the American system of governance might be improved if they adopted an ancient Choctaw mode of governance, with the execu-tive branch split between a civil chief who promoted peace at home and a war chief who battled external enemies.[25]

Indians discussed such issues in their homes, debating societies, and council houses, but they also shared their perspectives with outsiders. While still an undergraduate at Delaware College, Allen Wright gave popular temperance lectures in Philadelphia. Jacob Pitchlynn Folsom was one of several Dartmouth graduates who spoke at the 1854 com-mencement. Combating prevailing stereotypes, Folsom titled his speech

"The Indian of Fiction and of History," and, according to local newspapers, it was the crowd's favorite that day. Peter Pitchlynn traveled across the United States on the lyceum circuit, educating Americans about Choctaw history, culture, schooling, and governance. Educated Indians eagerly engaged the outside world, but did so critically, never losing sight of their own tribal inheritance.[26]

⚜

Referring to his people's educational feats, George Harkins declared, "I hope the day is rolling around when that detested being called the Indian and savage will stand on the same footing with the whites." Two decades earlier, Harkins, a star orator at Choctaw Academy, had given a convocation speech full of optimism about his people's future "amidst our white brethren." Since then, Harkins had experienced racial prejudice in ways subtle and overt. Harkins had cast a critical eye over crowded dorms, protested after John Riddle was expelled for interfering as an overseer whipped a slave, testified before Congress about financial mismanagement at Choctaw Academy, and castigated Indian removal as illegal and immoral. Indians' educational goals had shifted since the early days of Choctaw Academy. Leaders like Harkins were, perhaps, even more driven to demonstrate Indians' intellectual equality with whites, though they no longer expected to enjoy the kind of dual citizenship that James McDonald had imagined. Instead, Choctaws and other Indian nations embarked on a separate project of nation building.[27]

Native people restructured their nations, moving away from kinship-based polities toward modern nation-states. For the Choctaws and Cherokees, in particular, this process began earlier in the nineteenth century, with the advent of republican governments created by democratic elections and regulated by written constitutions. Removal, however, was a major turning point, dissolving hopes of sharing power under the US federalist system while encouraging Indians to think creatively about their separate destiny. In the aftermath of removal, the Choctaws and many other Indian people redoubled their efforts at state-building because they saw transformation as necessary for survival in the modern world. When speaking to groups of fellow Choctaws, Peter Pitchlynn cast political changes as revision, not revolution. The Choctaws developed a republican constitution that created a three-branch government. In the executive branch, hereditary mikos were replaced by three democratically elected chiefs who represented each district. The Constitution of 1860 further consolidated power by creating a single principal chief. The legislative branch was embodied in the General Council, formerly composed of captains who represented powerful lineages but now staffed by elected representatives. Laws, once handed down orally, were now printed in Doaksville and disseminated throughout the nation and beyond. Perhaps the most novel branch was the judicial. Before removal, families of victims primarily dealt with matters of crime and punishment, but in Indian Territory the Choctaw Nation developed an extensive judicial system overseen by a Supreme Court.[28]

Choctaw Academy alumni were instrumental in revising Choctaw governance, dominating every branch from the 1850s through the 1880s. Principal Chiefs included Alfred Wade, owner of the treasured math workbook, and jack-of-all-trades Peter Pitchlynn. Adam Christie, a prize-winning essayist, served as a member of the General Council, becoming Speaker for his district. Among the first Supreme Court justices was John Page, a monitor who served as a leader during the student protests. Thompson McKinney, too, had been active in those protests. McKinney, like many graduates, later took on myriad positions in his nation, though his career was among the most distinguished. An assistant teacher at Choctaw Academy, McKinney continued teaching in the Choctaw Nation, then served as a National School Board Trustee, tribal diplomat, and, finally, Principal Chief.[29]

Schools played a crucial role in the way Indian leaders reimagined their nations. When the Chickasaws began to build their own national academies, the superintendent of schools declared, "Our object in all this is to teach, not only our scholars, but the Nation." Education, traditionally the province of the Indian family, had become a service financed and organized by the national governments. That privilege engendered obligation. Students, knowing that their schooling had been supported by their national treasuries, stated again and again that they felt compelled to "be useful to my people." Joseph Pitchlynn Folsom, who attended mission schools and Choctaw Academy before going to Dartmouth, felt a mixture of accomplishment and anxiety a few months before his college graduation, worrying that people back home "will kill me with such questions as these: 'What do you expect to do? What will you make of yourself, a minister, a doctor, a lawyer? What can you do? What *will* you do anyhow?'" Graduates like Folsom were expected to become the professional backbone of modern Indian nations.[30]

The meaning and purpose of education exerted a powerful influence on both the individual and collective psyche, but schools were also focal points of nationhood in a more physical sense. The Choctaws' flagship male academy, Spencer, developed a lending library open to all Choctaw citizens. Spencer and other national academies often hosted meetings of the district councils or even the Choctaw General Council. Meanwhile, local interest groups met at neighborhood schools, discussing district concerns and drafting petitions (usually in Choctaw) that they sent to the General Council. When the Choctaw council house was destroyed during the Civil War, the legislature moved to nearby Armstrong Academy. Particularly in the aftermath of traumatic events like removal and the Civil War, whose attendant violence and dislocation tore at traditional ties of kin and community, schools emerged as the vital heart of a surviving nation, touchstones of support, points of pride, sources of self-understanding, and augurs of future promise.[31]

The rise of Indian school systems inaugurated an era of prosperity—the so-called Golden Age of Indian Territory—that lasted until the Civil War. While acknowledging the tragic loss of the Choctaw homeland, Peter Pitchlynn declared of Indian Territory: "This is our country, it is our home and we love it." In addition to schools, the emigrants built national capitols, council houses, mills, churches, and ceremonial grounds. Major towns like Doaksville boasted shops, including a blacksmith, tailor, carpenter, shoemaker, cabinetmaker, and loommaker, in addition to Henry Folsom's medical practice. All across Indian Territory, Choctaw Academy graduates like Folsom owned and worked in such businesses, forming the core of the Native middle class. Capitalizing on their proximity to the Oregon Trail, Potawatomis like Joseph Bourassa built toll bridges, ferries, inns, horseracing tracks, and taverns, and they bought extra goods from travelers who had overpacked, reselling their discards at a profit. Adam Nail, the Choctaw Academy doctor who led the student rebellion, built a practice in Indian Territory, inspiring his son, grandson, and two great-grandsons to follow in his footsteps. Even as he gained professional respectability, Nail remained a whistleblower, critiquing those who seemed to get rich at the expense of their neighbors. Those on the receiving end of Nail's attacks decorated their houses with expensive carpets, mahogany furniture, and Chickering pianos. In "domestic comforts," one traveler noted, wealthy Indians were "not merely rivaling but absolutely excelling many of the whites along the border."[32]

Despite the prosperity of its scattered towns, Indian Territory's economic development was primarily a rural endeavor. Native nations regarded land as collective domain, which meant that all citizens could start farms or ranches and then sell or consume the products of their labor. While portions of the new Choctaw homeland were rocky or arid,

Figure 12.3 Choctaw Academy alumnus Robert M. Jones and his wife Susan Colbert, ca. 1870. Jones operated twenty-eight trading posts, two steamboats, and six plantations. At the height of Jones's wealth, he owned three hundred slaves, making him one of the largest slaveholders in North America. Robert L. Williams Collection, Courtesy of the Research Division of the Oklahoma Historical Society.

the lowlands contained good farmland. Surveying the prairies around the Red River, George Harkins said that they reminded him of "the rich lands about Lexington, Kentucky." In the grasslands, families raised horses, cattle, and hogs. They farmed the alluvial soils near the rivers, and by 1842, a decade after removal, crop yields in Indian Territory were finally respectable, thanks to much back-breaking labor and a period of merciful weather. Continuing a tradition practiced by their ancestors for over a thousand years, Native people in Indian Territory grew corn as their main food crop, but they increasingly relied on a newer cash crop: cotton. As Native farmers discovered, the climate of eastern Indian Territory supported the cultivation of short-staple cotton, which they baled and shipped down the Red River for sale in the port of New Orleans.[33]

~❧ 9 ❧~

By supporting the education of females and non-elites, the Choctaw Nation extended some rights of citizenship to a broader range of people, but people of African descent were not among the beneficiaries. Slavery grew dramatically in mid-nineteenth-century Indian Territory. Fewer than 600 slaves removed with the Choctaws, but, on the eve of the Civil War, that number had quadrupled to over 2,300, a trend replicated in the Cherokee, Chickasaw, and Creek nations. During removal, the US government had encouraged this development by designing slaves as one of the only forms of "movable property" able to accompany Indians to their new western lands. Accelerating a project begun in the East, the Choctaw government signaled its commitment to racial slavery by enacting a series of laws designed to enhance the power of masters while limiting that of slaves and even free blacks. In the 1830s and 1840s, the General Council decreed that no person of African descent could become a citizen or hold office and that foreign free blacks could not emigrate to the Choctaw Nation. Under these new laws, slaves could not own guns, and they could be whipped by the Lighthorse police for "infringing on any of the Choctaw rights." The General Council went further than Kentucky by declaring "teaching slaves how to read, to write, or to sing in meeting houses or schools, or in any open place, without the consent of the owner, or allowing them to sit at table with him, shall be sufficient ground to convict persons of favoring the principals and notions of abolitionism."[34]

The Choctaw Nation, like other slaveholding societies, left much to masters' discretion, which meant that, in practice, Choctaws maintained a wide range of relationships with people of African descent. Although the General Council outlawed it, many blacks demanded access to the nation's new school system and, though strictly barred from the national academies, they enrolled in local schools. Some free blacks attended neighborhood schools, while enslaved people, as time permitted, went to weekend schools. Peter Pitchlynn was among the Choctaw masters who encouraged literacy, at least among some of his slaves. Because Pitchlynn traveled frequently, he depended on these slaves to manage his property, especially after his children left home. In beautiful penmanship, Pitchlynn's enslaved overseer Solomon kept his master abreast of local news, requested supplies, and projected yields for cotton, potatoes, corn, and pumpkins. But on the Pitchlynn plantation, literacy extended outside the trusted overseer. Pitchlynn's slaves also wrote to family members living in other parts of the nation, and read and interpreted the Bible, among other books, for themselves. The pursuit of such education was facilitated by the relative autonomy that enslaved people enjoyed during Pitchlynn's frequent absences, a circumstance that led some Choctaws to claim that Pitchlynn had "a big plantation of free negroes" and was thereby "violating the Laws of the Nation."[35]

Overall, however, African Americans were more likely to be found working on the grounds of Choctaw schools than learning inside of them. To build their national academies, the Choctaws and other Southern Indian nations leased slave labor from nearby Indian masters. Labor was scarce and expensive in Indian Territory, and even abolitionist ministers associated with the schools resorted to this strategy. Slaves cleared scrub oak and cottonwood trees; sawed wood; built classrooms, libraries, springhouses, and dorms; and prepared nearby fields for cultivation. After applying finishing touches—painting the clapboards, affixing signs for "Pitchlynn Hall" and the like—some slaves remained on campus to maintain the buildings and grounds and to work in the nearby fields that fed the students.[36]

Among the slaves at Spencer Academy was Wallis Willis, a musician who composed the famous song "Swing Low, Sweet Chariot." Alexander

Reid, a teacher at Spencer, transcribed the lyrics and melodies and later taught them to the Fisk University choir. The song became a global sensation after the Fisk choir toured the United States and Europe, performing at Queen Victoria's Golden Jubilee, but its roots remained in Indian Territory, born of the experiences of an enslaved man. Willis was inspired by the nearby Red River, which he likened to the biblical river Jordan. Watching the muddy river make its slow, meandering way toward the Mississippi, Willis imagined that he, too, would one day be carried far away from his earthly labors, taken to his eternal reward in a chariot like the prophet Elijah.[37]

Marginalized within Indian nations, some African Americans sought freedom elsewhere. Indian Territory was born in a changing borderlands region, neighboring the newly independent Republic of Mexico and just north of its rebellious state Coahuila y Tejas. Slaves knew that Mexico held out the promise of both land and liberty, thanks in part to visiting Mexican soldiers seeking new recruits to help them subdue the Texans. Though debt peonage still ensnared many Indians, Mexico—with the exception of Texas—had banned black slavery in 1829. Choctaw Academy alumnus Pierre Juzan was among those whose slaves escaped. According to Juzan, who lived in the Pushmataha District bordering Mexico, small groups of Mexicans were "discovered in the night prowling about my house," encouraging locals to abscond with them. After threatening Juzan's life, the visitors and four of his slaves fled southward. Juzan chased them southward, but, without a party of warriors at his side, would not cross the border. Juzan asserted that he did not fear Mexicans but rather the "hostile tribes" of Comanche that dominated northern Mexico. Whether or not they shared Juzan's fear of Comanches, so many slaves attempted escape into Mexico that one of the chief duties of the Choctaw Lighthorse police force became border patrol and slave catching.[38]

The chaotic aftermath of removal created opportunities for some slaves but misery for many others. An enslaved woman named Lucy never forgave her master Richard Harkins, a Choctaw Academy alumnus, for forcing her to leave behind many of her family members and move to a remote plantation, where he refused to give them days off to celebrate Christmas. One wonders about other aspects of Harkins's personality, given that members of the Pitchlynn family expressed anxiety when Peter's daughter Lavinia became engaged to him. Lavinia insisted on marrying Harkins, reprimanded her father for his long absences, and told him that she wanted a family life and a home. For twelve years, Lavinia built the lifestyle she had imagined, but that all changed one December day in 1858. Richard had set off after breakfast to look for a stray ox, but did not return for the midday meal. After Richard's horse was found wandering in a canebrake, the saddle rotated under its belly, Lavinia was "nearly crazy" with worry. Lavinia suspected Prince, a young enslaved man who had been acting strangely, and asked male family members to intervene. After the posse tied Prince to a stake and whipped him, Prince confessed, describing how he had asked Richard to help him roll over a log and then, when his master's back was turned, struck him repeatedly with the blunt end of an axehead. His aunt Lucy, Prince explained, had long begged him to do it. After he was untied from the stake, Prince led the posse to Richard's body, weighed down with a rock at the bottom of Little River, before jumping in to drown himself. Lavinia's brother-in-law cursed Prince, saying he had wanted "to roast the devil." Lucy "did not confess a thing," but she suffered the death the posse had planned for Prince, the traditional death of enemies taken in war, when she was burned beside Prince's body.[39]

Lycurgus Pitchlynn, Peter's eldest son, was a member of the posse and witnessed it all: Prince, after he led them to the deep place near Ashley Ford in the Little River, screaming like a madman, claiming that he had seen the ghost of his master; Richard's bloated body and broken head, with a mouth full of leaves; his sister, the schoolteacher, turned into a "roaring maniac," claiming, "It was the white blood in Lucy that planned the death of her husband." Lycurgus wrote his father, "I wish to God you would sell every accursed negro you have or send them to Liberia." Richard Harkins's murder turned Lycurgus against slavery, but he could not imagine incorporating those who might be liberated into his own nation. Citing violence and fears over amalgamation, Lycurgus, like many Americans before him, deemed separation the best course.[40]

❧❧

As they rebuilt in Indian Territory, Choctaws scrutinized inhabitants of their own nation, but they also thought critically about their relationship to other nations. Due to their progress in "civilization," exemplified by their school system, the Choctaws came to see themselves as a beckon to the "wild Indians in the West" and mentors to other relocated eastern Indians. Even if their neighbors scoffed at Choctaws' self-aggrandizing rhetoric, they sought counsel from educated Choctaws. As the nations of Indian Territory developed court systems, Robert M. Jones, a Choctaw Academy graduate who became a teacher and a member of the board of trustees, added lawyer to his resume, defending clients of various tribal backgrounds. Noting Peter Pitchlynn's successes in dealing with the federal government, several other Indian nations hired Pitchlynn as an attorney. The first to do so were the Chickasaws, who instructed him to press claims for land and resources illegally taken during removal. Because the Chickasaw language was very similar to that of the Choctaws, Chickasaw tribal leaders also asked Pitchlynn to translate legal documents for them and act as an interpreter when they visited Washington. In return, the Chickasaw Nation paid Pitchlynn 15 percent of every dollar recovered from the federal government. Thereafter, visiting delegations from several Indian nations, including the Delawares and Wyandots, hired Pitchlynn to represent them as they negotiated treaties or sought redress.[41]

In the late 1840s, as the US Congress considered a bill that would unite all of Indian Territory under one territorial government, legal issues brought diverse tribes together once again. Through multi-tribal councils, ball games, and dances, the nations of Indian Territory had worked hard to overcome past conflicts and embrace brotherhood. Cherokee leaders urged "the rising generation" to "greet and receive each other as relations, and become united as one." At a great council, Mushulatubbee argued that after the US betrayals of the removal era, all Indian people should walk "the white path of Peace: may it reach far to the West, and long be travelled." These united nations used their collective power to oppose the proposed bill. Such a bill would invite a greater federal presence in Indian Territory and pave the way for thousands of new, non-Indian residents. Moreover, each nation wanted to maintain its own sovereignty, especially with regard to territorial integrity and the right to self-governance.[42]

On January 20, 1849, Peter Pitchlynn spoke against the bill before the US House of Representatives, remonstrating on behalf of the nations of

Indian Territory. Pitchlynn lectured Congress on the vast cultural differences that separated tribes, their varied languages, and their occupation of "different platforms in civilization." Pitchlynn's legal angle, though, was probably most effective. He explained that dissolving the national boundaries of Indian Territory's tribes would violate every one of their removal treaties and would, therefore, undermine the legality of those agreements. Pitchlynn concluded, "We wish simply to be let alone, and permitted to pursue the even tenor of our way." The Choctaw's plea swayed the House against the bill. For the time being, at least, the nations of Indian Territory were free to pursue their individual nationalisms, complete with school systems tailored according to each nation's means and preference.[43]

Around the same time that Alfred Wade's family donated his arithmetic book to the Oklahoma Historical Society, James Culberson preserved another Choctaw memory of removal. Culberson recorded the stories his father, Tushpa, told on his deathbed. Tushpa had been a boy of ten when Mississippi whites stormed into his village and burned down houses, threatening that delaying removal would bring further violence. As his family and neighbors prepared for the long journey, they selected Ishtaya, or Willis Folsom, to be the fire-bearer. Folsom gathered ashes from the village's sacred fire and carefully bundled them, so that they could be reignited, an ancient fire for a new town in Indian Territory. Packing seeds and what few possessions they could carry, the 100-member party set out for the West, sleeping on the damp ground in wet clothes, slogging knee-deep in muck through the swamps that surrounded the Mississippi River. When they finally reached the mighty river, two children fell off the raft, so Tushpa's brave father Kanchi dove in and rescued them. What happened next was seared into Tushpa's memory: his father, caught in the "swirling, twisting mass of brush, trees and refuse . . . never came to the surface again." Some were so disturbed by Kanchi's death that they wanted to return, but the party pushed on, making it to Indian Territory in 1834.

Fifty years later, it was Tushpa's dying wish that James "keep the family together and give them some chance for an education." Tushpa elaborated, linking education to being "a good citizen," saying that schooling would give Choctaws the ability to write their own histories, preserving stories like his. Fourteen-year-old James was already well prepared to comply. A student at Spencer Academy, James would graduate, then go to college in the United States, return home to enter politics, and eventually become attorney general of the Choctaw Nation. He married a schoolteacher and together they championed the education of all Choctaws.[44]

The story of Tushpa and his family reveals how, in just a few generations, schooling became central to Choctaw identity. Back in the early nineteenth century, all three Choctaw district chiefs had enthusiastically supported the introduction of mission schools, and Mushulatubbee had fostered the creation of Choctaw Academy. But early schools enrolled mostly elites like Alfred Wade. Tushpa came from an ordinary Choctaw family and never had an opportunity to go to school, a situation exacerbated by removal. Growing up in Indian Territory, Tushpa appreciated the way that his nation expanded access to schooling and was determined that his children and grandchildren would benefit from it. Other Choctaws echoed Tushpa's sentiments. One citizen, who had little formal education, wrote that he was desperate to send his son to school, for "I can not think of rasin him up in ignorance." A teacher at one of the female academies said that Choctaws repeatedly told him, in various ways, that they needed schools "to maintain their station among the nations of the earth." Peter Pitchlynn's nephew Hiram, who went on to earn his medical degree in Indiana, explained that education would allow him to "take my stand and be a man among men." Although Choctaw Academy could not sustain a shared great path, Indians used their experiences there to pave a different road. Education had become intertwined with the Choctaws' vision of themselves and their place in a changing world. In creating Indian schools controlled by Indians, Choctaws upheld education as a means to reclaim power.[45]

Conclusion

Paths to the Future

In 1846, fifteen years after leading one of the first removal groups to Indian Territory, Peter Pitchlynn returned to the land of his birth. He remembered, "Here I killed an alligator, there I killed a deer, here I slept one night, and then there was the spot my horse fell when I was bounding though the woods in full speed." The south wind passing through the tall pines made a soft moan, reminding Pitchlynn of the white wolf who, according to oral tradition, mourned the Nameless Choctaw and his lover. Going back to his family's home, Pitchlynn found that the old "cedar log mansion" was now occupied by a white family. They allowed Pitchlynn to come inside, and he scanned the house, noting that the interior was almost unchanged. Walking outside, Pitchlynn could still make out the imprint of a wayward cannonball that had struck the exterior wall during the War of 1812. The family graveyard was intact, though Pitchlynn must have suspected that, in time, undergrowth would hide the original markers.[1]

Further exploration revealed more profound changes. Surveying the plantations that had swallowed up the land of his birth, Pitchlynn felt like a mourner. Gone were the clusters of rivercane once full of deer and bears, and the tall oaks that shaded fishing spots along the creeks and rivers. The trees had long since been girded and left to die, replaced by vast cotton fields worked by hundreds of slaves, whose work songs rang out like dirges across the ravaged delta. "This once was a healthy country, but it is now a very sickly one," Pitchlynn lamented. "I scarcely know any of the places which were once familiar to me."[2]

Pitchlynn finally found comfort when he visited Nanih Waiya, the Choctaws' sacred mound. Walking the winding earthen rampart that led up to the mound's eighty-foot summit, Pitchlynn imagined that he could see generations of his matrilineal kin before him, and he recalled the stories his people told about that ancient time. Long ago, the Choctaws lived in the west, a land plagued by disease and violence. The chiefs and medicine men took action, using a sacred pole to lead the people on an epic journey in search of a new home. The journey took many years and claimed so many lives that the dead came to outnumber the living. Choctaws refused to leave their kin behind, so they carried their remains on their backs. Finally, the sacred pole led them to a place with rich soil and plentiful game, and here they constructed a mound to contain the bones of their people. Nanih Waiya means "bending mountain," but Choctaws also affectionately called her Iholitopa Ishki or "Beloved Mother," noting how she helped them remake their nation in a new place.[3]

Some oral traditions suggested that if the Choctaw people strayed from Nanih Waiya, the nation would die, but removal had come, and the nation had survived. Choctaws had overcome the tumult of the past and would persist into the future. The world was fundamentally a place of change, and Choctaws could and would change with it. Even though American imperialism had forced them into diaspora, Peter Pitchlynn knew that they would survive. The true lesson of Nanih Waiya was that the Choctaws were a resilient people.[4]

For millions of Americans, the age of Jackson brought not freedom and opportunity but fracture and loss. Yet the story of Great Crossings also demonstrates that absolute power is an illusion. Of US imperialism, Pitchlynn remarked, "This is a new thing with us, but this is not the end." The Indians, settlers, and slaves who once lived at Great Crossings used their experiences to imagine new roles in a changed world.[5]

~≈≽~

Great Crossings could not accommodate the diverse dreams of those who converged there. Once heralded as "the land of promise," Kentucky's opportunities quickly narrowed. The wealthiest families owned vast estates, while most white men, though politically empowered, were poor and landless. With regard to people of color, Kentuckians diverged from earlier inclusive impulses to emphasize racial difference and hierarchy as Indians were "removed" and slavery expanded. The number of free African Americans declined over time, and they held fewer rights than the Revolutionary generation. In 1845, a white mob in Lexington attacked the office of Cassius Clay's *True American*, an anti-slavery newspaper, and then marched to a free black neighborhood, where they tarred and feathered an African American man. The perpetrators were dressed as Indians. The real Indians of Great Crossings were anomalous, lacking a place in an increasingly binary society. "Kentucky," Peter Pitchlynn concluded, "was not a proper place for Indians to live in." Many of those who came together at Great Crossings would take diverse paths into the expanding US empire, where they would attempt to find a new staging ground for their aspirations.[6]

Even elites like Richard Mentor Johnson sought opportunities in the next American West. After Choctaw Academy closed, Johnson was still in debt. First begging for, then demanding the "just patronage of the Government," Johnson reminded his colleagues, "I have fought for freedom and gained it for my country." Eventually, he wheedled $2,000 out of Congress, allegedly to recoup building expenses for Choctaw Academy dormitories. Like his accounts, Johnson's political fortunes had plummeted. He failed in his bid to become the 1844 Democratic presidential candidate and lost the Kentucky governor's race four years later. Turning his gaze west, Johnson offered his former Washington colleagues unsolicited advice, such as "extend the laws of the U.S. over citizens in Oregon." Great Britain's competing claim gave Johnson an opportunity to castigate his old foe as "the most grasping, the most presumptuous, the most tyrannical nation on earth." Johnson accepted leadership over the Oregon Convention held in Cincinnati, then offered to raise a company for the Mexican War, suggested that they might be paid by "working the mines of Santee Fee." Johnson claimed that he would also accept "a foreign mission to any point whatever," or "the office of Governor for Mexico, California, or new Mexico." His colleagues may have cringed. Certainly, they were unable to imagine complying with the desperate pleas of an old warrior, nearly seventy and beginning to suffer from dementia. Johnson finally regained elected office in 1850, ending his political career where it began, in the

Kentucky House of Representatives. He died of a stroke two weeks into his term.[7]

Other whites who had been associated with Choctaw Academy continued to look for opportunities in Indian affairs. Teacher Daniel Vanderslice sought an appointment as an emigration agent, telling the commissioner of Indian affairs that he would force the minority of Choctaws who remained in the Deep South to join their kin in Indian Territory. Whites were desperate to seize every acre of the emerging cotton kingdom, but most aspiring planters would be disappointed, for the best land was already sold. Back in 1830, after the Indian Removal Act was passed but before the Choctaws emigrated, their federal agent William Ward started to survey land and set aside choice plantations for his family members. Most successful was Junius Ward, the son of William Ward and his wife Sally, Richard Johnson's sister. Junius was among those whom Pitchlynn blamed for despoiling the Choctaw homeland, for he became a wealthy cotton planter in Mississippi. Junius still spent much of his time in Kentucky, using the proceeds of his Mississippi fortune to construct one of the grandest of antebellum mansions, Ward Hall, which

Figure C.1 Ward Hall, 1856. Clay Lancaster Slide Collection, Courtesy of the University of Kentucky Special Collections Research Center.

still stands in Georgetown. Capitalizing on their inside knowledge and connections, the Wards and their relations followed Junius down the river, developing cotton or sugar plantations on lands recently vacated by Indians.[8]

Though few would match the Wards' success, millions of Americans followed similar paths, seeking their fortunes in the Deep South and far West. It was not long before Americans discovered that the Corps of Topographical Engineers had been mistaken in characterizing Indian Territory as the "Great Desert," a place "almost wholly unfit for cultivation." By the mid-1840s, the region's long drought abated and environmental conditions improved. Texans moseyed into the Choctaw and Chickasaw nations, cutting timber and grass for their ever-growing cattle ranches, and selling their wares, including bootleg whiskey, in violation of both federal and Indian law. Other whites sought more permanent residence. Land speculators operating out of Arkansas advertised in newspapers throughout the South and Midwest, would sell plots in Indian Territory "subject to the extinguishment of Indian title." One observer noted how such schemes created panic in Indian Territory, calling to mind "in very vivid colours, the difficulties which they have had to encounter East of the Mississippi."[9]

In treaties, the United States pledged to set aside Indian Territory for Native nations who had suffered removal "to the end of time," but Indians noted with alarm how quickly signs of the apocalypse seemed to accumulate. In 1853, when Congress extended territorial status over Nebraska, Peter Pitchlynn protested, explaining that Indians there "hold it upon the same terms that we hold this country." When they heard that the federal government planned to extend jurisdiction over Indian Territory, the Choctaw chiefs and tribal council wrote a protest petition to the president: "We doubt whether a single man of our tribe ever emigrated without first receiving a distinct assurance that in the West, he would be forever secure from the operation of the whiteman's law." President James K. Polk, however, continued the legacy of fellow Democrat Andrew Jackson, asserting that the United States should extend its empire wherever Americans wished to settle.[10]

Indian removal was a pivotal event in US history because it established a precedent for invoking white supremacy to seize the lands of other peoples. The writer Ralph Waldo Emerson captured popular thought when he predicted, in 1844, that "the strong British race" would dominate the continent, seizing the American West and much of Mexico. In the aftermath of the Mexican War, the United States violated the Treaty of Guadalupe Hidalgo by denying the rights of citizenship to former Mexicans. Over the following decades, most Mexican Americans lost their land through fraud, violence, and lack of legal redress, methods that would have seemed familiar to Choctaws who tried to claim land in Mississippi under Article 14 of their removal treaty.[11]

No longer did politicians and intellectuals tout amalgamation as a means to create an inclusive empire. Anxieties over interracial sex, widely propagated during the election of 1836, mounted throughout the nineteenth century. In 1858, as Abraham Lincoln ran for Senate, many voters asked him about the future of African Americans. Lincoln assented that he could envision emancipation, but not equality. In one of his famous debates with Stephen Douglas, Lincoln remarked, "I do not understand that because I do not want a negro woman for a slave, I must necessarily want her for a wife." Lincoln continued, "I will add to this that I have never seen to my knowledge a man, woman, or child who is in favor of producing a perfect equality, social and political, between negroes and white men. I recollect of but one distinguished instance . . . Col. Richard M. Johnson." The Illinois crowd reportedly roared with laughter, incredulous that, not so long ago, a national political figure embraced such a radical vision of the American family.[12]

After Richard Mentor Johnson died, his brothers John and Henry went to the next court session in the state capital at Frankfort and testified that they were Richard's only two surviving siblings and, furthermore, that Richard "left no widow, children, father or mother living." In the eyes of the law, Richard Mentor Johnson and Julia Chinn were never legally married, and thus their children were illegitimate. Adaline had long since died, but Imogene stood to gain most of her father's remaining property, including thousands of acres of Bluegrass farmland. Unfortunately, like many other mixed-race children of white planters, Imogene was cheated out of much of her inheritance by white relatives.[13]

Imogene's parents must have feared this outcome, for they had already given her many tools to provide for herself and her family. Imogene and her husband Daniel Pence already owned considerable property, much of it sold or given to them by Richard. Employing the Italian method of bookkeeping taught to her by Thomas Henderson, Imogene kept track of her property in a ledger, proving a much more responsible accountant than her father. On the farm deeded to them by Richard, Imogene and Daniel built a two-story brick house in the neoclassical style, adorning the interior with elaborate woodwork. Over time, the Pences added to their holdings, buying adjacent acreage and a paper mill on the Elkhorn. The couple provided ably for their four children who lived to adulthood and their many grandchildren and great-grandchildren. In her ledger, Imogene carefully recorded the generous gifts that she and Daniel gave their descendants: a farm, the "Old Rogers' place," for their daughter Malvina upon her marriage to Robert Lee; two decades later, when the house belonging to Malvina and Robert's daughter Mary burned down, her grandparents provided furniture, food, livestock, and $720 toward a new home.[14]

Imogene and Daniel also built a schoolhouse on their property and hired a private teacher. By the time that they had grandchildren, Kentucky had developed a public school system, but the Pences likely feared racial prejudice. When their children were young, white mobs burned several free black schools in the Bluegrass region. Since the Pence children, legally speaking, were "white," it is more likely that their parents considered sending them to a white school. But local white children or even the teachers might antagonize the Pences, whose appearances ranged from fair blonds to those with darker complexions and wavy black hair. No matter their physical appearance, the Pences' ancestry was known to everyone in Scott County. As Richard had done when she was a child, Imogene might have wanted to control the circumstances of her children's education to minimize their exposure to racism and violence.[15]

While Richard Johnson's brothers John and Henry callously disinherited their niece, other members of the Johnson family maintained ties. Imogene and Daniel did business with William Johnson, Imogene's cousin, buying and selling land and mules. When Richard Mentor Johnson died, he left his house and farm at White Sulphur to Thomas W. Scott, the widower of his late daughter Adaline. Scott was supposed to hold the estate in trust for his and Adaline's son Robert Johnson Scott.

Thomas, however, sold the estate when he moved his family, which included a second wife and several children, to Illinois. The patriarch may have used the money to pay for Robert's education, for the boy would go on to become a doctor in Missouri. The buyer was Richard Mentor Johnson Jr. The son of Richard's brother James, Richard Jr. was his namesake's ward who, as a boy, had starred in the pageant that welcomed General Lafayette to Great Crossings. As an adult, Richard Jr. maintained ties with his cousin Imogene and the Pence family. He sold the White Sulphur estate to Daniel Pence, who owned it jointly with his sons-in-law, Robert Lee and Josiah Pence. Such extensive property-swapping suggests that at least some family on either side of the color line maintained cordial relations.[16]

Despite mounting racial prejudice, the Pences decided not to seek opportunities elsewhere. Their family ties, wealth, and education gave them enough power and opportunities in Great Crossings to build a satisfying life there. Josiah Pence, who owned a partial share of White Sulphur plantation, used the farm to develop and patent a horse-drawn seed-gatherer, and he later aided Cyrus McCormick in inventing the mechanical reaper. He and his wife Mary Jane lived a comfortable life-style, entertaining guests who included Frank and Jesse James. The Jameses' parents hailed from nearby Stamping Ground, and though Frank and Jesse had grown up in Missouri, they came back to Kentucky to visit family and friends. They chose to stay at the Pences' home because two of Josiah's brothers were members of the James gang, having ridden with Frank and Jesse during the Civil War in William Quantrill's infamous guerrilla unit. Although the descendants of Richard Johnson and Julia Chinn were likely shunned by many Bluegrass gentry, they were still connected to an expansive and empowering network that included planters, scientists, generals, and outlaws.[17]

The Pences were also bound by blood to many enslaved people, and yet their wealth and social position depended on slaveholding. Among the wedding gifts that the Pences gave to their children were enslaved people, typically one or two adults in their twenties and several children. These may have been nuclear families, for Imogene and Daniel tried not to break up families. They once went to great lengths to accommodate one of their slaves, John Samuels, whose wife's master moved with her and the children to Missouri. Eventually, Daniel Pence was able to sell John Samuels to a planter who lived eleven miles away from Samuels's wife. Soon thereafter, Samuels's master hired out his wife as a cook, so that the family got to live under one roof for the first time. This happy outcome made the Pences feel like benevolent masters, and the Samuels family certainly appreciated their efforts, passing down the story through the generations. Still, the story remains one rooted in human trafficking.[18]

Imogene Pence may have had half-brothers or half-sisters, for her father had relationships with other black women after her mother's death. Richard Johnson's colleagues noted his subsequent affairs with two of Julia Chinn's nieces, but oral tradition holds that there were others. Documentary evidence, too, suggests that Richard Johnson may have had a son from one of these unions. Following Richard Johnson's death, the Johnson family paid for the education of Theodore Jusan, a free man of color. Jusan's genealogy is unclear, but the 1850 census shows that one Malvina Jusan, a young "mulatto" woman, lived in Richard Mentor Johnson's household. The evidence is merely suggestive, but it is certainly possible that Theodore Jusan was the son of Richard Mentor Johnson and the grandson of the Choctaw Pierre Juzan, who, as a student at the Academy, had an affair with an enslaved woman named Dicy. As a young man, Jusan attended Elutherin College, a radical Indiana institution that was co-ed, integrated, and anti-slavery. Jusan left college to join the Union Army. He must have been fair in appearance, for he enlisted in in 1861, before black troops were admitted. He died on February 1, 1862, during the Battle of Green River in his home state of Kentucky.[19]

As a Union soldier, Theodore Jusan helped pave the way for the liberation of four million African Americans, though the path to meaningful citizenship was circuitous, beset by a thousand devils. A border state, Kentucky had been pro-Union during the war, yet many slaveholders resented emancipation. In 1866, the head of Kentucky's Freedmen's Bureau reported that black veterans were often "*scourged, beaten, shot at,* and driven from their homes and families." Kentucky's levels of anti-black violence, including lynching, rape, and the burning of freedmen's schools, rivaled that of the Deep South, as the Ku Klux Klan sought to use violence and intimidation to prevent African Americans from voting and exercising other civil rights. In the aftermath of the Civil War,

Kentucky abandoned its former image as an inclusive frontier state with moderate politics in favor of a neo-Confederate identity.[20]

In 1876, freedpeople in Great Crossings began to receive circulars urging them to become homesteaders on the high plains of northern Kansas. That very year, those lands had been ceded by representatives from the Lakota, Northern Cheyenne, and Arapaho nations. As Americans, North and South, sought to reconcile after the Civil War, they joined together to conquer the West. Paradoxically, the Plains Wars were waged in the name of brotherhood and peace, as Americans used violence to force Indians to cede vast swaths of these homelands and crowd onto reservations. For Native people of the Plains, Kansas was another lost homeland, a further compromise of autonomy. But when freedpeople of Great Crossings thought of the place, a different history came to mind: the days of Bleeding Kansas, when Jayhawkers and abolitionists had fought for free soil and free men. Maybe there was still a Promised Land somewhere in America.[21]

The freedpeople of Scott County were at the forefront of a massive black exodus to Kansas. Among those who boarded the westbound train on March 1, 1878, were former slaves who had been owned by Richard Johnson or his daughter Imogene: Mary Johnson, her son Joseph and his family; Thomas Johnson and his family; plus Beverly, Herring, Hiram, and Travis Samuels and their families. They paid the fare to Ellis, Kansas, then drove teams of horses and wagons for two days, finally arriving at their destination: Nicodemus. The town was named after a slave in early Jamestown who, according to the emigrants, "predicted that the white people would regret, some day, of having enslaved the colored people." Nicodemus, they said, was the first slave in America to earn his freedom.[22]

When the emigrants finally arrived, the auspiciously named town looked quite different from the earthly paradise of their imaginations. Many from Scott County, reared amid rolling hills, blue-green grass, and stands of white oak and hickory trees, were shocked by how hard the country looked. "My eyes ached from looking so far and seeing nothing," Elvira Williams remembered. "I wondered if we could live there." As their eyes adjusted, the emigrants noticed smoke rising out of the ground, which, they learned, came from the fires of the dugout shelters that served as housing. Some were so discouraged that they returned to

Kentucky, complaining bitterly of the lies they had been sold by the conductors of the "Nicodemus Town Company." Most emigrants stayed, however, and they succeeded in coaxing wheat out of the dry earth. Nicodemus quickly developed into a prosperous community of seven hundred, the most famous all-black town in the West.[23]

The settlers of Nicodemus saw education as a hallmark of true freedom. Before the war, as slaves in Kentucky, many had struggled to become literate, and some had succeeded. In their oral traditions, the people of Nicodemus proudly remembered the hemp factory slaves who, after their overseer departed each evening, taught themselves to read, write, and work sums. Others recalled how they had risked grave punishment to read treasured Bibles by candlelight after a long day's work. After emancipation, the people of Nicodemus wanted to make sure that their children would not have to go to such lengths to acquire an education. Just after the emigrants arrived in Kansas, they began holding informal classes in their newly constructed dugouts. In 1879, less than two years after Nicodemus was established, the first full school term commenced in a small stone house, which was full to bursting: all the benches were taken, and children lined the floor along every wall. Among those who served on the five-member board of trustees, financing the school and hiring teachers, was John Samuels, one of the former slaves who had worked in the hemp factory and later perfected his skills in a makeshift library in the woods. Financial constraints were challenging—teachers doubled as janitors, and children had to share textbooks and other supplies—but the trustees stabilized the school, and it eventually grew to include a junior high. Those who went on to high school traveled to nearby Hill City, and some later returned to work as teachers at Nicodemus.[24]

The school became the focal point of the community. Parents and other family members served as teachers and trustees. On Sundays and holidays, when school was not in session, the community gathered at the school to sing hymns and listen to lectures. Schoolhouses were more than just buildings in which children learned. A profound break from past oppression, schools were symbols of hope, pride, and endurance, where a people who had suffered a profound trauma could regroup to create a better future for themselves and their descendants.[25]

❧

Like the settlers of Nicodemus, many Eastern Indians moved to the West during the nineteenth century. Removal forced an Indian diaspora, displacing 100,000 Native people: A terrible many would not go far, their bodies interred in shallow graves by the road; most would make new homes and new nations in Indian Territory; some would travel farther still, seeking new lives in new corners of the American empire.

George Washington Trahern, a star student at Choctaw Academy, was among the most successful children of the diaspora. Orphaned as a toddler, "Wash" Trahern grew up with his maternal grandparents. Though his family had little, Trahern built "air castles" in his mind, as he later put it. The young Choctaw studied elocution, a traditional path to power among his people, one that he could also cultivate at Choctaw Academy. After graduating in 1838, Trahern went west, seeing Indian Territory for the first time—the scrubby cottonwoods, empty corncribs, graveyards. He did not linger.[26]

By the following year, Trahern was one of at least seven hundred Choctaws who had crossed the border to seek opportunities in the Republic of Texas. Like most of his countrymen, Trahern went to Texas primarily for economic reasons. Becoming a cowboy, Wash started a ranch with his sister and brother-in-law. In addition to herding cattle, the trio bought Spanish horses from Mexico and sold them at a profit in Texas. As the Traherns and other Choctaws discovered, the international border created opportunity but also conflict. Mexico, which still disputed Texan independence, sought new recruits for its army, and some Choctaws, seeking revenge for unpunished murders and thefts by the "lawless and unprincipled" Texans, were persuaded to join. Others expressed admiration for Sam Houston, the Texas president who had formerly lived among the Cherokees and married an Indian woman. Houston, in the words of one Choctaw, "tells the truth about the [US] Government, they have lied and defrauded the poor Indians ever since they commenced buying any lands from them." But perhaps no Choctaw went further in supporting Sam Houston than George Washington Trahern, who became a Texas Ranger. Texas was then a dangerous place—every man was then "a minute man," according to Wash Trahern, who said that he relished the opportunity to fight "Mexicans and Indians." The "Indians" were Comanches, fierce warriors who had dominated the southern Plains for a century. Master horsemen who hunted bison, Comanches were jarringly different from the Choctaws, who cursed the way those "wild Indians" raided their plantations. Wash Trahern, for one, reveled in his new life as a Texan.[27]

Decades of Comanche and Apache raids meant that Mexico had only tenuous control over its northern border, a circumstance that Americans capitalized on during the Mexican War. The Choctaw Nation remained officially neutral, and few professed interest in going "to war to Mexico and get[ting] killed." But Wash Trahern cast his lot with the Americans. Alongside dozens of other Texas Rangers, he was captured while trying to hold San Antonio, and then spent a year and a half as a prisoner in the Castle of Perote in the Mexican state of Veracruz. During his captivity, Trahern bonded with other American prisoners, as they did hard labor, side by side. After his release, Trahern joined the US Army and fought under Zachary Taylor, who grew up in Louisville and commanded thousands of fellow Kentuckians eager to extend their nation's borders and thereby enhance their own opportunities. Continuing his work as a cowboy, Trahern drove cattle and supplied beef to Taylor's army, but he also fought alongside a regiment of Kentucky cavalry, talking horses and tactics with fellow soldiers. The war bred intimacy, making Trahern feel as though he belonged, as though he was an American. He later recalled telling "cock-and-bull" stories in Zachary Taylor's tent as the general sipped whiskey; receiving orders alongside future president of the Confederacy, then Colonel Jefferson Davis; and fighting at the Battle of Buena Vista near Henry Clay Jr., who died at the head of his regiment, the victim of a Mexican lancer.[28]

After the Mexican War, Trahern was one of many Choctaws who took advantage of US territorial gains by moving west again, this time to California. In 1849, just one year after gold was discovered at Sutter's Mill, Malvina Folsom, Peter Pitchlynn's daughter, noted that many of her neighbors had left, abandoning their farms and cattle herds "to get their fortune." Most departed from Boggy Depot, a growing Choctaw town from which they could take the "gold road" to California. Among the emigrants was William Brown, who reminded Peter Pitchlynn of their old Choctaw Academy days by writing, "excuse my poor hand writing, the specimen of old Kentuck!" Updating Pitchlynn and other Choctaws from his temporary home in Fresno, Brown described

California as "*inla!*" ("strange!"), marveling, "there are people from all parts of the world in this state." Indeed, the Gold Rush created a great path to California, making it the most ethnically diverse place in the world. Economic opportunity attracted not only local Californios, but also white and black Americans, Hawaiians, Latin Americans, Asians, Europeans, and Indians from across North America. William Brown made a little money but lost it through speculation, lamenting, "That is the mischief with this golden country."[29]

When he arrived in California, Trahern spent a week at a mining camp in the Sonoma Valley called Jimtown. A week's worth of panning earned him only $1.50 in gold, so Trahern decided to try a new venture. Partnering with a longtime friend and fellow Texas Ranger, John McMullin, Trahern drove cattle from the rancherias of Mexico and southern California to feed miners in the northern part of state. The two made a fortune. At their height, the partners owned over 12,000 head of cattle, and they built large ranches in California's San Joaquin Valley. After McMullin's death, Trahern continued to make shrewd investments, operating two vast farms on either side of the Stanislaus River, in addition to investing in stocks and serving as director of the local bank. Trahern was prescient and worldly enough to see beyond the gold boom and capitalize on diverse economic opportunities. Regarding California's future development, Trahern proclaimed, "I think it is going to be the greatest country in the world."[30]

Late in life, Wash Trahern was interviewed by the famous historian Hubert Howe Bancroft for his history of California. Bancroft was enthralled by this compact yet powerful man with iron-gray hair and shining black eyes. Trahern was an ideal interviewee because, in Bancroft's words, "His memory surpasses anything I have ever known." Trahern recalled every place he had ever been, each new acquaintance, every battle of the Mexican War. Strange then, that even when Bancroft pressed, Trahern remained doggedly vague about his early life, saying that he had "never been able to trace" his family and could "not particularly" recall anything of his schooldays.[31]

As Trahern knew, Hubert Howe Bancroft was among the most influential historians writing the story of America, a celebratory epic about a people favored by Providence and their march of progress across a continent. Such a narrative afforded Indians only bit parts, usually as adversaries temporarily blocking the path westward. Bancroft was interested in Indians but felt that they were culture-bound and primitive, thus more suited to be anthropological than historical subjects. In his five-volume foray into anthropology, *The Native Races*, Bancroft perpetuated popular stereotypes of Indians, calling them "dull of comprehension," "lazy," "filthy," and "wild." Trahern seemed the polar opposite: "quick of comprehension, enterprising and progressive." "Men such as he are the true builders of society," Bancroft wrote. "They are the ones to whom civilization is indebted by what it is. They are the ones whose lives are worthy of imitation. They are the ones, a record of whose lives will be read with profit and pleasure by future generations." In other words, Trahern was a man worthy of history. Bancroft noted that Trahern was "dark complexioned," but must have pushed that observation out of his mind as he lauded this perfect embodiment of the American man—a cowboy and a soldier, a self-made orphan who became rich. Bancroft's views were a product of Indian removal, when white policymakers and intellectuals cast Indians as foils so fundamentally different from whites that the two peoples could never peacefully co-exist. Like all myths, this one purposely manipulated history, shearing it of its complexity, obfuscating centuries of exchange that had brought colonizers and the colonized closer together.[32]

⟞⟝

By the time Bancroft interviewed Trahern, the Plains Wars had slowed and the United States had gained firmer control over the West, leaving no longitudinal leeway, no faraway "Indian Territory" in which to push Native people. Seeking to transform its Indigenous subjects, the federal government put education at the core of its new "Assimilation Policy," creating a coherent and comprehensive system of schooling as a means of acculturating Indians. While the federal government had supported Indian schooling since the early 1800s, its previous approach had been more relaxed, relying heavily on Indian money and, consequently, collaboration with Native nations. Particularly after the rise of school systems in Indian Territory, white critics argued that such an approach gave

Indians too much control. Native families insisted on shaping the curriculum, often refusing to allow their children to do manual labor. If the children were to work on farms, their families argued, such efforts were best expended at home. Families also pulled students out of school in the summers to help around the farm. If the children did not seem to progress quickly enough in their studies, families stopped sending them altogether. Even those who remained in school still had constant contact with their families, still practiced Native religions, and still spoke Indigenous languages at school. These children, white reformers feared, would never become true Americans. "Absorb all the resources of the Indians," one federal agent advised. Only then would Native people "adopt those improvements which will tend to their ultimate advancement."[33]

Beginning with the opening of Carlisle in 1879, the federal government developed a system of Indian boarding schools that refined and systematized policies originally developed at Choctaw Academy. Carlisle's superintendent, Richard Henry Pratt, was an army officer who, like Richard Mentor Johnson, had been active in Indian wars, and he played a leading role in shaping the policies that governed all boarding schools. Pratt insisted that students wear military-style uniforms and forced them through daily drills and a dress parade on Sundays, regulations that were adopted by other federal boarding schools. Pratt also relied on students to enforce discipline, setting up a moot court system similar to Choctaw Academy's Lycurgus court and appointing advanced students to act as monitors. Although Choctaw Academy piloted a manual labor program almost uniformly rejected by students and their families, later boarding schools made labor compulsory and featured it as a central component of the curriculum. Even into the twentieth century, the schools continued to teach blacksmithing and harness-making. By that time, such skills were obsolete in America's industrial economy but were in step with policymakers' views of Indians as an antiquated underclass. Like Richard Johnson, Pratt and other officials tried to limit students' visits to their home communities and screened their letters home. Those forced to stay at Choctaw Academy for years on end sometimes complained that they felt like captives; decades later, some of their counterparts at federal boarding schools were actual prisoners, captured by the army during the Plains

Wars, forced east to go to school while their families served time in prison camps. Homesickness contributed to mental health problems, especially depression, while the schools' cheap food and cramped dormitories led to high mortality rates, much higher than at Choctaw Academy. In many ways, Choctaw Academy anticipated these later boarding schools, which took its practices—and problems—to the extreme.[34]

The new schools also departed from Choctaw Academy in significant ways. Whereas Richard Johnson had constructed separate dorms for each Native nation, Pratt developed a policy of deliberately splitting up tribes, forcing students into living quarters where no one spoke their language so that they would be forced to learn English more quickly. This practice contributed to high rates of language loss at these later schools, but perhaps fostered an even greater sense of pan-Indian identity, which graduates carried into their adult lives as many became active in the Indian rights movements of the twentieth century. While Carlisle and other schools gave some Indian students leadership experience as monitors, they rarely hired them as teachers, another significant break from Choctaw Academy. Later schools also meted out extreme punishments, introducing pitch-black holding cells, where students could be put in solitary confinement and fed meager bread-and-water diets for days. The shift underwriting all of these changes was the fact that, in 1891, the federal government made schooling mandatory for all Indian children and, two years later, authorized federal agents to withhold rations and annuities from uncooperative families. There was no illusion of partnership, financial or otherwise, with Indian nations. Not surprisingly, Indian ambivalence about federal schooling that started at Choctaw Academy accelerated in the later nineteenth century, leading to fierce resistance in many Native communities.[35]

The Native nations of Indian Territory fought to retain their own school systems, but the Curtis Act, passed by Congress in 1898, authorized the Interior Department to seize 995 tribally controlled schools. The Choctaw Nation, which had the most extensive educational system, had to give up 160 neighborhood schools and 16 academies. Some became federal Indian boarding schools, and the rest were controlled by Oklahoma. After becoming a state in 1907, Oklahoma used former Indian schools as the building blocks of its public schools. Several tribally controlled schools were transformed into the state's earliest colleges and universities: a Creek mission school became the University of Tulsa, and the Cherokee Nation's flagship female academy became Northeastern State University.[36]

While many Indian students persisted in their pursuit of higher education, this takeover by the state and federal governments overwhelmingly benefited whites. The quality of Indian education suffered tremendously as the schools passed out of tribal control: the curriculum shrank from twelve to eight grades; school was in session nine instead of ten months a year; students, rather than staff, did custodial work, cooking, and maintenance; entrance exams were discontinued, making the academies less competitive. One study of the Cherokee Nation found that literacy rates reached a high of nearly 100 percent under their tribal school system in the late nineteenth century (13 percent higher than the US national average) but plummeted after the Oklahoma takeover, registering only 60 percent in 1969. For the tribal nations who had worked so hard to create and administer their own educational institutions, the thefts of their school systems were national tragedies, staggering losses of capital and autonomy, whose costs would be borne by succeeding generations of Indians. Not until the late twentieth century, following one hundred years of activism, would Indian nations regain the power to institute bilingual, bicultural schooling. Still, only those with sufficient capital that meet certain federal requirements have been able to do so.[37]

⟞≈⟞

Early US imperialism brought an era of rapid transformation characterized by the crossing of space and the meeting of cultures. Like Hubert Howe Bancroft, Americans like to think of their history as a narrative of progress, whereby the passage of time and settling of new lands enhance freedom. But as Creek chiefs once explained, a "new made" path was not automatically "a great path." The residents of Great Crossings remind us that progress cannot be taken for granted.[38]

In the aftermath of the Revolution, many of America's diverse people sought to build a great path paved by collaboration and alliance. Home to the first federal Indian school and a famous interracial family, Great Crossings was a meeting ground for those who sought to put inclusive ideals into practice. Many Indian nations made peace treaties with the United States, and some leaders, like James L. McDonald, envisioned dual citizenship. Native Americans considered Choctaw Academy a valuable study-abroad experience, in which they would learn to "walk in the paths of virtue," gaining the skills and experiences they would need to live in peace and plenty alongside American and Indian neighbors. Although many in the United States and some in Indian country held slaves, African Americans held out hope for a greater share of freedom in the empire of liberty. They drew on Revolutionary rhetoric to argue for emancipation, a tactic that proved successful in many northern states. Those who remained enslaved sought out routes to empowerment, sometimes with the help of white or Indian allies. Julia Chinn and Richard Johnson, imagining a brighter future, used their power to mold Great Crossings into a training ground that would prepare their daughters for freedom.[39]

The era of Jackson, however, bloodied and then divided the great path. Whites forged their empire of liberty by embracing a narrow definition of citizenship and excluding millions from a narrative of progress. Empowered by voters eager to seize western lands, the Jackson administration drowned out critical voices and scrapped accommodating Indian policies in favor of an aggressive and frequently violent push for removal. Once Native nations were removed to marginal enclaves, their homelands opened to white settlement. Slavery was at the vanguard of American imperialism, reshaping the culture and environment of the Deep South and many parts of the West. After the Civil War, African Americans seized freedom, but with that came a violent backlash from militant whites and retreat on the part of the federal government. In surveying the ascendant empire, Peter Pitchlynn agreed that the United States seemed like a force of nature, but a destructive and terrible one, "a mighty flood rolling over every thing with an irresistible force." Pitchlynn lamented that the United States was "determined to exercise that power over every inch of land from the Atlantic to the Pacific." Some

Indians and African Americans sought opportunities within the United States, while others fled to Canada, Mexico, or overseas.[40]

Yet the conquest was not complete. Indian nations retained their sovereignty and used it to rebuild their nations in Indian Territory. Extending intertribal connections forged at Choctaw Academy, the diverse nations of Indian Territory held peace councils, shared educational strategies, strengthened their national governments, and lobbied Congress for their collective rights. Diplomatically, Indian nations continually worked to find a place in a realm of divided sovereignty, reminding the federal government of treaty obligations and demanding a voice in Washington. African Americans lacked the sovereign rights of Indian nations, but they too worked to cultivate power as well as autonomous spaces. Imogene Johnson Pence, like her mother Julia Chinn, focused on her family, carving out opportunities for them in Kentucky. After the Civil War liberated Great Crossings' other African Americans, many of them also hoped to remain there, but the violence and lack of economic opportunities motivated dozens to leave and seek out a fuller freedom on the high plains of Kansas. Whatever their opinion of Great Crossings, its inhabitants came away believing that education could be empowering under the right circumstances. Seeking direct control over their children's schooling, they built grand academies in Indian Territory, makeshift classrooms in Plains dugouts, and tiny schoolhouses in rural Kentucky.

The Indians, settlers, and slaves who came together at Great Crossings linked education to their people's destinies, but no one, not even powerful whites, could control what people learned and how they chose to use that knowledge. In the 1830s, the students of Choctaw Academy argued that recent history should give Americans cause for concern, not celebration. Student-teacher August Buckholts implored local whites to remember US obligations, enshrined in treaties, to the first Americans. If the United States neglected this sacred duty, its people must "take care of the wrath to come." Fellow Choctaw Wash Trahern, who hid his own past as a historian from Bancroft, agreed. Drawing on Indian and European intellectual traditions, Trahern asserted that societies declined and fell due to moral decay. It seemed a divine judgment, and no nation, not even the United States, was exempt from what Wash Trahern called "the will of the Mighty Ruler above." As a teacher in the Choctaw school system argued, it was just as likely that "the U.S. would share the fate of warlike Rome and classic Greece, as that all Indian tribes would cease to be." History suggested that empires, fraught and unstable, would eventually crumble to reveal the preexisting nations underneath.[41]

The residents of Great Crossings challenge not just the themes of American history but also the way the story has been told. In their essays, students at Choctaw Academy cast time not as a linear progression, but more like a recurring sine curve, moving up and down, repeating its cycles. This Indigenous model of time can help frame American history in a new light. Americans prize the seeds of virtue sown by the Revolutionary generation but often prefer to forget the deeds of violence that nourished their nation as it grew vast and powerful. Yet, as long as Americans cultivate amnesia regarding unpleasant historical truths, we continue to reap the legacies of the Jacksonian era, when the adolescent empire coalesced around principles of intolerance, exclusion, and racial injustice. For many Americans, the promise of liberty remains elusive, for the United States has not yet equally extended rights of citizenship or respected the autonomy promised in treaties. Circling back to old paths, however, also provides the opportunity to cultivate change. As the essayists of Choctaw Academy remind us, the epic of America is still being written.

NOTES

Abbreviations Used in Notes

BC   Bancroft Collection of Western and Latin Americana, The Bancroft Library, University of California, Berkeley

CA   Choctaw Academy

CK   Cyrus Kingsbury

CKC   Cyrus Kingsbury Collection, copy in WHC, originals in American Board of Commissioners for Foreign Missions Collection, Divinity Library Special Collections, Yale University

CRR   Choctaw Removal Records, Record Group 75, NARA

DMC   Lyman Copeland Draper Manuscript Collection, Microfilm Copy, State Historical Society of Wisconsin, Madison

DV   Daniel Vanderslice

FHS   Filson Historical Society, Louisville, Kentucky

GCBC   Great Crossings Baptist Church Records, James P. Boyce Centennial Library Archives and Special Collections, The Southern Baptist Theological Seminary, Louisville, Kentucky

GFC   Grant Foreman Collection, Oklahoma Historical Society, Oklahoma City, Oklahoma

GLOVEC Great Lakes-Ohio Valley Ethnohistory Collection, Erminie Wheeler-Voegelin Archives, Glenn A. Black Laboratory of Archaeology, Indiana University

GMA   Gilcrease Museum Archives, Tulsa, Oklahoma

JLM   James L. McDonald

JWCP   J. Winston Coleman Papers, Special Collections, University of Kentucky Libraries, Lexington

KHS   Kentucky Historical Society, Frankfort, Kentucky

KU   Kenneth Spencer Research Library, University of Kansas, Lawrence

LCM   Lula Craig Manuscript, Kenneth Spencer Research Library, University of Kansas, Lawrence

LOC   Library of Congress, Washington, DC

LROIA   Letters Received by the Office of Indian Affairs, NARA

LRSW	Letters Received by the Secretary of War, NARA
LSOIA	Letters Sent by the Office of Indian Affairs, NARA
LSSIT	Letters Sent by the Superintendent of Indian Trade, NARA
MDAH	Mississippi Department of Archives and History, Jackson
NARA	National Archives and Records Administration, Washington, DC
OKHS	Oklahoma Historical Society, Oklahoma City
OIA	Office of Indian Affairs
PABCFM	Papers of the American Board of Commissioners for Foreign Missions, microfilm copy, Houghton Library, Harvard University
PPP	Peter Perkins Pitchlynn
PPPC	Peter Perkins Pitchlynn Collection, Western History Digital Collections, presented by the University of Oklahoma Libraries, https://digital.libraries.ou.edu/whc/
PPPP	Peter Perkins Pitchlynn Papers, Gilcrease Museum Archives, Tulsa, Oklahoma
PU	Rare Books and Special Collections Department, Firestone Library, Princeton University
ROSW	Records of the Office of the Secretary of War, Record Group 107, NARA
RG	Record Group
RMJ	Richard Mentor Johnson
SBTS	Southern Baptist Theological Seminary, James P. Boyce Centennial Library Archives and Special Collections, Louisville, Kentucky
TH	Thomas Henderson
THP	Thomas Henderson Papers, Filson Historical Society, Louisville, Kentucky
TLM	Thomas L. McKenney
TLML	Thomas L. McKenney Letterbook, Choctaw Removal Records, 1825–1858, Box 5, NARA
UC	The Bancroft Library, University of California, Berkeley
UK	Special Collections, University of Kentucky Libraries, Lexington
VB	Papers of Martin Van Buren, microfilm copy, Library of Congress, Washington, DC
WHC	Western History Collections, University of Oklahoma Libraries, Norman, Oklahoma
WW	William Ward

Author's note: In most cases, quotations from English-language sources are presented verbatim, but, for the sake of clarity, I have occasionally corrected spelling and punctuation.

Introduction

1. James McDonald to the editor of the *Argus*, n.d. [1827?], TLML, NARA; TH to Greenwood LeFlore, September 13, 1828, LROIA, Choctaw Agency, roll 169, frame 510, NARA; CA Trustees' Report, November 22, 1826, LROIA, Schools, roll 773, frames 124–125, NARA; CA Quarterly Report, August 1, 1832, 26th Cong., 2nd sess., HD 109, no. 56; Frederick E. Hoxie, *This*

Indian Country: American Indian Political Activists and the Place They Made (New York: Penguin, 2012), 49–50.

2. J. E. Alexander, *Transatlantic Sketches, Comprising Visits to the Most Interesting Scenes in North and South America and the West Indies* (Philadelphia: Key and Biddle, 1833), 270; James Buckingham Silk, *The Eastern and Western States of America* (London: Fisher, Son, & Co., 1842), vol. 2, 450–469; Deposition of Samuel Wilson, April 15, 1777, in *Calendar of Virginia State Papers and Other Manuscripts, 1652–1781*, ed. William P. Palmer (New York: Kraus Reprint, 1968), 283.

3. James McDonald to the editor of the *Argus*, n.d. [1827?], TLML, NARA; James Barbour to TH, September 21, 1826, TLML, NARA; CA Board of Trustees to James Barbour, October 12, 1827, TLML, NARA; RMJ to David Folsom, September 12, 1828, LROIA, Schools, roll 169, frames 530–531, NARA; RMJ to TH, May 12, 1834, THP, folder 9, FHS. "Children of the forest" was a popular turn of phrase at that time. In addition to McDonald's letter, see, for example, *Kentucky Gazette*, March 28, 1835.

4. James McDonald to the editor of the *Argus*, n.d. [1827?], TLML, NARA; CA Quarterly Report, April 30, 1827, LROIA, Schools, roll 773, frame 648, NARA; CA List of Students, Fall 1827, TLML, NARA.

5. James McDonald to the editor of the *Argus*, n.d. [1827?], TLML, NARA.

6. James McDonald to the editor of the *Argus*; CA Trustees' Report, August 18, 1826, PPPC, box 5, folder 6, WHC.

7. CA Trustees' Report, August 18, 1826; *Argus of Western America*, August 4, 1824; *Cincinnati Daily Gazette*, June 22, 1835; Frances L. S. Dugan and Jacqueline P. Bull, eds., *Bluegrass Craftsman: Being the Reminiscenes of Ebenezer Hiram Stedman, Papermaker: 1808–1885* (Lexington: University of Kentucky Press, 1959), 76, 142.

8. Catherine E. Kelly, *Republic of Taste: Art, Politics, and Everyday Life in Early America* (Philadelphia: University of Pennsylvania Press, 2016), 50; CA Quarterly Report, November 1, 1827, TLML, NARA; Trustees' Report, July 1827, PPPC, box 5, folder 11, WHC; Trustees' Report, August 10, 1832, LROIA, Schools, roll 775, frames 758–764, NARA; *Niles Weekly Register*, November 4, 1826.

9. Emma Rouse Lloyd, "Clasping Hands with Generations Past," THP, folder 1, FHS.

10. William Blount to James Seagrove, January 9, 1794, James Robertson Papers, roll 801, Tennessee State Library and Archives, Nashville; Chief Payne to Enrique White, July 29, 1800, East Florida Papers, roll 43, P. K. Yonge Library of Florida History, Department of Special and Area Studies Collections, George A. Smathers Libraries, University of Florida, Gainesville; John Pitchlynn to Andrew Jackson, August 18, 1831, copy in PPPP, folder 105, GMA; Tom Hatley, *The Dividing Paths: Cherokees and South Carolinians through the Era of Revolution* (New York: Oxford University Press, 1995); Gregory A. Waselkov, "Indian Maps of the Colonial Southeast," in *Powhatan's Mantle: Indians in the Colonial Southeast*, ed. Waselkov, Peter H. Wood, and Tom Hatley (Lincoln: University of Nebraska Press, 2006), 435–502; James Taylor Carson, *Making an Atlantic World: Circles, Paths, and Stories from the Colonial South* (Knoxville: University of Tennessee Press, 2007); Angela Pulley Hudson, *Creek Paths and Federal*

Roads: Indians, Settlers, and Slaves and the Making of the American South (Chapel Hill: University of North Carolina Press, 2010).

11. The controversy over whether Johnson actually killed Tecumseh is discussed in greater detail in Chapter 2.

12. Eliga H. Gould, *Among the Powers of the Earth: The American Revolution and the Making of a New World Empire* (Cambridge, MA: Harvard University Press, 2012), 1–4; Jedidiah Morse, *The American Geography; or, A View of the Present Situation of the United States of America* (Elizabethtown, NJ: Shepard Kollock, 1789), 469; David Andrew Nichols, *Red Gentlemen and White Savages: Indians, Federalists, and the Search for Order on the American Frontier* (Charlottesville: University of Virginia Press, 2008), 10–11, 201; Eliga H. Gould, *The Persistence of Empire: British Political Culture in the Age of the American Revolution* (Chapel Hill: University of North Carolina Press, 2000), 134; Carmen E. Pavel, *Divided Sovereignty: International Institutions and the Limits of State Authority* (New York: Oxford University Press, 2015), 20–21.

13. Honor Sachs, *Home Rule: Households, Manhood, and National Expansion on the Eighteenth-Century Kentucky Frontier* (New Haven, CT: Yale University Press, 2015), 5; Quotation from "Annexation," *Democratic Review* 17 (July 1845): 5.

14. Speech of Richard Mentor Johnson, February 1820, Senate, Annals of Congress, 16th Cong., 1st sess., 345–359; Thomas Jefferson to George Rogers Clark, December 25, 1780, in *The Papers of Thomas Jefferson*, vol. 4, ed. Julian P. Boyd (Princeton, NJ: Princeton University Press, 1951), 237–238; Gary B. Nash, *Forging Freedom: The Formation of Philadelphia's Black Community, 1720–1840* (Cambridge, MA: Harvard University Press, 1988), 4.

15. Leslie M. Harris, *In the Shadow of Slavery: African Americans in New York City, 1626–1863* (Chicago: University of Chicago Press, 2003), 93–94; Nathan O. Hatch, *The Democratization of American Christianity* (New Haven, CT: Yale University Press, 1989); Daniel Chinn was Richard Johnson's longtime valet and accompanied him when he traveled. *The Liberator*, July 25, 1845; Leland Meyer, *The Life and Times of Colonel Richard M. Johnson of Kentucky* (New York: Columbia University Press, 1932), 324.

16. Kathleen DuVal, *Independence Lost: Lives on the Edge of the American Revolution* (New York: Random House, 2015), 271–273; John Craig Hammond, *Slavery, Freedom, and Expansion in the Early American West* (Charlottesville: University of Virginia Press, 2007), 1–3; Nash, *Forging Freedom*, 148–152, 180, 189.

17. Reginald Horsman, *Race and Manifest Destiny: The Origins of American Racial Anglo-Saxonism* (Cambridge, MA: Harvard University Press, 1981), Chapter 6; Speech of Richard Mentor Johnson, February 1820, Annals of Congress, Senate, 16th Cong., 1st sess., 357; Reprint of a letter from TH, June 20, 1835, in *Louisville Advertiser*, July 3, 1835.

18. Nicholas Guyatt, *Bind Us Apart: How the First American Liberals Invented Racial Segregation* (New York: Basic, 2016), 117–132; Thomas Jefferson to Benjamin Hawkins, February 18, 1803, in *Thomas Jefferson: Writings*, ed. Merrill D. Peterson (New York: Library of America, 1984), 1113–1116; Thomas Jefferson to Edward Coles, August 25, 1814, in Merrill D. Peterson, ed., *Thomas Jefferson: Writings* (New York: Library of America, 1984), 1345; Gilbert Imlay, *A Description of the Western Territory of North America* (Dublin: William Jones, 1793), 187–199.

19. John Filson, *The Discovery, Settlement, and Present State of Kentucky* (London: John Stockdale, 1793), 61; Silk, *Eastern and Western States*, vol. 3, 7–8; Matthew Carey, *Some Notices of Kentucky, Particularly of Its Chief Town Lexington* (Philadelphia, 1828); James A. Ramage and Andrew S. Watkins, *Kentucky Rising: Democracy, Slavery, and Culture from the Early Republic to the Civil War* (Lexington: University Press of Kentucky, 2011), 3, 84, 237–239; Marion B. Lucas, *A History of Blacks in Kentucky: From Slavery to Segregation, 1760–1891* (Frankfort: Kentucky Historical Society, 2003), 111–112; Sachs, *Home Rule*, 6, 43; Emma Rouse Lloyd, "Clasping Hands with Generations Past," THP, folder 1, FHS.

20. Ramage and Watkins, *Kentucky Rising*, 142–145; "The Hunters of Kentucky" broadside, 1815, FHS. Intriguingly, "the half horse, half alligator" originated during a fight between two Kentucky boatmen over a Choctaw woman. Christian Schultz witnessed the fight in Natchez, Mississippi, and recorded it in *Travels on an Inland Voyage through the States of New-York, Pennsylvania, Virginia, Ohio, Kentucky and Tennessee and through the Territories of Indiana, Louisiana, Mississippi and New-Orleans* (New York: Isaac Riley, 1810), vol. 2, 145.

21. Jedidiah Morse, *Report to the Secretary of War of the United States on Indian Affairs* (New Haven, CT: Converse, 1822), 82.

22. Herman J. Viola, *Thomas L. McKenney: Architect of America's Early Indian Policy* (Chicago: Swallow Press, 1974), 36, 41–42; Nichols, *Red Gentlemen and White Savages*, 201; John C. Calhoun, "Regulations for the Civilization of the Indians," February 29, 1820, RG 75, entry 116, Data Book for the Civilization Fund, NARA; Benjamin Rush, "On the Mode of Education Proper in a Republic," in *American Educational Thought: Essays from 1640–1940*, ed. Andrew J. Milson, Chara Haeussler Bohan, Perry L. Glanzer, and J. Wesley Null (Charlotte, NC: Information Age, 2010), 67; Andrew Hughes to Lewis Cass, August 7, 1831, LROIA, Schools, roll 775, frame 142, NARA; A. H. Sevier to Lewis Cass, April 23, 1832, LROIA, Schools, roll 775, frame 690, NARA.

23. Seth Rockman, "Jacksonian America," in *American History Now*, ed. Eric Foner and Lisa McGirr (Philadelphia: Temple University Press, 2011), 60; Winthrop D. Jordan, *White over Black: American Attitudes toward the Negro, 1550–1812* (Chapel Hill: University of North Carolina Press, 1968), 546–569; Sachs, *Home Rule*, 139–141.

24. Harold D. Tallant, *Evil Necessity: Slavery and Political Culture in Antebellum Kentucky* (Lexington: University Press of Kentucky, 2003), 39–56; Lucas, *History of Blacks in Kentucky*, 53–54; *Freedom's Journal*, November 2, 1827, emphasis in original; Nash, *Forging Freedom*, 3, 234–245; Harris, *In the Shadow of Slavery*, 96.

25. Thomas Jefferson to William Henry Harrison, February 27, 1803, in Merrill, ed., *Thomas Jefferson: Writings*, 1118.

26. James Axtell, *The Invasion Within: The Contest of Cultures in Colonial North America* (New York: Oxford University Press, 1985); Rebecca Kugel, "Of Missionaries and Their Cattle: Ojibwa Perceptions of a Missionary as Evil Shaman," *Ethnohistory* 41 (1994): 227–244; Margaret Connell Szasz, *Indian Education in the American Colonies, 1607–1783* (Lincoln: University of Nebraska Press, 2007); Theda Perdue, "Women, Men, and American Indian Policy: The Cherokee Response to 'Civilization,'" in *Negotiators*

of Change: Historical Perspectives on Native American Women, ed. Nancy Shoemaker (New York: Routledge, 1995), 90–114.

27. Talk of the Florida Delegation of Indians to James Barbour, in Gad Humphreys to James Barbour, May 18, 1826, LROIA, Seminole Agency, roll 800, NARA; Talk of Winnebagos [Ho-Chunk] to John H. Kinzie, January 6, 1831, LROIA, Schools, roll 775, frames 256–257, NARA; Thomas Williamson to Harvey, July 31, 1848, LROIA, Schools, roll 784, frames 199–200, NARA.

28. Ralph Waldo Emerson, "The Young American," in *The Collected Works of Ralph Waldo Emerson,* ed. Robert E. Spiller (Cambridge, MA: Harvard University Press, 1971), 230; David Folsom to Jeremiah Evarts, May 9, 1824, CKC, box 2, folder 7, item 36, WHC.

29. David Folsom to TLM, October 1, 1818, Native American Collection, Clements Library, University of Michigan, Ann Arbor.

30. Robert J. Berkhofer, *Salvation and the Savage: An Analysis of Protestant Missions and American Indian Response, 1787–1862* (Lexington: University Press of Kentucky, 1965), 1–2, 28–29; Speech of Noonday, January 11, 1827, "Extracts from Mr. Lykin's Journal," in Isaac McCoy, *History of Baptist Indian Missions* (Washington, DC: William M. Morrison, 1840), 299; WW to James Barbour, April 15, 1826, LROIA, Choctaw Agency, roll 169, frames 344–345, NARA.

31. Quotation from Speech of George Washington Trahern, February 23, 1838, 26th Cong., 2nd sess., HD 109, no. 137, p. 118. "Facing east" is borrowed from Daniel K. Richter's masterful synthesis *Facing East from Indian Country: A Native History of Early America* (Cambridge, MA: Harvard University Press, 2003). *Great Crossings* also employs ethnohistorical methodology and draws inspiration from works that illuminate multivalent perspectives. See especially DuVal, *Independence Lost;* Jonathan Todd Hancock, "A World Convulsed: Earthquakes, Authority, and the Making of Nations in the War of 1812 Era" (Ph.D. diss., University of North Carolina at Chapel Hill, 2013); Karl Jacoby, *Shadows at Dawn: An Apache Massacre and the Violence of History* (New York: Penguin, 2009); Ari Kelman, *A Misplaced Massacre: Struggle over the Memory of Sand Creek* (Cambridge, MA: Harvard University Press, 2013).

32. Choctaw Delegation to Congress, February 18, 1825, in Thomas L. McKenney, *Memoirs, Official and Personal* (New York: Paine & Burgess, 1846), vol. 2, 121.

33. Speech of John C. Calhoun, February 4, 1817, Annals of Congress, House of Representatives, 14th Cong., 2nd sess., pp. 853–854.

Chapter 1

1. Charles Lanman interview with Peter Pitchlynn, in "Peter Pitchlynn, Chief of the Choctaws," *Atlantic Monthly* 25 (1870): 496–497.

2. PPP Biographical Information from Peter Hudson, PPP Vertical File, OKHS; W. David Baird, *Peter Pitchlynn: Chief of the Choctaws* (Norman: University of Oklahoma Press, 1972), 5–6; Ben James to Governor Blount, June 30, 1792, copy in Peter James Hudson Collection, box 1, folder 15, OKHS; Horatio B. Cushman, *History of the Choctaw, Chickasaw, and Natchez Indians,* ed. Angie Debo (Norman: University of Oklahoma Press, 1969), 242.

3. Pitchlynn Family Genealogy, compiled by Sandra Moore Riley, PPP Vertical File, OKHS; Dan Poland to W. David Baird, July 7, 1976, PPPC, box 7, folder

8; Theda Perdue, *"Mixed-Blood" Indians: Racial Construction in the Early South* (Athens: University of Georgia Press, 2003); Andrew K. Frank, *Creeks and Southerners: Biculturalism on the Early American Frontier* (Lincoln: University of Nebraska Press, 2005); Kathleen DuVal, *The Native Ground: Indians and Colonists in the Heart of the Continent* (Philadelphia: University of Pennsylvania Press, 2006). Miko is often rendered as "mingo," though miko is the preferred Choctaw spelling. Marcia Haag and Henry J. Willis, eds. and trans., *A Gathering of Statesmen: Records of the Choctaw Council Meetings, 1826–1828* (Norman: University of Oklahoma Press, 2013), 39, n. 17.

4. John Pitchlynn to PPP, June 13, 1834, PPPC, box 1, folder 41, WHC; Baird, *Peter Pitchlynn*, 7–10; PPP to "Dear Brother," September 23, 1846, PPPC, box 1, folder 109, WHC.

5. John Pitchlynn to PPP, June 15, 1824, PPPP, folder 24, GMA; John Pitchlynn to PPP, March 14, 1824, PPPP, folder 23; PPP to Edmund Folsom, January 7, 1829, PPPP, folder 67; Armstrong Census of 1831, 23rd Cong., 1st sess., SD 512, no. 246.

6. PPP to "Dear Brother," September 23, 1846, PPPC, box 1, folder 109, WHC; Charles Dickens, *American Notes for General Circulation* (New York: Penguin, 1972), 210; PPP to unknown, January 12, 1835, copy, PPP Vertical File, OKHS; Mushulatubbee to John Eaton, January 16, 1831, LROIA, Choctaw Agency, roll 169, frames 871–872, NARA.

7. Lanman, "Peter Pitchlynn," 486; Richard A. Sattler, "Cowboys and Indians: Creek and Seminole Stock Raising, 1700–1900," in *American Indian Culture and Research Journal* 22 (1998): 79–100; Cushman, *History of the Choctaw*, 169, 176.

8. Patricia Galloway, *Choctaw Genesis, 1500–1700* (Lincoln: University of Nebraska Press, 1995); James Taylor Carson, *Searching for the Bright Path: The Mississippi Choctaws from Prehistory to Removal* (Lincoln: University of Nebraska Press, 1999); Greg O'Brien, *Choctaws in a Revolutionary Age, 1750–1830* (Lincoln: University of Nebraska Press, 2002).

9. Arthur DeRosier Jr., *The Removal of the Choctaw Indians* (Knoxville: University of Tennessee Press, 1970), 36; Talk to the Choctaw General Council, October 17, 1827, in *Reports and Proceedings of Col. McKenney, on the Subject of his Recent Tour among the Southern Indians* (Washington: Gales & Seaton, 1828), 31.

10. PPP interview with Lanman, "Peter Pitchlynn," 486; John Edwards, "The Choctaw Indians in the Middle of the Nineteenth Century," in *Chronicles of Oklahoma* 10 (1932): 420–421.

11. PPP Diary, PPPC, box 6, folder 1, WHC; Pitchlynn Family Genealogy, compiled by Riley, PPP Vertical File, OKHS; Gideon Lincecum to PPP, June 13, 1846, PPPC, box 1, folder 106, WHC; Lanman, "Peter Pitchlynn," 486.

12. PPP interview with Lanman, "Peter Pitchlynn," 486; Israel Folsom to James Monroe, March 8, 1821, Israel Folsom Letter, MDAH; Cushman, *History of the Choctaw*, 250, 291, 332; David Folsom to RMJ, January 19, 1825, CKC, box 2, folder 6, item 15, WHC; David Folsom to TLM, October 1, 1818, Native American Collection, Clements Library, University of Michigan, Ann Arbor.

13. PPP interview with Lanman, "Peter Pitchlynn," 486.

14. Robert Bell to John C. Calhoun, October 1, 1824, LROIA, Schools, roll 772, frames 11–14, NARA.

15. Kidwell, *Choctaws and Missionaries*, 24–32, 42–44, 60–65; Hannah Pride to Thomas Thacher, August 5, 1821, Hannah and William Pride Papers, MDAH;

Kingsbury to Jeremiah Evarts, August 13, 1827, CKC, box 2, folder 6, item 40, WHC; Kingsbury to Peter Porter, Annual Report for 1828, CKC, box 3, folder 8, item 31, WHC.

16. Kingsbury to Samuel Worcester, May 5, 1820, CKC, box 3, folder 10, item 2, WHC; Kingsbury to Samuel Hubbard, April 26, 1822, CKC, folder 9, item 33; Kidwell, *Choctaws and Missionaries*, 38–57; *MeasuringWorth*, accessed January 2, 2014, http://www.measuringworth.com/uscompare.

17. Agreement between ACBFM and the Choctaws for the Establishment of Mission Schools, July 28, 1823, CKC, box 2, folder 7, item 4, WHC; Louis Coleman, *Cyrus Byington: Missionary and Choctaw Linguist* (Kearney, NE: Morris, 1996), 1–6, 21–23; Kidwell, *Choctaws and Missionaries*, 53–54, 82–86; Samuel Worcester to Choctaw Chiefs, n.d. [1820?], Native American Collection, Clements Library.

18. Edwards, "Choctaw Indians in the Middle of the Nineteenth Century," quotation on p. 420.

19. CK to Peter Porter, Annual Report for 1828, CKC, box 3, folder 8, item 31, WHC; Kidwell, *Choctaws and Missionaries*, 33; CK to Evarts, September 12, 1821, CKC, box 3, folder 10, item 4, WHC.

20. William Pride to Thomas Thacher, November 29, 1825, Pride Papers, MDAH; Kingsbury to James Barbour, Annual Report for 1826, CKC, box 3, folder 8, item 12, WHC; Hannah Pride to Thomas Thacher, August 5, 1821, Pride Papers, MDAH.

21. Cyrus Kingsbury to Jeremiah Evarts, August 13, 1827, CKC, box 2, folder 6, item 40, WHC; Kingsbury to James Barbour, Annual Report for 1826, CKC, box 3, folder 8, item 12; Joel Wood to Cyrus Kingsbury, April 12, 1822, CKC, box 3, folder 9, item 27; Quarterly Report, Spring Place Mission, September 29, 1832, LROIA, Schools, roll 775, frames 683–686, NARA.

22. Taliaferro Journal, August 23, 1836, Chippewa Files, Folder August–December 1836, GLOVEC; Cyrus Kingsbury to TLM, February 8, 1830, LROIA, Schools, roll 774, frame 467, NARA.

23. Colin G. Calloway, *The Indian History of an American Institution: Native Americans and Dartmouth* (Hanover: Dartmouth College Press, 2010), 12; Adam Hodgson, *Remarks during a Journey through North America* (Westport: Negro Universities Press, 1970), 287.

24. Petition of Robert Cole, June 6, 1821, CKC, box 3, folder 9, item 39, WHC; Kingsbury to Evarts, October 9, 1823, CKC, box 2, folder 7, item 9; Kingsbury to Slocomb, August 17, 1825, CKC, box 3, folder 9, item 16.

25. Cyrus Kingsbury to John C. Calhoun, General Remarks on Mission Schools, October 1823, CKC, box 3, folder 8, item 44, WHC; Cyrus Kingsbury to the ABCFM, November 24, 1830, CKC, box 1, folder 1, item 1; Speech of PPP to the General Council, n.d., PPPP, folder 80A, GMA; List of Trade License Applications, 1825, LROIA, Choctaw Agency, roll 169, frame 256, NARA.

26. List of current and past students at Mayhew, May 1824, CKC, box 3, folder 8, item 23, WHC; Robert Bell to Elbert Herring, September 29, 1832, LROIA, Schools, roll 775, frames 406–414, NARA; Ledger, Schools Established among the Indian Tribes, 1824, RG 75, entry 116, Data Book for the Civilization Fund, NARA; Kingsbury to the Secretary of War, Annual Report of 1826, LROIA, Schools, roll 773, frame 220, NARA.

27. Robert F. Berkhofer Jr., *Salvation and the Savage: An Analysis of Protestant Missions and American Indian Response, 1787–1862* (Lexington: University Press of Kentucky, 1965), 61–63; Robert Bell to Elbert Herring, September 29, 1832, LROIA, Schools, roll 775, frame 413, NARA; James L. McDonald to Thomas L. McKenney, April 25, 1826, LROIA, Choctaw Agency, roll 169, frame 327, NARA; James L. McDonald to Thomas L. McKenney, January 31, 1826, LROIA, Choctaw Agency, roll 169, frames 315–317, NARA; Cushman, *History of the Choctaw*, 78.

28. Kingsbury to Evarts, July 19, 1824, CKC, box 2, folder 7, item 2, WHC; Kingsbury to Evarts, August 8, 1825, CKC, box 2, folder 6, item 47.

29. Cyrus Kingsbury to unknown, July 5, 1825, CKC, box 3, folder 8, item 48, WHC; Margaret Connell Szasz, *Indian Education in the American Colonies, 1607–1783* (Lincoln: University of Nebraska Press, 2007), 142; Students at Cornwall School, recorded March 1, 1821, by Jedidiah Morse, in *Report to the Secretary of War of the United States on Indian Affairs* (New Haven, CT: Converse, 1822), appendix 265–266; Kidwell, *Choctaws and Missionaries*, quotation on p. 103.

30. James L. McDonald to TLM, October 25, 1825, LROIA, Schools, roll 772, frames 610–611, NARA; L. R. Bakewell to James Barbour, September 2, 1825, LROIA, Choctaw Agency, roll 169, frames 152–158, NARA; McDonald to McKenney, August 9, 1819, LRSW, M221, M-33(13), NARA.

31. McDonald to McKenney, August 9, 1819, LRSW, M221, M-33(13), NARA; TLM to Isaac Tyson and Andrew Ellicott, March 27, 1818, Letters Sent by the Superintendent of Indian Trade, M16, roll 5, vol. E, pp. 4–5, NARA.

32. TLM to John McKee, April 15, 1818, M16, Letters Sent by the Superintendent of Indian Trade, vol. E, p. 18, NARA; Thomas L. McKenney, *Memoirs, Official and Personal* (New York: Paine & Burgess, 1846), vol. 2, 110–114; TLM to John C. Calhoun, August 10, 1819, LRSW, M-33 (13), NARA; McDonald to TLM, August 9, 1819, LRSW, M-33 (13), NARA; Frederick E. Hoxie, *This Indian Country: American Indian Political Activists and the Place They Made* (New York: Penguin, 2012), 51–52.

33. TLM to Calhoun, November 20, 1820, LRSW, roll 90, M-111 (14), NARA; McKenney, *Memoirs*, vol. 2, 116.

34. Kidwell, *Choctaws and Missionaries*, 93–95; Herman J. Viola, *Thomas L. McKenney: Architect of America's Early Indian Policy* (Chicago: Swallow Press, 1974), 125–126.

35. WW to TLM, July 24, 1824, CRR, Misc. Choctaw Removal Records, box 2, NARA; Mushulatubbee to PPP, October 10, 1824, PPPC, box 1, folder 3, WHC; John Pitchlynn to WW, October 17, 1824, PPPC, box 1, folder 7.

36. David Folsom to Cyrus Byington, December 24, 1824, DMC 10YY111; Kidwell, *Choctaws and Missionaries*, 18, 22.

37. McKenney, *Memoirs*, vol. 2, 116.

38. James L. McDonald to John C. Calhoun, January 20, 1825, LROIA, Choctaw Agency, roll 169, frames 178–182, NARA; Arthur DeRosier Jr., *The Removal of the Choctaw Indians* (Knoxville: University of Tennessee Press, 1970), 81–82; Treaty of 1825, proclaimed February 19, 1825, in Charles J. Kappler, ed., *Indian Affairs: Laws and Treaties* (Washington, DC: Government Printing Office, 1904), vol. 2, 211–214.

39. Choctaw Delegation to Congress, February 18, 1825, reprinted in McKenney, *Memoirs*, 120–122; McKenney, *Memoirs*, 113; Hoxie, *This Indian Country*, 93–94.

40. McDonald to McKenney, October 25, 1825, LROIA, Schools, roll 772, frames 610–611, NARA.

41. John Pitchlynn to McKenney, January 27, 1825, LROIA, Choctaw Agency, roll 169, frame 195, NARA; McKenney to Joshua Tennison, June 17, 1825, LSOIA, roll 2, vol. 2, p. 50, NARA; David Folsom to Cyrus Byington, December 24–26, 1824, DMC, 10YY111; Cyrus Kingsbury to James Barbour, July 6, 1825, 26th Cong., 2nd sess., HD 109, no. 2, pp. 5–6.

42. Resolution of the Choctaw General Council, August 27, 1825, copy in CRR, Misc. Choctaw Removal Records, box 5, TLML, NARA; CK to Evarts, July 19, 1824, CKC, box 2, folder 7, item 2, WHC; CK to Evarts, August 8, 1825, CKC, box 2, folder 6, item 47.

43. Mushulatubbee et al. to Andrew Jackson, December 23, 1830, 23rd Cong., 1st sess., SD 512, vol. 2, pp. 205–206; WW to James Barbour, April 15, 1826, LROIA, Choctaw Agency, roll 169, frame 346, NARA; CK to Evarts, July 19, 1824, CKC, box 2, folder 7, item 2, WHC; CK to Evarts, August 8, 1825, CKC, box 2, folder 6, item 47.

44. CK to unknown, July 5, 1825, CKC, box 3, folder 8, item 48, WHC; Israel Folsom to PPP, September 17, 1841, PPPP, folder 301, GMA; Meyer, *Life and Times*, 301–302; RMJ paraphrased in John Pitchlynn to PPP, January 10, 1835, PPPC, box 1, folder 45, WHC; CK to Evarts, August 8, 1825, CKC, box 2, folder 6, item 47, WHC.

45. David Folsom to McKenney, June 27, 1826, LROIA, Choctaw Agency, roll 169, frames 276–280, NARA; McDonald to McKenney, April 27, 1826, LROIA, Choctaw Agency, roll 169, frame 319, NARA; McKenney to Kingsbury, August 3, 1825, 26th Cong., 2nd sess., HD 109, no. 3, pp. 8–9; McKenney to Kingsbury, October 20, 1825, 26th Cong., 2nd sess., HD 109, no. 9, p. 14; Resolution of the Choctaw General Council, August 27, 1825, TLML, NARA; Greenwood Leflore to James Barbour, January 9, 1828, LROIA, Schools, roll 773, frame 1160, NARA.

46. Committee upon Schools Report to the General Council, n.d., PPPP, folder 381A, GMA.

47. David Folsom to Students of CA, August 15, 1826, published in *The Western Luminary*, October 25, 1826; Cyrus Kingsbury to the Choctaw General Council, October 24, 1825, LROIA, Schools, roll 772, frames 585–587, NARA; RMJ to OIA, September 27, 1825, LROIA, Schools, roll 772, frame 537, NARA.

48. Paraphrase of elders' speech in WW to TH, April 13, 1828, THP, folder 4, FHS.

Chapter 2

1. Edgar Hume Erskine, *Lafayette in Kentucky* (Frankfort, KY: Transylvania College and the Society of the Cincinnati in the State of Virginia, 1937), 101–102; Ebenezer Hiram Stedman, *Bluegrass Craftsman: Being the Reminiscences of Ebenezer Hiram Stedman, Papermaker: 1808–1885*, ed. Frances L. S. Dugan and Jacqueline P. Bull (Lexington: University of Kentucky Press, 1959), 74–76, 142.

2. *Missouri Intelligencer*, July 2, 1825.

3. Leland Meyer, *The Life and Times of Colonel Richard M. Johnson of Kentucky* (New York: Columbia University Press, 1932), 7–29.

4. Meyer, *Life and Times*, 23–51; *Kentucky Gazette*, November 17, 1826. Bryan's Station is sometimes spelled "Bryant's Station."

5. Lindsey Apple, Frederick A. Johnston, and Ann Bolton Bevins, eds., *Scott County, Kentucky: A History* (Georgetown, KY: Scott County Historical Society, 1993), 34, 43; Isaac W. Skinner, *Kentucky; a Poem* (Frankfort, 1821), 13.

6. Stephen Aron, *How the West Was Lost: The Transformation of Kentucky from Daniel Boone to Henry Clay* (Baltimore: Johns Hopkins University Press, 1999), esp. 156; John Filson, *The Discovery, Settlement, and Present State of Kentucky* (London: John Stockdale, 1793), 61; Harry Toulmin, *A Description of Kentucky in North America: To Which Are Prefixed Miscellaneous Observations Respecting the United States*, ed. Thomas D. Clark (1793; Lexington: University of Kentucky Press, 1945), 91; Lowell H. Harrison and James C. Klotter, *A History of Kentucky* (Lexington: University Press of Kentucky, 1997), 44, 99; Frederika Teute, "Land, Liberty and Labor in the Post-Revolutionary Era: Kentucky as the Promised Land" (Ph.D. diss., Johns Hopkins University, 1988), 404–411; Honor Sachs, *Home Rule: Households, Manhood, and National Expansion on the Eighteenth-Century Kentucky Frontier* (New Haven, CT: Yale University Press, 2015), 39, 44, 76; Apple, Johnston, and Bevins, eds., *Scott County*, 46–50.

7. Lewis Collins, *Historical Sketches of Kentucky* (Maysville, KY: Collins, 1847), 376–377; Reminiscences of Benjamin Tuley, August 25, 1841, DMC, 30CC45; *Kentucky Reporter*, August 12, 1812; *Kentucky Gazette*, July 17, 1804.

8. Speeches by Richard M. Johnson, December 11, 1811, and March 9, 1812, in Annals of Congress, 12th Cong., 1st sess., p. 456, 1191–1192; *Extra Globe*, August 5, 1840, quoted in Meyer, *Life and Times*, 31.

9. James A. Ramage and Andrea S. Watkins, *Kentucky Rising: Democracy, Slavery, and Culture from the Early Republic to the Civil War* (Lexington: University Press of Kentucky, 2011), 116–120; RMJ, Account of the Battle of the Thames before the people of Oswego, DMC, 30CC37; *Lexington Intelligencer*, November 27, 1840; John O'Fallon to William Henry Harrison, April 21, 1834, John O'Fallon Papers, FHS.

10. *American Republic*, April 10, 1812, quoted in Meyer, *Life and Times*; Interview with Judge Ben Monroe, n.d., DMC, 30CC16; Lewis Collins, *Historical Sketches of Kentucky* (Covington, KY: Collins & Co., 1874), vol. 2, 404–410; Account of James Coleman, December 27, 1816, Johnson Family Papers, Richard M. Johnson folder, FHS; Account of Robert McAfee, *Kentucky Gazette*, January 6, 1817; William Emmons, *Authentic Biography of Col. Richard M. Johnson of Kentucky* (New York: Henry Mason, 1833), 33–38.

11. Thomas L. McKenney, *Memoirs, Official and Personal* (New York: Paine & Burgess, 1846), vol. 1, 181–182; Joseph N. Bourassa on the Death of Tecumseh, July 2–3, 1868, DMC, 23S165; Stedman, *Bluegrass Craftsman*, 76.

12. Alan Taylor, *The Civil War of 1812: American Citizens, British Subjects, Irish Rebels, and Indian Allies* (New York: Knopf, 2010).

13. James Y. Kelly interview with Leland Meyer, April 2, 1929, in *Life and Times*, 478; *Niles' Register*, March 12, 1814, p. 37; Margaret Bayard Smith to Mrs. Kirkpatrick, 1816, in Gaillard Hunt, ed., *The First Forty Years of Washington Society in the Family Letters of Margaret Bayard Smith* (New York: Frederick

Ungar, 1965), 129; McKenney, *Memoirs*, vol. 1, 180; Collins, *Historical Sketches of Kentucky*, 379.

14. Stedman, *Bluegrass Craftsman*, 76; Robert Bolt, "Vice President Richard M. Johnson of Kentucky: Hero of the Thames—Or the Great Amalgamator?" *Register of the Kentucky Historical Society* 75 (1977): 195; Meyer, *Life and Times*, 244; *Niles' Register*, January 30, 1819; *Kentucky Gazette*, March 26, 1819.

15. Meyer, *Life and Times*, 286–289; *Speech of Col. Richard M. Johnson of Kentucky on a Proposition to Abolish Imprisonment for Debt, Submitted by Him to the Senate of the United States, January 14, 1823* (Boston: Society for the Relief of the Distressed, 1823).

16. *The Spirit of '76*, May 12, 1826; Meyer, *Life and Times*, Chapter 5; WW to RMJ, May 29, 1819, Papers of RMJ, Library of Congress, Washington, DC.

17. Henry Clay to Langdon Cheves, June 11, 1821, *The Papers of Henry Clay*, ed. James F. Hopkins (Lexington: University of Kentucky Press, 1963), vol. 3, 88–89; Henry Clay to Langdon Cheves, October 3, 1821, *The Papers of Henry Clay*, 121–125; Henry Clay to Nicolas Biddle, January 3, 1824, *The Papers of Henry Clay*, 558–560; *MeasuringWorth*, accessed September 5, 2015, http://www.measuringworth.com/uscompare. See also the Papers of Richard Mentor Johnson at the Library of Congress, which detail the politician's ongoing financial problems.

18. John W. Hall, *Uncommon Defense: Indian Allies in the Black Hawk War* (Cambridge, MA: Harvard University Press, 2009), 70–72; Lucy Eldersveld Murphy, *A Gathering of Rivers: Indians, Métis, and Mining in the Western Great Lakes, 1737–1832* (Lincoln: University of Nebraska Press, 2000), 101–103; *American Sentinel* (Georgetown, KY), September 10, 1824.

19. RMJ to TH, April 26, 1826, THP, folder 2, FHS.

20. RMJ to Capt. A. Partriege, January 4, 1816, Papers of RMJ, LOC; Meyer, *Life and Times*, 156–159; Ronald Lawrence Pitcock, "Regulating Illiterates: 'Uncommon' Schooling at the Choctaw Academy" (Ph.D. diss., University of Kentucky, 2001), 115.

21. *Kentucky Gazette*, March 19, 1819; Extract of a letter from Rev. Staughton to the Secretary of War, August 3, 1819, in Jedidiah Morse, *Report to the Secretary of War of the United States on Indian Affairs* (New Haven, CT: Converse, 1822), Appendix 166–167; Evelyn Crady Adams, "Kentucky's Choctaw Academy, 1819–1842: A Commercial Enterprise," *Filson Club Quarterly* 26 (1952): 28–36.

22. Hume, *Lafayette in Kentucky*, 102; National Historical Landmark Nomination, Nicodemus Historic District, 2013, National Park Service, p. 61; WW to James Barbour, July 12, 1825, LROIA, Choctaw Agency, roll 169, frame 222, NARA; Kingsbury to Evarts, August 8, 1825, CKC, box 2, folder 6, item 47, WHC; RMJ to War Department, September 27, 1825, 26th Cong., 2nd sess., HD 109, no. 5. Julia's work preparing for the school is not described in detail, but other documents confirm that she regularly paid for school and plantation goods and supervised seamstresses. See, for example, RMJ to TH, February 26, 1826, THP, folder 2, FHS; RMJ to TH, March 4, 1826, THP, folder 2, FHS.

23. Johnson-Chinn Family Papers, private collection; "Chine," *Oxford English Dictionary*, accessed February 10, 2006, http://www.oed.com; "Chin," *Forebears*, accessed February 10, 2016, http://forebears.io/surnames/chin; Judge James Y. Kelly Manuscript, in Meyer, *Life and Times*, 477; *Kentucky Sentinel*, June 10, 1835; Annette Gordon-Reed, *The Hemingses of Monticello: An*

American Family (New York: Norton, 2008), 80, 108; LCM, folder 2, pp. 12–16, KU.

24. Meyer, *Life and Times*, 47, 303–306, 318–319; Margaret Bayard Smith to Mrs. Kirkpatrick, 1816, in *The First Forty Years of Washington Society in the Family Letters of Margaret Bayard Smith*, ed. Gaillard Hunt (New York: Frederick Ungar, 1965), 129; Personal communication with Brenda Brent Wilfert, December 14, 2014; Letter from TH, reprinted in *Louisville Advertiser*, July 3, 1835; Dialog recorded in LCM, folder 2, pp. 12–16, KU. The LCM is based on oral history and interviews with elderly members of the community of Nicodemus, Kansas, an Exoduster town settled in part by ex-slaves from the Johnson plantation.

25. Gordon-Reed, *Hemingses of Monticello*, 106–107, 281, 353; Kent Anderson Leslie, *Woman of Color, Daughter of Privilege: Amanda America Dickson, 1849–1893* (Athens: University of Georgia Press, 1995); Martha Hodes, *White Women, Black Men: Illicit Sex in the Nineteenth-Century South* (New Haven, CT: Yale University Press, 1997); Joshua D. Rothman, *Notorious in the Neighborhood: Sex and Families across the Color Line in Virginia, 1787–1861* (Chapel Hill: University of North Carolina Press, 2003); Timothy J. Lockley, "Crossing the Race Divide: Interracial Sex in Antebellum Savannah," *Slavery and Abolition* 18 (1997): 159–173; James Patriot Wilson to Patrick Wilson, April 1803, Misc. Collections, American Philosophical Society, Philadelphia, PA.

26. Pauli Murray, ed., *States' Laws on Race and Color* (Athens: University of Georgia Press, 1997); Gordon-Reed, *The Hemingses of Monticello*, 87, 409; Hodes, *White Women, Black Men*, 122, 199–200.

27. Sharon Block, *Rape and Sexual Power in Early America* (Chapel Hill: University of North Carolina Press, 2006), esp. 241; *Running a Thousand Miles for Freedom; or the Escape of William and Ellen Craft from Slavery* (London: William Tweedie, 1860), 16–17; Harriet Ann Jacobs, *Incidents in the Life of a Slave Girl*, ed. Lydia Marie Child (London: William Tweedie, 1862), 81.

28. Emily Clark, *The Strange History of the American Quadroon: Free Women of Color in the Revolutionary Atlantic World* (Chapel Hill: University of North Carolina Press, 2013), 64; Kathleen DuVal, "Indian Intermarriage and Métissage in Colonial Louisiana," *William and Mary Quarterly* 65 (2008): 267–304; Claire A. Lyons, *Sex among the Rabble: An Intimate History of Gender & Power in the Age of Revolution, Philadelphia, 1730–1830* (Chapel Hill: University of North Carolina Press, 2006), 353; Hodes, *White Women, Black Men*, 49–50; Myers, *Forging Freedom*, 57, 132.

29. RMJ to Humphrey Marshall, May 26, 1840, Humphrey Marshall Papers, folder 1, FHS; LCM, folder 2, pp. 16–17, KU; Recollections of John Wilson, 17CC16, DMC; Rhys Isaac, "Monticello Stories Old and New," in *Sally Hemings & Thomas Jefferson: History, Memory, and Civic Culture*, ed. Jan Ellen Lewis and Peter S. Onuf (Charlottesville: University Press of Virginia, 1999), 120; *Cincinnati Daily Gazette*, June 22, 1835; *Indiana Daily Democrat*, July 17, 1835; *Lexington Observer & Kentucky Reporter*, July 1, 1835; François Furstenburg, "Atlantic Slavery, Atlantic Freedom: George Washington, Slavery, and Transatlantic Abolitionist Networks," *William and Mary Quarterly* 68 (2011): 247–286; Stedman, *Bluegrass Craftsman*, 76; Kelly Manuscript, in Meyer, *Life and Times*, 477.

30. Today, some Johnson family members believe that it was Henry Johnson who destroyed Richard's correspondence with Julia. This would make sense; after

Richard's death, Henry and another brother, John, testified that Richard "left no widow, children, father or mother living" and then claimed his property. Personal Correspondence, Brenda Brent Wilfert, December 13, 2014; Fayette County Order Book no. 13, June 11, 1851, p. 136.

31. Ann Bolton Bevins, *A History of Scott County, as Told by Select Buildings* (Georgetown, KY: Bevins, 1981), 272–273; *American Sentinel* (Georgetown, KY), September 10, 1824; RMJ to TH, April 30, 1828, THP, folder 4, FHS; *Louisville Advertiser*, July 3, 1835; LCM, folder 2, p. 15, KU; *The Argus of Western America*, June 20, 1827; RMJ to TH, December 9, 1829, THP, folder 1, FHS.

32. *American Sentinel* (Georgetown, KY), September 10, 1824; RMJ to TH, February 26, 1826, THP, folder 2, FHS; RMJ to TH, March 4, 1826; RMJ to TH, December 9, 1829, both THP, folder 1, FHS.

33. 1820 United States Federal Census, Records of the Bureau of the Census, M33, roll 27, p. 131, NARA; RMJ to TH, January 13, 1826, THP, folder 2, FHS; RMJ to TH, December 8, 1825, THP, folder 1, FHS. For women as "deputy husbands" and managers of "housefuls," see Laurel Thatcher Ulrich, *Good Wives: Image and Reality in the Lives of Women in Northern New England, 1650–1750* (New York: Knopf, 1982), 37; Ellen Hartigan-O'Connor, *The Ties That Buy: Women and Commerce in Revolutionary America* (Philadelphia: University of Pennsylvania Press, 2009), 14.

34. RMJ to TH, February 26, 1826, RMJ to TH, March 4, 1826, both THP, folder 2, FHS; Hartigan-O'Connor, *Ties That Buy*, 69, 140–141.

35. RMJ to TH, December 31, 1825, THP, folder 1, FHS; RMJ to TH, January 13, 1826, THP, folder 2, FHS. This "stone house" may be the small building preserved on the original Choctaw Academy site to the immediate left of where the big house once stood.

36. Gordon-Reed, 301; *The Liberator*, July 25, 1845; Meyer, *Life and Times*, 324; *Lexington Observer and Kentucky Reporter*, July 22, 1835.

37. Lucas, *History of Blacks in Kentucky*, 14; Interview of Addie Murphy by J. C. Meadors, August 13, 1938, in "Slave Interviews, Notes and Data on Kentucky Slavery," typescript by J. Winston Coleman, JWCP, UK; Stedman, *Bluegrass Craftsman*, 76; Hartigan-O'Connor, *Ties That Buy*, 172–173; John Styles, "Involuntary Consumers? Servants and Their Clothes in Eighteenth-Century England," *Textile History* 33 (2002): 9–21.

38. RMJ to TH, March 7, 1828, THP, folder 4, FHS; Interview of Addie Murphy by J. C. Meadors, August 13, 1938, JWCP, UK; *Louisville Advertiser*, July 3, 1835.

39. Interview of Addie Murphy by J. C. Meadors, August 13, 1938, JWCP, UK; *American Sentinel* (Georgetown, KY), September 10, 1824. Johnson's financial dealings are detailed in the Papers of Richard Mentor Johnson at the Library of Congress.

40. RMJ to TH, December 31, 1825, THP, folder 1, FHS; RMJ to TH, January 13, 1826, THP, folder 2, FHS; RMJ to TH, n.d., THP, folder 17, FHS.

41. Gary B. Nash, *Forging Freedom: The Formation of Philadelphia's Black Community, 1720–1840* (Cambridge, MA: Harvard University Press, 1988), 148; Gordon-Reed, *Hemingses of Monticello*, 324; Myers, *Forging Freedom*, 2–3, 11; *American Sentinel*, September 10, 1824; Hartigan-O'Connor, *Ties That Buy*, 186.

42. John Norvell to John McLean, January 23, 1832, The Papers of John McLean, container 6, roll 3, LOC; *Louisville Advertiser*, July 3, 1835.

43. Speech of RMJ on the Missouri Question, February 1820, Annals of Congress, Senate, 16th Cong., 1st sess., 345–359, quotations on pp. 346, 348; *Georgetown Weekly Times*, June 5, 1872; Nicholas Guyatt, *Bind Us Apart: How the First American Liberals Invented Racial Segregation* (New York: Basic, 2016), 175–176.

44. Speech of RMJ on the Missouri Question, February 1820, Annals of Congress, Senate, 16th Cong., 1st sess., 345–359; RMJ to TH, January 13, 1826, THP, folder 2 FHS.

45. Scott County Order Book C, May 20, 1828, p. 111, October 5, 1832, p. 382, both in KHS; Lucas, *History of Blacks in Kentucky*, 84–85; Meyer, *Life and Times*, 295–296.

46. RMJ to Francis B. Blair, June 16, 1835, Blair-Lee Family Papers, box 14, folder 3, PU; RMJ to Humphrey Marshall, May 26, 1840, Humphrey Marshall Papers, folder 1, FHS; GCBC Minutes, April 20, 1828, book 2, pp. 169–170, SBTS.

47. LCM, folder 2, p. 18, KU; Gordon-Reed, *Hemingses of Monticello*, 639; Lucas, *History of Free Blacks in Kentucky*, 111–112.

48. Honor Sachs, *Home Rule: Households, Manhood, and National Expansion on the Eighteenth-Century Kentucky Frontier* (New Haven, CT: Yale University Press, 2015), 147; RMJ to TH, December 7, 1835, RMJ to TH, February 26, 1836, both in THP, folder 10, FHS; RMJ to Francis P. Blair, June 16, 1835, Blair-Lee Family Papers, box 14, folder 3, PU.

49. RMJ to Adaline Johnson Scott, December 12, 1833, THP, folder 8, FHS; Scott County Deed Book L, November 9, 1832, p. 126, KHS. See Chapter 8 and the Conclusion for more on Imogene and Adaline as Richard's heirs.

50. RMJ to TH, January 6, 1826, THP, folder 2, FHS; Stedman, *Bluegrass Craftsman*, 76; *Louisville Advertiser*, July 3, 1835, reprint of a letter from TH.

51. Benjamin Perley Poore, *Perley's Reminiscences of Sixty Years in the National Metropolis* (Philadelphia: Hubbard Brothers, 1886), 153, 164.

52. Heather Andrea Williams, *Self-Taught: African American Education in Slavery and Freedom* (Chapel Hill: University of North Carolina Press, 2005), 24–26.

53. Nash, *Forging Freedom*, 202, 269; *The Philanthropist, or Cincinnati Weekly Herald*, February 26, 1836; Lucas, *History of Blacks in Kentucky*, 140–144.

54. Myers, *Forging Freedom*, 101–102; Lawrence A. Cremin, *American Education: The National Experience, 1783–1876* (New York: Harper & Row, 1980), 229; Daniel Walker Howe, *What Hath God Wrought: The Transformation of America, 1815–1848* (New York: Oxford University Press, 2007), 451.

55. LCM, folder 7, pp. 29–31, KU.

56. LCM, folder 7, pp. 33–34, KU; RMJ to TH, December 31, 1825, THP, folder 1, FHS.

57. Lucas, *History of Blacks in Kentucky*, 140–144.

58. RMJ to Francis P. Blair, June 16, 1835, Blair-Lee Family Papers, box 14, folder 3, PU; Letter from TH, printed in *Louisville Advertiser*, July 3, 1835; Emma Rouse Lloyd, "Clasping Hands with Generations Past," THP, folder 1, FHS; Shelly D. Rouse, "Colonel Dick Johnson's Choctaw Academy: A Forgotten Educational Experiment," *Ohio Archaeological and Historical Publications* 25 (1916): 92–93; Lindsey Apple, Frederick A. Johnston, and Ann Bolton Bevins, *Scott County, Kentucky: A History* (Georgetown, KY: Scott County Historical Society, 1993), 76; GCBC Minutes, book 2, SBTS; Thomas Henderson, *An Easy*

System of the Geography of the World: By Way of Question and Answer, Principally Designed for Schools (Lexington, KY: Thomas T. Skillman, 1813), 140.

59. RMJ to TH, December 8, 1825, THP, folder 1, FHS; Letter from TH printed in *Louisville Advertiser,* July 3, 1835.

60. Myers, *Forging Freedom,* 78–89; RMJ to TH, January 13, 1826, THP, folder 2, FHS. On Johnson's reminders, see, for example, RMJ to TH, December 2, 1825, RMJ to TH, January 13–14, 1826, both in THP, folder 1, FHS; RMJ to TH, n.d., THP, folder 17, FHS.

61. Frederick Marryat, *A Diary in America: With Remarks on Its Institutions* (Philadelphia: Carey and Hart, 1839), vol. 1, 159; *Lexington Observer & Kentucky Reporter,* July 1, 1835; *The Torch Light* (Hagerstown, MD), June 11, 1835; *Louisville Advertiser,* July 3, 1835; RMJ to Adaline Johnson Scott, December 12, 1833, THP, folder 8, FHS.

62. William Emmons, *Authentic Biography of Colonel Richard M. Johnson of Kentucky* (Boston, 1834), 57; RMJ speech of January 12, 1820, Annals of Congress, House of Representatives, 16th Cong., 1st sess.

63. For examples of kinship terms, see RMJ to Adaline Johnson Scott, December 12, 1833, THP, folder 8, FHS; RMJ to TH, March 7, 1828, THP, folder 4, FHS; RMJ to TH, January 13, 1826, folder 2, FHS; RMJ to Marshall, May 26, 1840, Marshall Papers, folder 1, FHS.

Chapter 3

1. John Bond to James Barbour, October 9, 1826, LROIA, Schools, roll 773, frames 17–18, NARA; CA Trustees' Report, October 12, 1827, TLML, NARA; RMJ to TH, March 28, 1834, THP, folder 9, FHS; Speeches reprinted in *Daily National Intelligencer,* December 21, 1826.

2. *Daily National Intelligencer,* December 21, 1826.

3. Speeches reprinted in *Daily National Intelligencer,* December 21, 1826.

4. CK to ABCFM, July 24, 1826, CKC, box 3, folder 9, item 15, WHC; RMJ to James Barbour, August 20, 1826, GFC, box 9, folder 2, OKHS; TLM to Secretary of War, December 9, 1825, TLML, NARA; CK to McKenney, October 11, 1825, 26th Cong., 2nd sess., HD 109, no. 12, p. 17.

5. CK to Jeremiah Evarts, April 28, 1828, CKC, box 3, folder 9, item 1, WHC; Interview of Susannah Lyles by Brother Cushman, n.d., CKC, box 3, folder 9, item 38; Greenwood Leflore to CK, August 8, 1828, CKC, box 3, folder 9; CK to Jeremiah Evarts, August 8, 1825, CKC, box 2, folder 6, item 47; TH to Lewis Cass, July 22, 1833, LROIA, roll 776, frame 203, NARA.

6. John Johnston to Charles Cist, October 22, 1847, copy in Miami folder 1834–1847, GLOVEC; Lee Compere to Thomas L. McKenney, May 20, 1828, LROIA, Creek Agency, roll 221, frames 704–707, NARA; Herman J. Viola, *Thomas L. McKenney: Architect of America's Early Indian Policy* (Chicago: Swallow Press, 1974), 193; Chickasaw Chiefs to James Barbour, March 11, 1828, LROIA, Schools, roll 773, frames 945–947, NARA; Robert Bell to Thomas L. McKenney, March 12, 1830, LROIA, Schools, roll 774, frames 276–277, NARA.

7. RMJ to McKenney, July 25, 1828, LROIA, Schools, roll 773, frames 1084–1086, NARA; William Clark to RMJ, April 16, 1830, LROIA, Schools, roll 774, frames 312–315, NARA; TH and Trustees of CA to John Eaton, November 17,

1829, LROIA, Schools, roll 774, frame 98, NARA; CA Quarterly Report, April 30, 1827, LROIA, Schools, roll 773, frames 648–651, NARA; TLM to James Barbour, December 1, 1827, LSOIA, vol. 4, p. 162, NARA; John Doughterty to RMJ, November 23, 1832, PPPC, box 1, folder 33, WHC.

8. Creek Chiefs to James Barbour, April 1, 1826, LROIA, Schools, roll 773, frames 60–62, NARA.

9. R. David Edmunds, *The Potawatomis: Keepers of the Fire* (Norman: University of Oklahoma Press, 1978), esp. 218–229; Isaac McCoy to Lewis Cass, June 30, 1827, LROIA, Michigan Superintendency, roll 419, frames 984–985, NARA; Potawatomi Contract with CA, May 4, 1827, copy in Potawatomi 1826–1827 folder, GLOVEC.

10. RMJ to TH, January 30, 1826, THP, folder 2, FHS; RMJ to Thomas L. McKenney, April 1, 1826, LROIA, Schools, roll 773, frames 147–149, NARA; WW to TH, February 21, 1826, THP, folder 2, FHS; Speech of George Harkins, reprinted in *Daily National Intelligencer*, December 21, 1826. On Indian identity, see Gregory Evans Dowd, *A Spirited Resistance: The North American Indian Struggle for Unity, 1745–1815* (Baltimore: Johns Hopkins University Press, 1992); Nancy Shoemaker, "How Indians Got to Be Red," *American Historical Review* 102 (1997): 625–644; Nancy Shoemaker, *A Strange Likeness: Becoming Red and White in Eighteenth-Century North America* (New York: Oxford University Press, 2004). For sample contracts, see copies in TLML.

11. John Ross to Andrew Jackson, September 1, 1834, LROIA, Schools, roll 776, frames 913–915, NARA; Elbert Herring to Benjamin Reynolds, December 11, 1834, RG 75, Chickasaw Removal Records, book 1, p. 31, NARA; John Connolly to RMJ, August 25, 1832, PPPP, folder 116, GMA; CA Quarterly Report, January 31, 1831, LROIA, Schools, roll 775, frames 78–81, NARA; Richard Cummins to William Clark, May 7, 1838, LROIA, Schools, roll 778, frames 771–772, NARA; WW to TLM, February 1, 1827, LROIA, Schools, roll 773, frames 891–892, NARA; Elbert Herring to Lewis Cass, May 5, 1836, LROIA, Schools, roll 777, frame 847, NARA.

12. RMJ to TH, February 14, 1831, THP, folder 6, FHS; WW to TH, July 29, THP, folder 2, FHS; Theda Perdue, *Cherokee Women: Gender and Culture Change, 1700–1835* (Lincoln: University of Nebraska Press, 1999).

13. Expenses for Horatio Grooms, November 1834, LROIA, Schools, roll 776, frames 717–719, NARA; TH to RMJ, December 9, 1830, LROIA, Schools, roll 775, frames 114–115, NARA; RMJ to Elbert Herring, November 9, 1833, LROIA, Schools, roll 776, frames 237–239, NARA; To the Public from John Pitchlynn, Andrew Weir, and Sylvester Pearl, November 7, 1834, 26th Cong., 2nd sess., HD 109, no. 87; RMJ to TH, February 3, 1830, THP, folder 6, FHS.

14. J. L. Douglas to TH, July 23, 1838, PPPP, folder 204, GMA; CA Quarterly Report, September 30, 1843, LROIA, Schools, roll 781, frame 634, NARA; DV to William Medill, June 27, 1847, LROIA, Schools, roll 783, frame 1215, NARA; RMJ to TLM, November 22, 1826, LROIA, Schools, roll 773, frame 166, NARA; DV to William S. Crawford, July 28, 1843, LROIA, Schools, roll 781, frame 624, NARA; RMJ to TH, December 19, 1827, THP, folder 3, FHS.

15. George A. Pettitt, "Primitive Education in North America," *University of California Publications in American Archaeology and Ethnology*, vol. 43 (1946): 59–73, quotation on p. 59; John Edwards, "The Choctaw Indians in

the Middle of the Nineteenth Century," *Chronicles of Oklahoma* 10 (1932): 421; John R. Swanton, *Source Material for the Social and Ceremonial Life of the Choctaw Indians* (Tuscaloosa: University of Alabama Press, 2001), 119–120.

16. J. T. Hadden to Jeremiah Evarts, June 28, 1824, PABCFM, unit 6, roll 755, frame 1171; List of Choctaw Students at Choctaw Academy, 1 Dec 1825, LROIA, Schools, roll 772, frames 512–513, NARA; List of Choctaw Students at Choctaw Academy, 1826, roll 773, frame 117; WW to TH, April 13, 1828, THP, folder 4, FHS.

17. *Daily National Intelligencer,* July 11, 1828; TH to Lewis Cass, January 23, 1837, LROIA, Schools, roll 778, frames 155–156, NARA; RMJ to TH, March 23, 1828, THP, folder 4, FHS; Student Lists, compiled from LROIA, Schools, NARA.

18. CA Quarterly Report, May 1, 1826, LROIA, Schools, roll 773, frames 95–100, NARA; TH Report, November 25, 1825, PPPC, box 5, folder 3, WHC; RMJ to TH, December 13, 1826, THP, folder 2, FHS; John Mullay to William Medill, July 27, 1846, LROIA, roll 783, frame 451, NARA.

19. Regulations of CA, January 1, 1834, LROIA, Schools, roll 781, frames 566–570, NARA; Certificate of John Bond, October 4, 1826, LROIA, Schools, roll 773, frame 19, NARA; CA Quarterly Report, September 30, 1847, LROIA, Schools, roll 783, frame 1222, NARA; Receipt, March 18, 1826, LROIA, Schools, roll 773, frame 164, NARA; RMJ to William Crawford, March 4, 1840, 26th Cong., 2nd sess., HD 109, no. 161, p. 139.

20. CA Quarterly Report, August 1, 1828, PPPP, folder 65, GMA; CA Quarterly Report, January 1, 1843, roll 781, frames 572–589, NARA; TH to N. M. Henderson, May 13, 1832, THP, folder 7, FHS; CA Quarterly Report, November 1, 1833, PPPC, box 5, folder 27, WHC; List of Clothing Deficient, compiled by J. W. Barrow and Wall McCann, 1841, LROIA, Schools, roll 780, frames 241–244, NARA.

21. John K. Mahon, *History of the Second Seminole War, 1835–1842* (Gainesville: University of Florida Press, 1985), 185; J. Leitch Wright Jr., *Creeks and Seminoles: The Destruction and Regeneration of the Muscogulge People* (Lincoln: University of Nebraska Press, 1986), 231; John Pitchlynn to Andrew Jackson, August 18, 1831, PPPP, folder 105, GMA.

22. RMJ to TH, April 6, 1828, THP, folder 4, FHS; TH to War Department, March 28, 1831, 26th Cong., 2nd sess, HD 109, no. 44, p. 47; CA Quarterly Report, May 1, 1826, LROIA, Schools, roll 773, frames 95–100, NARA; TH to RMJ, December 18, 1837, 26th Cong., 2nd sess., HD 109, no. 134, p. 115. "Sons of the forest" was a popular way to describe Indians at that time.

23. All textbooks cited in this chapter come from CA textbook lists. Lindley Murray, *English Grammar, Adapted to the Different Classes of Learners* (Boston: T. Bedlington, 1825), 70; RMJ to TLM, November 22, 1826, LROIA, Schools, roll 773, frame 166, NARA; RMJ to TH, March 28, 1835, THP, folder 10, FHS; CA Quarterly Report, January 1, 1843, LROIA, Schools, roll 781, frames 572–589, NARA; Personal communication, email from Daryl Baldwin, February 15, 2016; Personal communication, email from David Costa, February 15, 2016. There are many other English sounds that would have been difficult for monolingual speakers of Indian languages; I offer only a few examples here to give the reader an idea of the vast linguistic diversity represented at Choctaw Academy.

24. WW to TH, December 16, 1825, THP, folder 1, FHS; James Crawford, *Hold Your Tongue: Bilingualism and the Politics of "English Only"* (Reading, MA: Addison-Wesley, 1992).

25. Murray, *English Grammar*, 44, 19–21; Noah Webster, *The Elementary Spelling Book; Being an Improvement on the American Spelling Book* (Wells River, VT: Ira White, 1835), 50; CA Quarterly Report, November 1, 1827, TLML, NARA; CA Quarterly Report, April 1, 1838, LROIA, Schools, roll 778, frames 922–923, NARA.

26. Murray, *English Grammar*, 274; Carolyn Eastman, *A Nation of Speechifiers: Making an American Public after the Revolution* (Chicago: University of Chicago Press, 2009); Caroline Winterer, *The Culture of Classicism: Ancient Greece and Rome in American Intellectual Life, 1780–1910* (Baltimore: Johns Hopkins University Press, 2002), 68; Sandra M. Gustafson, *Eloquence Is Power: Oratory and Performance in Early America* (Chapel Hill: University of North Carolina Press, 2000), xix–xxiii; CA Trustees' Report, July 1827, PPPC, box 5, folder 11, WHC; Merrill D. Peterson, ed., *Thomas Jefferson: Writings* (New York: Library of America, 1984), 188; Henry C. Benson, *Life among the Choctaw Indians and Sketches of the South-west* (New York: Johnson Reprint Co., 1970), 222.

27. RMJ to TH, December 17, 1825, THP, folder 1, FHS; RMJ to TH, January 13, 1826, THP, folder 2, FHS; RMJ to TH, March 23, 1828, THP, folder 4, FHS.

28. Colin G. Calloway, *Pen and Ink Witchcraft: Treaties and Treaty Making in American Indian History* (New York: Oxford University Press, 2013), quotations on pp. 30, 36; Robert Allen Warrior, *Tribal Secrets: Recovering American Indian Intellectual Traditions* (Minneapolis: University of Minnesota Press, 1994); Philip H. Round, *Removable Type: Histories of the Book in Indian Country, 1663–1880* (Chapel Hill: University of North Carolina Press, 2010), 11–12, 22, 38–56, 115; Lisa Brooks, *The Common Pot: The Recovery of Native Space in the Northeast* (Minneapolis: University of Minnesota Press, 2008); Craig S. Womack, *Red on Red: Native American Literary Separatism* (Minneapolis: University of Minnesota Press, 1999), 16; Shoemaker, *A Strange Likeness*, 63–66, 160 n. 32; Jill Lepore, *The Name of War: King Philip's War and the Origins of American Identity* (New York: Knopf, 1998), 67; Grayson B. Noley, "The History of Education in the Choctaw Nation from Precolonial Times to 1830" (Ph.D. diss., Pennsylvania State University, 1979), 94.

29. Timothy Walker to Ellis Falling, September 12, 1838, LROIA, Schools, roll 778, frames 945–947, NARA; WW to TH, July 29, 1826, THP, folder 2, FHS; RMJ to TH, March 23, 1828, THP, folder 4, FHS.

30. CA Trustees' Report, August 1, 1828, PPPC, box 5, folder 13, WHC; CA Quarterly Report, April 30, 1833, PPPC, box 5, folder 24, WHC; CA Quarterly Report, July 31, 1834, PPPC, box 5, folder 31, WHC.

31. Winterer, *Culture of Classicism*, 44; Colin B. Burke, *American Collegiate Populations: A Test of the Traditional View* (New York: Oxford University Press, 1982), 36–37, 44, 96, 105, 234; Lawrence A. Cremin, *American Education: The National Experience, 1783–1876* (New York: Harper & Row, 1980).

32. Burke, *American Collegiate Populations*, 131–138; Richard Turner, *A New Introduction to Book-Keeping, after the Italian Method* (Salem, MA: Cushing & Appleton, 1820); Samuel Milroy to RMJ, August 24, 1839, 26th Cong., 2nd sess., HD 109, no. 109, p. 132.

33. Robert Gibson, *The Theory and Practice of Surveying; Containing all the Instructions Requisite for the Skilful Practice of this Art* (New York: Evert Duyckinck, 1821); Viola, *Thomas L. McKenney*, 190–191.
34. Murray, *English Grammar*, 45, 82; Webster, *Elementary Spelling Book*.
35. Cremin, *American Education*, 394; Webster, *Elementary Spelling Book*, 29; Jesse Torrey, *The Moral Instructor; and Guide to Virtue: Being a Compendium of Moral Philosophy* (Philadelphia: Kimber and Sharpless, 1824), iv, 18, 20.
36. Jesse Olney, *A Practical System of Modern Geography; or a View of the Present State of the World*, 34th ed. (New York: Robinson, Pratt & Co., 1841), 147; S. G. Goodrich, *The Fourth Reader for the Use of Schools* (Louisville, KY: Morton and Griswold, 1839), 25; Charles A. Goodrich, *The Child's History of the United States Designed as a First Book of History for Schools*, 7th ed. (Boston: Carter, Hendee & Co., 1835), 22; CA Quarterly Report, February 1, 1828, TLML.
37. Thomas Henderson, *An Easy System of the Geography of the World; By Way of Question and Answer Principally Designed for Schools* (Lexington, KY: Thomas T. Skillman, 1813), 45; B. D. Emerson, *The Second-Class Reader: Designed for the Use of the Middle Class of Schools in the United States* (Boston: Russell, Odiorne, & Metcalf, 1834), 144; William H. McGuffey, *McGuffey's Newly Revised Second Reader* (Cincinnati: Winthrop B. Smith, 1844), 159–160; Torrey, *The Moral Instructor*, 252; Ruth Miller Elson, *Guardians of Tradition: American Schoolbooks of the Nineteenth Century* (Lincoln: University of Nebraska Press, 1964), 77.
38. Samuel G. Goodrich, *A Pictorial History of Greece: Ancient and Modern* (Philadelphia: Sorin & Ball and Samuel Agnew, 1846), 10; Gibson, *Theory and Practice of Surveying*, iii; Torrey, *The Moral Instructor*, 53–56; Alexander Fraser Tytler, *Elements of General History, Ancient and Modern* (Concord, NH: Horatio Hill, 1824), 19, 175, 182–192, 398.
39. Jedidiah Morse and Sidney Edwards Morse, *A New System of Geography, Ancient and Modern, for the Use of Schools*, 24th ed. (Boston: Richardson & Lord, 1824), 35; Goodrich, *Child's History*, 44.
40. Morse and Morse, *A New System of Geography*, 117; Henderson, *An Easy System of the Geography of the World*, 93.
41. Torrey, *The Moral Instructor*, 29–30; Goodrich, *Child's History*, 138.
42. Henderson, *An Easy System of the Geography of the World*, 1–14, 21, 130–141, 194–196; Wayne J. Urban and Jennings L. Wagoner Jr., *American Education: A History*, 3rd ed. (New York: McGraw Hill, 2004), 82.
43. RMJ to TH, January 9, 1828, THP, folder 4, FHS; Robert Ould to TLM, June 28, 1828, LROIA, Schools, roll 773, frames 1195–1197, NARA; CA Quarterly Report, August 1, 1828, LROIA, Schools, roll 773, frames 1010–1015, NARA; Ronald Rayman, "Joseph Lancaster's System of Instruction and American Indian Education, 1815–1838," *History of Education Quarterly* 21 (1981): 395–409.
44. Ebenezer Hotchkin to William Armstrong, July 1841, LROIA, Schools, roll 780, frames 642–645, NARA; CA Quarterly Report, January 1, 1843, LROIA, Schools, roll 781, frame 588, NARA.
45. Greenwood LeFlore to James Barbour, June 27, 1827, TLML, NARA; Resolutions of the General Council of Students of CA, June 1827, TLML, NARA; John Page to PPP, 1841, PPPC, box 1, folder 58, WHC; CA Quarterly

Report, January 31, 1832, PPPC, box 5, folder 19, WHC; Timothy J. Williams, *Intellectual Manhood: University, Self, and Society in the Antebellum South* (Chapel Hill: University of North Carolina Press, 2015), 175–178.

46. CA Trustees' Report, August 1, 1828, LROIA, Schools, roll 773, frames 1006–1008, NARA; Frances L. S. Dugan and Jacqueline P. Bull, eds., *Bluegrass Craftsman: Being the Reminiscences of Ebenezer Hiram Stedman, Papermaker: 1808–1885* (Lexington: University of Kentucky Press, 1959), 30–31; CA Medical Report, LROIA, Schools, roll 779, frame 307, NARA; RMJ to Cave Johnson, January 8, 1845, 28th Cong., 2nd sess., HR 193, p. 9; Robert Evans to William S. Crawford, October 21, 1841, LROIA, Schools, roll 780, frame 194, NARA; RMJ to TH, December 9, 1829, THP, folder 1, FHS.

47. JLM to TLM, January 25, 1827, LROIA, Schools, roll 773, frame 792, NARA; John Mullay to William Medill, July 27, 1846, LROIA, Schools, roll 783, frames 447–472, NARA; CA Quarterly Report, October 31, 1826, PPPC, box 5, folder 9, WHC; CA Quarterly Report, April 30, 1830, PPPC, box 5, folder 17, WHC.

48. CA Quarterly Report, January 31, 1826, PPPP, folder 22, GMA; CA Trustees' Report, November 22, 1826, roll 773, frames 124–125, NARA; William Staughton to TH, December 8, 1825, TLML, NARA; Trustees' Report, August 18, 1826, PPPC, box 5, folder 6, WHC; Trustees' Report, May 1, 1826, LROIA, Schools, roll 773, frame 127, NARA; CA Quarterly Report, May 1, 1826, LROIA, Schools, roll 773, frame 98.

49. TH to Greenwood LeFlore, September 13, 1828, LROIA, Choctaw Agency, roll 169, frames 510–513, NARA; Judge James Y. Kelly Manuscript, April 2, 1929, in Leland Meyer, *The Life and Times of Colonel Richard M. Johnson of Kentucky* (New York: Columbia University Press, 1932), 477; JLM to TLM, January 25, 1827, LROIA, Schools, roll 773, frames 790–796, NARA; RMJ to David Folsom, September 12, 1828, LROIA, Choctaw Agency, roll 169, frame 537, NARA; Trustees' Report, September 16, 1828, LROIA, Schools, roll 773, frame 1017, NARA; CA Quarterly Report, August 1, 1832, 26th Cong., 2nd sess., HD 109, no. 56, p. 58.

50. William Staughton to TH, December 8, 1825, TLML, NARA; William Staughton to James Barbour, December 22, 1825, LROIA, Schools, roll 772, frame 667, NARA; RMJ to TH, January 30, 1826, THP, folder 2, FHS; RMJ to TH, April 29, 1834, THP, folder 9, FHS; CA Quarterly Report, January 1, 1843, LROIA, Schools, roll 781, frames 572–589, NARA; CA Quarterly Report, August 1, 1828, LROIA, Schools, roll 773, frames 1010–1015, NARA; GCBC Minutes, book 2, SBTS.

51. CA Quarterly Report, April 30, 1827, LROIA, Schools, roll 773, frames 648–651, NARA; GCBC Minutes, December 6–7, book 2, SBTS; CA Quarterly Report, December 31, 1844, LROIA, Schools, roll 782, frames 1220–1223, NARA.

52. CA Quarterly Report, April 30, 1830, PPPC, box 5, folder 17, WHC; CA Quarterly Report, January 1, 1843, LROIA, Schools, roll 781, frame 588, NARA; TH to LeFlore, September 18, 1828, LROIA, Schools, roll 169, frame 510, NARA; CA Quarterly Report, November 1, 1827, TLML, NARA; Catherine E. Kelly, *Republic of Taste: Art, Politics, and Everyday Life in Early America* (Philadelphia: University of Pennsylvania Press, 2016), 50.

53. *Daily National Intelligencer,* December 21, 1826; *New Hampshire Observer,* February 27, 1826; *Niles Weekly Register,* December 10, 1825; RMJ to TH, February 10, 1828, THP, folder 4, FHS; *Kentucky Gazette,* November 4, 1825.

54. Henderson, *An Easy System of the Geography of the World,* 3.

Chapter 4

1. RMJ to David Folsom, September 12, 1828, LROIA, Choctaw Agency, roll 169, frames 520–522, NARA; Principal Chiefs of the Cherokee Nation to George Vashon, December 8, 1833, LROIA, Schools, roll 776, frames 988–989, NARA; RMJ to Henderson, March 1, 1830, THP, folder 6, FHS. For evaluations of Indian country's fine coffee, see, for example, Gregory A. Waselkov and Kathryn E. Holland Brand, eds., *William Bartram and the Southeastern Indians* (Lincoln: University of Nebraska Press, 1995), 156; Grant Foreman, ed., *A Traveler in Indian Territory: The Journal of Ethan Allen Hitchcock* (Norman: University of Oklahoma Press, 1996), 153, 198.

2. RMJ to David Folsom, September 12, 1828, LROIA, Choctaw Agency, roll 169, frames 522–524, NARA; RMJ to Elbert Herring, November 9, 1833, LROIA, Schools, roll 776, frame 237, NARA; TH to Greenwood Leflore, September 13, 1828, LROIA, Choctaw Agency, roll 169, frame 514, NARA; RMJ to TH, January 17, 1836, THP, folder 10, FHS; Thomas Chishom, John Jolly, Black Coat, and Walter Webber to George Vashon, December 8, 1833, LROIA, Schools, roll 776, frame 989, NARA; RMJ to TH, March 1, 1830, THP, folder 6, FHS.

3. RMJ to W. L. Morey, March 20, 1845, LROIA, Schools, roll 782, frame 857, NARA; TH to RMJ, December 27, 1830, CRR, Miscellaneous Choctaw Removal Records, Choctaw Academy folder, box 5, NARA; TH to RMJ, February 27, 1838, LROIA, Schools, roll 778, frames 906–907, NARA; RMJ to War Department, September 27, 1825, 26th Cong., 2nd sess., HD 109, no. 5, p. 10.

4. Gary B. Nash, *Forging Freedom: The Formation of Philadelphia's Black Community* (Cambridge, MA: Harvard University Press, 1988); Sean Wilentz, *Chants Democratic: New York City and the Rise of the American Working Class, 1788–1850* (New York: Oxford University Press, 1984); Harry L. Watson, *Liberty and Power: The Politics of Jacksonian America* (New York: Hill and Wang, 1990); Ellen Hartigan-O'Connor, *The Ties That Buy: Women and Commerce in Revolutionary America* (Philadelphia: University of Pennsylvania Press, 2009), 183.

5. Julie Winch, *Philadelphia's Black Elite: Activism, Accommodation, and the Struggle for Autonomy, 1787–1848* (Philadelphia: Temple University Press, 1988); Alexandra Harmon, *Rich Indians: Native People and the Problem of Wealth in American History* (Chapel Hill: University of North Carolina Press, 2010); David R. Roediger, *The Wages of Whiteness: Race and the Making of the American Working Class* (New York: Verso, 1999); Leslie M. Harris, *In the Shadow of Slavery: African Americans in New York City, 1626–1863* (Chicago: University of Chicago Press, 2003); Reginald Horsman, *Race and Manifest Destiny: The Origins of American Racial Anglo-Saxonism* (Cambridge, MA: Harvard University Press, 1981).

6. Christina Snyder, *Slavery in Indian Country: The Changing Face of Captivity in Early America* (Cambridge, MA: Harvard University Press, 2010), Chapter 1;

Daniel K. Richter, *Before the Revolution: America's Ancient Pasts* (Cambridge, MA: Harvard University Press, 2011), Chapter 1; Harmon, *Rich Indians*, Chapter 3; Claudio Saunt, "Taking Account of Property: Stratification among the Creek Indians in the Early Nineteenth Century," *William and Mary Quarterly* 57 (2000): 733–760; Lance K. Greene, "Ethnicity and Material Culture in Antebellum North Carolina," *Southeastern Archaeology* 30 (2011): 64–78; David R. Edmunds, *The Potawatomis: Keepers of the Fire* (Norman: University of Oklahoma Press, 1978), 227; first quotation from Foreman, ed., *A Traveler in Indian Territory*, 186; second quotation from Henry Vose to Peter Pitchlynn, September 13, 1831, PPPC, box 1, folder 26, WHC.

7. Regarding slaves, see John Pitchlynn to PPP, PPPP, June 15, 1824, folder 24, GMA; John Pitchlynn to PPP, PPPP, March 14, 1824, folder 23, GMA; PPP to Edmund Folsom, January 7, 1829, PPPP, folder 67; David W. Baird, *Peter Pitchlynn: Chief of the Choctaws* (Norman: University of Oklahoma Press, 1972), 45–46. For examples of Peter's accounts, see the following bills, all in PPPP at the GMA: from Raser and Co., November 1824–November 1825, folder 32; from Thomas Wofford, February–October 1826, folder 37; from Joseph Vaughn, November 1–December 3, 1827, folder 51. For masonry, see W. David Baird, *Peter Pitchlynn, Chief of the Choctaws* (Norman: University of Oklahoma Press, 1972), 18. For quote, see PPP Diary, December 25, 1828, PPPC, box 5, folder 2, WHC.

8. Marcia Haag and Henry Willis, trans. and eds., *A Gathering of Statesmen: Records of the Choctaw Council Meetings, 1826–1828* (Norman: University of Oklahoma Press, 2013), 99.

9. PPP, Journal of 1826, PPPC, box 6, folder 4, WHC; Baird, *Peter Pitchlynn*, 25–26.

10. JLM to TLM, September 30, 1826, LROIA, Schools, roll 773, frames 359–366, NARA; CA Quarterly Report, April 30, 1827, LROIA, Schools, roll 773, frames 648–651, NARA.

11. PPP to RMJ, October 5, 1826, LROIA, Schools, roll 773, frames 409–410, NARA; RMJ to the Professors of Transylvania University, March 11, 1827, PPPC, box 1, folder 10, WHC.

12. Lowell Harrison and James C. Klotter, *A New History of Kentucky* (Lexington: University Press of Kentucky, 1997), 151–152, Jefferson quote on p. 152; Leland Meyer, *The Life and Times of Colonel Richard M. Johnson of Kentucky* (New York: Columbia University Press, 1932), 42.

13. John D. Wright Jr., *Transylvania: Tutor to the West* (Lexington: University Press of Kentucky, 1980), Chapter 5; James A. Ramage and Andrea S. Watkins, *Kentucky Rising: Democracy, Slavery, and Culture from the Early Republic to the Civil War* (Lexington: University Press of Kentucky, 2011), 60, 71–74, 199, 234; William Trahern to PPP, April 18, 1833, PPPP, folder 127, GMA.

14. PPP to TLM, November 2, 1827, LROIA, Schools, roll 773, frames 810–811, NARA; JLM to PPP, May 5, 1827, PPPP, folder 43, GMA; JLM to PPP, March 3, 1827, PPPP, folder 41, GMA.

15. RMJ to TH, March 19, 1828, and April 28, 1828, THP, folder 4, FHS; RMJ to David Folsom, September 12, 1828, LROIA, Choctaw Agency, roll 169, frames 518–537, NARA.

16. PPP to TLM, November 2, 1827, LROIA, Schools, roll 773, frames 810–811, NARA; Lawrence A. Cremin, *American Education: The National Experience, 1783–1876* (New York: Harper & Row, 1980), 25–26; Philip Lindsley, *An Address Delivered in Nashville, January 12, 1825, at the Inauguration of the*

President of Cumberland College (Nashville: Joseph Norvell, 1825), 3; Philip Lindsley, *The Cause of Education in Tennesee: An Address Delivered to the Young Gentlemen admitted to the Degree of Bachelor of Arts, at the First Commencement of the University of Nashville, October 4, 1826* (Nashville: Hunt, Tardiff & Co., 1833); PPP's Nashville University Account, November 1, 1827–April 15, 1828, PPPP, folder 63A, GMA; George Harkins to PPP, December 20, 1827, PPPP, folder 52, GMA; J. Herron to PPP, February 19, 1828, PPPP, folder 58, GMA. The literal translation is "Exertion breaks the bow, relaxation weakens the mind." My thanks to Timothy J. Williams for his translation help.

17. RMJ to David Folsom, September 12, 1828, LROIA, Choctaw Agency, roll 169, frames 518–537, NARA; TH to Greenwood Leflore, September 13, 1828, LROIA, Choctaw Agency, roll 169, frames 508–515, NARA; Stagecoach Receipt, July 10, 1828, LROIA, Schools, roll 773, frame 1035, NARA.

18. TH to Greenwood LeFlore, September 13, 1828, LROIA, Choctaw Agency, roll 169, frame 513, NARA; James Axtell, *Beyond 1492: Encounters in Colonial North America* (New York: Oxford University Press, 1992), 135–136; Timothy J. Shannon, "Dressing for Success on the Mohawk Frontier: Hendrick, William Johnson, and the Indian Fashion," *William and Mary Quarterly* 53 (1996): 13–42; RMJ to the War Department, August 20, 1826, 26th Cong., 2nd sess., HD 109, doc. 28, p. 33; CA Quarterly Report, November 1, 1827, TLML, NARA.

19. Michael A. LaCombe, *Political Gastronomy: Food and Authority in the English Atlantic World* (Philadelphia: University of Pennsylvania Press, 2012).

20. James Barbour to TH, September 21, 1826, TLML, NARA; RMJ to Henderson, April 30, 1828, THP, folder 4, FHS; John Mullay to William Medill, July 27, 1846, LROIA, Schools, roll 783, frames 447–472, NARA.

21. RMJ to William S. Crawford, October 20, 1841, LROIA, Schools, roll 780, frames 206–216, NARA; J.C. Meadors interview with Addie Murphy, August 13, 1938, "Slave Interviews, Notes and Data on Kentucky Slavery," JWCP, UK; Thomas Chisholm, John Jolly, Black Coat, and Walter Webber to George Vashon, December 8, 1833, LROIA, Schools, roll 776, frames 987–990, NARA.

22. RMJ to William Wilkins, April 1, 1844, LROIA Schools, roll 782, frames 303–304; *Kentucky Sentinel*, August 5, 1835; Hartigan-O'Connor, *Ties That Buy*, 174.

23. RMJ to Francis P. Blair, June 16, 1835, Blair-Lee Family Papers, box 14, folder 3, PU; LCM, folder 2, p. 18, KU; GCBC Minutes, April 20, 1828, book 2, pp. 169–170, SBTS; GCBC Attendance Records, SBTS; J. N. Bradley, *History of the Great Crossings Baptist Church* (Georgetown, KY: Great Crossings Baptist Church, 1945), part 1; *Louisville Advertiser*, July 3, 1835; Obituary for Imogene Johnson Pence, copy in Chinn-Johnson Family Papers, private collection; Nash, *Forging Freedom*, 217–219; Kent Anderson Leslie, *Woman of Color, Daughter of Privilege: Amanda America Dickson, 1849–1893* (Athens: University of Georgia Press, 1995), 111; Harris, *In the Shadow of Slavery*, 143. Richard Johnson claimed that Julia Chinn began attending GCBC about 1818, but the church records indicate that she was not baptized until 1828. Whatever the timeline, both sources claim that she was devout.

24. RMJ to TH, January 13, 1826, THP, folder 2, FHS; RMJ to TH, December 19, 1827, THP, folder 3, FHS; RMJ to TH, March 8, 1832, THP, folder 7, FHS;

RMJ to Adaline Johnson Scott, December 12, 1833, THP, folder 8, FHS; RMJ to TH, April 30, 1828, THP, folder 4, FHS.

25. RMJ to TH, March 23, 1828, THP, folder 4, FHS; RMJ to TH, January 14, 1835, folder 10, FHS.

26. RMJ to TH, January 14, 1835, folder 10, FHS; TH to Greenwood LeFlore, September 13, 1828, LROIA, Choctaw Agency, roll 169, frame 514, NARA; Amrita Chakrabarti Myers, *Forging Freedom: Black Women and the Pursuit of Liberty in Antebellum Charleston* (Chapel Hill: University of North Carolina Press, 2011), 116; Ebenezer Hiram Stedman, *Bluegrass Craftsman: Being the Reminiscences of Ebenezer Hiram Stedman, Papermaker: 1808–1885*, ed. Frances L. S. Dugan and Jacqueline P. Bull (Lexington: University of Kentucky Press, 1959), 76; RMJ to TH, April 30, 1828, THP, folder 4, FHS; RMJ to Francis P. Blair, June 16, 1835, Blair-Lee Family Papers, box 14, folder 3, PU.

27. RMJ to TH, December 27, 1827, THP, folder 3, FHS; Stephanie McCurry, *Masters of Small Worlds: Yeoman Households, Gender Relations, and the Political Culture of the Antebellum South Carolina Low Country* (New York: Oxford University Press, 1997); RMJ to Francis P. Blair, June 16, 1835, Blair-Lee Family Papers, box 14, folder 3, PU.

28. *Louisville Advertiser*, July 3, 1835; *Easton Gazette*, July 30, 1831, reprinted from *Kentucky Reporter*, July 20, 1831; TH to Greenwood LeFlore, September 13, 1828, LROIA, Choctaw Agency, roll 169, frames 508–515, NARA; Joshua D. Rothman, *Notorious in the Neighborhood: Sex and Families across the Color Line in Virginia, 1787–1861* (Chapel Hill: University of North Carolina Press, 2003), Chapter 2; Martha Hodes, *White Women, Black Men: Illicit Sex in the Nineteenth-Century South* (New Haven, CT: Yale University Press, 1997), 49.

29. *Easton Gazette*, July 30, 1831, reprinted from the *Kentucky Reporter*, July 20, 1831; *Cincinnati Daily Gazette*, June 22, 1835; RMJ to Francis P. Blair, June 16, 1835, Blair-Lee Family Papers, box 14, folder 3, PU.

30. *Easton Gazette*, July 30, 1831, reprinted from the *Kentucky Reporter*, July 20, 1831; *Cincinnati Daily Gazette*, June 22, 1835; RMJ to Francis P. Blair, June 16, 1835, Blair-Lee Family Papers, box 14, folder 3, PU.

31. Snyder, *Slavery in Indian Country*, Chapter 7; RMJ to Elbert Herring, November 9, 1833, LROIA, Schools, roll 776, frames 237–239, NARA; James Gadsden to the Secretary of War, July 6, 1833, in *The Territorial Papers of the United States, Volume XXIV: The Territory of Florida, 1828–1834*, ed. Clarence Edwin Carter (Washington, DC: National Archives, 1959), 858–861; Choctaw Laws Passed before 1830, PPPC, box 7, folder 5, WHC; Haag and Willis, trans. and eds., *Records of the Choctaw Council Meetings*, 139, 142–143, 145.

32. Pierre Juzan to William Ward, July 5, 1829, LROIA, Choctaw Agency, roll 169, frame 673, NARA; Bill of Sale, Charles Juzan to Delilah Brashiers, June 2, 1829, Chancery Court Records, Livingston, Alabama, copy in Juzan Vertical File, OKHS; J. T. Hadden to Jeremiah Evarts, June 28, 1824, PABCFM, roll 755, frame 1171; *Daily National Intelligencer*, December 21, 1826.

33. GCBC, List of those Received by Baptism, n.d., SBTS; CA Quarterly Report, August 1, 1828, PPPP, folder 65, GMA.

34. RMJ to TH, December 28, 1827, THP, folder 3, FHS; George Clarke to RMJ, October 15, 1837, GFC, box 9, folder 2, OKHS; District Chiefs Pierre Juzan, James Fletcher, and John McKenny to PPP, October 7, 1840, PPPC, box 1, folder 57, WHC; 1850 United States Federal Census, Records of the Bureau

of the Census, Scott County, Kentucky, copy in FHS; Annette Gordon-Reed, *The Hemingses of Monticello: An American Family* (New York: Norton, 2008), 79–80.

35. RMJ to TH, December 27, 1827, THP, folder 3, FHS; Ella Wells Drake, "Choctaw Academy, 1825–1848: American Indian Education, Experience, and Response" (M.A. Thesis, University of Kentucky, 1999), 89.

36. RMJ to TH, January 10, 1835, THP, folder 10, FHS; TH to the Office of Indian Affairs, September 15, 1829, LROIA, Schools, roll 774, frame 90, NARA; RMJ to TH, April 16, 1834, THP, folder 9, FHS; RMJ to TH, March 7, 1828, THP, folder 4, FHS; RMJ to TH, December 7, 1838, THP, folder 10, FHS; RMJ to Henderson, March 24, 1830, THP, folder 6, FHS.

37. RMJ to TH, March 23, 1828, THP, folder 4, FHS; RMJ to TH, February 27, 1834, THP, folder 9, FHS.

38. RMJ to TH, March 24, 1830, THP, folder 6, FHS; *American Sentinel*, September 10, 1824; GCBC Minutes, June 7, 1828, book 2, p. 181, SBTS.

39. RMJ to TH, March 24, 1830, THP, folder 6, FHS; RMJ to TH, March 7, 1828, THP, folder 4, FHS. See also Kathleen Brown, *Good Wives, Nasty Wenches, and Anxious Patriarchs: Gender, Race, and Power in Colonial Virginia* (Chapel Hill: University of North Carolina Press, 1996).

40. RMJ to TH, December 27, 1827, THP, folder 3, FHS; RMJ to TH, March 7, 1828, THP, folder 4, FHS; Drake, "Choctaw Academy," 89.

41. *Louisville Advertiser*, July 3, 1835; L. Smith to B. W. Smith, May 25, 1844, Miscellaneous Manuscripts, FHS; RMJ to Henderson, n.d., THP, folder 17, FHS; RMJ to Henderson, December 9, 1829, THP, folder 1, FHS; RMJ to Henderson, January 13, 1826, THP, folder 2, FHS.

42. RMJ to TH, March 7, 1828, THP, folder 4, FHS; RMJ to David Folsom, September 12, 1828, LROIA, Choctaw Agency, reel 169, frame 524, NARA; Recommendation for Robert M. Jones, August 29, 1835, LROIA, Choctaw Agency West, reel 184, frames 344–346 (endorsed by Riddle and other Council members), NARA.

43. RMJ to TH, March 24, 1830, THP, folder 6, FHS; RMJ to TH, March 7, 1828, THP, folder 4, FHS.

44. RMJ to TH, March 7, 1828, THP, folder 4, FHS; RMJ to TH, n.d., THP, folder 17, FHS.

45. Gerald T. Hopkins, *A Mission to the Indians from the Indian Committee of Baltimore Yearly Meeting to Fort Wayne, in 1804* (Philadelphia: T. Ellwood Zell, 1864), 54; David Andrew Nichols, *Red Gentlemen and White Savages: Indians, Federalists, and the Search for Order on the American Frontier* (Charlottesville: University of Virginia Press, 2008), 11–12; RMJ to TH, March 7, 1828, THP, folder 4, FHS; RMJ to TH, March 19, 1828, March 23, 1828, April 16, 1834, all in THP, folder 9, FHS; *Easton Gazette*, July 30, 1831.

46. RMJ to Francis P. Blair, June 16, 1835, Blair-Lee Family Papers, box 14, folder 3, PU; RMJ to TH, April 30, 1828, THP, folder 4, FHS; TH to the Office of Indian Affairs, September 15, 1829, LROIA, Schools, roll 774, frame 90, NARA; CA Quarterly Report, October 31, 1830, LROIA, Schools, roll 774, frames 401–403, NARA; Drake, "Choctaw Academy," 92.

47. RMJ to TH, April 28, 1828, THP, folder 4, FHS; TLM to TH, March 17, 1828, 26th Cong., 2nd sess., HD 109, no. 37.

48. RMJ to TH, May 4, 1834, TH, folder 9, FHS; RMJ to TH, January 10, 1835, folder 10.

49. RMJ to David Folsom, September 12, 1828, LROIA, Choctaw Agency, roll 169, frames 518–537, NARA; RMJ to TH, March 7, 1828, THP, folder 4, FHS.

Chapter 5

1. TLM to John C. Calhoun, November 20, 1820, LRSW, M221, roll 90, M-111(14), NARA; JLM to PPP, May 20, 1827, PPPP, folder 44, GMA; JLM to PPP, May 5, 1827, PPPP, folder 43, GMA; JLM to PPP, July 1, 1828, PPPC, box 1, folder 14, WHC; TLM to Isaac Tyson and Andrew Ellicott, March 27, 1818, LSSIT, M16, roll 5, vol. E, pp. 4–5, NARA; Thomas L. McKenney, *Memoirs, Official and Personal* (New York: Paine & Burgess, 1846), vol. 2, 110.

2. McDonald to McKenney, August 9, 1819, LRSW, M221, M-33 (13), NARA; McDonald to PPP, July 1, 1828, PPPC, box 1, folder 14, WHC; Robert M. Jones to PPP, June 25, 1831, PPPC, box 1, folder 24, WHC; Hines County Tax Records, Personal Property, 1830, roll 2660, p. 47, MDAH; Charlotte Capers to Herman J. Viola, April 2, 1968, James L. McDonald Vertical File, MDAH.

3. Speech reprinted in *National Gazette*, August 14, 1830. Other Indian activists deployed similar tactics; see Andrew Denson, *Demanding the Cherokee Nation: Indian Autonomy and American Culture, 1830–1900* (Lincoln: University of Nebraska Press, 2004), 28–35.

4. JLM to PPP, January 27, 1829, PPPP, folder 68, GMA; JLM to PPP, July 1, 1828, PPPP, folder 14, GMA; JLM to PPP, March 29, 1830, PPPP, folder 79, GMA; JLM to TLM, April 25, 1826, LROIA, Choctaw Agency, roll 169, frame 328, NARA.

5. Cyrus Kingsbury to Thomas McKenney, February 8, 1830, LROIA, Schools, roll 774, frame 470, NARA; Speech of David Crockett, *Jackson Gazette*, June 26, 1830 (masthead incorrectly reads June 19).

6. Robert F. Berkhofer Jr., *Salvation and the Savage: An Analysis of Protestant Missions and American Indian Response, 1787–1862* (Lexington: University of Kentucky Press, 1965), 101; Board of Managers of the Baptist General Missionary Convention to the House and Senate, November 26, 1827, RG 233, 20th Cong., HD, Committee on Indian Affairs, folder 1, NARA; Joel Chandler Harris, *Stories of Georgia* (New York: American Book Company, 1896), 216.

7. Herman J. Viola, *Thomas L. McKenney: Architect of America's Early Indian Policy, 1816–1830* (Chicago: Swallow Press, 1974), 192–202; McKenney, *Memoirs, Official and Personal*, vol. 2, 116; TLM to TH, December 22, 1826, LSOIA, roll 3, pp. 267–268, NARA.

8. Ninian Edwards to General William Clark, August 9, 1829, September 4, 1827, in Ninian W. Edwards, *History of Illinois from 1778 to 1833 and Life and Times of Ninian Edwards* (Springfield: Illinois State Journal Company, 1870), 349.

9. Talk of Senatchewane, December 14, 1827, copy in Potawatomi folder 1826–1827, GLOVEC; Statement of the Choctaw chiefs and captains, October 17, 1827, LROIA, Choctaw Agency, roll 169, frames 428–430, NARA; TLM to James Barbour, October 17, 1827, in McKenney, *Memoirs*, vol. 1, 337.

10. RMJ to TH, March 23, 1828, THP, folder 4, FHS; Choctaw Academy Students to Friends and Countrymen, October 10, 1829, PABCFM, unit 6, vol. 4, roll 757, frames 667-669; TLM to TH, March 17, 1828, 26th Cong., 2nd sess., HD 109, no. 37.

11. RMJ to TH, March 19, 1828, THP, folder 4, FHS; RMJ et al. to the President, January 25, 1827, in McKenney, *Memoirs*, vol. 1, 315–316; RMJ to TH, February 14, 1831, THP, folder 6, FHS; RMJ to TH, March 24, 1830, THP, folder 6, FHS.

12. Cho-chus Micco to TH and RMJ, 1828, LROIA, Choctaw Agency, roll 169, frame 470, NARA; Greenwood Leflore to McKenney, February 22, 1828, LROIA, Choctaw Agency, roll 169, frame 548; RMJ to TH, March 19, 1828, THP, folder 4, FHS; PPP to McKenney, November 2, 1827, LROIA, Schools, roll 773, frames 810–811, NARA.

13. John Pitchlynn to PPP, February 15, 1828, PPPP, folder 57, GMA; John Pitchlynn to PPP, April 14, 1828, PPPP, folder 63, GMA; PPP Diary, PPPC, box 6, folders 1–2, WHC.

14. Draft letter, PPP to John Pitchlynn, November 27, 1828, PPPC, box 6, folder 2, WHC; PPP to "uncle," January 24, 1829, PPPC, box 6, folder 2; PPP to Principal Chiefs and Warriors of the Choctaw Nation, n.d., PPPP, folder 66B, GMA.

15. Draft letter, PPP to John Pitchlynn, November 27, 1828, PPPC, box 6, folder 2, WHC; PPP to Principal Chiefs and Warriors of the Choctaw Nation, n.d., PPPP, folder 66B, GMA; PPP Diary, PPPC, box 6, folder 1, WHC; Kathleen DuVal, "Debating Identity, Sovereignty, and Civilization: The Arkansas Valley after the Louisiana Purchase," *Journal of the Early Republic* 26 (2006): 25–58.

16. Draft letter, PPP to John Pitchlynn, November 27, 1828, PPPC, box 6, folder 2, WHC.

17. Daniel Walker How, *What Hath God Wrought: The Transformation of America, 1815–1848* (New York: Oxford University Press, 2007), 276–281.

18. Andrew Jackson to James Monroe, March 4, 1817, in *Papers of Andrew Jackson: Volume 4, 1816–1820*, ed. Harold Moser, David R. Hoth, and George H. Hoeman (Knoxville: University of Tennessee Press, 1994), 95–96; Robert V. Remini, *Andrew Jackson and His Indian Wars* (New York: Viking, 2001); Francis P. Prucha, "Andrew Jackson's Indian Policy: A Reassessment," *Journal of American History* 56 (1969): 527–539.

19. Reginald Horsman, *Race and Manifest Destiny: The Origins of American Racial Anglo-Saxonism* (Cambridge, MA: Harvard University Press, 1981), 116–128; C. H. Howell to PPP, March 22, 1837, PPPP, folder 183, GMA.

20. Lewis Cass, "Removal of the Indians," *North American Review* 30 (January 1830): 62–121, quotations on pp. 68, 77, 104; Andrew Jackson, Fifth Annual Message to Congress, December 3, 1833, *Compilation of the Messages and Papers of the Presidents, 1789–1897* (New York: Bureau of National Literature, 1897), vol. 3, 33.

21. Horatio B. Cushman, *History of the Choctaw, Chickasaw, and Natchez Indians*, ed. Angie Debo (Norman: University of Oklahoma Press, 1999), 192; J. E. Alexander, *Transatlantic Sketches, Comprising Visits to the Most Interesting Scenes in North and South America and the West Indies* (Philadelphia: Key and Biddle, 1833), 276; *Arkansas Gazette*, April 23, 1828; Kathleen DuVal, *The Native Ground: Indians and Colonists in the Heart of the Continent* (Philadelphia: University of Pennsylvania Press, 2007), 237–238.

22. Cass, "Removal of the Indians," 71; CK to David Greene, August 10, 1847, CKC, box 1, folder 2, item 3, WHC.

23. John C. Fitzpatrick, ed., *The Autobiography of Martin Van Buren* (Washington, DC: US Government Printing Office, 1920), 295; John W. Hall, *Uncommon Defense: Indian Allies in the Black Hawk War* (Cambridge, MA: Harvard University Press, 2009), 100; John Johnson to Charles Cist, October 22, 1847, copy in Miami folder 1834–1847, GLOVEC; McKenney, *Memoirs*, vol. 1, 262; Petition of Choctaw Chiefs, Headmen, and Warriors to John Quincy Adams, September 17, 1828, LROIA, Choctaw Agency, roll 169, frames 467–477, 481–483, NARA.

24. WW to John Eaton, October 15, 1829, LROIA, Choctaw Agency, roll 169, frames 676–677, NARA; Choctaw Academy Students to Friends and Countrymen, October 10, 1829, PABCFM, vol. 4, roll 757, frames 667–669.

25. Memorial of the Headmen and Warriors of the Creek Nation, January 24, 1832, RG 233, HD, 22st Cong., Committee on Indian Affairs, NARA.

26. *Laws of the State of Mississippi Passed at the Twelfth Session of the General Assembly* (Jackson: Peter Isler, 1829), 81–83; Clara Sue Kidwell, *Choctaws and Missionaries in Mississippi, 1818–1918* (Norman: University of Oklahoma Press, 1995), 130–132; CA Quarterly Report, November 1, 1829, LROIA, Schools, roll 774, frames 99–103, NARA; Choctaw Academy Students to Friends and Countrymen, October 10, 1829, PABCFM, vol. 4, roll 757, frames 667–669.

27. Choctaw Academy Students to Friends and Countrymen, October 10, 1829, PABCFM, vol. 4, roll 757, frames 667–669; Council of the Northeast District to the Office of Indian Affairs, November 17, 1829, LROIA, Schools, roll 774, frames 51–52, NARA.

28. Choctaw Academy Students to Friends and Countrymen, October 10, 1829, PABCFM, vol. 4, roll 757, frames 667–669; James P. Ronda, "'We Have a Country': Race, Geography, and the Invention of Indian Territory," *Journal of the Early Republic* 19 (1999): 743.

29. Choctaw Academy Students to Friends and Countrymen, October 10, 1829, PABCFM, vol. 4, roll 757, frames 667–669; Council of the Northeast District to the Office of Indian Affairs, November 17, 1829, LROIA, Schools, roll 774, frames 51–52, NARA.

30. Pierre Juzan to William Ward, July 5, 1829, LROIA, Choctaw Agency, roll 169, frame 673, NARA; Headmen of the Southeast District to John Eaton, November 20, 1829, LROIA, Choctaw Agency, roll 169, frames 641–642; David Folsom to WW, November 7, 1829, LROIA, Choctaw Agency, roll 169, frame 692; PPP Diary, PPPC, box 6, folder 1, WHC; D. W. Haley to Andrew Jackson, March 10, 1831, LROIA, Choctaw Agency, roll 169, frames 802–803, NARA.

31. Register of Debates, 21st Cong., 1st sess., pp. 312, 359; Indian Removal Act, Chapter CXLVIII, 21st Cong., 1st sess., Statutes at Large; Andrew Jackson to David W. Haley, October 15, 1829, *Papers of Andrew Jackson: Volume 7, 1829*, ed. Daniel Feller, Harold D. Moser, Laura-Eve Moss, Thomas Coens (Knoxville: University of Tennessee Press, 2007), 494–495.

32. Chiefs and Headmen of the Northeast and Southern Districts of the Choctaw Nation to John Eaton, June 2, 1830, LROIA, Choctaw Agency, roll 169, frames 702–708, NARA; Speech of PPP to General Council, n.d. [May 1830], PPPP, folder 80A, GMA; Kidwell, *Choctaws and Missionaries*, 134–137. On payments for the Folsom children's schooling, see Folsom to TLM, March 4, 1830, LROIA, Schools, roll 774, frames 335–336, NARA; Eaton to Folsom, December 2, 1830, LROIA, Schools, roll 774, frame 328.

33. H. S. Halbert, "Story of the Treaty of Dancing Rabbit Creek," *Publications of the Mississippi Historical Society* 6 (1902): 373–377; Arthur DeRosier Jr., *The Removal of the Choctaw Indians* (Knoxville: University of Tennessee Press, 1970), 120.
34. Halbert, "Treaty of Dancing Rabbit Creek," 380–385, quotations on p. 385.
35. Halbert, "Treaty of Dancing Rabbit Creek," 386–400, first two quotations on pp. 387, 389. Last three quotations from Reuben H. Grant to PPP, December 21, 1854, PPPC, box 2, folder 55, WHC; Basis of a treaty to be submitted to the Commissioners of the United States on behalf of the Choctaw Nation, PPPP, folder 86, GMA.
36. For the original Choctaw proposal, see Basis of a Treaty, September 25, 1830, PPPP, folder 86, GMA. For the ratified treaty, see Treaty with the Choctaws, September 15, 1830, RG 11, M668, Ratified Indian Treaties, roll 6, NARA. For Pitchlynn's opinion, see C. H. Howell to PPP, August 17, 1836, PPPP, folder 177, GMA.
37. Grant to PPP, December 21, 1854, PPPC, box 2, folder 55, WHC; James A. Folsom to PPP, October 30, 1831, PPPP, folder 109, GMA; WW to John Eaton, December 2, 1830, LROIA, Choctaw Agency, roll 169, frames 788–789, NARA; Harkins quoted in James Taylor Carson, *Searching for the Bright Path: The Mississippi Choctaws from Prehistory to Removal* (Lincoln: University of Nebraska Press, 1999), 124–125.
38. Treaty with the Choctaws, September 15, 1830, RG 11, M668, Ratified Indian Treaties, roll 6, NARA; Testimony of Grant Lincecum, December 8, 1834, RG 75, CRR, Misc. Choctaw Removal Records, box 2, NARA; Testimonies of Little Leader or Ha-p-as-ka-te-ne, John Carter, John Pitchlynn, Adam James, and Grabel Lincecum in RG 75, CRR, Misc. Choctaw Removal Records, box 2, NARA; Robert M. Jones to PPP, July 17, 1872, PPPC, box 4, item 55, WHC.
39. Testimony of Grant Lincecum, December 8, 1834, CRR, Misc. Choctaw Removal Records, box 2, NARA; Testimony of John Carter, December 8, 1834, CRR, Misc. Choctaw Removal Records, box 2, NARA; Ohoyo Tom et al. to Lewis Cass, December 6, 1833, LROIA, Choctaw Agency, roll 170, frames 484–485, NARA.
40. John Pitchlynn to PPP, March 10, 1833, PPPC, box 1, folder 36, WHC; John Walker and William Hall to Lewis Cass, September 6, 1833, LROIA, Schools, roll 776, frame 475, NARA; R. D. Hallin to PPP, July 13, 1830, PPPC, box 1, folder 17, WHC; Hinds County Tax Records, roll 2660, p. 47, MDAH; J. C. Hastings to PPP, February 26, 1830, PPPC, box 1, folder 15, WHC; JLM to PPP, March 18, 1831, PPPC, box 1, folder 21, WHC; JLM to Alexander McKee, March 30, 1831, PPPC, box 1, folder 22, WHC.
41. John Pitchlynn to PPP, February 21, 1833, PPPC, box 1, folder 35, WHC; John Pitchlynn to PPP, November 23, 1832, PPPC, box 1, folder 31, WHC; Moses Foster Jr. to PPP, September 20, 1831, PPPC, box 1, folder 27, WHC; "Brother" to PPP, August 8, 1834, PPPP, folder 146, GMA; John Pitchlynn to PPP, April 5, 1835, PPPC, box 1, folder 47, WHC; John Pitchlynn to PPP, January 10, 1835, PPPC, box 1, folder 45, WHC; JLM to PPP, March 18, 1831, PPPC, box 1, folder 21, WHC; Andrew K. Frank, *Creeks and Southerners: Biculturalism on the Early American Frontier* (Lincoln: University of Nebraska Press, 2005), 123.

42. Theda Perdue and Michael D. Green, *The Cherokee Nation and the Trail of Tears* (New York: Penguin, 2007); John Johnston to Charles Cist, October 22, 1847, copy in Miami folder 1834–1847, GLOVEC.

43. First quotation from Talk of Sena-ju-win (Swift Water), Report of a Council held with Gen. Wm. Clark and a deputation of Potawatomi Indians, August 21–26, 1830, copy in Potawatomi folder 1830, GLOVEC; second quotation from Daniel Walker How, *What Hath God Wrought: The Transformation of America, 1815–1848* (New York: Oxford University Press, 2007), 419. See also John W. Hall, *Uncommon Defense: Indian Allies in the Black Hawk War* (Cambridge, MA: Harvard University Press, 2009); John T. Ellisor, *The Second Creek War: Interethnic Conflict and Collusion on a Collapsing Frontier* (Lincoln: University of Nebraska Press, 2010).

44. Henry Vose to PPP, September 13, 1831, PPPC, box 1, folder 26, WHC; James A. Folsom to PPP, October 30, 1831, PPPP, folder 109, GMA; Notes on Robert M. Jones, Peter James Hudson Collection, box 1, folder 10, OKHS; Viola, *McKenney*, 198–199; JLM to TLM, April 25, 1826, LROIA, Choctaw Agency, roll 169, frame 327, NARA; McDonald to PPP, March 29, 1830, PPPP, folder 79, GMA.

Chapter 6

1. James A. Ramage and Andrea S. Watkins, *Kentucky Rising: Democracy, Slavery, and Culture from the Early Republic to the Civil War* (Lexington: University Press of Kentucky, 2011), 222–224.

2. Sam Hatch, CA Medical Report, May 1, 1833, LROIA, Schools, roll 776, frames 193–195, NARA; Sam Hatch, CA Medical Report, August 1833, LROIA, Schools, roll 776, frames 209–212, NARA; CA Quarterly Report, December 31, 1844, LROIA, Schools, roll 782, frames 1214–1216.

3. CA Quarterly Report, August 1, 1833, PPPC, box 5, folder 26, WHC; GCBC Minutes, July 6, 1833, book 2, p. 265, SBTS; *Louisville Advertiser*, July 3, 1835; Personal communication with Ann Bevins, June 29, 2011.

4. GCBC Minutes, July 6, 1833, book 2, p. 265, SBTS; Adam Jortner, "Cholera, Christ, and Jackson: The Epidemic of 1832 and the Origins of Christian Politics in Antebellum America," *Journal of the Early Republic* 27 (2007): 233–264; Charles M. Hudson, *The Southeastern Indians* (Knoxville: University of Tennessee Press, 1976), 340–365; PPP Diary, October 29, 1842, PPPP, folder 375, GMA, quoting the King James version of Jeremiah 17, verses 5 and 9.

5. PPP Diary, PPPC, box 5, folder 2, GMA; Phreno-Physiognomical Report on PPP by Gideon Lincecum, April 15, 1846, PPPP, folder 532, GMA.

6. Thomas Wall to Alexander McKee, April 28, 1831, PPPC, box 1, folder 23, WHC; Horatio Cushman, *History of the Choctaw, Chickasaw, and Natchez Indians*, ed. Angie Debo (Norman: University of Oklahoma Press, 1999), 342; Mushulatubbee to John Eaton, January 16, 1831, LROIA, Choctaw Agency, roll 169, frame 871, NARA.

7. Arthur DeRosier Jr., *The Removal of the Choctaw Indians* (Knoxville: University of Tennessee Press, 1970), 129, 161–169; John R. Swanton, *Source Material for the Social and Ceremonial Life of the Choctaw Indians* (Tuscaloosa: University of Alabama Press, 2001), 181.

8. Account of Thomas McGee, in Correspondence on the Subject of the Emigration of Indians, 23rd Cong., 1st sess., SD 512, vol. 1, 982–986.

9. Muriel H. Wright, "The Removal of the Choctaws to the Indian Territory, 1830–1833," in *Chronicles of Oklahoma* 6 (1928): 103–128; John Pitchlynn to PPP, June 14, 1833, PPPP, folder 132, GMA.

10. Armstrong Census of 1831, 23rd Cong., 1st sess., SD 512, no. 246; Barbara Krauthamer, *Black Slaves, Indian Masters: Slavery, Emancipation, and Citizenship in the Native American South* (Chapel Hill: University of North Carolina Press, 2015), 39; Grant Foreman, *Indian Removal: The Emigration of the Five Civilized Tribes of Indians* (Norman: University of Oklahoma Press, 1956), 95; W. David Baird, *Peter Pitchlynn: Chief of the Choctaws* (Norman: University of Oklahoma Press, 1972), 46; Daniel F. Littlefield Jr., "African-Descended People and Removal," in *Encyclopedia of American Indian Removal*, ed. Littlefield and James W. Parins (Santa Barbara, CA: Greenwood, 2011), vol. 1, 3–6; Wright, "Removal of the Choctaws," 119.

11. DeRosier, *Removal of the Choctaw Indians*, Appendix C: Removal Regulations of May 15, 1832.

12. Draft letter, PPP to Lewis Cass, May 2, 1832, PPPP, folder 113, GMA; Foreman, *Indian Removal*, 51–52; Alexis de Tocqueville, *Democracy in America*, trans. Arthur Goldhammer (New York: Library of America, 2004), 374–375.

13. Baird, *Peter Pitchlynn*, 42–43; Draft letter, PPP to Lewis Cass, May 2, 1832, PPPP, folder 113, GMA; Draft of a Song, PPPP, folder 110A, GMA.

14. J. Brown to George Gibson, February 2, 1832, SD 512, vol. 1, 438; PPP Diary, PPPC, box 5, folder 2, WHC; Foreman, *Indian Removal*, 51–52.

15. Foreman, *Indian Removal*, 52; DeRosier, *Removal of the Choctaw Indians*, 149 and Appendix C; Russell Thornton, *American Indian Holocaust and Survival: A Population History since 1492* (Norman: University of Oklahoma Press, 1987), 114–118.

16. John Johnston to Charles Cist, October 22, 1847, copy in Miami folder 1834–1847, GLOVEC; Grant Foreman, ed., *A Traveler in Indian Territory: The Journal of Ethan Allen Hitchcock* (Norman: University of Oklahoma Press, 1996), 150; R. David Edmunds, *The Potawatomis: Keepers of the Fire* (Norman: University of Oklahoma Press, 1978), 263; Report of Lieut. John G. Reynolds, March 31, 1837, *American State Papers: Military Affairs* (Washington, DC: Gales and Seaton, 1832), vol. 7, 867.

17. Draft letter, PPP to Lewis Cass, May 2, 1832, PPPP, folder 113, GMA; Michael L. Bruce, "'Our Best Men Are Fast Leaving Us': The Life and Times of Robert M. Jones," in *Chronicles of Oklahoma* 66 (1988): 295; John Pitchlynn to PPP, November 12, 1832, PPPP, folder 121, GMA; F. W. Armstrong to Gen. George Gibson, December 2, 1832, SD 512, vol. 1, 401.

18. "Journal of an Emigrating Party of Pottawattomie Indians, 1838," reprinted in *Indiana Magazine of History* 21 (1925): 325; Joseph Kerr to Lewis Cass, SD 512, vol. 1, 719–720. The "Trail of Tears" is more commonly associated with the Cherokees. However, a Cherokee minister who preached among the Choctaws in early Indian Territory confirmed that Choctaws invented the phrase. See T. L. Ballenger, "Joseph Franklin Thompson: An Early Cherokee Leader," *Chronicles of Oklahoma* 3 (1925): 288–289. For more on the history and memory of that phrase, see Theda Perdue, "The Legacy of Indian Removal," *Journal*

of Southern History 78 (2012): 23. Thanks to Theda Perdue for clarifying this for me.

19. Armstrong to Elbert Herring, September 20, 1833, LROIA, Choctaw Agency, roll 170, frames 286–288, NARA.

20. Armstrong to Elbert Herring, September 20, 1833, LROIA, Choctaw Agency, roll 170, frames 286–288, NARA.

21. Foreman, *Indian Removal*, 97–99; Joseph Kincaid to PPP, August 14, 1835, PPPP, folder 164, GMA; Armstrong to Herring, March 8, 1834, LROIA, Schools, roll 776, frames 519–528, NARA.

22. PPP Diary, PPPC, box 6, folder 2, WHC; *Cherokee Phoenix*, March 3, 1830; Michael C. Stambaugh, Richard P. Guyette, Erin R. McMurry, Edward R. Cook, David M. Meko, Anthony R. Lupo, "Drought Duration and Frequency in the U.S. Corn Belt during the Last Millennium," *Agricultural and Forest Meteorology* 151(2001): 154–162; Grant Foreman, ed., *A Pathfinder in the Southwest: The Itinerary of Lieutenant A.W. Whipple during his Explorations for a Railway Route from Fort Smith to Los Angeles in the years 1853 & 1854* (Norman: University of Oklahoma Press, 1941), 62.

23. Rhoda Pitchlynn to PPP, September 23, 1841, PPPC, box 1, folder 67, WHC; PPP to Thomas Wall, December 2, 1847, PPPP, folder 597, GMA; John Pitchlynn to PPP, n.d., PPPP, folder 124A, GMA; Rhoda to PPP, November 29, 1841, PPPP, folder 314, GMA.

24. Rhoda Pitchlynn to PPP, August 30, 1841, PPPC, box 1, folder 65, WHC; Rhoda Pitchlynn to PPP, September 23, 1841, PPPC, box 1, folder 67, WHC; Rhoda Pitchlynn to PPP, November 29, 1841, PPPP, folder 314, GMA; Rhoda Pitchlynn to PPP, December 22, 1841, PPPP, folder 320, GMA; Solomon to PPP, December 11, 1857, PPPC, box 3, folder 3, WHC.

25. Thornton, *American Indian Holocaust and Survival*, 94–99; Donna L. Akers, *Living in the Land of Death: The Choctaw Nation, 1830–1860* (East Lansing: Michigan State University Press, 2004), 113–114; Notes on Choctaw History, n.d., Peter James Hudson Collection, box 1, folder 13, OKHS; Louis Coleman, *Cyrus Byington: Missionary and Choctaw Linguist* (Kearney, NE: Morris, 1996), 55; Foreman, *Indian Removal*, 221.

26. Akers, *Living in the Land of Death*, xiii, xxxvi, 73; Nitakachi quoted in WW to John Eaton, March 2, 1831, LROIA, Choctaw Agency, roll 169, frames 949–950, NARA; E. A. Hitchcock to John C. Spencer, March 20, 1842, in Foreman, ed., *Traveler in Indian Territory*, 256; Armstrong to Harris, February 28, 1837, LROIA, Choctaw Agency, roll 170, frames 813–815, NARA; R. M. Jones, G. Harkins, and Pierre Juzan to C. A. Harris, May 5, 1838, LROIA, Choctaw Agency, roll 170, frame 892, NARA; Chiefs of the Piankashaw, Wea, and Peoria to William Clark, July 28, 1830, copy in Miami folder 1830–1833, GLOVEC.

27. Journal of a negotiation at the forks of the Wabash, October–November 1833, copy in Potawatomi folder 1833, GLOVEC; Council of 1834, Talk of Thomas Chisholm and John Rogers to Armstrong and Dodge, September 4, 1834, LROIA, Choctaw Agency, roll 170, frames 537–541, NARA.

28. Chiefs, Captains, and Warriors of the Arkansas District to David McClellan, April 3, 1834, LROIA, Choctaw Agency West, roll 184, frames 260–262, NARA; Ebenezer Hotchkin to Armstrong, July 23, 1838, LROIA, Schools, roll 778, frames 681–683, NARA.

29. Izumi Ishii, *Bad Fruits of the Civilized Tree: Alcohol & the Sovereignty of the Cherokee Nation* (Lincoln: University of Nebraska Press, 2008), 41–47, 83; CK to Jeremiah Evarts, December 25, 1830, CKC, box 2, folder 6, item 22, WHC.

30. Pitchlynn Family Genealogy, compiled by Sandra Moore Riley, PPP Vertical File, OKHS; Robert M. Jones to PPP, June 25, 1831, PPPC, box 1, folder 24, WHC. On Sophia and her stepchildren, see John Pitchlynn to PPP, June 13, 1834, PPPC, box 1, folder 41, WHC.

31. Armstrong to Herring, April 25, 1834, LROIA, Choctaw Agency, roll 170, frames 398–401, NARA.

32. Akers, *Living in the Land of Death*, 113–115; Swanton, *Social and Ceremonial Life of the Choctaw Indians*, 183.

33. John Pitchlynn to PPP, January 30, 1834, PPPC, box 1, folder 40, WHC; Michael P. Rogin, *Fathers and Children: Andrew Jackson and the Subjugation of the American Indian* (New York: Vintage, 1975), 4; John to PPP, August 20, 1833, PPPP, folder 135, GMA; John to PPP, June 13, 1834, PPPC, box 1, folder 41, WHC.

34. John to PPP, November 23, 1832, PPPC, box 1, folder 31, WHC; John to PPP, May 28, 1833, PPPP, folder 131, GMA; Samuel Garland to PPP, November 28, 1833, PPPC, box 1, folder 39, WHC; John to PPP, April 5, 1835, PPPC, box 1, folder 47, WHC; John to PPP, June 13, 1834, PPPC, box 1, folder 41, WHC; Samuel Garland to PPP, May 20, 1835, PPPP, folder 161, GMA; C. H. Howell, May 22, 1835, PPPP, folder 162, GMA; John to PPP, January 10, 1835, PPPC, box 1, folder 45, WHC; John to PPP, February 22, 1835, PPPP, folder 159, GMA; C. H. Howell to PPP, June 12, 1835, PPPP, folder 163, GMA; Sophia Pitchlynn to PPP, July 1, 1836, PPPP, folder 176, GMA.

35. Tonozekah, Tezawakuntah, and Sarazon to Lewis Cass, December 25, 1833, LROIA, Schools, roll 776, frames 392–393, NARA; William Davis to Elbert Herring, November 12, 1834, 26th Cong., 2nd sess., HD 109, no. 86; James Leach to T. Hartley Crawford, July 25, 1845, LROIA, Schools, roll 782, frame 1051, NARA; William Armstrong to Herring, March 8, 1834, LROIA, Schools, roll 776, frames 519–528, NARA; William Armstrong to Herring, March 13, 1834, LROIA, Schools, roll 776, frames 530–532, NARA; CA Quarterly Report, May 1, 1834, PPPC, box 1, folder 30, WHC.

36. Leonard Tarrant to Elbert Herring, February 28, 1833, LROIA, Schools, roll 776, frames 457–458, NARA; Tusknahaw, Opothle Yahola, Little Doctor, and Mad Blue to Leonard Tarrant, April 16, 1833, LROIA, Schools, roll 776, frame 460, NARA; Herring to Lewis Cass, May 5, 1836, LROIA, Schools, roll 777, frame 847, NARA. For other tribes, see, for example, A. C. Pepper to OIA, March 28, 1837, 26th Cong., 2nd sess., HD 109, no. 117; Elijah Hicks to Harris, June 6, 1838, LROIA, Schools, roll 778, frame 855, NARA.

37. Foreman, *Indian Removal*, 187–188; Jim Boy and David Barnett to C. A. Harris, April 17, 1838, LROIA, Schools, roll 778, frames 925–926, NARA; Thomas Henderson to Harris, May 21, 1838, LROIA, Schools, roll 778, frame 853, NARA.

38. CA Quarterly Report, May 1, 1829, LROIA, Schools, roll 774, frames 82–85, NARA; RMJ to TH, March 8, 1832, THP, folder 7, FHS.

39. TH to RMJ, December 27, 1830, CRR, Misc. Choctaw Removal Records, box 5, CA folder, NARA; RMJ to TH, March 14, 1834, THP, folder 9, FHS; WW to TH, September 3, 1831, THP, folder 6, FHS. For more on problems after Chinn's death, see Chapter 10.

40. Timothy Walker to Ellis Falling, September 12, 1838, LROIA, Schools, roll 778, frames 945–946, NARA; Timothy Walker, "On Stealing," LROIA, Schools, roll 778, frame 931, NARA.

41. TH to RMJ, December 27, 1830, CRR, Misc. Choctaw Removal Records, box 5, CA folder, NARA; RMJ to Herring, November 9, 1833, LROIA, Schools, roll 776, frames 237–239, NARA; CA Quarterly Report, August 1, 1831, PPPC, box 5, folder 18, WHC; Ella Wells Drake, "A Choctaw Academy Education: The Apalachicola Experience, 1830–1833," *Florida Historical Quarterly* 78 (2000): 289–308.

42. James Gadsden to Lewis Cass, May 20, 1833, LROIA, Schools, roll 776, frames 156–157, NARA.

43. TH to Elbert Herring, October 12, 1833, LROIA, Schools, roll 776, frames 228–229, NARA; TH to Elbert Herring, November 10, 1833, LROIA, Schools, roll 776, frames 241–243, NARA.

44. RMJ to Herring, November 9, 1833, LROIA, Schools, roll 776, frames 237–239, NARA; RMJ to Adaline Johnson Scott, December 12, 1833, THP, folder 8, FHS; Drake, "Choctaw Academy Education."

45. RMJ to Adaline Johnson Scott, December 12, 1833, THP, folder 8, FHS; TH to Cass, December 28, 1833, THP, folder 8, frames 245–246, FHS; TH to RMJ, March 5, 1834, LROIA, Schools, roll 776, frames 740–741, NARA.

46. John P. Bowes, *Exiles and Pioneers: Eastern Indians in the Trans-Mississippi West* (New York: Cambridge University Press, 2007), 79-80; Samuel Milroy to T. Hartley Crawford, October 23, 1839, LROIA, roll 361, frames 290–292, NARA; John W. Hall, *Uncommon Defense: Indian Allies in the Black Hawk War* (Cambridge, MA: Harvard University Press, 2009), 262; Talk of Red Bird to Isaac Ketchum in the *White Pigeon Republican*, August 28, 1839, copy in Potawatomi folder 1838–1840, GLOVEC.

47. James Logan to Armstrong, September 20, 1845, copy in GFC, box 9, folder 3, OKHS.

48. James Logan to Armstrong, September 20, 1845, copy in GFC, box 9, folder 3, OKHS; William Wilson to Armstrong, August 30, 1842, LROIA, Schools, roll 780, frames 689–696, NARA.

49. Michael Doran, "Population Statistics of Nineteenth Century Indian Territory," *Chronicles of Oklahoma* 53 (1976): 496; Foreman, ed., *Traveler in Indian Territory*, 157.

50. John W. Hall, *Uncommon Defense: Indian Allies in the Black Hawk War* (Cambridge, MA: Harvard University Press, 2009); Cushman, *History of the Choctaw*, 286.

Chapter 7

1. RMJ to TH, January 17, 1836, THP, folder 10, FHS; RMJ to TH, April 16, 1834, THP, folder 9, FHS; RMJ to Lewis Cass, October 1833, LROIA, Schools, roll 776, frames 278–279, NARA.

2. Hubert Howe Bancroft interview with George Washington Trahern, n.d., Biographical Materials relating to George Washington Trahern, BC, ms. C-D 843, 1-3, UC; Register of the Names of Choctaw Orphan Children, compiled by Middleton McKee, December 17, 1832, LROIA, roll 170, frames 167–178, NARA.

3. Bancroft interview with Trahern, esp. 57; Washington Trahern to Thomas L. McKenney, June 25, 1828, LROIA, Schools, roll 773, frames 1238–1239, NARA.

4. Speech of George Washington Trahern, February 23, 1838, 26th Cong., 2nd sess., HD 137, p. 118.

5. Elbert Herring to Barton Stone and the Inspectors of CA, June 6, 1834, LSOIA, roll 13, frames 15–17, NARA; Lewis Cass to M. Stokes, August 19, 1833, LSOIA, roll 11, frames 106–108, NARA; Extract from the Annual Report of the Indian Office to the Secretary of War, November 25, 1834, 26th Cong., 2nd sess., HD 109, no. 90.

6. Amanda J. Cobb, *Listening to Our Grandmothers' Stories: The Bloomfield Academy for Chickasaw Females, 1852–1949* (Lincoln: University of Nebraska Press, 2000), 28; Jesse Torrey, *The Moral Instructor, and Guide to Virtue: Being a Compendium of Moral Philosophy* (Philadelphia: Kimber and Sharpless, 1824), 154–156.

7. Leslie M. Harris, *In the Shadow of Slavery: African Americans in New York City, 1626–1863* (Chicago: University of Chicago Press, 2003), 119–126, 230–237.

8. Taliaferro Journal, August 23, 1836, Chippewa folder August–December 1836, GLOVEC; Cyrus Kingsbury to Thomas McKenney, February 8, 1830, LROIA, Schools, roll 774, frames 464–470, NARA; Laws of the Northeast District, recorded on June 12, 1837, by PPP, in *A Gathering of Statesmen: Records of the Choctaw Council Meetings, 1826–1828*, trans. and ed. Marcia Haag and Henry Willis (Norman: University of Oklahoma Press, 2013), 70; Resolution of the Choctaw General Council, November 8, 1834, copy in GFC, box 9, folder 2, OKHS.

9. Israel Folsom to PPP, February 20, 1841, PPPP, folder 259B, GMA. Emphasis in original.

10. TH to Lewis Cass, May 8, 1832, PPPC, box 5, folder 21, WHC; RMJ to TH, April 30, 1828, THP, folder 4, FHS; RMJ to TH, January 13, 1838, THP, folder 13, FHS.

11. Joseph N. Bourassa to N. D. Grover, February 20, 1833, 26th Cong., 2nd sess., HD 109, no. 60; Bourassa to Lewis Cass, February 21, 1833, 26th Cong., 2nd sess., HD 109, no. 61; Bourassa to Elbert Herring, April 18, 1833, LROIA, Schools, roll 775, frames 41–44, NARA.

12. William Staughton to TLM, March 10, 1826, LROIA, Schools, roll 773, frames 436–439, NARA; John P. Bowes, *Exiles and Pioneers: Eastern Indians in the Trans-Mississippi West* (New York: Cambridge University Press, 2007), 58; RMJ to TH, March 23, 1828, and April 30, 1828, THP, folder 4, FHS; Lyman C. Draper interview with Joseph N. Bourassa, July 2–3, 1868, DMC, 23S165; John Tipton to TH, October 21, 1831, THP, folder 6, FHS; CA Student List, August 1, 1832, LROIA, Schools, roll 775, frames 767–768, NARA; Joseph N. Bourassa to N. D. Grover, February 20, 1833, 26th Cong., 2nd sess., HD 109, no. 60; TH to NM Henderson, May 13, 1832, THP, folder 7, FHS; Joseph N. Bourassa to Lewis Cass, April 27, 1832, LROIA, Schools, roll 775, frames 708–710, NARA.

13. Trustees' Report, August 10, 1832, LROIA Schools, roll 775, frame 761, NARA; RMJ to TH, March 23, 1828, THP, folder 4, FHS; RMJ to TH, February 27, 1834, THP, folder 9, FHS; CA Student List, August 1, 1832, LROIA, Schools, roll 775, frames 767–768, NARA.

14. W. Trahern to PPP, April 18, 1833, PPPP, folder 127, GMA.
15. John Tipton to TH, June 5, 1832, THP, folder 7, FHS.
16. RMJ to TH, March 23, 1828, THP, folder 4, FHS; Joseph N. Bourassa to Lewis Cass, June 21, 1834, LROIA, Chicago Agency, roll 132, frames 367–368, NARA; RMJ to TH, February 10, 1835, THP, folder 10, NARA; Affidavit of Thomas L. McKenney [Potawatomi], May 6, 1835, THP, folder 10, NARA; RMJ to TH, March 8, 1838, THP, folder 13, NARA.
17. Joseph N. Bourassa to Lewis Cass, April 27, 1832, LROIA, Schools, roll 775, frames 708–710, NARA; John Tipton to Lewis Cass, May 13, 1832, LROIA, Schools, roll 775, frame 706, NARA; Joseph N. Bourassa to Lewis Cass, February 21, 1833, 26th Cong., 2nd sess., HD 109, no. 61.
18. Joseph N. Bourassa to Lewis Cass, June 4, 1833, LROIA, Schools, roll 776, frames 47–48, NARA; William Trahern to PPP, April 18, 1833, PPPP, folder 127, GMA.
19. 26th Cong., 2nd sess., HD 109, no. 62–65; Report from the Office of Indian Affairs to the Secretary of War, November 28, 1833, 23rd Cong., 1st sess., SD 1, no. 11, p. 199; Joseph N. Bourassa to Lewis Cass, November 9, 1833, LROIA, Schools, roll 776, frame 50, NARA; TH to RMJ, n.d. [1835?], LROIA, Schools, roll 777, frames 216–217, NARA; Henry N. Folsom to Herring, April 5, 1836, LROIA, Schools, roll 777, frame 715, NARA; RMJ to TH, January 10, 1835, THP, folder 10, FHS; Joseph Bourassa to Lewis Cass, June 4, 1833, LROIA, Schools, roll 776, frames 47–48, NARA; *Catalog of the Officers and Students of Transylvania University* (Lexington: J. Clarke, 1833).
20. Lowell H. Harrison and James C. Klotter, *A New History of Kentucky* (Lexington: University of Kentucky Press, 1997), 160; R. L. Jensen and J. L. Stone, "Benjamin Winslow Dudley and Early American Trephination for Posttraumatic Epilepsy," *Neurosurgery* 41 (1997): 263–268; William Trahern to Lewis Cass, LROIA, Schools, roll 776, frames 469–471, NARA; Receipt, April 30, 1835, LROIA, Schools, roll 777, frames 327–328, NARA; William Trahern to Lewis Cass, August 15, 1835, LROIA, Schools, roll 777, frame 549, NARA; *Catalog of the Officers and Students of Transylvania University.*
21. TH to Herring, April 18, 1833, 26th Cong., 2nd sess., HD 109, no. 65; Herring to TH, May 1, 1833, LSOIA, letterbook 10, p. 306, NARA; CA Quarterly Report, November 1, 1833, PPPC, box 5, folder 27, WHC.
22. Herring to John Tipton, June 8, 1832, LSOIA, vol. 8, p. 448, NARA; RMJ to TH, November 27, 1833, THP, folder 8, FHS; TH to RMJ, December 19, 1834, LROIA, Schools, roll 776, frames 791–792, NARA; John Mullay to Medill, July 27, 1846, LROIA, Schools, roll 783, frame 467, NARA; TH to Joel R. Poinsett, July 1, 1839, RG 107, ROSW, Confidential and Unofficial Letters, folder P, NARA; CA Quarterly Report, September 30, 1838, 26th Cong., 2nd sess., HD 109, no. 147.
23. W. Trahern to PPP, April 18, 1833, PPPP, folder 127, GMA; Henry Vose to PPP, September 14, 1831, PPPP, folder 107, GMA.
24. Samuel Milroy to RMJ, August 24, 1839, 26th Cong., 2nd sess., HD 109, no. 109; Lewis Cass to James Noble, January 5, 1826, copy in Potawatomi folder 1826–1827, GLOVEC; Student List, August 1, 1832, LROIA, Schools, roll 775, frames 767–768, NARA; Student List, October 31, 1834, LROIA, Schools, roll 776, frames 770–771, NARA; A. C. Pepper to TH, September

14, 1835, LROIA, Schools, roll 777, frame 354, NARA; A. C. Pepper to C. A. Harris, September 10, 1836, LROIA, Schools, roll 777, frames 880–882; A. C. Pepper to OIA, March 28, 1837, HD 109, no. 117.

25. RMJ to TH, May 12, 1834, THP, folder 9, FHS; Armstrong to Lewis Cass, May 20, 1834, THP, folder 9, FHS; Armstrong to Herring, July 18, 1835, LROIA, Schools, roll 777, frames 48–49, NARA.

26. George Vashon to RMJ, January 23, 1834, THP, folder 9, FHS; Allen Hamilton to T. Hartley Crawford, October 12, 1843, copy in Miami folder 1834–1827, GLOVEC.

27. CK to Samuel Worcester, May 5, 1820, CKC, box 3, folder 10, item 2, WHC; Clara Sue Kidwell, *Choctaws and Missionaries in Mississippi, 1818–1918* (Norman: University of Oklahoma Press, 1995), 144–145, 160; Louis Coleman, *Cyrus Byington: Missionary and Choctaw Linguist* (Kearney, NE: Morris, 1996), 49; Cyrus Kingsbury, Report on Schools in the Choctaw Nation, May 4, 1837, CKC, box 1, folder 2, item 17, WHC; Julie L. Reed, "A Nation's Charge: Cherokee Social Services, 1835–1907" (Ph.D. diss., University of North Carolina at Chapel Hill, 2011), 38; *Measuring Worth*, accessed January 21, 2014, http://www.measuringworth.com/uscompare.

28. Armstrong to Lewis Cass, April 4, 1833, LROIA, Schools, roll 170, frames 235–245, quotation on frame 236, NARA; Louis Coleman and Barbara Asbill Grant, *The Wheelock Story* (Durant, OK: Texoma Print Services, 2011), 14–19; Ramsay D. Potts, School Report for 1836, Pushmataha District, 26th Cong., 2nd sess., HD 109, no. 185; Alanson Alben to John Stuart, September 15, 1835, LROIA, Schools, roll 777, frame 525, NARA; William Wilson to Armstrong, October 13, 1838, LROIA, Schools, roll 778, frames 665–668, NARA; Statement of Indian Territory Schools, 1840, LROIA, Schools, roll 779, frame 513, NARA; C. A. Harris to S. G. Tillet, May 20, 1835, 26th Cong., 2nd sess., HD 109, no. 223; Choctaw Nation Schools Report, 1837, LROIA, Schools, roll 778, frame 36, NARA.

29. Leonard Tarrant to Elbert Herring, August 22, 1834, LROIA, Schools, roll 776, frame 970, NARA; RMJ to TH, February 27, 1834, THP, folder 9, FHS; quotation from Armstrong to Harris, October 31, 1838, LROIA, Schools, roll 778, frame 663, NARA.

30. Cass to M. Stokes, August 19, 1833, LSOIA, roll 11, pp. 106–108, NARA; Herring to TH, March 7, 1835, HD 109, no. 95, pp. 92–93.

31. TH to Cass, May 8, 1832, PPPC, box 5, folder 21, WHC; TH to RMJ, December 22, 1837, 26th Cong., 2nd sess., HD 109, no. 135; RMJ to TH, March 8, 1838, THP, folder 13, FHS; Colin G. Calloway, *The Indian History of an American Institution: Native Americans and Dartmouth* (Hanover, NH: Dartmouth College Press, 2010), 12; Adam Hodgson, *Remarks during a Journey through North America* (Westport, CT: Negro Universities Press, 1970), 287; Theda Perdue, "Women, Men, and American Indian Policy: The Cherokee Response to 'Civilization,'" in *Negotiators of Change: Historical Perspectives on Native American Women*, ed. Nancy Shoemaker (New York: Routledge, 1995), 90–114.

32. RMJ and TH, May 5, 1834, and June 3, 1834, THP, folder 9, FHS; CA Quarterly Report, July 31, 1834, PPPC, box 5, folder 31, WHC; Statement of O. P. Rood, January 1, 1845, CA Quarterly Report, LROIA, Schools, roll 782, frames 1218–1219, NARA.

33. Rush quoted in Caroline Winterer, *The Culture of Classicism: Ancient Greece and Rome in American Intellectual Life, 1780–1910* (Baltimore: Johns Hopkins University Press, 2002), 42; Alexis de Tocqueville, *Democracy in America*, trans. Arthur Goldhammer (New York: Library of America, 2004), 538; Abraham Lincoln to Jesse W. Fell, December 20, 1859, in *The Collected Works of Abraham Lincoln*, ed. Roy P. Basler (New Brunswick, NJ: Rutgers University Press, 1953), vol. 3, 511; Catherine E. Kelly, *Republic of Taste: Art, Politics, and Everyday Life in Early America* (Philadelphia: University of Pennsylvania Press, 2016), 18; Mary W. Helms, "Political Lords and Political Ideology in Southeastern Chiefdoms: Comments and Observations," in *Lords of the Southeast: Social Inequality and the Native Elites of Southeastern North America*, ed. Alex W. Barker and Timothy R. Pauketat, *Archaeological Papers of the American Anthropological Association* 3 (1992): 185–194.

34. RMJ to TH, June 3, 1834, THP, folder 9, FHS; Elbert Herring to TH, January 22, 1834, 26th Cong., 2nd sess., HD 109, no. 74; Herring to A. C. Pepper, December 23, 1835, LSOIA, roll 17, frames 350–351, NARA; RMJ to TH, April 16, 1834, and May 27, 1834, THP, folder 9, FHS.

35. TH to RMJ, February 27, 1838, LROIA, Schools, roll 778, frames 906–913, NARA; for printed essays, see 26th Cong., 2nd sess., HD 109, no. 137–140.

36. B. D. Emerson, *The Second-Class Reader: Designed for the Use of the Middle Class of Schools in the United States* (Boston: Russell, Odiorne, & Metcalf, 1834), 143; quotation from Torrey, *The Moral Instructor*, 252.

37. Winterer, *Culture of Classicism*, 3, 25, 70–71.

38. Winterer, *Culture of Classicism*, 68; CA Trustees' Report, July 1827, PPPC, box 5, folder 11, WHC; Merrill D. Peterson, ed., *Thomas Jefferson: Writings* (New York: Library of America, 1984), 188; Alexander Fraser Tytler, *Elements of General History, Ancient and Modern* (Concord, NH: Horatio Hill, 1824), 26; John Gillies, *The History of Ancient Greece, Its Colonies and Conquests from the Earliest Accounts till the Division of the Macedonian Empire in the East* (Philadelphia: Joseph Marot, 1829), 44–46, quotation on p. 44.

39. Like most Americans, the students probably read the classics in translation, though some of the students could read the original Greek or Latin. The advanced students read Tytler's *Elements of General History*, and a popular translation of Plutarch by John and William Langhorne, *Plutarch's Lives, Translated from the Original Greek; with Notes, Historical and Critical* (Philadelphia: Hickman and Hazzard, 1822); for quotation on mechanical arts, see vol. 1, p. 90. Peter Pitchlynn definitely read John Gillies, *The History of Ancient Greece* (which is based largely on histories written by Plutarch and Xenophon) and recommended it to young Choctaws. Less advanced students at Choctaw Academy might have encountered Greek history in Samuel Goodrich, *Peter Parley's Tales about Ancient and Modern Greece*, or Goodrich's *A Pictorial History of Greece: Ancient and Modern*. Choctaw Academy's textbook lists before 1840 are vague, though the school did use several history and geography texts from Goodrich's popular series.

40. Regular instruction in Latin was available at Choctaw Academy beginning in 1833 with the arrival of Isaac Gardner, though some students may have taken earlier tutorials in the subject from Thomas Henderson. CA Quarterly Report, November 1, 1833, PPPC, box 5, frame 27, WHC. On the Lancastrian system and translation, see Choctaw Academy Trustees' Report, August 1, 1828,

PPPC, box 5, folder 13, WHC; Quarterly Report, January 1, 1843, LROIA, Schools, roll 781, frame 588, NARA.

41. CA Quarterly Report, January 31, 1832, PPPC, box 5, folder 19, WHC; Constitution of the Eagletown Social and Intellectual Society (later called the "Eagletown Debating Society"), 1834, PPPP, folder 153, GMA; Peter Pitchlynn, Notes of a Speech in the Eagletown Debating Society, n.d., PPPP, folder 646, GMA. On debating societies elsewhere, see, for example, E. Merton Coulter, *College Life in the Old South as Seen at the University of Georgia* (Athens: University of Georgia Press, 1983), 119–120; Edmund P. Drago, *Charleston's Avery Center: From Education and Civil Rights to Preserving the African American Experience* (Charleston, SC: History Press, 2006), 36; Debate in the Senate, February 27, 1830, *Niles' Register*, vol. 38, p. 11.

42. Langhorne and Langhorne, eds. and trans., "Lycurgus," in *Plutarch's Lives*, vol. 1, 65–70; Gillies, *History of Ancient Greece*, 40–41.

43. Langhorne and Langhorne, eds. and trans., "Lycurgus," in *Plutarch's Lives*, vol. 1, 65–98. For quote on greed and conquest, see Gillies, *History of Ancient Greece*, 41.

44. Anthony P. F. Navarre and Antoine Bourbonnais to William Medill, March 30, 1846, LROIA, Schools, roll 783, frame 232, NARA; PPP to Lycurgus Pitchlynn, August 31, 1846, PPPC, box 1, folder 108, WHC.

45. G. W. Trahern, "On History," 26th Cong., 2nd sess., HD 109, no. 140, p. 122. For examples from their textbooks, see Tytler, *Elements of General History*, 13–16; Gillies, *History of Ancient Greece*, 11–22; Lindley Murray, *English Grammar, Adapted to the Different Classes of Learners* (Boston: T. Bedlington, 1825), 134; Robert Gibson, *The Theory and Practice of Surveying: Containing all the Instructions Requisite for the Skilful Practice of this Art* (New York: Evert Duyckinck, 1821), iii.

46. G. W. Trahern, "On History," 26th Cong., 2nd sess., HD 109, no. 140, p. 122. He adapted a quotation from Langhorne and Langhorne, "Lycurgus," in *Plutarch's Lives*, 79.

47. PPP to Lycurgus Pitchlynn, August 31, 1846, PPPC, box 1, folder 108, WHC; Gillies, *History of Greece*, 99, 167, 262–263, 296, 352; Langhorne and Langhorne, "Lysander," in *Plutarch's Lives*, vol. 2, 281–307; G. W. Trahern, "On History," 26th Cong., 2nd sess., HD 109, no. 140, p. 122.

48. Speech of August Buckholts, February 23, 1838, 26th Cong., 2nd sess., HD 109, no. 138, p. 120; Adam Christie, untitled essay, 26th Cong., 2nd sess., HD 109, no. 140, p. 123.

49. Adam Christie, untitled essay, 26th Cong., 2nd sess., HD 109, no. 140, p. 123; S. Augustus Mitchell, *Mitchell's Primary Geography, An Easy Introduction to the Study of Geography: Designed for the Instruction of Children in Schools and Families* (Philadelphia: Thomas, Cowperthwait & Co., 1840), 51; Jesse Olney, *A Practical System of Modern Geography; or a View of the Present State of the World*, 34th ed. (New York: Robinson, Pratt & Co., 1841), 63; Miss Francis, "The Lone Indian," in B. D. Emerson, *The Second-Class Reader: Designed for the Use of the Middle Class of Schools in the United States* (Boston: Russell, Odiorne, & Metcalf, 1834), 34–36.

50. Stow Persons, "The Cyclical Theory of History in Eighteenth Century America," *American Quarterly* 6 (1954): 147–163; John O'Sullivan, "The Great Nation of Futurity," *United States Democratic Review* 6 (1839): 427.

51. Mrs. Phelps, "Advantage of Studying History," in Emerson, *Second-Class Reader*, 144; Torrey, *Moral Instructor*, 252; Lewis Cass, "Decay of the Indians," in S. G. Goodrich, *The Fourth Reader for the Use of Schools* (Louisville, KY: Morton and Griswold, 1839), 304.

52. Margaret Malamud, *Ancient Rome and Modern America* (West Sussex: Wiley-Blackwell, 2009), 18–26, Calhoun quoted on p. 23; Washburn quoted in Colin Calloway, *Pen and Ink Witchcraft: Treaties and Treaty Making in American Indian History* (New York: Oxford University Press, 2013), 147.

53. Christie essay, 26th Cong., 2nd sess., HD 140, pp. 122–123; Trahern speech, 26th Cong., 2nd sess., HD 140, p. 118.

54. Trahern speech, 26th Cong., 2nd sess., HD 140, p. 118; Christie essay, 26th Cong., 2nd sess., HD 140, p. 123.

Chapter 8

1. *Kentucky Sentinel*, June 3, July 8, 1835; *Lexington Observer & Kentucky Reporter*, July 8, 1835; *The Graphic* (Georgetown, KY), February 13, 1958; Treaty of Mississinewa, October 16, 1826, copy in Potawatomi Files, 1826–1827, GLOVEC; Personal communication, email from John Bickers, February 16, 2016; quotation from RMJ note on a letter, John Jones to Elbert Herring, April 27, 1835, GFC, box 9, folder 2, OKHS.

2. RMJ to CA Harris, August 24, 1836, LROIA, Schools, roll 777, frames 790–792, NARA.

3. RMJ to CA Harris, August 24, 1836, LROIA, Schools, roll 777, frames 790–792, NARA; *Kentucky Sentinel*, July 8, 1835; *Lexington Observer & Kentucky Reporter*, July 8, July 15, and July 22, 1835 (quotation from July 8); *Lexington Intelligencer*, July 7, 1835; *New York American*, August 5, 1835; *Vermont Phoenix*, July 24, 1835; RMJ to TH, January 14, 1835, THP, folder 10, FHS. On freedom of movement, see *Running a Thousand Miles for Freedom; or the Escape of William and Ellen Craft from Slavery* (London: William Tweedie, 1860).

4. William Staughton to TLM, March 10, 1826, LROIA, Schools, roll 773, frame 438, NARA.

5. William Staughton to TLM, March 10, 1826, LROIA, Schools, roll 773, frames 436–439, NARA.

6. TH to Lewis Cass, November 8, 1832, LROIA, Schools, roll 775, frame 533, NARA; List of Students, compiled by TH, October 31, 1834, LROIA, Schools, roll 776, frames 770–771, NARA; Physician's Report, by Samuel Hatch, to the Trustees of Choctaw Academy, August 1833, LROIA, Schools, roll 776, frames 209–212, NARA; John Jones to John Tipton, January 17, 1835, LROIA, Schools, roll 777, frames 542–543, NARA; CA Quarterly Report, 30 April 1827, LROIA, Schools, roll 773, frames 648–651, NARA; PPP to T. Hartly Crawford, March 2, 1841, LROIA, Schools, roll 780, frames 450–451, NARA.

7. Contract between John Jones and TH, June 1, 1834, LROIA, Schools, roll 776, frame 751, NARA; Receipt from John Jones, July 25, 1834, LROIA, Schools, roll 776, frame 753, NARA; Contract between John Jones and TH, July 25, 1834, LROIA, Schools, roll 776, frame 755, NARA; Ella Wells Drake, "Choctaw Academy, 1825–1848: American Indian Education, Experience, and Response" (M.A. Thesis, University of Kentucky, 1999), 77–78; John Jones to John Tipton, January 17, 1835, LROIA, Schools, roll 777, frames 542–543, NARA; Tipton to Elbert Herring, January 30, 1835, LROIA, Schools, roll

777, frame 540, NARA; John Jones to Elbert Herring, April 27, 1835, LROIA, Schools, roll 777, frames 544–547, NARA.

8. John Jones to John Tipton, January 17, 1835, LROIA, Schools, roll 777, frames 542–543, NARA.

9. RMJ to TH, April 1, 1836, THP, folder 10, FHS; RMJ to TH, May 4, 1834, THP, folder 9, FHS.

10. Jacob Holt to TH, February 24, 1834, THP, folder 9, FHS; Handbill from the Election of 1836, Colonel Richard M. Johnson Vertical Files, KHS; Leland Meyer, *The Life and Times of Colonel Richard M. Johnson of Kentucky* (New York: Columbia University Press, 1932), 262, 286–289.

11. Meyer, *Life and Times of Colonel Richard M. Johnson*, 264–267; Robert V. Remini, *Andrew Jackson: The Course of American Empire, 1767–1821* (Baltimore: Johns Hopkins University Press, 1977), 57–67; Norma Basch, "Marriage, Morals, and Politics in the Election of 1828," *Journal of American History* 80 (1993): 890–918; Allan Nevins, ed., *The Diary of John Quincy Adams, 1794–1845: American Diplomacy, and Political, Social, and Intellectual Life, from Washington to Polk* (New York: Charles Scribner, 1951), 431–432; on "warm friend," see John Norvell to John McLean, January 23, 1832, The Papers of John McLean, roll 3, LOC.

12. Meyer, *Life and Times of Colonel Richard M. Johnson*, 407–409; Handbill from the Election of 1836, Colonel Richard M. Johnson Vertical Files, KHS; *Kentucky Sentinel*, June 10, 1835; *Arkansas Weekly Gazette*, August 30, 1836; RMJ to TH, February 1, 1833, THP, folder 8, FHS; *Argus of Western America*, August 4, 1824.

13. *Kentucky Sentinel*, August 5, 1835; John Norvell to John McLean, January 23, 1832, McLean Papers, roll 3, LOC.

14. *Niles' Register*, May 23, May 30, June 6, 1835; *Daily National Intelligencer*, May 22, 1835.

15. Benjamin Perley Poore, *Perley's Reminiscences of Sixty Years in the National Metropolis* (Philadelphia: Hubbard Brothers, 1886), 153; *Kentucky Sentinel*, July 8, 1835; Harriet Martineau, "Washington in Jackson's Day; Southern Slavery," in *American Social History as Recorded by British Travellers*, ed. Allan Nevins (New York: Henry Holt, 1923), 193–194; *New-York Spectator*, February 19, 1835; Thomas Brown, "The Miscegenation of Richard Mentor Johnson as an Issue in the National Election Campaign of 1835–1836," *Civil War History* 39 (1993): 25; Alfred Balch to Jackson, April 4, 1835, Andrew Jackson Papers, series 1, roll 46, LOC.

16. *Salem Gazette*, August 23, 1836. See also Annette Gordon-Reed, *The Hemingses of Monticello: An American Family* (New York: Norton, 2008), 570.

17. Brown, "The Miscegenation of Richard Mentor Johnson"; *The Liberator*, August 20, 1836; *Salem Gazette*, October 14, 1836.

18. *The Torch Light* (Hagers-Town, Maryland), June 11, 1835; *Cincinnati Daily Gazette*, June 22, 1835; Recollections of John Wilson, Kentucky Manuscripts, DMC, 17CC16; *Salem Gazette*, August 28, 1835; *Louisville Advertiser*, July 3, 1835.

19. *Louisville Daily Journal*, June 12, 1835; *New York Herald*, July 11, 1835; *Lexington Observer and Kentucky Reporter*, July 1, 1835; *Cincinnati Daily Gazette*, June 18, June 19, June 24, 1835.

20. Letter from TH, June 20, 1835, reprinted in *Louisville Advertiser*, July 3, 1835, and *Lexington Observer and Kentucky Reporter*, July 29, 1835.

21. *Kentucky Sentinel*, June 17, July 22, August 12, 1835; L. Smith to B. W. Smith, May 25, 1844, Miscellaneous Correspondence, Smith Letter, FHS.

22. J. F. Henry to Mrs. M. W. Henry, September 19, n.y., Henry-Bacon Family Papers, Uncataloged, FHS; *Kentucky Sentinel*, June 10, 1835.

23. *Cincinnati Daily Gazette*, June 22, 1835; Frederick Marryat, *A Diary in America: With Remarks on Its Institutions* (Philadelphia: Carey and Hart, 1839), vol. 1, 159. See also Gordon-Reed, *The Hemingses of Monticello*, 275.

24. RMJ to Francis P. Blair, June 16, 1835, Blair-Lee Family Papers, box 14, folder 3, PU.

25. RMJ Speech on the Missouri Question, February 1820, Annals of Congress, Senate, 16th Congress, 1st sess., 346, 353–354; *Argus of Western America*, January 9, 1828; *Ohio Statesman*, January 26, 1841; *The Emancipator*, June 13, 1839.

26. Pence Family Bible, private collection; 1810 United States Federal Census, Records of the Bureau of the Census, M252, roll 8, p. 191, NARA; Ann Bolton Bevins, *A History of Scott County: As Told by Select Buildings* (Georgetown, KY: Bevins, 1981), 167; *Lexington Observer*, November 29, 1832; Scott County Deed Book L, November 9, 1832, p. 126, KHS.

27. Record of Expenses, September 30, 1836, LROIA, Schools, roll 777, frames 752–753, NARA; Great Crossings Attendance Records, June 7, 1828, GCBC Records, SBTS; GCBC Minutes, July 6, 1833, book 2, p. 265; Scott County Deed Book Q, June 30, 1841, p. 426, KHS; 1850 United States Federal Census, Slave Schedules, Ancestry, accessed January 14, 2014, http://www.ancestrylibrary.com; Amrita Chakrabarti Myers, *Forging Freedom: Black Women and the Pursuit of Liberty in Antebellum Charleston* (Chapel Hill: University of North Carolina Press, 2011), 120, 145–146.

28. Myers, *Forging Freedom*, 42, 51; Gordon-Reed, *The Hemingses of Monticello*, 409–410, 648–659.

29. Myers, *Forging Freedom*, 12–14; Joel Williamson, *New People: Miscegenation and Mulattoes in the United States* (New York: Free Press, 1980), 13, 17–19.

30. *Lexington Observer and Kentucky Reporter*, November 29, 1832; *The Torch Light*, June 11, 1835. Emphasis in original.

31. James Oliver Horton and Lois E. Horton, *In Hope of Liberty: Culture, Community, and Protest among Northern Free Blacks, 1700–1860* (New York: Oxford University Press, 1997), 209; Marion B. Lucas, *A History of Blacks in Kentucky: From Slavery to Segregation, 1760–1891* (Frankfort: Kentucky Historical Society, 2003), 61; Adam Rothman, *Slave Country: American Expansion and the Origins of the Deep South* (Cambridge, MA: Harvard University Press, 2005); John Craig Hammond, *Slavery, Freedom, and Expansion in the Early American West* (Charlottesville: University of Virginia Press, 2007), 170.

32. Michael Witgen, *An Infinity of Nations: How the Native New World Shaped Early North America* (Philadelphia: University of Pennsylvania Press, 2012); John W. Hall, *Uncommon Defense: Indian Allies in the Black Hawk War* (Cambridge, MA: Harvard University Press, 2009), 10–11; R. David Edmunds, *The Potawatomis: Keepers of the Fire* (Norman: University of Oklahoma Press, 1978), 3–4, 18, 153, 234–235; quotation from Testimony of White Cloud, Treaty of Prairie du Chien, August 1825, copy in Sac folder 1825–1827, GLOVEC.

33. W. David Baird, *Peter Pitchlynn: Chief of the Choctaws* (Norman: University of Oklahoma Press, 1972), 46; Bill of Sale, August 18, 1832, PPPP, folder 114, GMA; Laws of October 3, 1838, *The Constitution and Laws of the Choctaw Nation* (Park Hill, Cherokee Nation: John Candy, 1840), 28. For enslaved population figures, see Christine Bolt, *American Indian Policy and American Reform: Case Studies of the Campaign to Assimilate the American Indians* (London: Allen & Unwin, 1987), 152; James A. Ramage and Andrea S. Watkins, *Kentucky Rising: Democracy, Slavery, and Culture from the Early Republic to the Civil War* (Lexington: University Press of Kentucky, 2011), 238–239.

34. John P. Bowes, *Exiles and Pioneers: Eastern Indians in the Trans-Mississippi West* (New York: Cambridge University Press, 2007), 182; Andrew Hughes to William Clark, March 10, 1831, copy, Sac folder 1831, GLOVEC; PPP Diary, November 28, 1828, PPPC, box 5, folder 2, WHC; Deposition of John Pitchlynn, September 25, 1819, PPPP, folder 14, GMA; Christina Snyder, *Slavery in Indian Country: The Changing Face of Captivity in Early America* (Cambridge, MA: Harvard University Press, 2010), 204–205.

35. *Kentucky Sentinel*, July 8, 1835; *Lexington Observer & Kentucky Reporter*, July 8, July 15, and July 22, 1835; *Lexington Intelligencer*, July 7, 1835; *New York American*, August 5, 1835; *Vermont Phoenix*, July 24, 1835; *Union Herald*, July 6, 1838; *The Liberator*, July 25, 1845.

36. *Vermont Phoenix*, July 24, 1835; *New York American*, August 5, 1835; *Lexington Observer and Kentucky Reporter*, July 8, 1835.

37. *Norfolk Advertiser*, July 18, 1835; *Lexington Observer and Kentucky Reporter*, July 8, 1835; *Lexington Intelligencer*, July 7, 1835.

38. *Vermont Phoenix*, July 24, 1835, reprint of a Columbus, Ohio, letter dated July 6, 1835.

39. *Lexington Observer and Kentucky Reporter*, July 22, 1835; Amos Kendall to Martin Van Buren, VB, series 2, vol. 36, roll 21; RMJ to TH, May 4, 1834, THP, folder 9, FHS; *The Liberator*, July 25, 1845; James A. Peak to John Eaton, November 15, 1829, LROIA, Schools, roll 774, frames 225–226, NARA; TH to John Eaton, June 30, 1830, LROIA, Schools, roll 774, frame 382, NARA. Contemporary accounts say only that Parthena was beaten, but later testimony from a former Johnson slave offers greater detail about typical punishments for runaways. Interview of Addie Murphy by J. C. Meadors, August 13, 1938, "Slave Interviews, Notes and Data on Kentucky Slavery," typescript, JWCP.

40. Adam Rothman, *Slave Country: American Expansion and the Origins of the Deep South* (Cambridge, MA: Harvard University Press, 2005), Chapter 5; Edward E. Baptist, *The Half Has Never Been Told: Slavery and the Making of American Capitalism* (New York: Basic, 2014); Lucas, *History of Blacks in Kentucky*, 84–99; Ramage and Ramage, *Kentucky Rising*, 265–266; Emily Clark, *The Strange History of the American Quadroon: Free Women of Color in the Revolutionary Atlantic World* (Chapel Hill: University of North Carolina Press, 2013), 164.

41. *Lexington Observer and Kentucky Reporter*, July 22, 1835; Interview with John Wilson, n.d., DMC, 17CC16; *Union Herald*, July 6, 1838, reprint of June 15 letter from Lewis Tappan; *The Liberator*, July 25, 1845; Scott County Court Order Book C, October 5, 1832, p. 382, KHS.

42. W. R. Hallet to Martin Van Buren, January 12, 1837, VB, series 2, vol. 25, roll 16, LOC; *Cincinnati Daily Gazette*, June 18, 1835; Meyer, *Life and Times*, 311–312.

43. Unknown to Amos Kendall, August 12, 1839, VB, series 2, vol. 36, roll 21, LOC; Amos Kendall to Van Buren, August 22, 1839, VB, series 2, vol. 36, roll 21, LOC; *Kentucky Tribune*, September 22, 1843; Catherine Bragg to Catherine C. Gould, October 8, 1840, Miscellaneous Manuscripts, Catherine Bragg Letters, FHS. Only the newspaper article explicitly names Dinah, and I cannot be sure that this name is correct.

44. Scott County Deed Book Q, June 30, 1841, p. 426, KHS; RMJ to Adaline Johnson Scott, December 12, 1833, THP, folder 8, FHS.

45. RMJ to TH, February 26, 1836, THP, folder 10, FHS; Personal communication, Ann Bevins, June 29, 2011.

46. RMJ to C. A. Harris, August 24, 1836, LROIA, Schools, roll 777, frames 790–792, NARA; A. C. Pepper to C. A. Harris, August 8, 1836, LROIA, Schools, roll 777, frames 876–877, NARA; Resolution of the Miami Council West of Missouri, March 18, 1847, LROIA, Schools, roll 783, frames 770–771, NARA; Isaac McCoy to Crawford, April 22, 1839, LROIA, Schools, roll 779, frames 222–223, NARA; Herman Lincoln to William Medill, March 4, 1848, LROIA, Schools, roll 784, frames 305–310, NARA.

47. Brown, "The Miscegenation of Richard Mentor Johnson"; Kendall to Van Buren, August 22, 1839, VB, series 2, vol. 36, roll 21, LOC.

48. *National Banner and Nashville Whig*, August 24, 1836; RMJ to Henderson, March 23, 1828, THP, folder 4; RMJ to Henderson , January 14, 1835, THP, folder 10, FHS.

Chapter 9

1. Clara Sue Kidwell, *Choctaws and Missionaries in Mississippi, 1818–1918* (Norman: University of Oklahoma Press), 19, 64–65; Nail Family Genealogy, Nail Family Vertical File, OKHS; CK, Journal of the Mission at Mayhew, October 23, 1822, CKC, box 3, folder 8, item 47, WHC; CK to the ABCFM, November 24, 1830, CKC, box 1, folder 1, item 1, WHC; Susannah Nail to Mrs. Williams, June 24, 1826, CKC, box 3, folder 9, item 41, WHC; List of Choctaw Students Attending Schools in the States, GFC, box 9, folder 3, OKHS; Horace T. N. Benedict to Board of Inspectors, 1 October 1837, LROIA, Schools, roll 778, frame 533, NARA; RMJ to TH and Mr. Pence, February 26, 1838, THP, folder 13, FHS; Adam Nail to Trustees, April 3, 1839, LROIA, Schools, roll 779, frame 289.

2. Horace T. N. Benedict, CA Quarterly Report, January 1, 1838, LROIA, Schools, roll 778, frame 890, NARA; Benjamin Kenney and William Johnson to T. Hartley Crawford, July 12, 1839, LROIA, Schools, roll 779, frame 171, NARA; War Department to TH, April 4, 1838, THP, folder 13, FHS; Lawrence A. Cremin, *American Education: The National Experience, 1783–1876* (New York: Harper & Row, 1980), 355; James A. Ramage and Andrea Watkins, *Kentucky Rising: Democracy, Slavery and Culture from the Early Republic to the Civil War* (Lexington: University Press of Kentucky, 2011), 190.

3. Horace T. N. Benedict, Medical Report, April 2, 1838, LROIA, Schools, roll 778, frame 920, NARA (emphasis in original); Ramage and Watkins, *Kentucky Rising*, 209; Horatio B. Cushman, *History of the Choctaw, Chickasaw, and Natchez Indians*, ed. Angie Debo (Norman: University of Oklahoma Press, 1999), 169–170, 307; John R. Swanton, *Source Material for the Social and*

Ceremonial Life of the Choctaw Indians (Tuscaloosa: University of Alabama Press, 2001), 229–238. On the popularity of Indian doctors among whites, see, for example, the story of Shabbona, the uncle of Choctaw Academy student Joseph N. Bourassa. Interview with Joseph N. Bourassa, July 2–3, 1868, DMC, 23S165, pp. 189–190.

4. Manuscript of Israel Folsom, in Cushman, *History of the Choctaw*, 307; quotations from Noley B. Grayson, "The History of Education in the Choctaw Nation from Precolonial Times to 1830" (Ph.D. diss., Pennsylvania State University, 1979), 87–88.

5. James Mooney and Frans Olbrechts, *The Swimmer Manuscript: Cherokee Sacred Formulas and Medicinal Prescriptions* (DC: US Government Printing Office, 1932), 108; Catherine M. Cameron, Paul Kelton, and Alan C. Swedlund, *Beyond Germs: Native Depopulation in North America* (Tucson: University of Arizona Press, 2015); Paul Kelton, *Cherokee Medicine, Colonial Germs: An Indigenous Nation's Fight against Smallpox, 1518–1824* (Norman: University of Oklahoma Press, 2015); Theda Perdue and Michael D. Green, *The Cherokee Nation and the Trail of Tears* (New York: Penguin, 2007), 126; quotation from Henry N. Folsom to Elbert Herring, April 5, 1836, LROIA, Schools, roll 777, frame 715, NARA.

6. CA Medical Report, April 2, 1838, LROIA, Schools, roll 778, frame 920, NARA; CA Medical Report, October 1, 1838, LROIA, Schools, roll 778, frame 1181, NARA; CA Medical Report, April 3, 1839, LROIA, Schools, roll 779, frame 289, NARA; W. S. Crawford interview with Gardner, October 22, 1841, LROIA, Schools, roll 780, frame 171, NARA; David Wallace Adams, *Education for Extinction: American Indians and the Boarding School Experience, 1875–1928* (Lawrence: University Press of Kansas, 1995), 130–132; Benjamin Phillips, *Scrofula; Its Nature, Its Causes, Its Prevalence, and the Principles of Treatment* (Philadelphia: Lea and Blanchard, 1846), esp. 255; John Forbes, Alexander Tweedie, John Conolly, and Robley Dunglison, *Cyclopedia of Practical Medicine* (Philadelphia: Henry C. Lea, 1867), 139.

7. William Venable to Thomas Henderson, February 12, 1839, THP, folder 14, FHS; To "the public" from John Pitchlynn, Andrew Weir, Sylvester Pearl, November 7, 1834, 26th Cong., 2nd sess., HD 109, no. 87; TH to Lewis Cass, November 17, 1834, GFC, box 9, folder 2, OKHS; Angie Debo, *Rise and Fall of the Choctaw Republic* (Norman: University of Oklahoma Press, 1934), 77; George A. Pettitt, "Primitive Education in North America," *University of California Publications in American Archaeology and Ethnology* 43 (1946): 8–10.

8. Mooney and Olbrechts, *The Swimmer Manuscript*, 92; Swanton, *Ceremonial Life of the Choctaw Indians*, 227.

9. Adam Nail et al. to the War Department, October 28, 1839, LROIA, Schools, roll 779, frames 228–230, NARA.

10. Adam Nail et al. to the War Department, October 28, 1839, LROIA, Schools, roll 779, frames 228–230, NARA; RMJ to TH, March 14, 1834, THP, folder 9, FHS; RMJ to TH, February 12, 1834, THP, folder 9, FHS; John Mullay to William Medill, July 27, 1846, LROIA, Schools, roll 783, frames 454–55, NARA; Joshua Pilcher to Joel Poinsett, April 28, 1839, RG 107, ROSW, Confidential and Unofficial Letters Received, folder P, NARA; W. S. Crawford interview with Isaac Gardner, October 22, 1841, LROIA, Schools, roll 780, frames 167–172, NARA; CA Students to W. S. Crawford, October 19, 1841, LROIA, Schools, roll 780, frames 226–227, NARA.

11. Webber quoted in Principal Chiefs of the Cherokee Nation (West) to George Vashon, December 8, 1833, LROIA, Schools, roll 776, frame 988, NARA; F. Joyce to W.P. Thomasson, November 24, 1844, 28th Cong., 2nd sess., HR 193, pp. 7–8.

12. W. S. Crawford interview with Isaac Gardner, October 22, 1841, LROIA, Schools, roll 780, frames 167–172, NARA; Joshua Pilcher to Joel Poinsett, April 28, 1839, RG 107, ROSW, Confidential and Unofficial Letters Received, folder P, NARA (emphasis in original); C. A. Harris to Vanderslice, April 3, 1837, RG 75, Chickasaw Removal Records, entry 252, book 1, pp. 141–142, NARA; W. S. Crawford interview with O. P. Rood, October 21, 1841, 28th Cong., 2nd sess., HR 193, pp. 2–3; CA Quarterly Report, December 31, 1844, LROIA, Schools, roll 782, frames 1214–1216, NARA; Report of Conditions at CA, n.d. [1840–1841], PPPP, folder 66a, GMA; Robert Evans to W. S. Crawford, October 21, 1841, LROIA, Schools, roll 780, frames 195–196, NARA; Students to Crawford, October 19, 1841, LROIA, Schools, roll 780, frame 226, NARA.

13. George A. Pettitt, "Education in North America," 66; Adam Nail et al. to the War Department, October 28, 1839, LROIA, Schools, roll 779, frames 228–230, NARA; Americus Hay to William Medill, May 31, 1848, LROIA, Schools, roll 784, frames 163–165, NARA.

14. Izumi Ishii, *Bad Fruits of the Civilized Tree: Alcohol and the Sovereignty of the Cherokee Nation* (Lincoln: University of Nebraska Press, 2008); Debo, *Rise and Fall of the Choctaw Republic*, 47–48; Patrick J. Abbott, "American Indian and Alaska Native Aboriginal Use of Alcohol in the United States," *American Indian and Alaska Mental Health Research* 7 (1996): 1–13; Peter Pitchlynn, draft of a temperance speech, June 25, 1843, PPPP, folder 362, GMA; Peter Pitchlynn Speech to Red River Temperance Society, May 28, 1842, PPPP, folder 360, GMA.

15. CA Quarterly Report, February 1, 1835, PPPC, box 5, folder 32, WHC; CA Students to W. S. Crawford, October 19, 1841, LROIA, Schools, roll 780, frame 226, NARA; CA Quarterly Report, January 1, 1843, LROIA, Schools, roll 781, frames 572–589, NARA; William Wilson to William Armstrong, August 30, 1842, GFC, box 9, folder 3, OKHS.

16. Adam Nail et al. to the War Department, October 28, 1839, LROIA, Schools, roll 779, frames 228–230, NARA.

17. Adam Nail et al. to the War Department, October 28, 1839, LROIA, Schools, roll 779, frames 228–230, NARA ; Emma Rouse Lloyd, "Clasping Hands with Generations Past," THP, folder 1, FHS; RMJ to TH, April 16, 1834, THP, folder 9, FHS.

18. Adam Nail et al. to the War Department, October 28, 1839, LROIA, Schools, roll 779, frames 228–230, NARA; Armstrong to Herring, January 5, 1833, 26th Cong., 2nd sess., HD 109, no. 59; Report of PPP on CA to the General Council of the Choctaw Nation, n.d., PPPP, folder 277, GMA; Committee upon Schools Report, draft 3, n.d., PPPP, folder 381A, GMA.

19. CA Quarterly Report, January 1, 1843, LROIA, Schools, roll 781, frame 588, NARA; Joe K. Page to Elbert Costner, August 19, 1965, John Page Vertical File, OKHS; CA Quarterly Report, April 1, 1838, LROIA, Schools, roll 778, frames 922–923, NARA; Armstrong to Herring, May 1, 1834, 26th Cong., 2nd sess., HD 109, no. 79.

20. TH to T. Hartley Crawford, July 1, 1839, RG 107, ROSW, Confidential and Unofficial Letters, folder P, NARA (emphasis added); C. A. Harris to TH,

January 5, 1838, 26th Cong., 2nd sess., HD 109, no. 136; CA Quarterly Report, October 1, 1839, 26th Cong., 2nd sess., HD 109, no. 156; CA Quarterly Report, Trustees' Report, October 2, 1839, LROIA, Schools, roll 779, frame 302, NARA.

21. B. F. Kenney to Spencer, 1842, LROIA, Schools, roll 780, frame 987, NARA; Student list, July 1845, LROIA, Schools, roll 783, frame 442, NARA; Special Report on CA, John Mullay to William Medill, July 27, 1846, LROIA, Schools, roll 783, frames 447–472, NARA; *Haverhill Gazette* (MA), December 6, 1839.

22. RMJ to TH, April 26, 1826, THP, folder 2, FHS.

23. William Clarke to RMJ, March 24, 1837, LROIA, Schools, roll 778, frames 230–231, NARA; TH to RMJ, December 9, 1830, LROIA, Schools, roll 775, frames 114–115, NARA; Bill, Outfits for Outgoing Youth, June 30, 1837, LROIA, Schools, roll 778, frame 169, NARA; TH to Joel Poinsett, July 29, 1837, LROIA, Schools, roll 778, frames 196–197, NARA.

24. CA Students to W. S. Crawford, October 19, 1841, LROIA, Schools, roll 780, frames 226–227, NARA; PPP, Report of Conditions at CA, n.d [1840 or 1841], PPPP, folder 66a, GMA; RMJ to TH, December 9, 1829, THP, folder 1, FHS; District Chiefs to PPP, October 7, 1840, PPPC, box 1, folder 57, WHC; Joshua Pilcher to Joel Poinsett, April 28, 1839, RG 107, ROSW, Confidential and Unofficial Letters, folder P, NARA.

25. *Commercial Advertiser* (New York), May 28, 1838; W. S. Crawford interview with O. P. Rood, LROIA, Schools, roll 780, frames 187–190, NARA.

26. Students to W. S. Crawford, October 19, 1841, LROIA, Schools, roll 780, frame 226, NARA; Armstrong to Herring, January 5, 1833, 26th Cong., 2nd sess., HD 109, no. 59.

27. Israel Folsom to PPP, February 20, 1841, PPPP, folder 259b, GMA; Petition of the Chiefs and Headmen of the Miami Nation to President, September 19, 1843, LROIA, Schools, roll 781, frame 346, NARA; Creek chiefs cited in Report of the Commissioner of Indian Affairs, June 30, 1842, GFC, box 9, folder 3, p. 503, OKHS; John T. Ellisor, *The Second Creek War: Interethnic Conflict and Collusion on a Collapsing Frontier* (Lincoln: University of Nebraska Press, 2010), 116; Creek chiefs to J. S. Dawson, LROIA, Schools, roll 782, frame 198, NARA; Letter dictated by Thomas Leflore (written by Bazil Leflore) to William Armstrong, January 14, 1840, 26th Cong., 2nd sess., HD 109, no. 159.

28. Committee upon Schools Report to the General Council of the Choctaw Nation, draft, n.d. [1840 or 1841], PPPP, folder 381a, GMA; R. David Edmunds, *The Potawatomis: Keepers of the Fire* (Norman: University of Oklahoma Press, 1978), 19; James Fletcher, James Gardner, and John M. Kenney to William Armstrong, n.d. [July 1841], LROIA, Schools, roll 780, frames 10–12, NARA.

29. Petition of Citizens of Scott County, n.d., LROIA, Schools, roll 780, frames 988–990, NARA; John W. Forbes to Vanderslice, December 30, 1844, LROIA, Schools, roll 782, frames 1211–1212, NARA.

30. Petition of Citizens of Scott County, n.d., LROIA, Schools, roll 780, frames 988–990, NARA; CA Students to the Secretary of War [response to previous], n.d., LROIA, Schools, roll 780, frames 707–708, NARA.

31. RMJ to Richard L. Sparrow and George Davis, May 22, 1841, PPPP, folder 271, GMA; John N. Cabill to PPP, January 11, 1842, PPPP, folder 329a, GMA.

32. Petition of Citizens of Scott County, n.d., LROIA, Schools, roll 780, frames 988–990, NARA; Pilcher to Poinsett, April 28, 1839, in *Commercial Advertiser* (New York), reprinted from *Boston Daily Advertiser*.

33. Joseph Sinclear to William Medill, February 25, 1846, copy in Miami folder 1834–1847, GLOVEC; Kemewau, Joseph Bourassa, John Laleme, and Joseph Laframboise to Lewis Cass, October 8, 1831, copy in Potawatomi folder 1831, GLOVEC.

34. Report of the Board of Trustees, January 2–3, 1840, in RMJ to the OIA, January 17, 1840, 26th Cong., 2nd sess., HD 109, no. 158.

35. Report of the Board of Trustees, January 2–3, 1840, in RMJ to the OIA, January 17, 1840, 26th Cong., 2nd sess., HD 109, no. 158; Benedict to Trustees, October 1, 1837, LROIA, Schools, roll 778, frame 533, NARA.

36. CA Students, quoting Benjamin Kenney, to Secretary of War, n.d., LROIA, Schools, roll 780, frames 707–708, NARA; Joshua Pilcher to Joel Poinsett, April 28, 1839, RG 107, ROSW, folder P, NARA; Richard Johnson to Thomas Henderson, April 26, 1826, THP, folder 2, FHS.

37. Swanton, *Ceremonial Life of the Choctaw Indians*, 227.

Chapter 10

1. Charles Dickens, *American Notes for General Circulation* (New York: Penguin, 1972), 204, 210–211.

2. Armstrong to Crawford, February 22, 1840, 26th Cong., 2nd sess., HD 109, no. 159, p. 137; Armstrong to Crawford , May 17, 1840, 26th Cong., 2nd sess., HD 109, no. 165, p. 142; Choctaw Chiefs to Armstrong, n.d., LROIA, Schools, roll 780, frames 10–12, NARA; Choctaw Chiefs to John Bell, October 8, 1841, LROIA, Schools, roll 780, frames 441–442, NARA.

3. RMJ to TH, June 1, 1840, THP, folder 15, FHS; RMJ to PPP, January 29, 1841, PPPC, box 1, folder 59, WHC; CA Quarterly Report, July 1, 1840, LROIA, Schools, roll 779, frames 415–416, NARA; RMJ to TH, June 19, 1840, THP, folder 15, FHS.

4. RMJ to TH, June 28, 1840, and February 17, 1840, THP, folder 15, FHS; RMJ to TH, March 14, 1834, THP, folder 9, FHS; William Armstrong to Elbert Herring, July 18, 1835, LROIA, Schools, roll 777, frames 48–49, NARA.

5. DV to T. H. Crawford, January 16, 1843, LROIA, Schools, roll 781, frames 561–563, NARA; RMJ to John Eaton, March 20, 1831, LROIA, Schools, roll 774, frame 420, NARA; Joshua Pilcher to Joel Poinsett, April 28, 1839, RG 107, ROSW, Confidential and Unofficial Letters Received, folder P, NARA; War Department to RMJ, July 3, 1835, LROIA, Schools, roll 777, frames 229–230, NARA; RMJ to TH, February 1, 1833, THP, folder 8, FHS; War Department to RMJ, September 26, 1837, THP, folder 12, FHS; War Department to RMJ, March 17, 1840, THP, folder 15, FHS; quotation from DV to Jessup, June 30, 1841, LROIA, Schools, roll 780, frames 305–306, NARA.

6. See, for example, William Johnson to C. A. Harris, February 24, 1837, LROIA, Schools, roll 778, frame 222, NARA; TH to Lewis Cass, January 20, 1834, LROIA, Schools , roll 776, frames 733–734, NARA; TH to T. H. Crawford, October 1, 1839, LROIA, Schools, roll 779, frame 130, NARA; DV to John Bell, n.d. [1841], LROIA, Schools , roll 780, frames 279–280, NARA.

7. T. Hartley Crawford to Spencer, October 28, 1842, LROIA, Schools, roll 780, frames 1093–1094, NARA; T. Hartley Crawford to J. R. Poinsett, March 1, 1841, 26th Cong., 2nd sess., HD 109, p. 3; Papers of Richard Mentor Johnson, LOC; RMJ to TH, April 15, 1840, THP, folder 15, FHS; Colin B. Burke, *American Collegiate Populations: A Test of the Traditional View* (New York: Oxford

University Press, 1982), 40; JLM to TLM, January 25, 1827, LROIA, Schools, roll 773, frame 793, NARA; *MeasuringWorth*, accessed January 5, 2015, http://www.measuringworth.com/uscompare.

8. Gardner to DV, June 26, 1841, LROIA, Schools, roll 780, frames 562–563, NARA; Committee upon Schools Report to the General Council, n.d., PPPP, folder 381A, GMA; PPP to Crawford, October 21, 1841, LROIA, Schools, roll 780, frame 157, frames 202–204, NARA; List of Clothing Deficient, 1841, LROIA, Schools, roll 780, frames 241–244; John Page to PPP, n.d. [1841], PPPC, box 1, folder 58, WHC; PPP, Report on CA to General Council of the Choctaw Nation, n.d., PPPP, folder 277, GMA; Joseph Fisher to PPP, February 21, 1841, PPPP, folder 260, GMA; Israel Folsom to PPP, November 29, 1841, PPPP, folder 315, GMA; PPP, Report of Conditions at CA, n.d., PPPP, folder 66A, GMA.

9. Choctaw Delegates to C. A. Harris, April 7, 1838, LROIA, Choctaw Agency, roll 170, frames 876–878, NARA; Andrew Denson, *Demanding the Cherokee Nation: Indian Autonomy and American Culture, 1830–1900* (Lincoln: University of Nebraska Press, 2004), 11–12.

10. PPP to Crawford, February 1841, PPPP, folder 261, GMA. This letter reiterated several points made by Pitchlynn during their initial meeting on January 13, 1841, PPP Memorandum Book, January 13, 1841, PPPP, folder 325, GMA.

11. Resolutions of the Choctaw General Council, October 9, 1841, LROIA, Schools, roll 780, frames 65–68, NARA; Choctaw Chiefs to John Bell, October 8, 1841, LROIA, Schools, roll 780, frames 440–442, NARA; PPP to T. H. Crawford, March 2, 1841, LROIA, Schools, roll 780, frames 449–452, NARA.

12. Elbert Herring to Henry Vose, November 26, 1831, 26th Cong., 2nd sess., HD 109, no. 52, p. 54; War Dept. to PPP, July 28, 1832, 26th Cong., 2nd sess., HD 109, no. 173, p. 147; PPP Draft Speech to Choctaw General Council, August 7, 1841, PPPP, folder 289, GMA; Israel Folsom to PPP, September 24, 1841, PPPC, box 1, folder 68, WHC.

13. Allan Nevins, ed., *The Diary of John Quincy Adams, 1794–1845: American Diplomacy, and Political, Social, and Intellectual Life, from Washington to Polk* (New York: Charles Scribner's Sons, 1951), 502; W. Emmons to TH, July 21, 1840, THP, folder 15, FHS; Leland Meyer, *Life and Times of Colonel Richard M. Johnson of Kentucky* (New York: Columbia University Press, 1932), 432; *Commercial Advertiser* (New York), June 26, 1839; Daniel Walker Howe, *What Hath God Wrought: The Transformation of America, 1815–1848* (New York: Oxford University Press, 2007), 505, 575–578.

14. Thomas Wall to PPP, April 1, 1841, PPPC, box 1, folder 62, WHC.

15. Crawford to William Armstrong, April 9, 1840, 26th Cong., 2nd sess., HD 109, no. 164, p. 141; Copy of Congressional Record, December 31, 1840, House of Representatives, 26th Cong., 2nd sess., LROIA, roll 780, frames 473–474, NARA; CA Students to W. S. Crawford, October 19, 1841, LROIA, roll 780, frames 226–227, NARA; W. S. Crawford to War Department, October 27, 1841, LROIA, roll 780, frame 231, NARA; W. S. Crawford to John Spencer, October 27, 1841, LROIA, roll 780, frames 154–155, NARA.

16. T. Hartley Crawford to TH, March 13, 1841, THP, folder 16, FHS; PPP to "brother," n.d., PPPP, folder 261A, GMA; PPP to T. Hartley Crawford, March 15, 1841, LROIA, Schools, roll 780, frames 446–447, NARA.

17. TH to John Bell, March 31, 1841, LROIA, Schools, roll 780, frames 267–268, NARA; Choctaw Chiefs to PPP, October 9, 1841, LROIA, Schools, roll 780, frames 443–444, NARA.

18. Rhoda Pitchlynn to PPP, September 10, 1841, PPPP, folder 300, GMA; Rhoda Pitchlynn to PPP, November 29, 1841, PPPP, folder 314, GMA; Rhoda Pitchlynn to PPP, December 22, 1841, PPPP, folder 320, GMA; PPP to Rhoda Pitchlynn, April 18, 1842, PPPP, folder 356, GMA; Malvina Pitchlynn, Rhoda Pitchlynn, and Arabela Howell to PPP, September 6, 1841, PPPP, folder 296, GMA; Lycurgus Pitchlynn to PPP, August 23, 1842, PPPP, folder 365, GMA.

19. PPP to Choctaw General Council, n.d., PPPP, folder 277, GMA; Joseph Fisher to PPP, February 21, 1841, PPPP, folder 260, GMA; W. S. Crawford interview with Isaac Gardner, October 22, 1841, LROIA, Schools, roll 780, frames 167–172, NARA; PPP to Crawford, October 20, 1841, LROIA, Schools, roll 780, frame 165, NARA.

20. RMJ to PPP, January 29, 1841, PPPC, box 1, folder 59, WHC; PPP to Crawford, March 2, 1841, LROIA, Schools, roll 780, frames 449–452, NARA; W. S. Crawford interview with Isaac Gardner, October 22, 1841, LROIA, Schools, roll 780, frames 167–172, NARA.

21. RMJ to TH, January 10, 1841, THP, folder 16, FHS; RMJ to PPP, February 7, 1841, PPPC, folder 61, WHC; RMJ to John Bell, February 9, 1841, PPPP, folder 258, GMA; RMJ to Richard Smith, May 29, 1841, Miscellaneous Richard Mentor Johnson Papers, folder 3, FHS; Robert Evans to William S. Crawford, October 21, 1841, LROIA, Schools, roll 780, frame 198, NARA; RMJ to PPP, January 29, 1841, PPPC, folder 59, WHC.

22. Phreno-Physiognomical Report on PPP by Gideon Lincecum, April 15, 1846, PPPP, folder 532, GMA; Superintendency Contract, March 10, 1841, LROIA, Schools, roll 780, frame 929, NARA; Choctaw Chiefs to John Bell, October 8, 1841, LROIA, Schools, roll 780, frame 441, NARA; PPP to "brother," n.d., PPPP, folder 261A, GMA; PPP to Lycurgus Pitchlynn, July 8, 1849, PPPC, box 2, folder 14, WHC.

23. RMJ to Richard Smith, September 28, 1841, Miscellaneous Richard Mentor Johnson Papers, folder 3, FHS; RMJ to Office of Indian Affairs, n.d., LROIA, Schools, roll 780, frames 348–351, NARA; RMJ to T. H. Crawford, October 17, 1841, LROIA, Schools, roll 780, frames 338–340, NARA; W. S. Crawford interview with Gardner, October 22, 1841, LROIA, Schools, roll 780, frame 171, NARA. For letters from neighbors, some of which are in RMJ's handwriting, see LROIA, Schools, roll 780, frames 381–382, 384–385, 387, 777–778, 782, NARA.

24. Joseph Fisher to PPP, February 21, 1841, PPPP, folder 260, GMA; TH to Eaton, March 28, 1831, LROIA, Schools, roll 775, frame 87, NARA; CA Quarterly Report, April 1, 1841, LROIA, Schools, roll 780, frames 532–533, NARA.

25. W. S. Crawford interview with DV, October 21, 1841, LROIA, Schools, roll 780, frames 173–180, NARA.

26. Elliott J. Gorn, "Gouge and Bite, Pull Hair and Scratch": The Social Significance of Fighting in the Southern Backcountry," *American Historical Review* 90 (1985): 18–43; W. S. Crawford interview with DV, October 21, 1841, LROIA, Schools, roll 780, frames 173–180, NARA; W. S. Crawford interview with Robert Evans, October 21, 1841, LROIA, Schools, roll 780, frames 193–200, NARA; TH to Greenwood Leflore, September 13, 1828, LROIA, Choctaw Agency, roll 169, frames 508–515, NARA; Phreno-Physiognomical Report on PPP by Gideon Lincecum, April 15, 1846, PPPP, folder 532, GMA; Hiram Pitchlynn to PPP, October 12, 1850, PPPP, folder 657, GMA.

27. RMJ to W. S. Crawford, October 20, 1841, LROIA, Schools, roll 780, frame 212, NARA; Robert Evans to W. S. Crawford, n.d., LROIA, Schools, roll 780, frames 185–186, NARA; David Folsom to PPP, December 2, 1841, PPPP, folder 316, GMA; List of Boys Absent, August 29, 1841, PPPP, folder 293, GMA; Students to PPP, September 25, 1841, LROIA, Schools, roll 780, frames 182–183, NARA; Students to W. S. Crawford, October 19, 1841, LROIA, Schools, roll 780, frames 226–227, NARA.

28. Statement of OIA on CA, November 3, 1841, LROIA, Schools, roll 780, frame 240, NARA; Trustees to Crawford, September 25, 1841, LROIA, Schools, roll 780, frames 283–284, NARA; RMJ to TH, April 15, 1840, THP, folder 15, FHS; RMJ to Poinsett, January 12, 1840, LROIA, Schools, roll 779, frame 445, NARA; Armstrong to PPP, August 24, 1841, LROIA, Schools, roll 780, frame 222, NARA.

29. Jacob Folsom to PPP, October 20, 1841, PPPC, box 1, folder 69, WHC; RMJ to John Spencer, November 25, 1841, LROIA, Schools, roll 780, frames 365–368, NARA.

30. PPP to Crawford, January 23, 1842, LROIA, Schools, roll 780, frame 923, NARA; DD Mitchell to Crawford, December 4, 1841, LROIA, Schools, roll 780, frame 438, NARA; O. P. Rood to RMJ, November 28, 1841, LROIA, Schools, roll 780, frames 370–373, NARA.

31. Dickens, *American Notes*, 211; James Silk Buckingham, *The Eastern and Western States of America* (London: Fisher, Son, & Co., 1842), vol. 3, 20, 27, 30–32; Captain J. E. Alexander, *Transatlantic Sketches, Comprising Visits to the Most Interesting Scenes in North and South America and the West Indies* (Philadelphia: Key and Biddle, 1833), 278; Kay Gill, "The Galt House," in *The Encyclopedia of Louisville*, ed. John E. Kleber (Lexington: University Press of Kentucky, 2001), 327.

32. DV to PPP, November 24, 1841, PPPP, folder 313, GMA; O. P. Rood to RMJ, November 28, 1841, LROIA, Schools, roll 780, frames 370–373, NARA.

33. PPP Memorandum Book, 1841, PPPP, folder 325, GMA; PPP to Rhoda Pitchlynn, November 6, 1841, PPPP, folder 311, GMA; Memorial of Peter Pitchlynn to the House and Senate, April 1, 1842, Record Group 233, 27th Cong., HD, Committee on Indian Affairs, NARA.

34. Memorial of Peter Pitchlynn to the House and Senate, April 1, 1842, Record Group 233, 27th Cong., HD, Committee on Indian Affairs, NARA.

35. Power of Attorney, Chickasaw Delegation to PPP, March 10, 1841, PPPP, folder 262, GMA; R. H. Grant to PPP, June 23, 1841, PPPP, folder 275, GMA; Rhoda Pitchlynn to PPP, October 26, 1841, PPPC, box 1, folder 70, WHC; Charles Lanham, "Peter Pitchlynn: Chief of the Choctaws," *Atlantic Monthly* 25 (1870): 490; Horatio B. Cushman, *A History of the Choctaw, Chickasaw, and Natchez Indians*, ed. Angie Debo (Norman: University of Oklahoma Press, 1999), 235.

36. Cushman, *History of the Choctaw*, 342; L. Thomas to PPP, March 24, 1842, PPPP, folder 347, GMA; M. Bokee to PPP, September 12, 1854, PPPP, folder 869, GMA; Caroline M. Pitchlynn to "son," August 8, 1860, PPPP, folder 1804, GMA; Unknown to PPP, February 2, 1843, PPPP, folder 391, GMA; Henry Moss to J. L. Moss, November 12, 1845, PPPP, folder 511, GMA; Anson Eleason to Senator Huntington, November 11, 1845, PPPP, folder 514, GMA; Dickens, *American Notes*, 211.

37. L. Thomas to PPP, March 24, 1842, PPPP, folder 347, GMA; Henry Moss to J. L. Moss, November 12, 1845, PPPP, folder 511, GMA; Dickens, *American Notes*, 211.

38. Thomas Henderson, *An Easy System of the Geography of the World; By Way of Question and Answer, Principally Designed for Schools* (Lexington, KY: Thomas K. Skillman, 1813), 124; S. G. Goodrich, *The Fourth Reader for the Use of Schools* (Louisville, KY: Morton and Griswold, 1839), 176–179, 240–242.

39. Notes, June 5, 1846, PPPP, folder 540, GMA; Peter Pitchlynn to unknown, March 4, 1853, PPPP, folder 692, GMA.

40. *Niles' Register*, May 1, 1847; Howe, *What Hath God Wrought*, 822–823.

41. PPP to T. Hartley Crawford, January 13, 1842, LROIA, Schools, roll 780, frame 921, NARA (see also draft in PPPP, folder 354, GMA); T. Hartley Crawford to PPP, March 22, 1842, 27th Cong., 2nd sess., HD 231, pp. 36–37; RMJ to Crawford, April 4, 1842, LROIA, Schools, roll 780, frames 802–803, NARA; DV to Crawford, April 21, 1842, LROIA, Schools, roll 780, frame 1051, NARA; B. B. Franklin to PPP, February 20, 1842, PPPP, folder 339, GMA.

42. Receipt, B. Samuel for PPP, April 11, 1842, PPPP, folder 353, GMA; PPP to Choctaw General Council, 1845, PPPC, box 1, folder 91, WHC.

43. Crawford to Armstrong, April 19, 1845, PPPP, folder 479, GMA; Thomas W. Newlin to PPP, February 20, 1845, LROIA, Schools, roll 782, frames 1127–1128, NARA.

44. PPP, Draft Speech to General Council, August 7, 1841, PPPP, folder 289, GMA; Committee upon Schools Report to General Council, n.d. [likely May 1842], PPPP, folder 381A, GMA.

Chapter 11

1. John Beach to TH, January 22, 1842, copy in GFC, box 9, folder 3, OKHS.

2. CA Quarterly Report, June 28, 1841, LROIA, Schools, roll 780, frames 570–571, NARA; CA Quarterly Report, January 1, 1843, LROIA, Schools, roll 781, frame 585, NARA; CA Quarterly Report, March 31, 1843, LROIA, Schools, roll 781, frames 596–597, NARA; David and Augustus Garrett to William Clark, March 27, 1839, RG 107, ROSW, Confidential and Unofficial Letters Received, folder P, NARA; Augustus Garrett to Joshua Pilcher, April 12, 1839, RG 107, ROSW, Confidential and Unofficial Letters Received, folder P, NARA; RMJ to William Medill, November 30, 1845, LROIA, Schools, roll 783, frame 1264, NARA; RMJ to William Wilkins, April 1, 1844, LROIA, Schools, roll 782, frames 303–304, NARA; RMJ to Medill, May 10, 1847, LROIA, Schools, roll 782, frames 871–872, NARA.

3. CA Quarterly Report, December 31, 1844, LROIA, Schools, roll 782, frames 1214–1216, NARA; CA Quarterly Report, September 30, 1846, LROIA, Schools, roll 783, frame 561, NARA; John Mullay to William Medill, July 27, 1846, LROIA, Schools, roll 783, frame 457, NARA.

4. PPP to Crawford, October 20, 1841, LROIA, Schools, roll 780, frames 163–165, NARA; Pierre Juzan quoted in the *Daily National Intelligencer*, December 21, 1826.

5. Beach to TH, January 22, 1842, GFC, box 9, folder 3, OKHS.

6. Ethan Allen Hitchcock to John C. Spencer, April 30, 1842, LROIA, Schools, roll 780, frame 754, NARA.

7. Richard S. Elliott to William Medill, November 1, 1845, LROIA, Schools, roll 783, frames 680–682, NARA.

8. Creek Chiefs to J. S. Dawson, January 18, 1844, LROIA, Schools, roll 783, frames 198–199, NARA; Armstrong to Crawford, October 20, 1845, LROIA, Schools, roll 783, frame 573, NARA.

9. D. D. Mitchell to Crawford, August 20, 1842, LROIA, Council Bluffs Sub-Agency, roll 215, frame 494, NARA; James Logan to Judge Wilkins, August 13, 1844, LROIA, Schools, roll 782, frame 401, NARA; Armstrong to Crawford, May 2, 1844, LROIA, Schools, roll 782, frame 34, NARA; Armstrong to Crawford, July 14, 1839, 26th Cong., 2nd sess., HD 109, no. 151; Petition of the Chiefs and Headmen of the Miami Nation to the President, September 19, 1843, LROIA, Schools, roll 781, frames 346–347, NARA; Dr. Johnston Lykins to RMJ, November 23, 1845, LROIA, Schools, roll 782, frames 976–978, NARA; Richard S. Elliott to William Medill, November 1, 1845, LROIA, Schools, roll 782, frame 682, NARA (emphasis in original).

10. Dr. Johnston Lykins to RMJ, November 23, 1845, LROIA, Schools, roll 782, frames 976–978, NARA; RMJ to Medill, March 30, 1846, LROIA, Schools, roll 783, frames 228–229, NARA.

11. RMJ to William B. Lewis, September 12, 1841, LROIA, Schools, roll 780, frame 379, NARA.

12. Indenture, May 31, 1841, Scott County Deed Book Q, pp. 374–375, KHS; RMJ to Medill, December 13, 1847, LROIA, Schools, roll 782, frames 1149–1151, NARA; RMJ to Medill, December 10, 1845, LROIA, Schools, roll 783, frame 1269, NARA; RMJ to Medill, November 9, 1845, LROIA, Schools, roll 783, frame 1277, NARA. The Papers of Richard Mentor Johnson at the Library of Congress detail the politician's ongoing financial problems.

13. RMJ to Medill, May 30, 1847, LROIA, Schools, roll 783, frames 875–877, NARA; RMJ to James K. Polk, February 26, 1845, LROIA, Schools, roll 782, frame 855, NARA; RMJ to Spencer, November 13, 1842, LROIA, Schools, roll 780, frames 823–826, NARA.

14. Crawford to D. D. Mitchell, February 21, 1843, LSOIA, M-21, roll 33, frame 307, NARA; Crawford to D. D. Mitchell, April 29, 1843, LSOIA, M-21, roll 33, frame 468, NARA; Benjamin Marshall and Roly McIntosh to Crawford, February 10, 1843, LROIA, Schools, roll 781, frame 98, NARA; CA Quarterly Report, April 1, 1841, LROIA, Schools, roll 780, frames 532–533, NARA; CA Quarterly Report, December 31, 1844, LROIA, Schools, roll 782, frame 1205, NARA.

15. RMJ to Medill, November 9, 1845, LROIA, Schools, roll 783, frames 1272–1275, NARA; RMJ to Medill, November 21, 1846, LROIA, Schools, roll 783, frame 1259, NARA; Medill to A. J. Vaughan, November 10, 1846, LSOIA, M-21, roll 39, frame 13, NARA; Medill to RMJ, February 7, 1847, LSOIA, M-21, roll 39, frame 442, NARA.

16. Copy, Resolution of the House of Representatives, January 7, 1845, LROIA, Schools, roll 782, frames 773–774, NARA; *Daily National Intelligencer*, February 19, 1846; *Philadelphia Inquirer*, March 21, 1848; *New York Herald*, March 22, 1848; *The North Star*, April 6, 1849; Will P. Thomasson to William Medill, April 8, 1846, LROIA, Schools, roll 783, frame 519, NARA.

17. CA Quarterly Report, January 1, 1843, LROIA, Schools, roll 781, frames 572–589, NARA; Thomas Harvey to Medill, June 27, 1846, LROIA, Schools, roll 783, frame 180, NARA; RMJ to Richard Smith, July 11, 1846, LROIA, Schools,

roll 783, frame, 506, NARA; RMJ to Medill, July 15, 1846, LROIA, Schools, roll 783, frames 509–511, NARA; RMJ to Medill, August 20, 1846, LROIA, Schools, roll 783, frames 300–302, NARA; Dorothy V. Jones, "A Potawatomi Faces the Problem of Cultural Change: Joseph N. Bourassa in Kansas," *Kansas Quarterly* 3 (1971): 48–49.

18. RMJ to Medill, August 20, 1846, LROIA, Schools, roll 783, frames 300–308, NARA; Antoine Bourbonnaise to RMJ, December 3, 1846, LROIA, Schools, roll 783, frames 327–328, NARA.

19. Rules for the Government of the Students of the CA, n.d. [1846?], LROIA, Schools, roll 783, frames 433–436, NARA; CA Quarterly Report, September 30, 1843, LROIA, Schools, roll 781, frames 630–632, NARA; Anthony P. F. Navarre and Antoine Bourbonnaise to William Medill, March 30, 1846, LROIA, Schools, roll 783, frame 232, NARA.

20. CA Student List, October 1, 1837, LROIA, Schools, roll 778, frame 366, NARA; CA Student List, July 1, 1844, LROIA, Schools, roll 782, frame 523, NARA.

21. C. A. Harris to Gholson Kercheval, June 17, 1837, 26th Cong., 2nd sess., HD 109, no. 123, p. 109; CA Harris to AC Pepper, July 6, 1837, 26th Cong., 2nd sess., HD 109, no. 125, p. 110; Miami leaders quoted in Samuel Milroy to Crawford, March 17, 1840, 26th Cong., 2nd sess., HD 109, no. 160, p. 139; Register of the Names of Choctaw Orphan Children, compiled by M. Mackey, December 17, 1832, LROIA, Choctaw Agency, roll 170, frames 167–178, NARA; "Orphan," *Oxford English Dictionary*, accessed September 5, 2014, http://www.oed.com. See also John Beach to John Chambers, August 13, 1845, GFC, box 9, folder 3, OKHS; Allen Hamilton to Crawford, April 16, 1845, LROIA, Schools, roll 782, frames 805–806, NARA.

22. RMJ to William Wilkins, April 1, 1844, LROIA, Schools, roll 782, frames 303–304, NARA; CA Quarterly Report, June 30, 1843, LROIA, Schools, roll 781, frames 619–620, NARA; CA Quarterly Report, October 1, 1843, LROIA, Schools, roll 781, frame 636, NARA; John Bell (aka Joel Barrow), March 13, 1842, LROIA, Schools, roll 780, frames 793–797, NARA; Temperance Society Speech, Joel Barrow, 1843, LROIA, Schools, roll 782, frames 316–319, NARA.

23. John Bell (aka Joel Barrow) to RMJ, March 13, 1842, LROIA, Schools, roll 780, frames 793–794, NARA; RMJ to Crawford, March 13, 1842, LROIA, Schools, roll 780, frames 789–791, NARA; J. M. Porter, Review of CA Expenses, November 17, 1843, LROIA, Schools, roll 781, frames 700–703, 711, NARA; CA Quarterly Report, January 1, 1843, LROIA, Schools, roll 781, frames 576–577, NARA; RMJ to Wilkins, April 1, 1844, LROIA, Schools, roll 782, frames 303–304, NARA.

24. Temperance Society Speech, Joel Barrow, 1843, LROIA, Schools, roll 782, frames 316–319, NARA; John Bell (aka Joel Barrow) to Doctor Lykins, March 18, 1842, LROIA, Schools, roll 780, frames 1028–1029, NARA.

25. Jefferson Jenkins to William Medill, March 3, 1846, LROIA, Schools, roll 783, frame 544, NARA; RMJ to Medill, August 1, 1846, LROIA, Schools, roll 783, frames 286–289, NARA.

26. Isaac Folsom and James Fletcher Armstrong to War Department, June 30, 1843, LROIA, Schools, roll 781, frame 129, NARA; Henry C. Benson, *Life among the Choctaw Indians and Sketches of the South-west* (New York: Johnson Reprint Corporation, 1970), 163; RMJ to William Wilkins, April 1, 1844, LROIA, Schools, roll 782, frames 303–304, NARA; Affidavit signed by Philip

Gleason, Amy Cornells, Milly Frances, and Simmiwike, July 20, 1845, LROIA, Schools, roll 782, NARA; D. D. Mitchell to Capt. E. Trevor, November 17, 1843, LROIA, Schools, roll 782, frame 240, NARA.

27. Judge William Barnett to T. Hartley Crawford, September 9, 1845, LROIA, Schools, roll 782, frames 640–641, NARA; RMJ to Medill, May 30, 1847, LROIA, Schools, roll 783, frames 875–877, NARA; Armstrong to C. A. Harris, December 24, 1836, LROIA, Choctaw Agency, roll 170, frame 779, NARA; Articles of an Agreement between the Chickasaw and Choctaw Nations, January 17, 1837, LROIA, Choctaw Agency, roll 170, frames 799–800, NARA; Grant Foreman, ed., *A Traveler in Indian Territory: The Journal of Ethan Allen Hitchcock* (Norman: University of Oklahoma Press, 1996), 183, 199.

28. Crawford to Chickasaw Chiefs, October 8, 1842, RG 75, Chickasaw Removal Records, book 2, p. 234, NARA; Choctaw Chiefs to John Bell, October 8, 1841, LROIA, Schools, roll 780, frames 440–441, NARA; Chickasaw Chiefs to John Spencer, May 9, 1842, LROIA, Schools, roll 780, frame 716, NARA; Ramsay D. Potts to Armstrong, August 29, 1844, LROIA, Schools, roll 782, frames 71–73, NARA; Crawford to Richard French, February 17, 1844, RG 75, Chickasaw Removal Records, book 2, pp. 331–332.

29. Alfred Vaughan to Medill, May 31, 1848, LROIA, Schools, roll 784, frame 669, NARA; Medill to Vanderslice, June 29, 1848, LSOIA, roll 41, frame 59, NARA.

30. Medill to RMJ, June 20, 1848, RG 75, Chickasaw Removal Records, entry 252, NARA; Chickasaw Delegation to Medill, July 8, 1848, LROIA, Schools, roll 784, frames 62–63, NARA.

31. Thomas Harvey to Medill, July 25, 1848, LROIA, Schools, roll 784, frame 180, NARA; RMJ to Medill, July 2, 1848, LROIA, Schools, roll 784, frames 258–260, NARA; CA Quarterly Report, March 31, 1848, LROIA, Schools, roll 784, frames 661–662, NARA; CA Quarterly Report, June 30, 1848, LROIA, Schools, roll 784, frames 676–677, NARA; RMJ to Cochran, November 3, 1848, LROIA, Schools, roll 784, frames 265–266, NARA.

32. Vanderslice to Medill, July 31, 1848, LROIA, Schools, roll 784, frame 684, NARA; PPP to Lycurgus Pitchlynn, August 6, 1848, PPPP, folder 616, GMA; Medill to RMJ, June 20, 1848, RG 75, Chickasaw Removal Records, entry 252, NARA; Chickasaw Delegation to Medill, June 20, 1848, LROIA, Schools, roll 784, frame 59, NARA.

33. RMJ to John C. Spencer, November 28, 1841, Misc. Richard Mentor Johnson Papers, FHS.

Chapter 12

1. CA Report of November 25, 1825, PPPC, box 5, folder 3, WHC; CA Quarterly Report, November 1, 1827, TLML, NARA.

2. RMJ to Medill, July 17, 1847, LROIA, Schools, roll 783, frames 891–892, NARA; Alfred Wade Arithmetic Workbook, Mrs. C. B. Wade Collection, OKHS; Arthur DeRosier Jr., *The Removal of the Choctaw Indians* (Knoxville: University of Tennessee Press, 1970), Appendix C: Removal Regulations of May 15, 1832; Personal communication, email from Jessica Lundsford-Nguyen, December 5, 2014 (accession information).

3. "Wheelock in Chronological Sequence—1832–1932," in Wheelock Academy Vertical File, OKHS; Ramsay D. Potts, School Report for 1836, September 14, 1836, 26th Cong., 2nd sess., HD 109, no. 185, quotation on p. 153; Israel Folsom to PPP, December 7, 1841, PPPC, box 1, folder 71, WHC.

4. Committee upon Schools Report, n.d., PPPP, folder 381a, GMA; Act Providing for the System of Public Instruction in the Choctaw Nation, approved November 29, 1842, copy in CKC, box 1, folder 1, item 6, WHC; Armstrong to Crawford, October 25, 1844, LROIA, Schools, roll 782, frames 40–43, NARA.

5. PPP to General Council, n.d. [1842], PPPP, folder 374a, GMA; An Act Providing for the System of Public Instruction in the Choctaw Nation, approved November 29, 1842, copy in CKC, box 1, folder 1, item 6, WHC; Resolution passed by the Committee appointed by the Choctaw General Council to select a site for a School, March 27, 1842, LROIA, Schools, roll 780, frames 615–616, NARA.

6. Israel Folsom to PPP, June 20, 1842, PPPP, folder 361, GMA; PPP, Committee upon Schools Report, n.d., PPPP, folder 381A, GMA; Israel Folsom to PPP, January 16, 1842, PPPC, box 1, folder 76, WHC. For a sample contract, see Act of Choctaw General Council, October 7, 1845, LROIA, Schools, roll 782, frames 1072–1073, NARA.

7. Lycurgus Pitchlynn to PPP, May 12, 1846, PPPP, folder 537, GMA; Lycurgus Pitchlynn to PPP, June 18, 1846, PPPP, folder 543, GMA; PPP to Lycurgus, May 28, 1848, PPPP, folder 611, GMA; PPP to Lycurgus, August 31, 1846, PPPC, box 1, folder 108, WHC.

8. W. David Baird, "Spencer Academy: The Choctaw 'Harvard,' 1842–1900" (M.A. Thesis, University of Oklahoma, 1965), 95–96; Armstrong to Medill, October 20, 1846, LROIA, Schools, roll 783, frames 35–40, NARA. For a discussion of Green Corn among nineteenth-century Choctaws, see Clara Sue Kidwell, *Choctaws and Missionaries in Mississippi, 1818–1918* (Norman: University of Oklahoma Press, 1995), 205, n. 23; quotation from Ebenezer Hotchkin in Grant Foreman, *The Five Civilized Tribes* (Norman: University of Oklahoma Press, 1934), 79.

9. Myrtle Drain, "A History of Education of the Choctaw and Chickasaw Indians" (M.A. Thesis, University of Oklahoma, 1928), 56; Petition to General Council by School Committee in Pushmataha District," September 6, 1844, PPPP, folder 429, GMA; Armstrong to Crawford, October 25, 1844, LROIA, Schools, roll 782, frame 40, NARA; Armstrong to Lavinia Pitchlynn, May 9, 1842, PPPP, folder 358, GMA; Lycurgus Pitchlynn to PPP, July 14, 1841, PPPP, folder 285, GMA; Rhoda Pitchlynn to PPP, January 5, 1842, PPPC, box 1, folder 74, WHC; Hotchkin to Rutherford, July 7, 1848, LROIA, Schools, roll 784, frames 484–487, NARA.

10. Barbara Solomon, *In the Company of Educated Women* (New Haven: Yale University Press, 1985), 13–26, 62–65; Daniel Walker Howe, *What Hath God Wrought: The Transformation of America, 1815–1848* (New York: Oxford University Press, 2007), 463; Israel Folsom to PPP, September 13, 1841, PPPC, box 1, folder 66, WHC; Israel Folsom to PPP, December 7, 1841, PPPC, box 1, folder 71, WHC; Unknown [Member of General Council] to PPP, n.d., PPPP, folder 314A, GMA; Linda Kerber, "The Republican Mother: Women and the Enlightenment—An American Perspective," *American Quarterly* 28 (1976): 187–205; PPP to Spencer, January 4, 1842, LROIA, Schools, roll 780, frame 918, NARA.

11. Louis Coleman and Barbara Asbill Grant, *The Wheelock Story* (Durant, OK: Texoma Print Services, 2011), 14–19; Thomas J. Pitchlynn to PPP, February 10, 1846, PPPC, box 1, folder 10, WHC; PPP to Lycurgus Pitchlynn, August 31, 1846, PPPC, folder 108, WHC; Armstrong to Crawford, May 20, 1844, LROIA, Schools, roll 782, frames 9–10, NARA; William Garrett to PPP, May 15, 1847, PPPP, folder 583, GMA; PPP to Lycurgus, December 21, 1848, PPPC, box 2, folder 7, WHC; PPP to Lycurgus, January 19, 1850, PPPP, folder 649, GMA; Lycurgus to PPP, May 12, 1846, PPPP, folder 537, GMA; Alfred Wright to Armstrong, July 3, 1843, LROIA, Schools, roll 781, frames 53–61, NARA.

12. William Wilson to Armstrong, August 30, 1842, LROIA, Schools, roll 780, frames 689–696, NARA; Rutherford to Medill, October 11, 1848, LROIA, Schools, roll 784, frames 460–465, NARA; H. G. Rind to Armstrong, August 2, 1843, LROIA, Schools, roll 781, frame 50, NARA; Edmund M. Kenney, Report of Spencer Academy, August 29, 1844, LROIA, Schools, roll 782, frames 82–89, NARA; Schools Act of 1842, copy in CKC, box 1, folder 1, item 6, WHC; PPP to Choctaw General Council, August 7, 1841, PPPP, folder 289, GMA.

13. Committee upon Schools Report, n.d., PPPP, folder 381A, GMA; Edmund M. Kenney, Report of Spencer Academy, August 29, 1844, LROIA, Schools, roll 782, frames 82–89, NARA.

14. Philip H. Round, *Removable Type: Histories of the Book in Indian Country, 1663–1880* (Chapel Hill: University of North Carolina Press, 2010), 22; List of Books Printed in the Choctaw Language, 1848, CKC, box 3, folder 8, item 16, WHC; Cyrus Kingsbury to Thomas L. McKenney, February 15, 1830, LROIA, Schools, roll 774, frames 472–475, NARA; Cyrus Byington to Armstrong, August 25, 1842, LROIA, Schools, roll 780, frame 685, NARA; Alfred Wright to John Drennen, October 25, 1849, LROIA, Schools, roll 784, frames 898–902, NARA; *Choctaw Telegraph*, 1848–1850.

15. Israel Folsom to PPP, January 16, 1842, PPPC, box 1, folder 76, WHC; Lavinia Pitchlynn to PPP, December 14, 1841, PPPC, box 1, folder 72, WHC; Alfred Wade to PPP, July 5, 1845, PPPC, box 1, folder 95, WHC; Samuel Worcester to PPP, February 8, 1856, PPPC, box 2, folder 72, WHC; Robert M. Jones to the Secretary of War, August 30, 1835, LROIA, Choctaw Agency West, roll 184, frame 354, NARA; Thompson McKenney to Armstrong, September 1, 1838, LROIA, Schools, roll 778, frame 706, NARA.

16. PPP Speech to Choctaw General Council, August 7, 1841, PPPP, folder 289, GMA; PPP, Committee upon Schools Report, n.d., PPPP, folder 381A, GMA; Devon Mihesuah, *Cultivating the Rosebuds: The Education of Women at the Cherokee Female Seminary, 1851–1909* (Urbana: University of Illinois Press, 1998), 16–22; J. Vann to PPP, February 10, 1846, PPPC, box 1, folder 103, WHC; Henry C. Benson, *Life among the Choctaw Indians and Sketches of the South-west* (New York: Johnson Reprint Corporation, 1970), 181, 209.

17. Armstrong to Medill, October 20, 1846, LROIA, Schools, roll 783, frames 35–40, NARA; M. DuVal to Rutherford, November 22, 1847, LROIA, Schools, roll 784, frames 385–386, NARA (emphasis in original); Walter Lowrie to Medill, April 11, 1849, LROIA, Schools, roll 784, frames 1095–1096, NARA.

18. Articles of an Agreement between the Presbyterian Board of Foreign Missions and the Creek Nation, May 8, 1847, LROIA, Schools, roll 782, frames 956–958;

Samuel Bunch to Medill, June 22, 1846, LROIA, Schools, roll 783, frames 116–117, NARA; Creek chiefs to James Logan, November 25, 1847, LROIA, Schools, roll 784, frames 392–393, NARA.

19. Resolution of the Miami Council West of Missouri, March 18, 1847, LROIA, Schools, roll 783, frames 770–771, NARA; Isaac McCoy to Crawford, April 22, 1839, LROIA, Schools, roll 779, frames 222–223, NARA; Isaac McCoy to Crawford, July 23, 1844, LROIA, Schools, roll 782, frames 437–438, NARA; Herman Lincoln to Medill, March 4, 1848, LROIA, Schools, roll 784, frames 305–310, NARA.

20. Ruth Miller Elson, *Guardians of Tradition: American Schoolbooks of the Nineteenth Century* (Lincoln: University of Nebraska Press, 1964), 6; A. H. Mechlin to PPP, June 10, 1846, PPPP, folder 541, GMA; Ebenezer Hotchkins to Armstrong, August 7, 1845, LROIA, Schools, roll 782, NARA; PPP, Draft of a Speech Delivered at Ievkheli, June 25, 1843, PPPP, folder 362, GMA; N. A. Nold to PPP, March 16, 1846, PPPP, folder 528, GMA.

21. Drain, "History of the Education of the Choctaw and Chickasaw Indians," 64–65; *Indian Education: A National Tragedy—A National Challenge*, 1969 Report of the Committee on Labor and Public Welfare, 91st Cong., 1st sess. (Washington, DC: US Government Printing Office, 1969), 25; James A. Ramage and Andrea S. Watkins, *Kentucky Rising: Democracy, Slavery, and Culture from the Early Republic to the Civil War* (Lexington: University Press of Kentucky, 2011), 93–95; Frank Allen Balyeat, "Education in Indian Territory" (Ph.D. diss., Stanford University, 1927), 52, 101; Grant Foreman, ed., *A Traveler in Indian Territory: The Journal of Ethan Allen Hitchcock* (Norman: University of Oklahoma Press, 1996), 51, 24.

22. Isaac Folsom to PPP, January 14, 1842, PPPP, folder 331, GMA; Schools Act of 1842, copy in LROIA, Schools, roll 781, frame 112, NARA; Report of the Standing of Allen Wright, July 18, 1849, LROIA, Schools, roll 784, frame 946, NARA; Lycurgus Pitchlynn to PPP, n.d. [1853?], PPPP, folder 727, GMA; Colin G. Calloway, *The Indian History of an American Institution: Native Americans and Dartmouth* (Hanover, NH: Dartmouth College Press, 2010), 96–99; Report of Mary Rhoda Pitchlynn, November 29, 1854, PPPP, folder 898, GMA; List of Choctaw Students Attending Schools in the States, GFC, box 9, folder 3, OKHS.

23. See, for example, A. Hays to Crawford, March 22, 1843, LROIA, Schools, roll 781, frames 203–204, NARA; Unknown [Indiana Ashbury University official] to PPP, July 7, 1848, PPPP, folder 614, GMA.

24. E. W. Andrews to Medill, August 22, 1848, LROIA, Schools, roll 784, frames 17–18, NARA; E. W. Andrews to Medill, October 7, 1848, LROIA, Schools, roll 784, frames 22–24, NARA; Lewis Garland to PPP, April 23, 1839, PPPP, folder 218, GMA; Peter Jr. to PPP, February 6, 1854, PPPP, folder 746, GMA; Gustavus J. Orr to PPP, May 3, 1854, PPPC, box 2, folder 36, WIIC; Grant Foreman, ed., *A Pathfinder in the Southwest: The Itinerary of Lieutenant A.W. Whipple during his Explorations for a Railway Route from Fort Smith to Los Angeles in the Years 1853 & 1854* (Norman: University of Oklahoma Press, 1941), 35–36.

25. William Medill to Alvan Bond, May 4, 1849, RG 75, Chickasaw Removal Records, book 3, entry 252, pp. 65–66, NARA; Lycurgus Pitchlynn to PPP, February 27, 1856, PPPP, folder 1095, GMA; Jacob Folsom to PPP, February

28, 1843, PPPP, folder 394, GMA; Isaac Folsom to PPP, January 14, 1842, PPPP, folder 331, GMA; Sampson Folsom to PPP, June 22, 1848, PPPP, folder 613, GMA. For the communications revolution, see Richard R. John, *Spreading the News: The American Postal System from Franklin to Morse* (Cambridge, MA: Harvard University Press, 1996); David M. Henkin, *The Postal Age: The Emergence of Modern Communications in Nineteenth-Century America* (Chicago: University of Chicago Press, 2006); Daniel Walker Howe, *What Hath God Wrought: The Transformation of America, 1815–1848* (New York: Oxford University Press, 2007).

26. Leonidas Garland to PPP, January 2, 1850, PPPP, folder 647, GMA; Calloway, *Native Americans and Dartmouth*, 96–99; L. Thomas to PPP, March 24, 1842, PPPP, folder 347, GMA; Hugh H. Patten to PPP, December 29, 1845, PPPP, folder 520, GMA.

27. George Harkins to Greenwood Leflore, June 17, 1845, GFC, box 9, folder 9, item 3, OKHS; Speech of George Harkins, *Daily National Intelligencer*, December 21, 1826.

28. Committee upon Schools Report, n.d., PPPP, folder 381A, GMA; PPP, Notes of a Speech on Law, Delivered at the Eagletown Debating Society, n.d., PPPP, folder 646, GMA; PPP to Lycurgus Pitchlynn, January 19, 1850, PPPP, folder 649, GMA.

29. List of Choctaw Students Attending School in the States, n.d., GFC, box 9, folder 3, OKHS.

30. Superintendent Robinson quoted in Allen, "Education in Indian Territory," 164; J. P. Folsom to PPP, June 29, 1854, PPPP, folder 827, GMA. On being "useful to my people," see, for example, Joseph N. Bourassa to Lewis Cass, June 4, 1833, LROIA, roll 776, frames 47–48, NARA; William Burnett to RMJ, March 11, 1836, LROIA, roll 777, frames 627–628, NARA; John Bell to RMJ, March 13, 1842, LROIA, roll 780, frames 793–794, NARA.

31. PPP to Lycurgus Pitchlynn, August 31, 1846, PPPC, box 1, folder 108, WHC; Jacob Folsom to PPP, September 24, 1842, PPPP, folder 371, GMA; E. J. Hobsbawm, *Nations and Nationalism since 1780: Programme, Myth, Reality*, 2nd ed. (New York: Cambridge University Press, 1990), 46; Anthony D. Smith, *National Identity* (Reno: University of Nevada Press, 1991), 118.

32. PPP, speech draft, June 25, 1843, PPPP, folder 362, GMA; Armstrong to Crawford, April 5, 1842, LROIA, Schools, roll 780, frames 617–620, NARA; R. David Edmunds, "Indians as Pioneers: Potawatomis on the Frontier," *Chronicles of Oklahoma* 65 (Winter 1987–1988): 340–353; John P. Bowes, *Exiles and Pioneers: Eastern Indians in the Trans-Mississippi West* (New York: Cambridge University Press, 2007), 100–112; William S. Nail to Rella Looney, August 11, 1967, Nail Family Vertical File, OKHS; Thompson McKenney to PPP, May 12, 1857, PPPC, box 7, folder 1, WHC; Foreman, ed., *Traveler in Indian Territory*, 45, quotation on p. 49, n. 34.

33. Alexandra Harmon, *Rich Indians: Native People and the Problem of Wealth in American History* (Chapel Hill: University of North Carolina Press, 2010), 139; Sandra Faiman-Silva, *Choctaws at the Crossroads: The Political Economy of Class and Culture in the Oklahoma Timber Region* (Lincoln: University of Nebraska Press, 1997), 37, 52; Harkins quoted in WW to Eaton, December 8, 1830, LROIA, Choctaw Agency, roll 169, frame 812, NARA; Report of H. G. Rind,

July 27, 1842, LROIA, Schools, roll 780, frames 678–679, NARA; Byington to Rutherford, July 20, 1848, LROIA, Schools, roll 784, frame 470, NARA.

34. Michael Doran, "Population Statistics of Nineteenth Century Indian Territory," *Chronicles of Oklahoma* 53 (1976): 501; *The Constitution and Laws of the Choctaw Nation* (Park Hill, Cherokee Nation: John Candy, 1840), 11, 12, 19, 20–21; Copy of "An Act Prohibiting Free Negroes to Reside in the Nation," with Alfred Wright's comments, 1850, CKC, box 3, folder 9, item 53, WHC.

35. David Winship to S. B. Treat, July 13, 1848, CKC, box 2, folder 5, item 9, WHC; Solomon to PPP, December 11, 1857, PPPC, box 3, folder 3, WHC; Adam Burris to Suckey Burris, April 13, 1880, PPPC, box 4, folder 101, WHC; Rhoda Pitchlynn to PPP, November 29, 1841, PPPP, folder 314, GMA; Lycurgus Pitchlynn to PPP, January 3, 1859, PPPC, box 3, folder 39, WHC.

36. Edmund M. Kenney, Report of Spencer Academy, August 29, 1844, LROIA, Schools, roll 782, frames 82–89, NARA; Wesley Browning, Report of Chickasaw Academy, March 31, 1848, LROIA, Schools, roll 784, frames 439–440, NARA.

37. Baird, "Spencer Academy," 13–14, 22–23.

38. Pierre Juzan to PPP, February 24, 1839, PPPP, folder 217, GMA; Juzan to Armstrong, March 8, 1839, LRIOIA, Choctaw Agency, roll 171, frames 11–13, NARA; Juzan to Poinsett, May 14, 1839, LRIOIA, Choctaw Agency, roll 171, frames 59–61, NARA.

39. Thomas J. Pitchlynn to PPP, December 6, 1846, PPPP, folder 561, GMA; Lycurgus Pitchlynn to PPP, December 31, 1858, PPPC, box 3, folder 37, WHC; Lycurgus Pitchlynn to PPP, January 3, 1859, PPPC, box 3, folder 39, WHC; Loring S. W. Folsom to PPP, January 1859, PPPC, box 3, folder 38, WHC.

40. Lycurgus to PPP, January 3, 1859, PPPC, box 3, folder 39, WHC; Loring S. W. Folsom, January 1859, PPPC, box 3, folder 38, WHC.

41. Joseph Kincaid and Chief Mushulatubbee to the Secretary of War, August 8, 1835, LROIA, Choctaw Agency West, roll 184, frames 317–318, NARA; Israel Folsom to PPP, September 27, PPPC, box 1, folder 115, WHC; PPP Memorandum Book, 1841, PPPP, folder 325, GMA; Unknown to PPP, n.d., PPPP, folder 314a, GMA; Robert M. Jones to PPP, July 13, 1848, PPPC, box 2, folder 5, WHC; John Conner to PPP, January 30, 1860, PPPC, box 3, folder 53, WHC; PPP to John M. Armstrong, March 16, 1846, John Armstrong Papers, folder 31, GMA.

42. John Jolly and Black Coat to the Chiefs of the Choctaws, March 18, 1832, PPPC, box 1, folder 28, WHC; Talk of Mushulatubbee, September 1834, in Proceedings of a Council held at Fort Gibson, LROIA, Choctaw Agency, roll 170, frame 509, NARA.

43. Remonstrance of Col. Peter Pitchlynn, January 20, 1849, HR, Misc. Document no. 35, 30th Cong., 2nd session.

44. "Tushpa Crosses the Mississippi," 1834, as related to James Culberson, in *Native American Testimony: An Anthology of Indian and White Relations* (New York: Harper & Row, 1978), 191–197.

45. "Tushpa Crosses the Mississippi"; T. J. Pitchlynn to PPP, November 16, 1845, PPPP, folder 513, GMA; Byington to Armstrong, September 3, 1846, LROIA, Schools, roll 783, frames 52–55, NARA; Hiram Pitchlynn to PPP, May 10, 1849, PPPP, folder 639, GMA.

Conclusion

1. PPP to "Brother," September 23, 1846, PPPC, box 1, folder 109, WHC; Charles Lanman, "Peter Pitchlynn, Chief of the Choctaws," *Atlantic Monthly* 25 (1870): 486–497; PPP to John M. Armstrong, March 16, 1846, John Armstrong Papers, folder 31, GMA.

2. PPP to John M. Armstrong, March 16, 1846, John Armstrong Papers, folder 31, GMA; PPP to Lycurgus Pitchlynn, August 31, 1846, PPPC, box 1, folder 108, WHC.

3. PPP to John Armstrong, March 16, 1846, Armstrong Papers, folder 31, GMA; PPP to unknown [A. A. Halsey?], July 27, 1846, PPPP, folder 553, GMA; John R. Swanton, *Source Material for the Social and Ceremonial Life of the Choctaw Indians* (Tuscaloosa: University of Alabama Press, 2001), 8–9; Donna L. Akers, *Living in the Land of Death: The Choctaw Nation, 1830–1860* (East Lansing: Michigan State University, 2004), 3, 25.

4. Akers, *Living in the Land of Death*, 25; PPP, Draft Remonstrance against Proposed Territorial Bill, PPPP, folder 632, GMA.

5. PPP to unknown, March 4, 1853, PPPP, folder 692, GMA.

6. John Filson, *The Discovery, Settlement, and Present State of Kentucky* (London: John Stockdale, 1793), 61; Frederika Teute, "Land, Liberty and Labor in the Post-Revolutionary Era: Kentucky as the Promised Land" (Ph.D. diss., Johns Hopkins University, 1988), 404–411; Honor Sachs, *Home Rule: Households, Manhood, and National Expansion on the Eighteenth-Century Kentucky Frontier* (New Haven, CT: Yale University Press, 2015), 39, 44, 76; James A. Ramage and Andrea S. Watkins, *Kentucky Rising: Democracy, Slavery, and Culture from the Early Republic to the Civil War* (Lexington: University Press of Kentucky, 2011), 238; Marion B. Lucas, *A History of Blacks in Kentucky: From Slavery to Segregation, 1760–1891* (Frankfort: Kentucky Historical Society, 2003), 116; Daniel Vanderslice quoting PPP in interview with W. S. Crawford, October 21, 1841, LROIA, Schools, roll 780, frame 179.

7. RMJ to Medill, October 27, 1846, LROIA, Schools, roll 783, frame 321, NARA; RMJ to Medill, December 13, 1847, LROIA, Schools, roll 782, frame 1149, NARA; RMJ to Medill, March 30, 1846, LROIA, Schools, roll 783, frame 229, NARA; RMJ to Medill, December 10, 1845, LROIA, Schools, roll 783, frames 1269–1270, NARA; RMJ to W. L. Morey, March 20, 1845, LROIA, Schools, roll 782, frames 857–861, NARA; RMJ to General Worthington, June 20, 1843, Miscellaneous Richard Mentor Johnson Papers, FHS; RMJ to Robert John Walker, July 27, 1848, Miscellaneous Richard Mentor Johnson Papers, FHS; Leland Meyer, *The Life and Times of Colonel Richard M. Johnson of Kentucky* (New York: Columbia University Press, 1932), 472–473.

8. DV to Lieut. Hart, December 28, 1848, LROIA, Schools, roll 784, frames 997–999, NARA; Lindsey Apple, Frederick A. Johnston, and Ann Bolton Bevins, *Scott County, Kentucky: A History* (Georgetown, KY: Scott County Historical Society, 1993), 127; Ann Bolton Bevins, *A History of Scott County, as Told by Select Buildings* (Georgetown, KY: Bevins, 1981), 194–195.

9. Edwin James, comp., *Account of an Expedition from Pittsburgh to the Rocky Mountains* (London: Longman, Hurst, Rees, Orme, and Brown, 1823), vol. 3, 236; Michael C. Stambaugh, Richard P. Guyette, Erin R. McMurry, Edward

R. Cook, David M. Meko, Anthony R. Lupo, "Drought Duration and Frequency in the U.S. Corn Belt during the Last Millennium," *Agricultural and Forest Meteorology* 151(2001): 159; Resolution of the Choctaw General Council, October 7, 1842, LROIA, Choctaw Agency, roll 171, frame 176, NARA; Thomas Pitchlynn to PPP, January 24, 1842, PPPC, box 1, folder 77, WHC; *Arkansas Gazette*, October 8, 1835; John Stuart to Elbert Herring, January 28, 1836, LROIA, Choctaw Agency, roll 170, frame 762, NARA.

10. PPP to unknown, March 4, 1853, PPPP, folder 692, GMA; Petition of Choctaw Chiefs and Captains to the President, August 22, 1846, LROIA, Choctaw Agency, roll 171, frames 455–458, NARA.

11. Daniel Walker Howe, *What Hath God Wrought: The Transformation of America, 1815–1848* (New York: Oxford University Press, 2007), 365; Ralph Waldo Emerson, "The Young American," in *The Collected Works of Ralph Waldo Emerson, Vol. 1: Nature, Addresses, and Lectures*, ed. Robert E. Spiller (Cambridge, MA: Harvard University Press, 1971), 220.

12. Paul M. Angle, ed., *The Complete Lincoln-Douglass Debates of 1858* (Chicago: University of Chicago Press, 1958), 235.

13. Fayette County Order Book no. 13, June 11, 1851, p. 136, KHS.

14. Pence Ledger Book, private collection; Pence Family Bible, private collection; Bevins, *A History of Scott County*, 167, 263.

15. Bevins, *History of Scott County*, 167; Marion B. Lucas, *A History of Blacks in Kentucky: From Slavery to Segregation, 1760–1891* (Frankfort: Kentucky Historical Society, 2003), 140–144; Pence Family Album, private collection.

16. Pence Ledger Book; Bevins, *History of Scott County*, 172, 187; *Georgetown News-Graphic*, November 6, 2005; *Biographical Review of Cass, Schuyler, and Brown Counties, Illinois* (Chicago: Biographical Review Publishing, 1892), 196.

17. Apple et al., *Scott County*, 115; Interview with Brenda Brent Wilfert, December 14, 2014; Personal communication, Ann Bevins, June 29, 2011.

18. Pence Family Ledger, private collection; LCM, folder 7, pp. 34–35, KU.

19. 1850 United States Federal Census, Records of the Bureau of the Census, Scott County, Kentucky, copy in FHS; RMJ to TH, December 28, 1827, THP, folder 3, FHS; Ann Bevins, "Preserving Scott County: Theodore Johnson," Johnson-Chinn Family Papers, private collection; Steve Lannen, "Unearthing their Roots: A Diverse Kentucky Family Reunites," *Herald-Leader* (Lexington, KY), July 23, 2005.

20. Jacob F. Lee, "Unionism, Emancipation, and the Origins of Kentucky's Confederate Identity," *Register of the Kentucky Historical Society* 111 (2013): 199–233, quotation on pp. 229–230; George C. Wright, *Racial Violence in Kentucky, 1865–1940: Lynchings, Mob Rule, and "Legal Lynchings"* (Baton Rouge: Louisiana State University Press, 1990).

21. Ari Kelman, *A Misplaced Massacre: Struggling over the Memory of Sand Creek* (Cambridge, MA: Harvard University Press, 2013); LCM, folder 1, p. 6, KU; LCM, folder 6, p. 4; Nell Irvin Painter, *Exodusters: Black Migration to Kansas after Reconstruction* (New York: Knopf, 1977), 261.

22. LCM, folder 1, pp. 5–6, KU; LCM, folder 2, p. 11.

23. LCM, folder 3, 30–32, KU; LCM, folder 6, p. 2; LCM, folder 3, p. 26; Interview of Addie Murphy by J. C. Meadors, August 13, 1938, JWCP, folder 20, pp. 123–125, UK; Painter, *Exodusters*, 149–153.

24. LCM, folder 7, pp. 29–34, KU; LCM, folder 6, pp. 23, 30–32; National Historical Landmark Nomination, Nicodemus Historic District, 2013, National Park Service, p. 69.

25. LCM, folder 6, pp. 29–34, KU.

26. Hubert Howe Bancroft interview with George Washington Trahern, n.d., Biographical Materials relating to George Washington Trahern, BC, mss. C-D 843, passim, quotation on p. 57, UC.

27. Hubert Howe Bancroft interview with George Washington Trahern, n.d., Biographical Materials relating to George Washington Trahern, BC, mss. C-D 843, 4–5, UC; Peter E. Beau to Lewis Cass, February 27, 1833, LROIA, Choctaw Agency, roll 170, frames 339–343, NARA; James Fletcher and Isaac Folsom to Major Thomas T. Fauntleroy, May 6, 1842, LROIA, Choctaw Agency, roll 171, frames 188–189, NARA; Thomas Pitchlynn to PPP, May 5, 1854, PPPC, box 2, folder 37, WHC.

28. Brian DeLay, *War of a Thousand Deserts: Indian Raids and the U.S.-Mexican War* (New Haven, CT: Yale University Press, 2009); Jacob Folsom to PPP, July 31, 1845, PPPC, box 1, folder 96, WHC; Bancroft interview with Trahern, n.d., pp. 13–41, quotation on p. 24.

29. Malvina Pitchlynn Folsom to Lycurgus Pitchlynn, May 20, 1849, PPPC, box 2, folder 11, WHC; Thomas Pitchlynn to PPP, May 5, 1854, PPPC, box 2, folder 37, WHC; William P. Brown to PPP, March 10, 1856, PPPC, box 2, folder 73, WHC; Arthur DeRosier Jr., *The Removal of the Choctaw Indians* (Knoxville: University of Tennessee Press, 1970), 166; Susan Lee Johnson, *Roaring Camp: The Social World of the California Gold Rush* (New York: Norton, 2000).

30. Bancroft interview with Trahern, n.d., BC, passim, quotation on p. 63, UC; Charles L. Convis, "Daring Texas Ranger, Wealthy California Rancher," *San Joaquin Historian* 7 (1993): 3–15.

31. Bancroft's notes, n.d., Biographical Materials relating to George Washington Trahern, BC, mss. C-D 843, UC; Bancroft interview with Trahern, n.d., BC, pp. 1–3, 56–57, UC.

32. John Walton Caughey, *Hubert Howe Bancroft: Historian of the West* (Berkeley: University of California Press, 1946), 120–139; Hubert Howe Bancroft, *The Native Races*, vol. 1: *Wild Tribes* (San Francisco: A. L. Bancroft & Co., 1883), 570, 207, 32, xi; Bancroft's notes, n.d., Biographical Materials relating to George Washington Trahern, BC, UC.

33. Armstrong to Harris, October 31, 1838, LROIA, Schools, roll 778, frames 662–664, NARA; Armstrong to Medill, November 24, 1846, LROIA, Schools, roll 783, frame 78, NARA; Thomas Williamson to Harvey, Schools Report for 1848, LROIA, Schools, roll 784, frames 195–202, NARA; David Wallace Adams, *Education for Extinction: American Indians and the Boarding School Experience, 1875–1938* (Lawrence: University Press of Kansas), 60; John Beach to John Chambers, August 13, 1845, copy in GFC, box 9, folder 3, OKHS.

34. Adams, *Education for Extinction*; Tsianina Lomawaima, *They Called It Prairie Light: The Story of Chilocco Indian School* (Lincoln: University of Nebraska Press, 1994), quotation on p. 102; Brenda J. Child, *Boarding School Seasons: American Indian Families, 1900–1940* (Lincoln: University of Nebraska Press, 1998).

35. RMJ to TH, March 16, 1834, and May 12, 1834, THP, folder 9, FHS; Sally McBeth, *Ethnic Identity and the Boarding School Experience of West-Central Oklahoma Indians* (Washington, DC: University Press of America,

1983); Adams, *Education for Extinction*; Lomawaima, *They Called It Prairie Light*, 19–23.

36. Balyeat, "Education in Indian Territory," 25–26, 210; Joe C. Jackson, "Survey of Education in Eastern Oklahoma from 1907 to 1915," *Chronicles of Oklahoma* 29 (1951): 202–204.

37. Devon Mihesuah, *Cultivating the Rosebuds: The Education of Women at the Cherokee Female Seminary, 1851–1909* (Urbana: University of Illinois Press, 1998), 1–6; Amanda J. Cobb, *Listening to Our Grandmothers' Stories: The Bloomfield Academy for Chickasaw Females, 1852–1949* (Lincoln: University of Nebraska Press, 2000), 72–74; *Indian Education: A National Tragedy— A National Challenge*, 1969 Report of the Committee on Labor and Public Welfare, 91st Cong., 1st sess. (Washington, DC: US Government Printing Office, 1969), 25; Grayson B. Noley, "The History of Education in the Choctaw Nation from Precolonial Times to 1830 (Ph.D. diss., Pennsylvania State University, 1979), 237.

38. Talk from the Upper Creeks to John Stuart, February 4, 1774, quoted in Kathryn E. Holland Braund, *Deerskins and Duffels: Creek Indian Trade with Anglo-America, 1685–1815* (Lincoln: University of Nebraska Press, 1993), 57.

39. Speech of Pierre Juzan, *Daily National Intelligencer*, December 21, 1826.

40. PPP to unknown, March 4, 1853, PPPP, folder 692, GMA.

41. Speech of A. Buckholts, February 23, 1838, 26th Cong., 2nd sess., HD 109, no. 138, p. 120; George Washington Trahern Speech, HD 109, no. 137, p. 118; Trahern essay, HD 109, no. 137, p. 118; H.B. Wright to PPP, June 24, 1843, PPPP, folder 403, GMA.

INDEX

Italicized pages refer to illustrations.